The Conceptualization of Equality and Non-discrimination as Legal Standards

Nijhoff Law Specials

VOLUME 111

The titles published in this series are listed at *brill.com/nlsp*

The Conceptualization of Equality and Non-discrimination as Legal Standards

From Formal to More Substantive Equality

By

Titia Loenen

BRILL | NIJHOFF

LEIDEN | BOSTON

The Library of Congress Cataloging-in-Publication Data is available online at https://catalog.loc.gov
LC record available at https://lccn.loc.gov/2024922572

Typeface for the Latin, Greek, and Cyrillic scripts: "Brill". See and download: brill.com/brill-typeface.

ISSN 0924-4549
ISBN 978-90-04-53785-9 (paperback)
ISBN 978-90-04-53836-8 (e-book)
DOI 10.1163/9789004538368

This book is printed on acid-free paper and produced in a sustainable manner.

Contents

Acknowledgements

Equality issues have been the subject of my research and teaching for some 40 years. In many respects, these 40 years have witnessed profound developments in the conceptualization of equality and non-discrimination as legal standards across jurisdictions. This book is the result of my long term engagement with the topic. In writing it, I am greatly indebted to all those scholars, students and other people who have inspired me so much during these years by their shared commitment to human rights and the ideals of equality and non-discrimination. Time and again, by engaging with them in reading, writing and/or discussing, they made me think through and rethink my understandings of these crucial notions as legal concepts. There are too many to thank them all in person, but some people and work experiences stand out in shaping my thoughts.

When I started out, I was lucky to be hired as a junior assistant professor by Jenny Goldschmidt, who was leading an innovative research and teaching project in feminist legal studies at Leiden University Law School. I was also lucky to be teamed up with Rikki Holtmaat, who had already earned a name in feminist approaches to law. The three of us formed the tiny, but very active and fruitful section 'Women and Law'. I could not have had a more inspirational start of my working life. In this formative period I developed the foundations for my thinking on equality as a legal principle in my doctoral thesis.[1] Thanks to the particular expertise of my supervisors Jenny Goldschmidt and Evert Alkema in constitutional and human rights law, these two perspectives became part and parcel of my intellectual baggage.

Following Jenny to Utrecht University, and moving fully to this institution in 1995 as associate and later full professor in women's legal studies, significantly added to further broadening my expertise. At Utrecht University I came to work with two other wonderful experts in gender studies who proved to be of lasting influence, Susanne Burri and Marjolein van den Brink. Of all the people I worked with over the years, Jenny, Susanne and Marjolein stand out more than any other by the way in which they brought me enduring bonds of academic and social friendship. In Utrecht, the small section 'Women's

---

1 T. Loenen, *Verschil in gelijkheid. De conceptualisering van het juridische gelijkheidsbeginsel met betrekking tot vrouwen en mannen in Nederland en de Verenigde staten* (Difference in equality – the conceptualization of the legal principle of equality as regards women and men in the Netherlands and the United States), Doctoral thesis, Leiden University, 1992.

legal studies' was embedded over time in different departments of the Law School. This brought new opportunities for collaboration and engaging in new research areas. My colleagues from the vibrant social law department made me look with new eyes to how equality issues play out in areas such as social security and employment. Moving to the department of legal theory subsequently led to increasing collaboration with colleagues working in the field of legal theory, philosophy and socio-legal studies. This stimulated me to engage in the then raging debates on multiculturalism and human rights. Becoming one of the coordinators of the research programme on human rights led to a long-time, inspired collaboration with SIM, the Netherlands Institute of Human Rights, in particular with Ineke Boerefijn, Kees Flinterman, and later – again – Jenny Goldschmidt.

A final phase with a profound influence on the approach taken in this book started in 2013 when I returned to Leiden University. Thanks to the then Dean of the Law School and committed human rights expert, Rick Lawson, I was given the unique opportunity to design and develop an advanced LLM in European and International Human Rights Law. Teaching on the global and regional human rights systems from a comparative perspective greatly extended my knowledge of these systems; teaching a course on transnational non-discrimination law refreshed my comparative engagement with approaches to equality as a legal concept across jurisdictions.

During all of these periods, enduring inspiration for the present book has come from several other sources.

To start with, students have always played an important role. Whether it was regular law students I taught who were often sceptical of the topic or the committed ones who chose our courses as electives, they all sharpened my mind and induced me to always look for testing the validity of abstract theory and notions by providing concrete examples from everyday law and life. I am particularly grateful to the students of the advanced LLM in human rights at Leiden University for bringing perspectives from across the world into the classroom, which profoundly influenced me both as an academic and as a person.

In addition, the international network of scholars and other professionals I became part of over the years was a crucial source of inspiration for developing more global and diverse perspectives. Several extended research visits merit a special word of thanks. In 1990 a semester spent at New York University provided the opportunity to visit several leading feminist legal scholars, including Sylvia Law who hosted me, Frances Olsen, Martha Fineman and Martha Minow. The latter's book 'Making all the difference' had a lasting influence on my understanding of equality.[2] In 1994, several months of guest lecturing in the new South Africa at the Universities of the Western Cape and of Cape Town also proved to have a profound influence on shaping my thoughts on equality; particularly in terms of the crucial importance of context and including Global South perspectives. In 2005 my participation in the multidisciplinary 2004/2005 Fulbright New Century Scholars project 'Towards Equality: the global empowerment of women' brought me together with some 30 other scholars from the US and around the world to work for a year on this common theme. The unique and diverse composition of this group, with strong and vocal input from Global South perspectives, left their distinct marks on my thinking ever since.

It is impossible to do justice to the inspiration I received from the many people I met at conferences, but a particular highlight was the international conference Peter Rodrigues and I organized ourselves in 1998 on comparative perspectives on non-discrimination law.[3] Of similar significance was the international expert seminar on religious pluralism and human rights in Europe which we organized at Utrecht University in 2006 on the occasion of the inaugural lecture by Abdullahi An-Naím, who was appointed on the rotating *G.J. Wiarda* Chair.[4]

Another enduring source of inspiration has come from the editorial board of the main Dutch human rights law journal, the *NJCM-Bulletin*, of which I was part for around 30 years. I will always cherish the memories of the many passionate discussions we had, which were happily matched with a strong feeling of companionship.

Some final words of special thanks are due to several of my former and current colleagues who commented on one or more draft chapters of this book: Adriaan Bedner, Marjolein van den Brink, Susanne Burri, Jenny Goldschmidt, Aart Hendriks and Nadia Sonneveld. It was a great pleasure to discuss these drafts with them and I hope I have done justice to their insightful comments and reflections.

2 M. Minow, *Making all the difference. Inclusion, exclusion, and American law*, Ithaca/London, Cornell University Press, 1990.

3 The keynote lectures and a selection of the papers were published in T. Loenen and P. Rodrigues (eds), *Non-discrimination law: comparative perspectives*, The Hague/London/Boston, Kluwer Law International, 1999.

4 It resulted in a compilation of his lecture and the papers presented at this seminar in M.L.P. Loenen and J.E. Goldschmidt (eds), *Religious pluralism and human rights in Europe: where to draw the line?* Intersentia, Antwerpen/Oxford, 2007.

Last, but certainly not least, I thank Ruud, my 40-year life companion, who has been there for me from the very start of my working life with his warm, loving and cheerful presence. I can only hope we will enjoy many more wonderful years together.

Leiden, August 2024

Abbreviations

ACHPR	African Charter of Human and Peoples' Rights
ACHR	American Convention on Human Rights
CEDAW	Convention on the Elimination of all forms of Discrimination Against Women
CESCR	Committee on Economic, Social and Cultural Rights
CJEU	Court of Justice of the EU
CRPD	Convention on the Rights of Persons with Disabilities
ECHR	European Convention on Human Rights
ECtHR	European Court of Human Rights
ETC	Equal Treatment Commission (*Commissie Gelijke behandeling*)
HRC	Human Rights Committee
IACtHR	Inter-American Court of Human Rights
ICCPR	International Covenant on Civil and Political Rights
ICERD	International Convention on the Elimination of all forms of Racial Discrimination
ICESCR	International Covenant on Economic, Social and Cultural Rights
NIHR	Netherlands Institute for Human Rights (*College voor de Rechten van de Mens*)
OHCHR	Office of the UN High Commissioner for Human Rights
PCIJ	Permanent Court of International Justice
UDHR	Universal Declaration of Human Rights

Overview of Case Law

American Convention on Human Rights

IACtHR, 19 January 1984, *Advisory Opinion OC-4/84 on proposed amendments to the naturalization provision of the constitution of Costa Rica*

IACtHR, 17 September 2003, *Advisory Opinion OC-18/03 on Juridical condition and rights of the undocumented migrants*

IACtHR, 16 November 2009, *González et al. ('Cotton Field') v. Mexico* (Preliminary objections, merits, reparations, and costs)

IACtHR, 28 November 2012, *Artavia Murillo e.a. ('In vitro fertilization'), v. Costa Rica* (Preliminary objections, merits, reparations and costs)

IACtHR, 1 September 2015, *Gonzales Lluy v. Ecuador* (Preliminary objections, merits, reparations and costs)

IACtHR, 24 November 2017, *Advisory Opinion OC-24/17 on Gender identity, and equality and non-discrimination of same-sex couples*

IACtHR, 15 July 2020, *Workers of the Fireworks Factory in Santo Antônio de Jesus and their families v. Brazil* (Preliminary objections, merits, reparations and costs)

Canada

Supreme Court, *Ontario Human Rights Commission v. Simpson-Sears* [1985] 2 SCR 536

Supreme Court, *Andrews v. Law Society of British Columbia* [1989] 1 SCR 143

Supreme Court, *Eldridge v. British Columbia* [1997] 3 SCR 624.

Supreme Court, *Law v. Canada* [1999] 1 SCR 497

Supreme Court, *Corbiere v. Canada (Minister of Indian and Northern Affairs)* [1999] 2 SCR 203

Supreme Court, *R. v. Kapp* [2008] 2 SCR 483

Supreme Court, *Alberta v. Cunningham* [2011] 2 SCR 670

Supreme Court, *Fraser v. Canada* [2020] 3 SCR 113

EU

CJEU, 12 February 1974, *Sotgiu*, C-152/73

CJEU, 31 March 1981, *Jenkins*, C-97/80

CJEU, 12 July 1984, *Hofmann*, C-184/83

CJEU, 4 December 1986, *Federatie Nederlandse Vakbeweging (FNV)*, C-71/85

CJEU, 13 May 1986, *Bilka*, C-170/84
CJEU, 11 June 1987, *Teuling-Worms*, C-30/85
CJEU, 13 July 1989, *Rinner-Kühn*, C-171/88
CJEU, 13 December 1989, *Ruzius-Wilbrink*, C-102/88.
CJEU, 8 November 1990, *Dekker*, C-177/88
CJEU, 7 February 1991, *Nimz*, C-184/89
CJEU, 14 July 1994, *Webb*, C-32/93
CJEU, 15 December 1994, *Helmig*, C-399/92
CJEU, 17 October 1995, *Kalanke*, C-450/93
CJEU, 30 April 1996, *P v S*, C-13/94
CJEU, 11 November 1997, *Marschall*, C-409/95
CJEU, 17 February 1998, *Grant*, C-249/96
CJEU, 17 June 1998, *Hill/Stapleton*, C-243/95
CJEU, 28 March 2000, *Badeck*, C-158/97
CJEU, 6 July 2000, *Abrahamsson*, C-407/98
CJEU, 7 December 2000, *Schnorbus*, C-79/99
CJEU, 19 March 2002, *Lommers*, C-476/99
CJEU, 30 September 2004, *Briheche*, C-319/03
CJEU (Grand Chamber), 1 April 2008, *Maruko*, C-267/06
CJEU, 30 September 2010, *Roca Álvarez*, C-104/09
CJEU, 18 November 2010, *Kleist*, C-356/09
CJEU (Grand Chamber), 16 July 2015, *Chez*, C-83/14
CJEU, 24 November 2016, *Parris*, C-443/15
CJEU (Grand Chamber), 14 March 2017, *Achbita*, C-157/15
CJEU, 19 October 2017, *Otero Ramos*, C-531/15
CJEU, 8 May 2019, *Villar Láiz*, C-161/18
CJEU, 26 January 2021, *Szpital Kliniczny*, C-16/19
CJEU (Grand Chamber), 3 June 2021, *Hungary v. European Parliament*, Case C-650/18
CJEU (Grand Chamber), *Wabe* and *Müller*, 15 July 2021, C-804/18 and C-341/19
CJEU, 24 February 2022, *TGSS*, C-389/20
CJEU, 13 October 2022, *SCRL*, C-344/20

European Convention on Human Rights

ECtHR, 23 July 1968, *Belgian Linguistics*, appl. no. 2126/64
EComHR, 12 July 1978, *X. v. United Kingdom*, appl. no. 7992/77
EComHR, 12 March 1981, *X. v. United Kingdom*, appl. no. 8160/78
EComHR, 3 December 1996, *Konttinen v. Finland*, appl. no. 24949/94
ECtHR, 24 February 1998, *Botta v. Italy*, appl. no. 21439/93

ECtHR, 27 March 1998, *Petrovic v. Austria*, appl. no. 20458/92
ECtHR (Grand Chamber), 6 April 2000, *Thlimmenos v. Greece*, appl. no. 34369/97
ECtHR, 14 May 2002, *Zehnalova and Zehnal v. the Czech Republic*, appl. no. 38621/97
ECtHR, 11 January 2005, *Phull v. France*, appl. no. 35753/03.
ECtHR (Grand Chamber), 12 April 2006, *Stec and others v. the United Kingdom*, appl. nos. 65731/01 and 65900/01
ECtHR, 12 December 2006, *Burden and Burden v. the United Kingdom*, appl. no. 13378/05
ECtHR (Grand Chamber), 13 November 2007, *D.H. and others v. the Czech Republic*, appl. no. 57325/00
ECtHR (Grand Chamber), 29 April 2008, *Burden v. the United Kingdom*, appl. no. 13378/05
ECtHR, 9 June 2009, *Opuz v. Turkey*, appl. no. 33401/02
ECtHR (Grand Chamber), 22 December 2009, *Sejdić and Finci v. Bosnia and Herzegovina*, appl. nos. 27996/06 and 34836/06
ECtHR (Grand Chamber), 16 March 2010, *Oršuš and Others v. Croatia*, appl. no. 15766/03
ECtHR, 20 May 2010, *Alajos Kiss v. Hungary*, appl. no. 38832/06
ECtHR, 10 March 2011, *Kiyutin v. Russia*, appl. no. 2700/10
ECtHR (Grand Chamber), 22 March 2012, *Konstantin Markin v. Russia*, appl. no. 30078/06
ECtHR, 24 April 2012, *Yordanova and others v. Bulgaria*, appl. no. 25446/06
ECtHR, 24 July 2012, *B.S. v. Spain*, appl. no. 47159/08
ECtHR, 11 December 2012, *Sampani and others* v. Greece, appl. no. 59608/09
ECtHR, 15 January 2013, *Eweida and others v. the United Kingdom*, appl. nos. 48420/10, 59842/10, 51671/10 and 36516/10
ECtHR, 17 October 2013, *Winterstein and others v. France*, appl. no. 27013/07
ECtHR (Grand Chamber), 1 July 2014, *S.A.S. v. France*, appl. no. 43835/11
ECtHR, 23 February 2016, *Çam v. Turkey*, appl. no. 51500/08
ECtHR, 22 March 2016, *Guberina v. Croatia*, appl. no. 23682/13
ECtHR (Grand Chamber), 24 May 2016, *Biao v. Denmark*, appl. no. 38590/10
ECtHR, 30 June 2016, *Taddeucci and McCall v. Italy*, appl. no. 51362/09
ECtHR, 25 July 2017, *Carvalho Pinto de Sousa Morais v. Portugal*, appl. no. 17484/15
ECtHR (Grand Chamber), 5 September 2017, *Fábián v. Hungary*, appl. no. 78117/13
ECtHR, 3 October 2017, *Alexandru Eneche v. Romania*, appl. no. 16986/12
ECtHR, 11 December 2018, *Belli and Arquier-Martinez v. Switserland*, appl. no. 65550/13
ECtHR, 24 October 2019, *J.D. and A v. the United Kingdom*, appl. nos. 32949/17 and 34614/17
ECtHR, 13 October 2020, *Adám and others v. Romania*, appl. nos. 8114/17 and five others
ECtHR, 11 May 2021, *Yocheva and Ganeva v. Bulgaria*, appl. no. 18592/15
ECtHR, 6 July 2021, *Gruba and others v. Russia*, appl. no. 66180/09
ECtHR, 26 October 2021, *Toplak and Mrak v. Slovenia*, appl. no. 34591/19 and 42545/19

ECtHR, 31 May 2022, *Arnar Helgi Lárusson v. Iceland*, appl. no. 23077/19
ECtHR, 31 May 2022, *X and others v. Albania*, appl. no. 73548/17 and 45521/19
ECtHR (Grand Chamber), 13 July 2022, *Advisory Opinion on the difference in treatment between landowners' associations "having a recognised existence on the date of the creation of an approved municipal hunters' association" and landowners' associations set up after that date*, Request No. P16-2021-002
ECtHR (Grand Chamber), 11 October 2022, *Beeler v. Switzerland*, appl. no. 78630/12

South Africa

Supreme Court, *Motala and another v. University of Natal*, 1995 (3) BCLR 374
Constitutional Court, *Brinks v. Kitshoff*, [1996] ZACC 9
Constitutional Court, *President of the Republic of South Africa and Another v. Hugo*, [1997] ZACC 4
Constitutional Court, *Harksen v. Lane and others*, [1997] ZACC 12
Constitutional Court, *City Council of Pretoria v. Walker* [1998] ZACC 1
Constitutional Court, *National Coalition for Gay and lesbian equality and others v. Minister of Home Affairs*, [1999] ZACC 17
Constitutional Court, *Christian Education South Africa v. Minister of Education*, [2000] ZAC C11
Constitutional Court, *Minister of Finance v. Van Heerden*, [2004] ZACC 3
Constitutional Court, *Port Elizabeth Municipality v. various Occupiers*, [2004] ZACC 7
Constitutional Court, *Minister of Home Affairs and another v. Fourie and another*, [2005] ZACC 19
Constitutional Court, *MEC for Education: Kwazulu-Natal and Others v. Pillay*, [2007] ZACC 21
Constitutional Court, *Hassam v. Jacobs*, [2009] ZACC 19
Constitutional Court, *Solidarity and others v. Department of correctional services and others*, [2016] ZACC 18
Constitutional Court, *Minister of Constitutional Development and another v. South African Restructuring and Insolvency Practitioners Association and others*, [2018] ZACC 20
Equality Court, *September v. Subramoney NO and Others*, (EC10/2016) [2019] ZAEQC 4.
Constitutional Court, *Mahlangu and Another v. Minister of Labour and Others*, [2020] ZACC 24
Constitutional Court, *Sithole and Another v. Sithole and Another*, [2021] ZACC 7
Constitutional Court, *Women's Legal Centre Trust v. President of the Republic of South Africa and Others*, [2022] ZACC 23

Constitutional Court, *Blind SA v. Minister of Trade, Industry and Competition and others*, [2022] ZACC 33

United States

US Supreme Court, *United States v. Carolene products*, 304 US 144 (1938).
US Supreme Court, *Korematsu v. United States*, 323 US 214 (1944)
US Supreme Court, *Brown v. Board of Education*, 347 US 483 (1954)
US Supreme Court, *Palmer v. Thompson*, 403 US 217 (1971)
US Supreme Court, *Griggs v. Duke Power Co*, 401 US 424 (1971)
US Supreme Court, *Roe v. Wade*, 410 US 113 (1973)
US Supreme Court, *Geduldig v. Aiello*, 417 US 484 (1974)
US Supreme Court, *Washington v. Davis*, 426 US 229 (1976)
US Supreme Court, *Craig v. Boren*, 429 US 190 (1976)
US Supreme Court, *Trans World Airlines v. Hardison*, 432 US 63 (1977)
US Supreme Court, *Dothard v. Rawlinson*, 433 US 321 (1977)
US Supreme Court, *Personnel Administrator of Massachusetts v. Feeney*, 442 US 256 (1979)
US Supreme Court, *Mississippi University for Women v. Hogan*, 458 US 718 (1982)
US Supreme Court, *Wards Cove Packing Co. v. Atonio*, 490 US 642 (1989)
US Supreme Court, *Adarand Constructors v. Federico Pena*, 515 US 200 (1995)
US Supreme Court, *Airways v. Barnett*, 535 US 391 (2002)
US Supreme Court, *Obergefell v. Hodges*, 576 US 644 (2015)
US Supreme Court, *Bostock v. Clayton Country*, 590 US 644 (2020)
US Supreme Court, *Dobbs v. Jackson Women's Health Organization*, 597 US 215 (2022)
US Supreme Court, *SFFA v. President and fellows of Harvard College*, 600 US 181 (2023)

Miscellaneous

African Court of Human and Peoples' Rights, 15 July 2020, *Kambole v. United Republic of Tanzania*, appl. no. 018/2018
Centrale Raad van Beroep (Central Appeals Tribunal), 14 May 1987, *Rechtspraak Sociale Verzekering* 1987, 246
Centrale Raad van Beroep (Central Appeals Tribunal), 7 May 2009, ECLI:NL:CRVB:2009:BI2440
Centrale Raad van Beroep (Central Appeals Tribunal), 9 mei 2017, ECLI:NL:CRVB:2017:1639

Gerechtshof Den Haag (Court of Appeal The Hague), 14 February 2023, ECLI:NL:GHDHA:2023:173

Hoge Raad (Supreme Court), 19 September 1990, ECLI:NL:HR:1990:ZC4387.

Permanent Court of International Justice, *Minority Schools in Albania*, PCIJ Series A/B, no. 64 (1935)

Supreme Court of India, 16 November 1992, *Indra Sawhney v. Union of India*

Supreme Court of India, 6 September 2018, *Navtej Singh Johar v. Union of India*

Supreme Court of India, 25 March 2021, *Lt Col Nitisha v. Union of India*

CHAPTER 1

Introduction

1.1 Goal and Approach of the Book

The second half of the 20th century saw the worldwide adoption of legally binding equality and non-discrimination standards (equality standards for short). At the global and regional level a wide variety of human rights treaties testify to this. They all contain equality standards, and some are devoted entirely to eliminating discrimination.[1] At the national level this development is reflected in the adoption of equality standards in many constitutions, bills of rights, and specific anti-discrimination laws.[2]

Article 26 of the International Covenant on Civil and Political Rights (ICCPR) is a prominent example of this development:

> All persons are equal before the law and are entitled without any discrimination to the equal protection of the law. In this respect, the law shall prohibit any discrimination and guarantee to all persons equal and effective protection against discrimination on any ground such as race, colour, sex, language, religion, political or other opinion, national or social origin, property, birth or other status.

Its twin convention, the International Covenant on Economic, Social and Cultural Rights (ICESCR), also contains a general and similarly formulated right to equal treatment and non-discrimination.[3] As a far majority of member

---

1 In the context of this study, the main treaties at the UN level consist of the International Covenant on Civil and Political Rights (ICCPR, 1966), the International Covenant on Economic, Social and Cultural Rights (ICESCR, 1966), the International Convention on the Elimination of All Forms of Racial Discrimination (ICERD, 1965), the Convention on the Elimination of All Forms of Discrimination Against Women (CEDAW, 1979) and the Convention on the Rights of Persons with Disabilities (CRPD, 2006). The main regional treaties are the European Convention on Human Rights (ECHR, 1950), The American Convention on Human Rights (ACHR, 1969) and the African Charter on Human and Peoples' Rights (ACHPR, 1981).

2 For equality standards in national constitutions see the website of the Comparative Constitutions Project, https://comparativeconstitutionsproject.org/.

3 Article 2(2) ICESCR: 'The States Parties to the present Covenant undertake to guarantee that the rights enunciated in the present Covenant will be exercised without discrimination of any kind as to race, colour, sex, language, religion, political or other opinion, national or

 DOI:10.1163/9789004538368_002

states of the United Nations has ratified both covenants, and almost all states have at least ratified one of the two, this shows equality and non-discrimination have become universally accepted as general and overarching legal standards.[4] Arguably, equality is foundational for the very idea of human rights as rights inherent to all human beings. As the Inter-American Court of Human Rights (IACtHR) formulated it: 'The notion of equality springs directly from the oneness of the human family and is linked to the essential dignity of the individual'.[5]

At the same time, what these standards entail or should entail in more concrete detail is often subject to much controversy and both legal and public debate, and may differ widely between jurisdictions. Many topical equality issues attest to this. Regarding racial discrimination, for example, there seems to be universal recognition that this form of discrimination is unacceptable, but what does this mean if applied in concrete situations? Should states always follow a race-blind approach, or may they also adopt affirmative action measures to undo past or systemic discrimination? Does a right to equal treatment regardless of sex or gender mean that women should always be treated the same as men, or should it allow for making exceptions if this meets with strong opposition by cultural or religious norms and practices? And what about the gendered division of labour regarding paid work and care-taking activities which is prevalent in most countries in the world? Does equality law have a role to play in achieving more shared responsibility between parents? Turning to issues of equal treatment regardless of sexual orientation or gender identity: does equality as a legal standard mean that same-sex couples must have access to marriage on an equal basis as different-sex couples? Does the right to non-discrimination include discrimination on the basis of gender identity? And how do discrimination on the basis of sexual orientation or gender identity relate to discrimination on the basis of sex? Are they included under the (often more extensive) protection accorded to the latter? Ongoing issues regarding discrimination on the basis of religion also figure worldwide, be it about the question whether banning certain religious expressions such as the

---

social origin, property, birth or other status.' For an overview of the main equality provisions in international and regional human rights conventions see L. Carlson, *Comparative discrimination law: historical and theoretical frameworks*, Brill Research Perspectives in Comparative Discrimination Law, Brill, 2017 and M. Mwakagali, *International human rights law and discrimination protections. A comparison of regional and national responses*, Brill Research Perspectives in Comparative Discrimination Law, Brill, 2019.

4 For the ratification status of UN human rights treaties see https://indicators.ohchr.org/.

5 IACtHR, 19 January 1984, *Advisory opinion OC-4/84 on proposed amendments to the naturalization provision of the constitution of Costa Rica*, par. 55.

wearing of a headscarf or burqa or, in the opposite way, requiring women to wear it, are acceptable or not. Regarding persons with disabilities, a general commitment to approaching the prohibition of discrimination as including a right to reasonable accommodation seems to be emerging across jurisdictions, but how far this right reaches in concrete situations is up for a lot of debate.

More generally, current discussions regarding the meaning of equality and non-discrimination as legal standards often raise the question to what extent they can or cannot address the structural and systemic disadvantage faced by vulnerable and marginalized groups suffering from all sorts of discrimination in society. Can it reach the underlying root causes of such forms of disadvantage, which are often ingrained in the very fabrics of society?

Though equality and non-discrimination standards often play a prominent role in these types of discussion, their actual role in addressing them in any legal system is often unclear. If anything, they may differ widely between jurisdictions. No commonly accepted agreement seems to exist about applying these standards in concrete situations. Also within a jurisdiction, application of these standards may remain unclear and raise a lot of questions. As such, it is not surprising that the right to equality has been characterized as elusive and hard to grapple with.[6]

In this study I intend to clarify why this is so and improve understanding of how equality – and its more specific manifestation as a prohibition of discrimination – operate as legal concepts and standards. Interestingly, equality as a legal concept has shown itself to be very dynamic. Particularly over the past fifty years or so, in many jurisdictions conceptualizations of equality have been evolving from rather limited notions centring on formal equality into broader and multi-layered understandings grounded in more substantive readings of equality. These include the notions of indirect discrimination, (reasonable) accommodation and positive discrimination or positive action.[7] This development has been driven largely by judicial interpretation and application of legal equality standards in a variety of jurisdictions. As a result, conceptualizations of equality have become all the more complex.

I will explore these legal concepts and explain how different conceptualizations matter and may result in different outcomes in legislation, case law and policy. This also entails exploring the limitations of equality and

6 Cf. Albertyn and Goldblatt, who call it 'this most difficult of rights', C. Albertyn and B. Goldblatt, Chapter 35. Equality, in: S. Woolman and M. Bishop (eds), *Constitutional Law of South Africa*, 2007, p. 2; Fredman refers to equality as 'elusive', see the preface of S. Fredman, *Discrimination law*, Oxford, Oxford University Press, 2022 (3rd edition).

7 For the way in which I use these and other concepts see below, Section 1.3.

non-discrimination as legal standards to address social realities of inequality and discrimination.

By taking an analytical and explanatory approach as my starting point, this work differs in a principled way from normative theories and studies on discrimination law, which propagate a particular theory or approach as the proper or best way forward. The books by Fredman, Khaitan, McGolgan and Solanke on discrimination law are prominent examples of the latter.[8] Rather than seeking to develop a normative theory of equality and non-discrimination as legal standards, this study does not intend to defend a particular conceptualization of equality and non-discrimination. Instead, it will focus on discussing the consequences of particular approaches and the dilemma's and difficulties involved in choosing between them. I hope this analysis will contribute to making the legal notion of equality less elusive.

With its focus on analyzing legal understandings of equality and non-discrimination, this study is predominantly directed to readers with a legal background, such as legal scholars and practitioners, judges and other professionals involved with equality and non-discrimination law, including activists, and law students. I hope it can also be relevant for persons with other disciplinary backgrounds involved in equality and non-discrimination law.

In the following chapters I explore the main concepts which have been developed in equality and non-discrimination law and theory – such as formal and substantive equality, direct and indirect discrimination, (reasonable) accommodation, positive discrimination or positive action and intersectional discrimination – and how different conceptualizations may impact the outcome of applying them in legal practice.

1.2 Methods

In analyzing the main concepts developed in equality and non-discrimination law and theory mentioned above, I understand these notions not as fixed or rigid categories which can be divided in separate and watertight compartments, but as specific types or models which share sufficient basic and general features to set them apart. In this way I intend to provide a meaningful, overarching analytical framework for better understanding how they are conceptualized and work across jurisdictions, while at the same time acknowledging

8 S. Fredman, *Discrimination law*, Oxford, Oxford University Press, 2022 (3rd edition); T. Khaitan, *A theory of discrimination law*, Oxford, Oxford University Press, 2015; A. McColgan, *Discrimination, equality and the law*, Oxford, Hart Publ., 2014; I. Solanke, *Discrimination as stigma: a theory of anti-discrimination law*, Bloomsbury, 2017.

that within these types or models many differences and varieties may exist between jurisdictions, including hybrid types and models. Being preoccupied with painting a broad picture, my analysis cannot do justice to the complex variety in which equality standards operate in more detail in different jurisdictions. It will necessarily gloss over many of the nuances, subtleties and/or inconsistencies within jurisdictions, but I hope it will provide a meaningful general framework for studying these in more detail.

A *caveat* is in order here. The general and overarching understanding I present does not lay claim to absolute truth or to being the only or best possible understanding. It is *my* best understanding as I have developed it over the past decades and I hope it will be meaningful for the reader. It is also important to point out that 'my best understanding' as presented is not the same as what I would consider *normatively* to be the best way to approach equality as a legal standard. My normative position may be apparent from other publications,[9] but as mentioned already above, my endeavour in this book is of an explanatory nature to help clarify the various conceptualizations of equality and non-discrimination in the legal realities of the jurisdictions in which they operate. This may help explain how these concepts work when applied in legal practice, why they often turn out to be quite fuzzy, the types of difficulties and bottlenecks they pose in their application, and how different conceptualizations may lead to different outcomes.

My conceptual analysis is based on a combination of legal theory perspectives and doctrinal legal research methods. Firstly, it draws on insights from legal and political/philosophical theory on equality and discrimination. The available scholarship on this topic is vast and provides a wealth of conceptual analyses and insights to which this study is profoundly indebted.[10] Secondly,

9 Starting with my dissertation in 1992, my normative position favours a more substantive reading of equality as a legal standard and has not changed significantly since then. See T. Loenen, *Verschil in Gelijkheid. De conceptualisering van het juridische gelijkheidsbeginsel met betrekking tot vrouwen en mannen in Nederland en de Verenigde Staten*, (Difference in equality. The conceptualisation of the legal principle of equality regarding women and men in the Netherlands and the United States), Doctoral thesis, Zwolle, Tjeenk Willink, 1992; T. Loenen, Rethinking sex equality as a human right, *Netherlands Quarterly of Human Rights*, 1994, p 253–270.

10 A starting point for readers not acquainted with the topic could be the *International Journal on Discrimination and the Law*, the publications in the *Brill Research Perspectives in Comparative Discrimination Law* and the overview of publications by members of the worldwide, multidisciplinary network of activists, advocates, and academics working in the field of anti-discrimination law, coordinated by the Berkeley Center on Comparative Equality & Anti-Discrimination Law, https://www.law.berkeley.edu/research/berkeley-center-on-comparative-equality-anti-discrimination-law/our-library/.

legal doctrine and case law regarding equality and discrimination as developed in a wide variety of jurisdictions provide crucial sources.

As judicial bodies often play a central and even driving role in developing legal notions of equality and discrimination, the latter source takes pride of place. At the national level, these jurisdictions include several countries which are well-known for their contributions to the development of the various conceptualizations of equality and discrimination in their judicial review of the applicable equality standards, such as the US, Canada and South-Africa. I also refer to equality cases in my own country, the Netherlands. Even if these are language wise not easily accessible to foreign readers and are mostly of a soft-law character, a conceptually rich jurisprudence has been developed under the Dutch General Equal Treatment Act.[11] At the regional level, the European Court of Human Rights (ECtHR) and the Court of Justice of the EU (CJEU) provide a wealth of relevant case law, which has been very influential in shaping approaches to equality standards in European countries, but also far beyond. In addition, the Inter-American Court of Human Rights (IACtHR) has also started to develop a significant line of jurisprudence on equality issues. Last but not least, at the global level, the conceptualization of equality and non-discrimination developed by the supervisory bodies to the international human rights conventions is a relevant source, though contrary to the regional human rights courts, the interpretation of equality standards by these treaty bodies constitute soft-law only. Nevertheless, as will become clear in this study, they may also exert considerable influence on conceptual developments.

Given the conceptual focus and overarching purpose of this study, it does not seek to provide a comprehensive, comparative law analysis of the equality and non-discrimination standards in the jurisdictions mentioned. It uses a selection of cases and other materials from across this variety of jurisdictions

---

11 The Dutch *Commissie Gelijke Behandeling* (Equal Treatment Commission) and its successor, the *College voor de Rechten van de Mens* (Netherlands Institute for Human Rights), have played a particularly important role in this respect by dealing with a very large number of equal treatment complaints under the Dutch equal treatment legislation (up to 100–200 cases each year since 1994). Though their decisions have the legal status of opinions and are not legally binding, they have been quite influential in shaping equality and non-discrimination standards in the Netherlands in more concrete detail. They are available in Dutch only. See more extensively S. Burri, Combating pregnancy discrimination in the Netherlands. The role of equality bodies, in: B. Havelková and M. Möschel (eds), *Anti-discrimination law in civil law jurisdictions*, Oxford University Press, Oxford 2019, Chapter 7, p. 158–1175 and in the same book T. Loenen, The impact of anti-discrimination law in the Netherlands. A case study of discrimination on grounds of religion in employment, Chapter 11, p. 233–243.

to illustrate how equality and non-discrimination standards can be understood in more limited or more far reaching terms; what types of difficulties and dilemmas are attached to the application of the various conceptualizations of equality and discrimination; and how different conceptualizations may result in very different outcomes. If I identify certain developments or approaches to equality in the subsequent chapters as 'general', 'frequent' or 'usual' and the like, it is within the context of this selection of jurisdictions.

1.2.1 *Limitations of This Study*

I realize that a focus on jurisdictions which have been playing a prominent role in developing and shaping equality standards entails a prevalence of Western perspectives and developments. It risks to leave out legal experiences and practices in many other countries and parts of the world not included in the selection. As such, this study cannot and does not claim to be grounded in some sort of 'universal' way of looking at equality and non-discrimination standards. At the same time, developments discussed in the following chapters show how understandings of equality as a legal concept in Global South jurisdictions have gained increasing prominence. They have become more and more influential in shaping notions of equality and discrimination throughout the world, including in Western jurisdictions. A particularly important role is played by the Constitutional Court of South Africa. In this sense, legal conceptualizations of equality standards are becoming much more globally informed than before. The internet revolution and rise of digital technologies have greatly helped the possibilities for such types of mutual influencing.

My focus on analyzing conceptual understandings of equality and non-discrimination standards creates another type of limitation. So far, interpretations of the legal concepts discussed in the subsequent chapters have to a large extent been based on equality and non-discrimination standards regarding groups facing discrimination on the basis of sex, race and religion. This may be explained by the fact that these grounds usually have much longer roots in equality and non-discrimination standards than categories such as disability, age, sexual orientation or gender identity. As a consequence, conceptual understandings of equality standards developed largely from case law regarding the former grounds. This is reflected in the prominent place they occupy in this study. Discrimination on the basis of disability provides an exception as far as the development of the concept of reasonable accommodation is concerned. As will be addressed in Chapter 6, the coming into being of the CRPD in 2006 has exerted (and still is exerting) a profound influence on shaping the meaning of this particular legal concept.

A third limitation derives from the dynamic character of equality as a legal concept referred to above. Its development into a much more multi-layered notion is not definite or finished, but ongoing. As the following chapters intend to show, the concepts of direct and indirect discrimination as well as the notions of positive discrimination or positive action seem to have become quite crystallized across jurisdictions, but lack of (reasonable) accommodation as a distinct form of discrimination and intersectional discrimination are still very much underdeveloped as legal concepts. As a consequence, the chapters discussing the latter are of a more tentative nature.

1.3 Terminology

As many jurisdictions may use the same words for different things or different words for the same things, a few remarks are in order about the terminology I use in this study. As a general starting point, I do not use any fixed definitions of the various notions of equality and discrimination figuring in this study as I try to capture their overarching features and look for commonalities in their understanding across jurisdictions. As a consequence, I use terminology rather loosely in a general sense and prefer formulations which span jurisdictions rather than wording particular to a specific jurisdictions. Nevertheless, as some of the terminology I use may not be self-evident or raise questions, some further explanation regarding the following terms may be useful to the reader. Of course, if I discuss particular equality standards or specific case law in a particular jurisdiction, I will use the corresponding terminology.

1.3.1 *Equality and Non-discrimination Standards*

I use the terms 'equality standards' or 'equality and non-discrimination standards' interchangeably and as generic terms for all sorts of legal standards covering a right to equal treatment or non-discrimination. So they may cover a wide range of more specific formulations in terms of, for example, equal protection of the law, equality before the law, granting rights 'without distinction' or 'without 'discrimination' of any kind or on particular grounds, et cetera.

1.3.2 *Formal and Substantive Equality*

Formal and substantive equality are commonly distinguished in academic literature and jurisprudence. In general terms, a formal equality approach starts from the presumption that all persons should be treated the same and is preoccupied with the question to what extent and in which situations differential treatment can nevertheless be justified. Substantive equality, on the other hand, is not concerned with equal or unequal treatment as such, but with the unequal outcome of a treatment, so regardless whether it results from the treatment being different or the same. In this study I use this general understanding of formal and substantive equality as a starting point and link it to the classic, Aristotelian notion of equality often referred to in legal theory, which holds that 'like case should be treated alike, and unalike cases unalike in accordance with their unalikeness'. In several jurisdictions this two-limbed notion has been taken on board, the second one having been tied expressly to a substantive equality approach. (See for further elaboration Chapter 3). As such it is part of legal doctrine.

To avoid confusion, this rather 'thin' and legally informed understanding of formal and substantive equality is to be distinguished from the way in which substantive equality is also often perceived as a 'thick', that is much more expressly normative conception of what equality and non-discrimination standards should try to achieve. Fredman's elaboration of substantive equality as a four-dimensional concept directed at redressing disadvantage (the redistribution dimension), addressing stigma, stereotyping and violence (the recognition dimension), facilitating social inclusion and political voice (the participation dimension) and accommodating difference and structural change (the transformative dimension), is a prime example.[12]

1.3.3 *Discrimination; Sensitive, Protected and Suspect Grounds*

Discrimination language is not always used in the same way across jurisdictions, but it is usually reserved for differences in treatment on the basis of certain grounds that are considered to require more stringent justification to be allowed. The latter is how I use the terminology, unless indicated otherwise. Grounds deserving such higher protection are often referred to as 'protected' grounds or 'suspect' grounds. In my own work I also used the terminology of 'sensitive' grounds. In this study I use these three terms interchangeably. The 'classic' list of grounds legally identified as protected grounds usually include race, sex and religion (already included in the Charter of the United Nations in 1945), as well as colour, political or other opinion, national or social origin, property and birth (included in addition to these grounds in the Universal Declaration of Human Rights (UDHR) and in the ICCPR and ICESCR). In more recent times, in many jurisdictions the list of protected grounds has been extended significantly, for example by including sexual orientation, disability, age and gender identity. (For further elaboration see Chapter 4.) Particularly

12 S. Fredman, *Discrimination law*, Oxford, Oxford University Press, 2022 (3rd edition).

the first three grounds – race, sex and religion – have played a prominent role in shaping the development of non-discrimination standards and as such will figure prominently in the subsequent chapters. Though using the categories of 'race' and 'sex' can be considered problematic,[13] I follow this terminology, as it is figuring in the far majority of legal texts and documents.

1.3.4 *Indirect Discrimination and Disparate Impact Discrimination*

The concept of indirect discrimination has developed over time in several jurisdictions. As will be discussed in Chapter 5, it has attained more or less common features across jurisdictions. In some jurisdictions the terminology of 'disparate impact' or adverse impact' discrimination is used. I use these terms as interchangeable.

1.3.5 (*Reasonable*) *Accommodation*

Using the terminology of 'reasonable accommodation' is more complicated. Denial of reasonable accommodation has taken on a quite specific meaning in the CRPD, in which it figures as a distinct, *sui generis* form of discrimination applicable in the context of disability. Thus, for example, discrimination on the basis of disability is at stake if office space is not adjusted to the specific, individual needs of an employee in a wheel chair, unless this would impose a disproportionate burden on the employer. As will be elaborated in Chapter 6, this specific conceptualization of reasonable accommodation as a right to *individual* accommodation does not fully align with similar notions of an obligation to accommodate the particular needs of persons or groups as part of equality and non-discrimination standards more generally. Thus, for example, several jurisdictions require accommodation of religious practices, for instance by granting an exemption from having to work on Saturday for persons adhering to the Jewish religion or adjusting dress codes to allow for the wearing of religious symbols. Other jurisdictions have also required accommodation of the needs of other groups protected by non-discrimination standards, such as the need of legal regulation of the relationship of same-sex partners as an alternative to marriage. As the terminology used for such obligations in different jurisdictions is quite varied and not consistent, I use (reasonable) accommodation

13 Using the category of 'race' sits uneasily with the idea that there is only a single human race. As approached in the ICERD, racial discrimination is to be understood in a broad way as discrimination on the basis of race, colour, descent or national or ethnic origin (Article 1(1)). 'Sex' as a category is now often disregarded and replaced by the terminology of 'gender'. This acknowledges the socially constructed nature of the categories of 'man' and 'woman' as well as these being broader and more fluid categories than the traditional binary notion.

as a generic term to refer to this type of obligation. By placing 'reasonable' between brackets I intend to avoid conflating the general and broader notion of a duty of accommodation existing in several jurisdictions with the particular way in which 'reasonable accommodation' is defined under the CRPD.

1.3.6 *Positive Discrimination and Positive Action*

Positive discrimination, reverse discrimination, benign discrimination, preferential treatment, affirmative action, ameliorative measures, remedial measures, temporary special measures or positive action: depending on the jurisdiction concerned, all these terms may refer to a highly contested topic. Do equality standards allow for measures or polices which make deliberate and express use of protected categories such as race or sex to benefit and improve the position of structurally disadvantaged groups? Formulations in terms of 'discrimination'– regardless the addition of 'positive' or 'benign' – usually denote a reluctance to accept this type of measures or policies as an acceptable way to improve the position of disadvantaged groups. Formulations avoiding the term discrimination and instead using terms like 'positive action' or 'ameliorative measures', tend to represent more positive attitudes to such measures. In view of the wide variety of terminology used in legal practice and the sensitivities attached to it, it is impossible to use legally neutral terminology. For this reason I use all the above terms interchangeably and often use 'positive discrimination' and 'positive action' in tandem, as in the title of Chapter 7. When discussing particular case law on the topic, I will use the terminology common to the jurisdiction concerned.

1.3.7 *Structural or Systemic Discrimination*

I understand structural or systemic discrimination in a general sense as discrimination that encompasses pervasive patterns of prejudice or disadvantageous treatment of (members of) a particular group across various areas of law and society. It is not about incidental discrimination or prejudice, but about 'multiple forms of compounded disadvantage'.[14]

1.3.8 *Intersectional Discrimination*

Intersectional discrimination, multiple discrimination and compound or aggravating discrimination are sometimes used as interchangeably, sometimes to denote distinct forms of discrimination. I generally use the terminology

---

14 Cf. D.B. Oppenheimer, What is 'systemic racism?' How is it different from racist acts caused by bigotry, prejudice or bias? Paper, 6 July, 2020, p. 1; available at SSRN https://ssrn.com/abstract=3644684 or http://dx.doi.org/10.2139/ssrn.3644684.

'intersectional discrimination' in the way it was deployed by Crenshaw in relation to the particular predicament faced by black women in the US compared to either white women or black men; that is as discrimination on the basis of a combination of two or more protected grounds resulting in a distinct type of discrimination.[15]

1.4 Outline of the Subsequent Chapters

An overview of the main scope and content of the subsequent chapters is provided to clarify to the readers what to expect and to enable easy navigation through the book and quickly find any particular topic.

Chapter 2 sets the stage by discussing the historical background and development of equality as a legal concept, including its links with equality as a political and philosophical notion and ideal, before turning to the general features of equality as a legal standard and some of the questions it raises.

The historical background explores the role of the state as the guarantor of equal and inalienable rights in liberal theory and the broadening personal scope of equality as a legal standard ('equality of whom') by gradually including not just a rather small group of mainly white, male citizens, but all human beings regardless of sex, race and other identity or status markers. This development is reflected in provisions regarding equal treatment and non-discrimination becoming part and parcel of international human rights conventions and national constitutions. In addition, the material scope of equality ('equality of what') is discussed. This element is often central to political and philosophical discussions on equality and is perhaps the most contested element. In classical liberal theory equality is limited to liberty and freedom rights, but over the course of time equality claims often have come to be extended to include (elements of) social and economic equality.

Besides on its personal and material scope, the reach of equality as a legal standard depends to a large extent on its conceptual scope. This scope may vary greatly, particularly depending on equality being interpreted in a formal or a substantive way. Similarly, conceptualizing discrimination in a broad way by including modalities of discrimination such as indirect discrimination, a lack of (reasonable) accommodation, positive discrimination/positive action,

15 K. Crenshaw, Demarginalising the intersection of race and sex: a Black feminist critique of antidiscrimination doctrine, feminist theory and antiracist politics, *University of Chicago Legal Forum*, 1989, p. 139–167.

and intersectional discrimination, makes a considerable difference. Such varieties in the conceptual scope of equality and non-discrimination standards are the focus of the book and are explored in the subsequent chapters.

Chapter 3 is devoted to the crucial distinction between formal and substantive equality. In a legal context, these notions have developed their own, distinct meaning. Taking the Aristotelian notion of equality as a starting point the chapter reflects on the one hand on the demand that 'likes should be treated alike', which represents a requirement of formal equal treatment. On the other hand, it delves into the question what the requirement that 'unalikes should be treated unalike in accordance with their unalikeness' adds to this. By its reference to the need to take differences into account, the second part of the Aristotelian notion of equality links it to the relevance of the outcome of the treatment, rather than the treatment itself being equal. A concern with the unequal impact of a treatment is the hallmark of a substantive equality approach. As human beings differ from each other in myriad ways, both approaches have to come to terms with the question which differences are relevant in which contexts, and which are not. If anything, it puts on the table what may be regarded as a core issue of conceptualizing legal equality and equality theory more generally: how to respond to human difference and inequality? The chapter discusses how formal and substantive equality approaches differ in this respect. It also clarifies how both bring along their own difficulties and dilemmas when they are applied in concrete cases. As both formal and substantive equality focus on unjustified treatment, be it unjustified unequal treatment or unjustified equal treatment, equality analysis inevitably involves all sorts of normative assessments and appreciation. Unsurprisingly, then, they can be up for a lot of discussion depending on the perspectives taken.

Chapter 4 provides an analysis of the general features of non-discrimination as a legal standard. It starts with an exploration of the distinguishing characteristics of discrimination, including its relationship with equality as a legal concept. Generally speaking, non-discrimination can be seen as a particular articulation of equality. Discrimination is first and foremost concerned with differential treatment on the basis of 'sensitive' or 'protected' grounds. Treating people differently on the basis of such grounds is usually perceived as 'suspect'. In addition to the most 'classic' grounds such as race, sex and religion, these have come to cover an increasing number of other categories, such as disability, sexual orientation and gender identity. The chapter discusses how grounds have been identified as sensitive or protected grounds and explores the complexities of legally defining and delimitating grounds of discrimination.

It also goes into the proliferation of the number of grounds identified as 'protected grounds' in many jurisdictions, before turning to what is core to non-discrimination law: the way in which differential treatment in rules or policies on the basis of protected grounds leads to a demand of stronger justification to be acceptable. More stringent judicial review, then, is a fundamental characteristic of the application of non-discrimination standards. The types of stricter review developed show strong similarities across jurisdictions. To conclude the chapter, some of the difficulties and dilemmas of differentiating discrimination review according to the particular ground involved are discussed.

Chapter 5 delves into the concept of indirect discrimination which developed over the years and can be said to have become – in one way or another – part and parcel of the conceptualization of non-discrimination by national and regional courts and global human rights bodies. A prohibition of indirect discrimination in addition to direct discrimination significantly expands the reach of non-discrimination standards by bringing seemingly neutral classifications having a disproportionate negative impact on groups protected by these standards within their purview. With its focus on the outcome of a treatment rather than the treatment itself, it belongs to the realm of substantive equality approaches. The general features and core elements of the concept of indirect discrimination are explored, including the ways in which disproportionate impact may be construed and standards of judicial review have been developed.

By problematizing the unequal, disadvantageous effects of an equal treatment as an equality issue, the notion of indirect discrimination may have a considerable potential for addressing more structural and systemic levels of discrimination. Yet, whether this potential can materialize depends to a large extent on the strictness or leniency with which it is applied in legal practice. Again, the consequences of different approaches for the outcome of concrete cases are illustrated with examples from across jurisdictions.

Chapter 6 explores a modality of discrimination which is closely related to indirect discrimination and sometimes conceived as a particular part of this notion, but also as a *sui generis* modality of discrimination: lack of (reasonable) accommodation. Similar to the concept of indirect discrimination, application of the notion of (reasonable) accommodation is triggered by the unequal impact of a treatment on a group protected by non-discrimination standards. As such, the concept of (reasonable) accommodation is also tied to a substantive equality approach.

The concept of (reasonable) accommodation is much less crystallized than indirect discrimination, which has established itself as a broadly accepted, distinct concept and manifestation of discrimination with very similar general features across jurisdictions. A duty of reasonable accommodation as part of discrimination analysis has gained considerable traction with the adoption of the CPRD in 2006, in which it occupies a prominent place. The CRPD has identified it as a distinct form of discrimination: not accommodating the particular, individual needs of disabled persons may amount to discrimination. The CRPD has become very influential globally. The Convention is widely ratified and its approach to (reasonable) accommodation has been followed in many national jurisdictions. At the same time, the particular context and focus of the notion of reasonable accommodation in the CRPD as a form of accommodation which is limited to individual adjustments and to persons with disabilities, seems to contribute to confusion about (reasonable) accommodation as a much broader concept in equality and non-discrimination law.

The idea that a lack of accommodation of certain individuals or groups may constitute a form of discrimination was present in legal practice before the terminology of (reasonable) accommodation was used and long before the CRPD-model of reasonable accommodation gained prominence. Anyway, manifestations of notions of (reasonable) accommodation in legal practice are quite fragmented and not fully aligned. As mentioned before, (reasonable) accommodation is in many respects an underdeveloped concept in the legal practice of jurisdictions.

Chapter 7 discusses positive discrimination or positive action, which is a highly contested issue in most jurisdictions. With its focus on correcting factual inequalities, affirmative action fits very well in a substantive equality approach. After providing an overview of the general features of positive discrimination or positive action, diverging views on its legitimacy and instrumentality are discussed. Being aware of these views is helpful in understanding the different choices that can be and are made regarding legal approaches to remedial measures in different jurisdictions, which are explored in more detail.

As it turns out, a central feature of the different legal approaches to affirmative action regards the question whether equality and non-discrimination are to be perceived in a symmetrical or asymmetrical way. Is a distinction based on sex or race to improve the position of women or disadvantaged racial groups to be regarded with equal suspicion as using such a distinction to the detriment of these categories? In jurisdictions adhering to the former, judicial review translates into more lenient scrutiny of remedial measures. At the same time, also within the latter type of jurisdiction approaches to remedial policies meet with their own distinct difficulties. Particularly the demarcation of the groups to benefit from affirmative action may pose serious dilemmas.

Chapter 8 addresses intersectional discrimination. This type of discrimination occurs when discrimination on two or more grounds coincide to create a distinct type of discrimination, which is qualitatively different from discrimination on the basis of the grounds taken separately. Intersectional discrimination has received increasing attention as it creates unique forms of discrimination. Discrimination suffered by black women at the intersection of race and gender is a classic example. Though it has been much discussed in academic literature, as a legal concept it has been hardly developed yet. Conceptually, intersectional discrimination poses tough questions for equality and non-discrimination law that do not seem to have been clearly answered yet in any jurisdiction. This chapter will try to bring a bit more clarity by looking at various ways in which intersectional discrimination has been dealt with so far in judicial analysis of equality standards.

Chapter 9 brings together the main lines and understandings developed in the preceding chapters by reflecting on some general trends regarding the conceptualization of equality as a legal standard that stand out across jurisdictions.

CHAPTER 2

Historical Background and General Characterization of Equality as a Legal Concept

2.1 Introduction

The Universal Declaration of Human Rights (UDHR), adopted in 1948 by the United Nations, opens by proclaiming in Article 1 that 'All human beings are born free and equal in dignity and rights'. Article 2 immediately follows up on this by providing that 'Everyone is entitled to all the rights and freedoms set forth in this Declaration, without distinction of any kind, such as race, colour, sex, language, religion, political or other opinion, national or social origin, property, birth or other status.' Together these Articles reflect the double meaning of the equality principle as a meta-juridical and juridical norm. In its meta-juridical meaning, the equality principle refers to the inherently equal human dignity of all human beings, whereas in its juridical shape, it grants equal entitlement to all rights and freedoms bestowed on them without distinction of any kind, including – but not limited to – distinctions on the basis of race, sex, religion and several other specifically articulated grounds. Historically, this approach to the human person is not at all self-evident. The idea of the equality of all human beings is a rather new fundamental premise which only gained general acceptance by becoming incorporated in wide array of fundamental legal norms and standards in the course of the 20th century.

This chapter discusses the historical background and development of equality as a legal concept and some of its links with equality as a meta-juridical or political/philosophical notion and ideal. In doing so, it will highlight its distinct character and how this translates into answering the questions 'equality of whom?' and 'equality of what?' (Section 2.2) before turning to the importance of how its legal conceptual scope is conceived for the reach equality standards may have (Section 2.3). This conceptual scope is the focus of the subsequent chapters. As it may vary widely between jurisdictions, the actual reach of equality standards may also differ widely as a consequence. The remaining sections of this chapter briefly discuss several other topics to keep in mind throughout this study for understanding the wider context in which equality standards are shaped and developed: the separation of powers and the role of courts (Section 2.4), the horizontalization of equality standards (Section 2.5)

DOI:10.1163/9789004538368_003

and the limits of law in changing all sorts of dominant standards and the resulting inequalities prevalent in law and society (Section 2.6).

2.2 Historical Development of Equality as a Legal Concept

The historical development of equality as a legal concept is to a large extent a product of the Western liberal tradition. It evolved only more recently into a globally embedded standard, as evidenced by its inclusion at the very beginning of the UDHR.[1] In this development, three elements seem crucial for understanding the contemporary (potential) reach of equality as a legal standard: the role of the state as the guarantor of equal freedoms and rights; the broadening personal scope of equality as a legal standard by gradually including not just a selected group of mainly white, male citizens, but all human beings regardless of sex, race and other identity or status markers; and last but not least, the broadening material scope of equality as a legal standard by increasing state regulation of all sorts of social and economic issues. In classical liberal theory, equality pertained to a small number of equal liberty and freedom rights, but in contemporary realities, equality claims often have come to include (elements of) social and economic equality. Particularly the latter element of the reach of the legal principle of equality ties in closely with political and philosophical debates on equality as a meta-juridical concept and is probably the most contested element.

2.2.1 *The State as the Guarantor of Equal Fundamental Rights*

The role assigned to the state for guaranteeing fundamental rights is firmly rooted in classical liberal theory, as exemplified by the ideas of one of its most prominent thinkers, John Locke (1632–1704). Locke's ideas greatly influenced Enlightenment thinkers and politicians and resonate in political documents such as the American Declaration of Independence of 1776 and the French Declaration of the Rights of Man and of the Citizen of 1789.

For Locke, in the 'state of nature', all men are free and equal and live in liberty. In this natural state, they have inalienable rights to 'life, liberty, health and possession' in order to be able to lead their lives and take care of themselves. As he put it:

1 This is not to say the UDHR is not criticized for being based predominantly on Western conceptions of human rights, notwithstanding efforts by UNESCO to include broader perspectives in the drafting process, see M. Goodale (ed), *Letters to the contrary. A curated history of the UNESCO human rights survey*, Stanford, Stanford University Press, 2018.

> The state of nature has a law of nature to govern it, which obliges everyone, and reason which is that law, teaches all mankind who will but consult it, *that being all equal and independent, no one ought to harm another in his life, health, liberty or possessions*; (...).[2] [emphasis added]

As each men's inalienable rights may not always be respected by their fellow men, they voluntarily relinquish part of their liberty by establishing a political community (the state) to protect these rights. To do so, the state is responsible for creating general and clear legal rules applicable to all, independent and impartial administration of justice and law enforcement. Importantly, the legitimacy of state power and its exercise depends on the proper protection of the inalienable rights of its subjects.[3]

Several points stand out in this classical liberal approach. First of all, the freedom to lead one's life as one sees fit and to enjoy the fruits of one's labour without interference by others, is paramount. Individual liberty is the default position, which the state has to protect. At the same time, as all rights bearers share in the right to individual liberty, *equal* protection of these rights must also be an inherent part of state obligations. Secondly, and perhaps contrary to what seems often neglected when discussing liberal theory: this approach starts from the need to protect individual rights from encroachments by other human beings, so from a horizontal focus of fundamental rights. A horizontal focus is not to overlook, of course, that once the state is established, its very power may also (or even more so) pose considerable threats to the fundamental rights of its subjects. In this situation, the vertical working of fundamental rights becomes an overriding concern. The role of the state is thus an ambiguous one: it poses potentially the most serious threats to the fundamental rights of its subjects, but is also the supreme power responsible for guaranteeing these rights. Thirdly, and this seems also quite often neglected, liberal theory does not disqualify state interference as a matter of principle. On the contrary, organizing an effective judicial system clearly requires some far reaching state regulation and other sorts of involvement. In this respect, liberal theory necessarily accepts a certain degree of state action to guarantee fundamental individual rights as part and parcel of the liberal state's *raison d'être*. To *what extent* state action is deemed necessary to protect the fundamental rights of all, however, remains a crucial question to answer and a bone of contention between different strands of liberal thought.

2 J. Locke, *Two treatises of Government*, 1689, Book II, 2.6.

3 Locke, *Two treatises*, 1689, Book II, 6.87–89.

What is most important to note at this point: the fundamental idea that the state is bound to protect the inalienable or fundamental rights of its subjects has been widely accepted and embedded in the formation of liberal, democratic states throughout the world. In this sense, the historical, liberal attribution of the role of guarantor of equal fundamental rights to the state has not changed as a matter of principle. This is borne out by the state legally being the duty bearer in guaranteeing the fundamental rights standards included in the international human rights conventions it has ratified.[4] What has changed over time, however, is the legal scope or reach of this role. The scope has increased in two ways: first of all, in terms of the subjects to be recognized as bearers of equal and inalienable rights (personal scope) and thus requiring equal protection by the state; secondly, in terms of the type of rights and freedoms to be regarded as fundamental rights (material scope).

2.2.2 *Equality of Whom – Personal Scope*

Historically, regarding all human beings as inherently equal and possessing equal rights, is a quite recent development. Looking again at the Western tradition, this change in perspective only came about in the 20th century.[5]

Though in Greek Antiquity the idea of the equality of all human beings was not completely absent (the Stoics are often mentioned as an example), this notion was not part of dominant thinking and practice. Even in the most equality dominated period of Athenian democracy, equality notions were limited to free Greek citizens. Women and enslaved people were excluded as a matter of principle. One of the greatest philosophers of Antiquity, Aristotle, adhered to this position, as he considered them lacking in their capacity for reason which was the basis for the equal citizenship bestowed on free Greek men. Roman times did not witness fundamental changes in such ways of thinking.

The rise of Christianity provided some more space for the idea of basic human equality, as Christian belief holds all human beings to be equal in the eyes of God, but this idea had little practical meaning. In the institutionalized

4 All states in the world have ratified at least one or more human rights treaties. This holds true even for North-Korea. See the overview of the status of treaty ratification on the website of the UN Office of the High Commissioner for Human Rights (OHCHR), https://indicators.ohchr.org/.

5 The brief sketch which follows is largely based on L.C. Winkel, Enige opmerkingen over de geschiedenis van het gelijkheidsbeginsel in het recht (Some remarks on the history of the equality principle in law), in: C.W. Maris (ed.), *Gelijkheid en recht* (Equality and law), Deventer/Zwolle, Van Loghum Slaterus/Tjeenk Willink, 1988, p. 99–112. For a more detailed historical overview see e.g. S.A. Lakoff, *Equality in political philosophy*, Cambridge, Harvard University Press, 1964.

thinking of the Church, such equality pertained exclusively to the afterlife, not to life on earth. In this dualist type of thinking, exemplified by the writings of Augustine, inequalities in earthly life were perceived to be the result of just punishment by God for the fall from paradise.[6] It was only in the early modern period that the foundation was laid for a more genuinely egalitarian perception of human beings. The work of John Locke referred to above is a clear example.

The 18th century Enlightenment period, which drew heavily on Lockean ideas, is generally regarded as the cradle of the modern perception of the inherent equality of all human beings, with the French *Déclaration des Droits de l'Homme et du Citoyen* (Declaration of the Rights of Man and of the Citizen) of 1789 often cited as one of its clearest political manifestations.

If we take a closer look, however, the age of Enlightenment did not bring about full inclusion of all human beings in the notion of equality. The French Declaration mentioned is a case in point. Despite its lofty language in Article 1 that 'Human beings are born and remain free and equal in rights', not everyone was indeed perceived as fully or equally human and meant to be included in the notion of 'human beings'. The Declaration neither intended to end slavery, which existed in many of the French overseas territories, nor to include women as bearers of equal rights.[7] As a response to the latter, in 1791 Olympe de Gouges formulated a *Déclaration des Droits de la Femme et de la Citoyenne'*, in which she spelled out the rights of women by reformulating the 1789 Declaration Article by Article.[8] The declaration of De Gouges was completely ignored by the powers that be, as was 'A Vindication of the Rights of Woman' by Mary Wollstonecraft.[9] The idea that equality could only pertain to men was too self-evident, including for most Enlightenment thinkers; Montesquieu, Rousseau and Kant were no exceptions.[10]

6 Lakoff, Equality in political philosophy, 1964, p. 21–22.

7 The more radical French Government that took power under Robespierre did abolish slavery in 1794.

8 For a comparison of the two declarations in English see the entry on Wikipedia 'Declaration of the Rights of Woman and of the Female Citizen'.

9 M. Wolstonecraft, *A vindication of the rights of women*, 1792.

10 For an overview of the approach by these and several other prominent thinkers in Western philosophy to women's (in)equality see S.M. Okin, *Women in Western political thought*, Princeton, Princeton University Press, 1979 and M.J. Gunning, *Gewaande rechten. Het denken over vrouwen en gelijkheid van Thomas van Aquino tot de Bataafsche Constitutie* (Supposed rights. Thinking on women and equality from Thomas of Aquino to the Batavian Consititution), Zwolle, W.E.J. Tjeenk Willink, 1991.

An important explanation for the exclusion of women from a common human equality can be found in the widespread idea existing at the time that women do not have the same rational capacities as men, as they are governed by their bodies and emotions rather than reason. This type of thinking remained dominant for a long time.[11] Recognition of women's inherent equality only came about in the 20th century. During the course of the 19th century, a small group of well-educated women emerged, who started to take up social and public roles and their performance made the argument of their inferiority and lesser rational capacities hard to maintain. At the same time, women started to organize themselves in an increasingly vocal emancipation movement, adding political to social pressure for recognition of their fundamental equality and equal rights. In the first half of the 20th century this development culminated in the extension of the vote to women in most Western countries. In addition, the growing economic role of women in the labour market presumably was a major influence in the wider acceptance of women's equality and may have been enhanced by the two world wars, when many men were fighting at the front.[12] However this may be, after World War II women were explicitly included in the fundamental equality proclaimed by the UDHR.

For non-white people, recognition of their fundamental equality also took a long time to materialize. Like women, they did not partake in the lofty equality ideas of the Enlightenment. The abolishment of the slave trade at the beginning of the 19th century did not fundamentally change things. The institution of slavery continued for quite some time, and as the US experience shows, abolishing slavery did not necessarily entail legally equal rights for whites and non-whites alike.[13] It is sobering to realize that even Abraham Lincoln, famous for his commitment to end slavery, did not fully depart from white-superiority thinking and opposed bestowing equal rights on black people:

> I will say then that I am not, nor ever have been, in favor of bringing about in any way the social and political equality of the white and black races, that I am not, nor ever have been, in favor of making voters or jurors of negroes, nor of qualifying them to hold office, nor to intermarry with white people; (…) [T]here must be the position of superior and inferior,

11 Idem.

12 This commonly held belief has been challenged as too simplified, see P. Summerfield, Women, war and social change: women in Britain in World War II, In: A. Marwick (ed), *Total war and social change*, London, Palgrave Macmillan, 1988, p. 95–118.

13 For an overview of the history of slavery see D. Harrison, *Geschiedenis van de slavernij: van Mesopotamië tot moderne mensenhandel* (History of slavery: from Mesopotamia to modern human trafficking. Translated from Norwegian), Utrecht, Omniboek, 2019.

> and I as much as any other man am in favor of having the superior position assigned to the white race. I say upon this occasion I do not perceive that because the white man is to have the superior position the negro should be denied everything.[14]

Dominant US thinking in terms of white superiority continued well into the 20th century and resulted in a full blown system of racial segregation and oppression, mostly so in the Southern states where it was legally backed up by pervasive segregation laws. An important legal turning point came about in 1954 with the Supreme Court judgement in *Brown v. Board of Education*, characterizing racial segregation as 'inherently unequal' and thus unconstitutional.[15]

For colonial people under European rule the situation was comparable: they were not regarded as equals in any fundamental way. Colonialism was much more than an economically based and profit driven system, it was ultimately grounded in and justified by thinking in terms of white superiority.[16] A change in this type of thinking also had to wait until the 20th century, when decolonization movements gained strength and forced European powers to reconsider their position and attitudes. World War II was also a major catalyst in changing dominant views on racial equality. Here again, the UDHR manifests this change by proclaiming that all human beings are entitled to the rights enshrined in it, without distinctions on the basis of race or colour.

This brief overview shows how since World War II the idea of the inherent equality of all human beings and their equal entitlement to fundamental rights has legally gained global traction.[17] As a legal standard, equality has since then become part and parcel of international human rights conventions and national constitutions. In this legal setting, equality provisions are usually formulated in terms of a right to equality of all before the law and to the equal protection of the law, and are very often closely linked to a prohibition of discrimination. Thus, for example, Article 26 of the International Covenant on Civil and Political Rights (ICCPR) provides:

---

14 A. Lincoln, *Charleston speech*, 18 September 1858. Available at https://www.nps.gov/liho/learn/historyculture/debate4.htm (last accessed 29 March 2024).

15 US Supreme Court, *Brown v. Board of Education*, 347 US 483 (1954).

16 See e.g. R. Ross, Introduction. Reflections on a theme, in: R. Ross (ed), *Racism and colonialism. Essays on ideology and social structure*, Studies in Overseas History vol. 4, The Hague/Boston/London, Martinus Nijhoff Publ., 1982, p. 1–9.

17 In Dworkin's terms it could be said that an abstract, 'egalitarian plateau' has been reached, cf. R. Dworkin, Comment on Narveson: in defense of equality, *Social Philosophy and Policy*, 1983, p. 24–40, at p. 25.

> All persons are equal before the law and are entitled without any discrimination to the equal protection of the law. In this respect, the law shall prohibit any discrimination and guarantee to all persons equal and effective protection against discrimination on any ground such as race, colour, sex, language, religion, political or other opinion, national or social origin, property, birth or other status.

With varieties in their specific formulation, largely similar provisions have been included in all major international and regional human rights conventions.[18] As all states have ratified at least one or more human rights conventions containing such explicit equality provisions, they have legally bound themselves to implement and enforce these norms.[19]

To conclude, in the present time a right to equality before the law and to non-discrimination for all is clearly established – which is not to say that what this right entails in more detail and in concrete cases is not contested or may not vary widely between jurisdictions.

2.2.3 *Equality of What – Material Scope*

General acceptance of equality as an abstract standard pertaining to all human beings without distinctions of any kind, does not silence discussions on its more concrete content: what is its object and focus? This element is often central to political and philosophical discussions on equality and is arguable the most contested element. Aristotle's much referred to characterisation of equality as a requirement to 'treat like cases alike, and unalike cases unalike in proportion to their unalikeness', leaves the 'equality of what' question open.[20] Equality as such does not give an answer and can be said to be a merely

18 For an overview of equality provisions in IHRL see L. Carlson, *Comparative discrimination law: historical and theoretical frameworks*, Brill Research Perspectives in Comparative Discrimination Law, Brill, 2017; M. Mwakagali, *International human rights law and discrimination protections. A comparison of regional and national responses*, Brill Research Perspectives in Comparative Discrimination Law, Brill, 2019. An overview of almost all national constitutions is available on the website of the Comparative Constitutions Project, https://comparativeconstitutionsproject.org/.

19 The ICCPR is ratified by 173 countries, China being one of the major exceptions. China did ratify several other human rights treaties including equality and non-discrimination provisions, such as the ICESCR, the ICERD and the CEDAW. For an overview of ratifications of all human rights treaties see the website of the Office of the High Commissioner for Human Rights (OHCHR), https://indicators.ohchr.org/.

20 Aristotle, *Ethics*, Book V (Justice), London, Penguin Classics, 1976.

formal or 'empty' notion in its own right, not a substantive concept.[21] It has to be filled out.[22]

Many contemporary political and philosophical theories seek to provide such content. They mostly focus on questions of distributive justice, to which equality is usually closely linked.[23] Such theories come up with a wide variety of answers to the question 'equality of what?'. Libertarian approaches view equality almost entirely in terms of equal freedom, which is the paramount interest to be protected by the state. As a consequence, libertarians see no role for the state beyond maintaining public order. Everything else is to be left to free enterprise and market forces.[24] In this perspective, any claims for more social and economic equality pose unacceptable threats to individual freedom. With this singularly strong focus on liberty, libertarians regard equality and freedom rather as an opposition. On the other side of the spectrum we find theories claiming a strict socio-economic equality. Thus the French revolutionary Babeuf claimed the right of everyone to be provided with the same level of material goods and services. To realize this he advocated the abolishment of private property.[25] In between these extremes figure many other approaches, such as theories focusing on equality of welfare, resource equality or equality of opportunity.[26]

When discussing equality as a *legal* concept and standard, answering the question 'equality of what' is fundamentally different. The 'what' of the state's obligation to guarantee equal protection of the law and non-discrimination to all its subjects – that is its material scope – is determined by the larger legal context in which these equality standards operate in a specific state or jurisdiction.

2.2.3.1 Prevailing Law as the Frame of Reference for Equality as a Legal Standard

For equality as a legal standard the frame of reference for the state's duties, including its implementation and enforcement by administrative and judicial powers, is legally defined. It consists of all prevailing law. This is a crucial

21 P. Westen, The empty idea of equality, *Harvard Law Review* 1982, p. 537–590.

22 S. Gosepath, *Equality, The Stanford Encyclopedia of Philosophy* (Summer 2021 Edition), Edward N. Zalta (ed), p. 4. https://plato.stanford.edu/archives/sum2021/entries/equality/.

23 Gosepath, *Equality*, 2021, p. 2.

24 Idem, p. 8.

25 F-N. Babeuf, *Manifeste des égaux*, 1796. Translated from French into English and included in L.P. Pojman and R. Westmoreland (eds.), *Equality. Selected readings*, New York/Oxford, Oxford University Press, 1997, p. 49–52.

26 For an overview of these and several more theories see Gosepath, *Equality*, 2021, p. 6–13.

difference indeed with philosophical discussions on the material scope of equality and is to be kept in mind at all times. Contrary to what Westen famously argued in a seminal publication in the eighties of the last century, equality as a *legal* concept and standard is not empty, or rather, its content is filled out by the larger legal framework in which it operates.[27]

As will become clear in the subsequent chapters, emphasizing this difference between the meaning of equality in political and philosophical theories of justice and equality as a legal standard is not denying their mutually influencing and overlapping character. To distinguish is not to separate in watertight compartments. Political and philosophical discussions on equality may and do resurface either implicitly or explicitly in all sorts of discussions regarding the interpretation and application of legal equality standards in concrete cases. Where, for instance, positive discrimination or positive action is concerned, judgments on its legal acceptability in a certain jurisdiction are often highly influenced by underlying philosophical views on equality as directed at equal opportunities or at (more) socio-economic equality as such.

2.2.3.2 Extension of State Action over Time

Similar to the expanded personal scope of legal equality standards, historical developments show a significant broadening of the material scope of those standards in probably most if not all jurisdictions. Whereas in Locke's time state regulation was mostly limited to a few areas such as administration of justice, maintaining public order and levying taxes, over time, all around the world the scope of state power and regulation has increased tremendously. Contemporary states tend to deal with a wide range of social and economic issues, often including education, employment, health care, social welfare and climate change. The greatly increased reach of what is sometimes termed 'the Administrative State' may be applauded or criticized, but it seems here to stay.[28]

This expansive reach of state action may be further stimulated in states which have given legal recognition to social, economic and cultural rights (social rights for short) in addition to classical civil and political rights. Many contemporary jurisdictions have included both types of rights in their

---

27 P. Westen, The empty idea of equality, *Harvard Law Review* 1982, p. 537–590.

28 Cf. C.R. Sunstein and A. Vermeule, *Law & Leviathan: redeeming the administrative state*, Cambridge, Massachusetts, The Belknap Press of Harvard University Press, 2020.

constitutions.[29] In addition, about 170 countries have ratified the International Covenant on Economic, Social and Cultural Rights.[30] If taken seriously, inclusion of social rights in the overarching fundamental rights framework of a state entails a much larger ambition and reach of state regulation covering large areas of social life and welfare. In jurisdictions where this has happened, close links may become apparent between applying legal equality standards and political and philosophical theories on distributive equality or justice.

Anyway, the larger the resulting span of state control and regulation, the larger the reach of legal equality standards. As Tussmann and tenBroek already noted in 1949: 'Whenever an area of activity is brought within the control or regulation of government to that extent equality supplants liberty as the dominant ideal and constitutional demand.'[31] Thus, for example, if a state decides to provide free education to children, equality standards are engaged if it excludes black children or girls. If it sets up a health care or social security scheme, it must comply with equality standards. In short, if the larger legal framework in a specific jurisdiction provides for laws, policies or other measures to promote more social and economic equality, to that extent legal equality standards apply. States may not be obliged to set up all sorts of social policies and benefits, but if they do they have to respect equality and non-discrimination standards.[32]

It may be clear that the more state action expands, the more complicated equal protection of all rights and freedoms will become, if only because rights and interests cannot all be realised at the same time and for everyone or may conflict. For example, under conditions of scarce resources, providing for education, health care or housing needs may compete and will require difficult choices regarding what or which groups should be prioritized. In such and many other situations, a balance has to be struck, in which equality standards may play an important role. Striking a balance is ultimately a *legal* decision. In democratic states such decisions are usually taken by the legislative powers, but may be subject to review by judicial bodies.

---

29 See for an overview the Comparative Constitutions Project website, https://comparativeconstitutionsproject.org/.

30 The largest country absent from the list of ratifications is the United States.

31 J. Tussman and J. tenBroek, The equal protection of the laws, *California Law Review* 1949, p. 341–381, at p. 380.

32 See e.g. ECtHR (Grand Chamber), 12 April 2006, *Stec and others v. the UK*, appl. nos. 65731/01 and 65900/01; in the same way Supreme Court of Canada, *Eldridge v. British Columbia* [1997] 3 SCR 624, par. 73.

2.3 Equality as a Legal Standard – Conceptual Scope: What Equality?

Notwithstanding the expansive reach of legal equality standards in both their personal and material scope sketched above, the question whether these standards are themselves narrowly or broadly conceived and interpreted in the specific jurisdiction in which they operate, is even more crucial to understand their actual and practical reach in a particular society or country. I call this their legal *conceptual* scope and this is the main focus of this study.

The legal conceptual scope of equality has shown itself to be dynamic and may vary greatly between jurisdictions. In my understanding, the most important differences between jurisdictions stem from the way in which they embrace a formal or (more) substantive notion of equality, which is in turn closely linked to the way in which they have adopted distinct modalities of discrimination in the application of equality standards, such as indirect discrimination, (reasonable) accommodation and positive discrimination or positive action.[33]

2.3.1 *Formal and Substantive Equality*

The conceptual scope of legal equality standards may vary greatly depending on equality being interpreted in a formal or a substantive sense. Equality may be legally interpreted as a requirement of formal equal treatment only, but also as demanding substantive equal treatment. A formal equality approach's primary concern is with unjustified unequal treatment, whereas a substantive equality approach is not so much interested in the treatment itself, but concerned about the unequal outcome of a treatment, regardless the treatment being the same or different. The latter interpretation considerably widens the reach of equality standards. As will be elaborated in Chapter 3, in a legal context, the concepts of formal and substantive equality are to be distinguished from the philosophical notions of formal and substantive equality referred to above. Within the dynamics of law, they have developed their own specific meaning.

2.3.2 *Equality and Discrimination – Protected Grounds and Modalities of Discrimination*

The way in which equality as a legal standard is linked to legal prohibitions of discrimination is also a very important aspect of its conceptual scope in law. As a legal standard, equality is closely linked to prohibitions of discrimination.

33 For the way in which I use these terms in this study see Chapter 1.

Equality and non-discrimination mostly operate as legal twins, though they are not usually conceptualized as identical twins.[34] Discrimination has a strong pejorative ring to it.[35] Discrimination is generally speaking perceived as a specific type of equality issue dealing with distinctions on the basis of race, sex and other 'sensitive' grounds, which are often listed in equality and non-discrimination provisions such as Article 2 UDHR and Article 26 ICCPR.[36] In many jurisdictions they are referred to as 'protected' or 'suspect' grounds.[37] Historical experience has taught us to be wary of these types of classifications for their often detrimental and exclusionary effects on women and members of racial, religious or other minority groups. For this reason these groups are considered to deserve special protection under equality and non-discrimination standards. As will be elaborated in the subsequent chapters, distinctions on the basis of sex, race and other sensitive grounds usually trigger higher scrutiny if they are subjected to judicial review and thus require stronger justification to be acceptable than if 'ordinary', non-sensitive ones are involved; they are generally approached as presumptively unjustified for their suspect character. As Fredman remarks, this recognition constitutes 'one of the biggest leaps in twentieth century struggles for equality'.[38]

Legal discussions on equality tend to focus on differential treatment on the basis of these sensitive or protected grounds rather than on the myriad number and range of 'ordinary' classifications used in law for purposes of regulating society, which are not in any way sensitive. This is where the notion of discrimination steps in. Discrimination is usually seen as a specific articulation of the notion of equality. In many jurisdictions, equality standards are often elaborated in more detail in non-discrimination law. As a consequence non-discrimination rather than equality as such is often the focal point of court cases and jurisprudence. This is reflected in this study, which deals predominantly with equality issues in respect of sensitive or protected grounds and devotes separate chapters to various modalities of discrimination.

The specific reach of non-discrimination provisions depends very much on their conceptual scope and the way in which they are linked to either formal or

34 In this study, both are included under the plural 'equality standards'.

35 W. McKean, *Equality and discrimination under international law*, Oxford, Clarendon Press, 1983, p. 10.

36 And many others, see overview in M. Mwakagali, *International human rights law and discrimination protections. A comparison of regional and national responses*, Brill Research Perspectives in Comparative Discrimination Law, Brill, 2019.

37 For the way in which I use the terminology of 'sensitive', protected' and 'suspect' grounds see Chapter 1.

38 S. Fredman, *Discrimination law*, Oxford, Oxford University Press, 2022, p. 9.

more substantive approaches to equality. Again, this may vary greatly between jurisdictions. Is discrimination in a particular jurisdiction perceived as including just direct discrimination, or also indirect discrimination? As will be elaborated in Chapter 5, the latter interpretation is linked to a substantive notion of equality rather than a formal one, and gives a prohibition of discrimination considerably more bite. Similar questions regarding the conceptual legal scope and relationship with a formal or substantive equality approach are highly relevant for topics such as (reasonable) accommodation (Chapter 6), positive discrimination or positive action (Chapter 7) and intersectional discrimination (Chapter 8). The different ways in which these modalities of discrimination can be legally conceived and approached may result in major differences in the actual implementation of equality standards and widely differing outcomes in concrete cases.

To sum up, as a legal standard, equality has its own specific dynamics and in its legal elaboration it may be conceptualized in a variety of ways between jurisdictions. Before elaborating this in the subsequent chapters, a few more words are in order here on several topics to keep in mind throughout this study for understanding the wider context in which equality standards are shaped and developed.

2.4 Equality Standards, Separation of Powers Principles and the Role of Courts

As a legal standard, equality is first and foremost a norm for the state. In general terms it requires states to treat their subjects as inherently equal and to ensure their equality before the law. Laws have to be general in nature and apply to all. In an absolute sense, such equality is impossible to adhere to. Laws classify by their very nature and thus differentiate all the time between different groups of subjects. This has been referred to as the paradox of legal equality.[39] This paradox is resolved by requiring classifications to be reasonable. The same treatment is so to speak the default position, for differences in treatment sufficient reasons are required to justify them.[40] Non-discrimination standards come in when sensitive or suspect classifications are

39 Tussman and tenBroek, Equal protection of the laws, 1949, p. 344.

40 Idem; in the same vein McKean, who gives many sources for the dominant idea that the principle of equality means that classifications are only acceptable if sufficient reasons for differences in treatment exist, W. McKean, *Equality and discrimination under international law*, Oxford, Clarendon Press, 1983, p. 3–5.

at stake, such as classifications on the basis of sex and race. Generally speaking for such classifications a much stronger justification is required (see further Chapters 3 and 4).

As mentioned above, the reach of equality standards expands with the expanding scope of government action and control. In democratic states governed by rule of law and separation of powers principles, the primary competence to decide governmental reach lies with the legislative power; it establishes the overall framework of laws and policies in which equality standards apply. It also decides which mandates for interpreting and enforcing equality standards are to be given to the other branches of government or to specialized institutions such as national human rights institutes or equality bodies, which may accordingly play an important part in their elaboration. In most democratic jurisdictions, a special position is usually reserved for the judiciary by given it competence to check such powers.[41] As a result, courts often play an important, if not crucial role in developing the conceptual scope and ultimate reach of equality standards.

2.4.1 *The Role of Judicial Bodies in Developing the Conceptual Scope and Reach of Equality Standards*

The role of courts in developing the scope and reach of equality standards may be considerable. It depends on a variety of factors, including their legal mandate and the use made of this mandate.

2.4.1.1 Legal Mandates for Equality Review

The role of courts is first of all determined by the legal mandate they have been granted to review laws, policies and other state or non-state action. For international courts such powers derive from the applicable international treaties, for national courts from the prevailing constitutional or statutory arrangements. The resulting influence judicial bodies can exert on shaping equality standards may vary greatly between jurisdictions. In countries with a strong tradition of constitutional review, the judiciary usually plays a core role. Similarly, in regional human rights systems, human rights courts have been given competence to develop an – often extensive – jurisprudence on a wide

41 In fact, a far majority of jurisdictions have adopted some form of judicial review, see J. Phang, Book review of Erin F. Delaney and Rosalind Dixon (eds), *Comparative judicial review*, Edward Elgar, 2018, *International Journal of Constitutional Law* (I·CON), 2019, p. 721–725.

variety of fundamental rights, including equality rights.[42] In fact, judicial interpretation has come to the fore as a driving force in the dynamic developments and expanding scope of equality standards.

The role of courts in shaping equality standards is also greatly influenced by the legal space they have for ordering remedies and reparations. Here again considerable differences may exist across jurisdictions. For the ECtHR, for example, its judgments are primarily envisaged as largely declaratory of a violation of fundamental rights, without specifying remedies. Implementation and enforcement is expressly left to the Committee of Ministers of the Council of Europe.[43] The CJEU's role in developing legal standards such as equality and non-discrimination is primarily shaped by the preliminary ruling procedure in which it clarifies the interpretation of EU law, leaving it to the member states to apply these standards in their domestic jurisdictions. The Inter-American counterpart of the ECtHR, the IACtHR, has a much broader mandate and has developed this into a broad approach to remedies and reparations, including collective and structural ones in addition to individual compensation.[44] In national jurisdictions the range of remedies and reparations judicial bodies can provide may similarly differ considerably depending on the domestic arrangements. No matter how important this topic is for the ultimate effectiveness of equality standards, it falls beyond the scope of this study. The same applies to the actual enforcement mechanisms available.

2.4.1.2 Use Made of Legal Mandates – Judicial Interpretation as a Driving Force of Conceptual Developments

In addition to the legal competence granted to judicial bodies, the actual use made of such competence is an important factor in the role played by courts. Legal traditions and practices may range from a very narrow or legalistic approach to judicial interpretation, such as the 'originalist' approach adhered to by several members of the US Supreme Court, to a broad, evolutive

42 Of course, all sorts of procedural regulations and admissibility criteria may put barriers on bringing cases to court to start with.

43 Article 46 ECHR.

44 Article 63(1) American Convention on Human Rights. Collective reparations are often based on the UN *Basic Principles and Guidelines on the Right to a Remedy and Reparation for Victims of Gross Violations of International Human Rights Law and Serious Violations of International Humanitarian Law*, which include not just restitution and compensation, but also rehabilitation, satisfaction and 'guarantees of non-repetition'. The latter in particular is broad and relevant to address structural causes of human rights violations.

approach generally adhered to by human rights courts.[45] Similar diversity may exist between jurisdictions regarding the range of remedies and reparations deployed on the basis of the legal mandate granted to judicial bodies.

In both instances, differing views on separation of powers principles and the proper relationship between the legislative and judicial branches of Government come into play; courts have to negotiate the tensions between robust fundamental rights protection and the deference due to the other branches of Government.[46] For international courts, their very position as an international rather than domestic body may bring its own perspectives on the discretion to be left to – in this setting – the States parties, rather than any of the particular branches. Here again, different courts may have quite different approaches.[47]

Interestingly, in many jurisdictions the role of courts in developing equality standards (and fundamental rights standards more generally) has increased significantly over the past decades. Human rights tribunals in particular have played an active and influential role by their dynamic and evolutive interpretation of fundamental rights, including equality and non-discrimination standards. This development is part of a much wider trend of judicialization.[48] Arguably, judicial interpretation has been the driving force behind conceptual developments of equality standards across jurisdictions. Particularly case law regarding race, sex and religion have played a central role. More recently, case

45 See for the former e.g. L.B. Solum, Originalism versus Living Constitutionalism: The conceptual structure of the great debate, *Northwestern University Law Review*, 2019, p. 1243–1296; for the latter see F. Pascual-Vives, Evolutive interpretation as a method of interpretation in Public International Law, in: F. Pascual-Vives *Consensus-Based Interpretation of Regional Human Rights Treaties*, Chapter 4, Brill, 2019.

46 This is no different in a jurisdiction such as South Africa, where broad powers of constitutional review, including remedial powers, are widely accepted. See *Special issue*: Separation of powers, the judiciary and the politics of constitutional adjudication, *South African Journal on Human Rights*, 2020, no. 4.

47 Thus the 'margin of appreciation' doctrine developed by the ECtHR suggests a more deferential approach than the 'conventionality control doctrine' of the IACtHR, which claims a particularly strong form of judicial supremacy for the IACtHR. See for the former e.g. J. Gerards, The Margin of Appreciation doctrine, the Very Weighty Reasons test and grounds of discrimination, in M. Balboni (ed), *The principle of discrimination and the European Convention of Human Rights*, Editoriale Scientifica, 2017, p. 27–61; for the latter see e.g. E. Ferrer Mac-Gregor, Conventionality control. The new doctrine of the Inter-American Court of Human Rights, *International Journal of American Law*, 2015, p. 93–99.

48 Judicialization is a particular form of legalization; it is legalization with a central role for courts and other judicial bodies. Critics warn against this trend as a form of judicial overreach and the advent of a 'juristocracy'. Cf. R. Hirschl, *Towards Juristocracy: The origins and consequences of the New Constitutionalism*, Harvard, Harvard University Press, 2004.

law regarding disability has proven influential by putting the concept of reasonable accommodation in the limelight (see further Chapter 6). The resulting jurisprudence developed by judicial bodies figures prominently in this study.

As interestingly, international, regional and national courts applying equality and other fundamental rights standards also show increasing awareness of each other's jurisprudence and often seem influenced by developments elsewhere in the interpretation of these standards under their own, specific mandates.[49] This type of conceptual exchange has been facilitated tremendously by the information revolution under way since the advent of personal computers and the internet. As a result – and notwithstanding all sorts of varieties – major conceptual developments in equality standards, including, for example, the development of the notion of indirect discrimination or reasonable accommodation, seem to be increasingly shared across jurisdictions. In addition, this type of enhanced harmonisation often leads to levelling up of human rights protection rather than levelling down, and may sometimes even turn 'soft law' standards developed by semi-judicial bodies into 'hard law' standards applied by courts. A case in point is the way in which the approach to violence against women by the CEDAW Committee as an issue of gender based discrimination has been taken on board in the case law of the ECtHR and the IACtHR.[50]

At the same time, the principle of the separation of powers puts important limits on the role of courts in holding governments to account for how they implement their obligations under equality standards and other fundamental rights. Much has been written on this topic, particularly in the context of

49 This influence can be either explicit, when a judicial body explicitly refers to other bodies, or implicit, when it adopts clearly similar lines of reasoning in its interpretation of equality standards. South Africa, Columbia and Argentina are some of the countries which are well-known for drawing inspiration from global and regional fundamental rights standards. Judicial bodies in European jurisdictions tend to look in particular to the jurisprudence of the ECtHR and the CJEU. Cf. M. Killander, Interpreting regional human rights treaties, 2010 *SUR – International Journal on Human Rights*, 2010, p. 145–169; L. Lixinski, Treaty interpretation by the Inter-American Court of Human Rights: expansionism at the service of the unity of international law, *European Journal of International Law*, 2010, p. 585–604; L. Burgorgue-Larsen, "Decompartmentalization": the key technique for interpreting regional human rights treaties, *International Journal of Constitutional Law (I·CON)*, 2018, p. 187–2013.

50 ECtHR, 9 June 2009, *Opuz v. Turkey*, appl. no. 33401/02; IACtHR, 16 November 2009, *González et al. ('Cotton Field') v. Mexico* (Preliminary Objections, Merits, Reparations, and Costs).

judicial review of social rights.[51] Social rights realization often requires the development of all sorts of – often costly – policies and positive state action, which are generally deemed to belong to the discretionary competence of political and legislative powers rather than judicial bodies. Courts adjudicating social rights claims have to deal with this tension. As will become clear in the subsequent chapters, similar issues and dilemmas emerge in interpreting and applying equality standards by courts, particularly where substantive equality approaches are involved.

2.5 Horizontalization of Equality Standards

A further point to mention here concerns the horizontal reach of legal equality standards. Over time, equality standards have become increasingly regarded as not just a norm in the vertical relationship between state and individual, but also between private individuals. Usually, such obligations for individuals to provide equal treatment and refrain from discrimination are established by way of more specific statutory regulation and have a much more limited material scope, such as employment or the access to goods and services in the public sphere. In this setting, duty-bearers are mostly identified on the basis of a specific function they perform, such as being an employer or a provider of certain goods and services.[52] As the resulting obligations for private persons interfere more directly with individual freedom, this development may meet with (even) more contestation than obligations for state actors.[53]

Compared to constitutional or treaty provisions, statutary equality and non-discrimination law usually provides for much more detailed elaboration of

51 See a.o. J. King, *Judging social rights*, Cambridge, Cambridge University Press, 2012; S. Fredman, Review article: Coming of age: socio-economic rights as human rights, in: S. Fredman and M. Campbell (eds), *Social and economic rights and constitutional law*, Cheltenham, Elgar Publ., 2016; E. Cameron, A South African perspective on the judicial development of socio-economic rights, in: L. Lazarus, C. McCrudden and N. Bowles (eds.), *Reasoning rights. Comparative judicial engagement*, Oxford, Hart Publ., 2014, p. 319–338.

52 Cf T. Khaitan, *A theory of discrimination Law*, Oxford, Oxford University Press, 2015, p. 66.

53 See e.g. the brief discussion on this in A. McColgan, *Discrimination, equality and the law*, Oxford, Hart Publ, 2014, p. 63–66 and a Belgian compilation of contributions entirely devoted to this topic: *Vrijheid en gelijkheid. De horizontale werking van het gelijkheidsbeginsel en de nieuwe antidiscriminatiewet* (Freedom and equality. The horizontal working of the equality principle and the new antidiscrimination act), Antwerpen/Apeldoorn, Maklu, 2003. Nevertheless, horizontal reach has been accepted as a matter of principle also in what is arguably the most liberal of all states, the US; see e.g. Title VII of the Civil Rights Act, which covers discrimination in employment.

what equality standards entail in concrete areas of society. In this way, they may figure in their own particular way as prominent focal points for shaping conceptual approaches to these standards.

Horizontalization of equality standards has also increased in a more indirect way. In international human rights law more generally, fundamental rights have come to be interpreted as including certain positive obligations for the state to prevent and redress human rights violations by private actors.[54] This also applies where discrimination is at stake. Thus, for instance, the responsibility of the state is engaged in combatting violence against women as a form of gender based discrimination in both the public and private sphere.

Anyway, whether the state or private actors are the duty bearers, the actual and practical reach of obligations to provide equal treatment and refrain from discrimination will depend to a large extent on how a specific jurisdiction defines the conceptual scope of equality standards. The notions of formal and substantive equality, direct and indirect discrimination, (reasonable) accommodation, positive discrimination or positive action, and intersectional discrimination, have an equally important bearing on the application of equality standards in vertical and horizontal relationships.

2.6 Equality and 'Dominant Standards' in Law and Society – the Limits of Law in Addressing Systemic Discrimination

A final point to keep in mind when addressing the reach of legal equality standards regards the limits of law as such. Law does not operate in a vacuum or from a *tabula rasa* point of departure. Legal equality standards are no exception.

Law and society have been shaped by historical developments and power relations and do not constitute a neutral playing field on which equality standards apply. Worldwide, women, disabled persons and members of a wide variety of racial, religious and sexual minority groups face structural inequalities that have become ingrained in law and society. Over time, all sorts of dominant standards and frames of reference evolved in which these groups do not fit or only to a much lesser degree than the 'reference man'. Thus, for instance, women face the consequences of long time societal patterns relegating them predominantly to the private sphere of the home and excluding them from

54 See for this development in the context of the ECHR J. Gerards, *General principles of the European Convention on Human Rights*, Cambridge, Cambridge University Press, 2023 (2nd ed).

the public sphere. Granting them equal rights does not undo the resulting inequalities at the stroke of a pen. Similarly, when South Africa abolished the *Apartheid* system, the equal rights granted to all non-white people did not do away with their poverty and structural inequalities in access to education, housing or health care and the like. Overcoming such systemic inequality in social reality requires profound societal change and transformation. As socio-legal scholars have demonstrated time and again, law is a limited instrument to achieve such change. An important question, then, is to what extent the application of legal equality standards can be helpful in reaching structural inequalities and be instrumental in bringing about systemic, transformative change. When and where do they reach their limits as legal instruments? Though this question is far beyond the reach of this book to answer, the limits of law in tackling systemic forms of discrimination and changing the dominant standards prevalent in our societies will resurface time and again in the subsequent chapters.

2.7 Concluding Remarks

As the above sketch of its historical background and characteristics show, equality as a legal standard is to be distinguished from political and philosophical understandings of equality. As a legal standard, it is a dynamic concept with its own, distinct features and scope. Over time, its scope has been considerably expanded. In terms of personal scope expansion resulted in the inclusion of all human beings as 'inherently equal' and deserving of equal rights, regardless characteristics such as race, sex or religion. In terms of material scope, expansion flows from the expanding reach of state regulation of society.

Notwithstanding this broad personal and material scope, the actual impact of equality as a legal standard depends to a large extent on its conceptual scope. This scope may vary greatly, particularly depending on equality being interpreted in a formal or a substantive way. Similarly, conceptualizing discrimination in a broad way by including modalities of discrimination such as indirect discrimination, a lack of reasonable accommodation, positive discrimination/positive action, and intersectional discrimination, may make a huge difference. Such varieties in the conceptual scope of equality and non-discrimination standards are the focus of the book and are explored in the subsequent chapters. Chapter 3 starts with the fundamental distinction to be made between formal and substantive approaches to equality as a legal standard.

CHAPTER 3

Formal and Substantive Equality

3.1 Introduction

The importance of the particular conceptualization of equality as a legal principle for the outcome of applying legal equality standards cannot be overemphasized. In this respect, two different conceptions of or approaches to equality can be identified: a formal equality approach and a substantive equality approach.[1] I distinguish the two as types or models and not as fixed, rigid concepts, which acknowledges the existence of all sorts of varieties within these models across jurisdictions.

Generally speaking, a formal equality approach can be characterized by a focus on equality of the *treatment* as such. If all human beings are inherently equal, they should be granted the same rights and duties, in particular regardless characteristics such as birth, race, sex, disability or any other sensitive status. In an absolute sense, a formal equality approach would entail abstracting from any individual or group characteristics of people to realize a strict legal equality; all people should be treated the same, always and everywhere. In legal reality, such an absolute formal equality cannot possibly exist. As soon as the state regulates, classification and thus differentiation occurs. Traffic regulations differentiate between car drivers and pedestrians, tax law may treat people with high and low incomes differently, and electoral law distinguishes on the basis of age.

A substantive equality approach can be characterized as not focusing on the equality of the treatment as such, but on the equal *outcome* of the treatment. The latter may indeed require differential treatment. A person suffering from a particular illness is not helped by being treated the same as a healthy person, but requires a specific, differential treatment to return to health. This approach to equality can also be based on the inherent equality of all human beings: on this basis, their individual needs and circumstances must be taken into account to genuinely realize their (equal) rights. As with formal equality, substantive equality in an absolute sense cannot be realized in legal reality; to treat all people always and everywhere in accordance with their individual characteristics and circumstances is impossible to achieve. It would mean

1 For the choice of the terminology used for the various concepts figuring in this chapter see Chapter 1.

DOI:10.1163/9789004538368_004

that all regulation would have to provide for open norms and standards which enable fully individualized, personalized treatment. Take as an example a tax law system organized on the basis of the equality to pay principle, which taxes high incomes by a higher percentage than low incomes. This differential taxation takes into account a highly relevant difference in view of the tax system's purpose. Yet, such a progressive income tax would not necessarily meet the standards of absolute substantive equality, as it does not provide the proper yardstick for each and every individual case. Though as a general rule people with a higher income will have a better ability to pay than people with a low income, this is not always the case. Some people with a high income may, for instance, have much less money left due to a disability. To take into account such very specific, individual circumstances influencing the ability to pay in order to achieve a more equal outcome, the tax system would have to provide for a system of personal deductions, allowing for a (more) fully individualized assessment of the ability to pay.

From the above two conclusions can be drawn. Firstly, both a formal and a substantive equality approach can be linked to the meta-juridical idea of the inherent equality and equal worth of all human beings. Secondly, in legal reality, neither of the two approaches can be realized in an absolute sense, that is for each and every individual, always and everywhere. This means both approaches have to come to terms with something in between: classifications which are based on generalizations and as such are group-based. In this sense, then, I would say that the often perceived opposition between a formal equality approach being individualistic and substantive equality being group-based is not entirely correct.[2] Both approaches can be conceived as demanding a fully individualized or personalized treatment if taken to their logical extreme, but in legal practice both have to deal with group-based classification.[3] The different ways in which they do, however, is of crucial importance due to their diverging starting points. Formal equality takes equal treatment as the default position, whereas substantive equality takes equal outcomes as its primary yardstick.

Compared to a formal equality approach, a substantive equality approach significantly broadens the scope of equality standards, but also adds another layer of complexity to their application. Overall, a formal equality approach is the most common approach in most jurisdictions and has been developed

2 See e.g. Fredman, *Discrimination Law*, 2022, p. 15.

3 This is also an important issue I will return to in Chapter 8 when discussing the difficulties and dilemma's connected to taking an intersectional perspective, if the latter is taken to an ever increasing degree of differentiation.

much more fully in legal doctrine and practice than substantive equality.[4] Nevertheless, an explicitly substantive equality approach can be found in various jurisdictions, notably in South Africa and Canada. Many more jurisdictions have implicitly or explicitly embraced at least some elements of a more substantive equality approach by applying the concepts of '(reasonable) accommodation' (see paragraph 3.4.2 below and Chapter 6) and 'indirect discrimination' (see Chapter 5), or allowing positive discrimination or positive action (Chapter 7). All of these respond to the unequal impact of a treatment.

Overall, a worldwide trend seems to be moving towards a more substantive approach. In Europe, the jurisprudence of the CJEU and ECtHR have been developing in this direction, particularly by the development of the concept of 'indirect discrimination' and by taking on board the notion of '(reasonable) accommodation'.[5] In the Americas, the Inter-American Court of Human Rights has taken the lead in interpreting the Inter-American Convention on Human Rights as requiring substantive equality.[6] Last but not least, the UN human rights treaty bodies have adopted a more substantive, outcome oriented equality approach.[7] Though their treaty interpretation constitutes soft law only, their influence on regional and national courts can be quite considerable.[8]

This chapter explores the notions of formal and substantive equality in more detail in the sections below, including the difficulties and limitations involved in their legal application. The Aristotelian definition of equality already mentioned in Chapter 2 (Section 2.2.3) provides a useful starting point for doing so.

4 Many legal scholars criticize the dominant approach to equality as being largely limited to a formal approach, see Fredman, *Discrimination Law*, 2022; Khaitan, *Theory of Discrimination Law*, 2015; McGolgan, *Discrimination, equality and the law*, 2014. Smith calls formal equality 'the most widespread' understanding of equality, A. Smith, Equality constitutional adjudication in South Africa, *African Human Rights Journal*, 2014, p. 609–632, p. 611.

5 For an overview of the European approaches to equality see M. Balboni (ed.), *The principle of discrimination and the European Convention of Human Rights*, Editoriale Scientifica, 2017 and T. Giegerich (ed.), *The European Union as the protector and promotor of equality*, Springer 2020.

6 See e.g. IACtHR, 24 November 2017, *Advisory Opinion OC-24/17 on Gender identity, and equality and non-discrimination of same-sex couples*, par. 61–62; Inter-American Court of Human Rights, 15 July 2020, *Workers of the Fireworks Factory in Santo Antônio de Jesus and their families v. Brazil* (Preliminary objections, merits, reparations and costs), par. 199.

7 The supervisory committees of the ICESCR) and the CEDAW are most explicit in this respect, see CESCR, *General Comment No. 20 of 2012 on Non-discrimination in economic, social and cultural rights (Art. 2, para.2 of the ICESCR)*; CEDAW-Committee, *General recommendation No. 25 of 2004, on Article 4, paragraph 1, of the Convention on the Elimination of All Forms of Discrimination against Women (temporary special measures)*.

8 The regional human rights courts do not interpret human rights in a vacuum and in their decisions refer to interpretations by treaty bodies on a regular basis.

A formal equality approach can be said to limit itself to the first part, requiring like cases to be treated alike. The second part of the Aristotelian definition, by demanding in addition that unalike cases are to be treated unalike in proportion to their unalikeness, ties in with a substantive conception of equality by suggesting that, depending on the circumstances, differential treatment may be required to achieve an equal (or at least more equal) outcome. Though formal equality may indeed also result in an equal outcome if cases are alike, in many instances where cases are unalike it does not. Crucially, if cases are indeed unalike, formal equality may allow for a difference in treatment, but it does not provide in itself an obligation to treat persons differently to reach a (more) equal outcome. For a fully substantive equality approach, then, adhering to both limbs is indispensable.

3.2 Formal Equality: Like Cases Must Be Treated Alike

Under a formal equality approach, equal treatment is the default position. All the state's subjects are presumptively 'like cases' which must be treated the same. An equality issue only arises when people are not treated alike. As classifications are inevitable as soon as laws and policies enter the stage, the equality principle demands a proper justification for any differential treatment.[9] *Unjustified unequal treatment*, then, is the problem a formal equality approach is concerned with.

3.2.1 *Justifying Unequal Treatment*

In legal life, courts usually play a crucial role in deciding the question whether differential treatment is justified or not when such treatment is challenged before judicial bodies. The precise formulation of the review criteria used to decide whether a classification can be justified may differ between jurisdictions, but overall two main elements stand out. To be justified, differential treatment has to pursue a legitimate goal and the means employed must bear a 'reasonable and objective' or 'proportional' relationship to this goal.[10]

9 Cf. E.W. Vierdag, *The concept of discrimination in international law*, The Hague, Martinus Nijhoff, 1973, p. 12.

10 See e.g. the classic judgment of the ECtHR of 1968 in the *Belgian Linguistics case* : '(...) the Court, following the principles which may be extracted from the legal practice of a large number of democratic States, holds that the principle of equality of treatment is violated if the distinction has no objective and reasonable justification. (...) A difference of treatment in the exercise of a right laid down in the Convention must not only pursue a legitimate aim: Article 14 (art. 14) is likewise violated when it is clearly established that there

3.2.1.1 Legitimate Goal and Reasonable and Objective Relationship between Means and End

For many instances of differential treatment it may not be very difficult or controversial to decide whether they are based on a relevant difference which may justify differential treatment. The difference between people with a high or low income is irrelevant in view of receiving a building permit for an extension to a house, whereas for receiving a minimum welfare benefit or a progressive income tax system this difference will be highly relevant. Similarly, setting a minimum age limit of eighteen for the right to vote makes sense, whereas setting a maximum age would not: all mature, adult people are like cases in view of electoral rights, whereas minors are not.

These examples show two things. First of all, the relevance of any difference is to be decided in view of the specific purpose or goal of a rule or measure. This highlights the importance of who decides about the goals set. As already pointed out in Chapter 2, in democratic states organized on the basis of the rule of law, the competence to set goals is primarily the prerogative of legislative powers. Deciding about goals is thus the result of political choices. The latter means a lot of controversy may exist regarding the goals itself. For example, establishing a tax system based on ability to pay may meet with opposition by people who favour a flat tax system. Nevertheless, for purposes of deciding whether like cases are treated alike, the goals set by the competent state organs are a given, unless the goals as such are not legitimate.[11]

Secondly, the examples show that a classification has to be *adequate* in view of the specific goals of a rule or measure; that is, the classification must provide

---

is no reasonable relationship of proportionality between the means employed and the aim sought to be realised.'(ECtHR 23 July 1968, *Belgian Linguistics case*, appl. no. 2126/64, par. 10). At the global level, the supervisory bodies to the ICCPR and the ICESCR consider differential treatment justified if the criteria for differentiation used are reasonable and objective and serve a legitimate aim, see HRC, *General Comment No. 18: Non-discrimination* (1989), par. 13 and CESCR, *General Comment No. 20, Non-discrimination in economic, social and cultural rights* (2009), par. 13.

11 I leave aside here the problems which may be involved in identifying the goals of a law or measure as such. Goals can be multiple or fuzzy. The search for goals may raise 'notorious and practical problems', see K.W. Simons, Overinclusion and underinclusion: a new model, *University of California Los Angeles Law Review* 1988/89, p. 447–528, p. 460; O. Fiss, Groups and the Equal Protection Clause, *Philosophy and Public Affairs* 1976, p. 107–177, p. 118–128; J. Gerards, *Judicial review in equal treatment cases*, Leiden/Boston, Martinus Nijhoff, 2002, p. 35–41. I return to this issue further below when discussing the case *Burden v. UK*.

a suitable means to achieve the end pursued.[12] This adequacy requirement demands a certain rationality and proportionality between means and ends. It may also be referred to as a requirement of 'fit'.[13] A progressive income tax system is an adequate instrument to tax people according to their ability to pay as taxing people with a high income at a higher percentage fits this purpose. One could also say that people with high and low income are relevantly 'unalike' groups for tax purposes. Similarly, setting the right to vote at eighteen is an adequate way to limit this right to people who can be considered sufficiently mature; the age requirement fits this goal. The examples also illustrate that the classifications chosen do not provide a 'perfect' fit with the end to be achieved. They are based on generalizations which need not match with the realities of every individual case. Thus, setting the right to vote at eighteen may exclude younger people who are in fact mature, or include people over eighteen who are not. This 'under- and overinclusion' or 'misfit' is inevitable, unless granting the right to vote would be based on an individualized assessment of each person's maturity. As such a system is unfeasible, the age of eighteen is used as an indicator or 'proxy' of maturity.[14] In the example of the tax system, a similar 'misfit' may occur if, as mentioned before, a person with a high income also bears unusually heavy financial burdens, for instance due to a disability.

The existence of 'misfit' raises the important question how much of it is still acceptable. For purposes of granting the right to vote to mature people only, setting the age at sixteen or twenty instead of eighteen will probably also be regarded as acceptable, whereas setting it at ten or 40 would definitely not provide sufficient fit with this purpose. The degree of fit required is indeed a question which may be answered differently between jurisdictions. Overall, regarding non-sensitive or non-suspect classifications the degree of misfit allowed is usually large, with wide discretion being left to governmental authorities. Where sensitive classifications are concerned, that is where discrimination enters the equal protection scene, stronger requirements of fit are usually adopted in judicial review. This heightened scrutiny in discrimination review will be explored more extensively in Chapter 4.

12 Loenen, *Verschil in gelijkheid*, 1992, p. 213. Vierdag speaks about 'truthfulness' of a classification, that is it being based on factual truth, Vierdag, *Concept of discrimination*, 1973, p. 62.

13 Simons, Overinclusion and underinclusion, 1988/89, p. 451.

14 Proxies are usually based on statistical generalizations and are often used in legal classifications. Cf. F. Schauer. Statistical (and non-statistical) discrimination, in: *The Routledge Handbook of the ethics of discrimination*, 2017, Chapter 3, p. 42–53.

3.2.1.2 Normative Appreciation as Part and Parcel of Justifying Unequal Treatment

Though in many instances the above reasonableness or rationality review may be pretty straightforward, in many others it may entail much more than a rather factual exercise and inevitably include significant degrees of normative appreciation which may vary with the perspective taken.[15]

Sometimes this normative appreciation becomes particularly focused on assessing whether differential treatment can be justified by the existence of a sufficiently relevant difference between the cases concerned. In some jurisdictions this 'comparability' question is added as a distinct element in judicial review of unequal treatment challenges. Thus, for instance, the ECtHR has added it as a distinct element to its standard of review under Article 14 ECHR.[16]

In other instances normative appreciation comes in particularly prominently by including an assessment of broader goals and interests the government may justifiably take into account when differentiating between different categories. This may then result in a wider proportionality test balancing all sorts of interests involved in assessing whether differential treatment can be justified. In academic literature this has sometimes been called proportionality *stricto sensu*.[17] Here again, in some jurisdictions this type of proportionality review is explicitly formulated as a distinct element of judicial review, as it is

15 Loenen, *Verschil in gelijkheid*, p. 212–216. See in a similar way Vierdag, who points to a 'volitive' element in addition to the 'cognitive' element involved in deciding about the adequacy (in his words 'truthfulness') of a classification, Vierdag, *Concept of discrimination*, p. 62.

16 Whereas 'comparability' was not a separate part of the review standard formulated in the landmark judgment in the *Belgian Linguistic case* of 1968 (appl. no. 2126/64), the ECtHR now includes it as a distinct element in its formulation of the review criteria to be applied under Article 14 ECHR: 'Article 14 ECHR is violated if persons *in relevantly similar situations* are treated differently without an objective and reasonable justification, that is if the difference in treatment does not pursue a legitimate aim and if there is no reasonable relationship of proportionality between the means employed and the aim sought to be realised' [emphasis added]. See e.g. ECtHR (Grand Chamber), 29 April 2008, *Burden v. UK*, appl. no. 13378/05, par. 60 and similarly in Advisory Opinion of 13 July 2022 'on the difference in treatment between landowners' associations "having a recognised existence on the date of the creation of an approved municipal hunters' association" and landowners' associations set up after that date', Request No. P16–2021–002; At the same time, the Court often skips it as a separate inquiry in its actual assessment of a case, see M. Sjöholm, *Gender-sensitive norm interpretation by regional human rights law systems*, Brill/Nijhoff, 2018, p. 196.

17 See e.g. J. Gerards, *Judicial review in equal treatment cases*, Leiden/Boston, Martinus Nijhoff, 2002, p. 53–54.

in the case law of the Inter-American Court of Human Rights.[18] In others it is approached as part of the required proportionality between means and ends or figures much more implicitly.

All in all, as will be further explored in Chapter 4 when discussing discrimination review, the various elements in judicial review distinguished above (legitimacy of the goal; comparability of cases and fit or proportionality between means and ends; consideration of wider interests) may receive different emphasis in different jurisdictions. In yet other jurisdictions, they are not clearly distinguished; or if distinguished as distinct steps, application in actual cases may show the steps are not neatly followed at all.[19] As a result, equality analysis and review by courts has been identified as muddled and unpredictable.[20] Interestingly, the ECtHR shows it is aware of this critique. In the separate opinion in *Fábián v. Hungary*, the concurring judges remarked that the 'choice of comparator will often change the outcome of the case, and the judicial choice of comparators is sometimes criticized for being arbitrary or lacking in a consistent rationale'.[21]

If I see this correctly, what makes this type of review indeed so elusive – and somehow inevitably so – is due to two factors. First of all, the above elements are profoundly intertwined and cannot really be separated. Trying to do so may be a laudable effort to create more transparency, but may in fact also enhance confusion rather than being helpful. Formulating a neat set of separate steps to take in assessing whether a difference in treatment is justified may obfuscate the inevitably fuzzy boundaries between them. Secondly, assessments of all the above elements ultimately depend to a significant degree on the perspective taken (which is a matter of choice rather than being grounded in clearly

---

18 See the Advisory Opinion of the IACtHR of 2017 on gender identity and same-sex couples, par. 81, in which the Court distinguishes three elements: the legitimacy of the aim; the relationship between means and ends; and 'In addition, there must be a strict proportionality analysis of the measure by which the benefits of adopting the measure in question must be clearly more advantageous than the restrictions it imposes on the treaty-based principles it affects', par. 81.

19 Thus, for example, it has been noted that the ECtHR 'frequently postpones the analysis of comparability to the justification phase', Sjöholm, *Gender-sensitive norm interpretation by regional human rights systems*, p. 196.

20 As Xenidis remarks, the comparison test has often met with profound critique 'for obfuscating deep-reaching moral judgments … behind a screen of apparent objectivity and scientific neutrality', R. Xenidis, *The concept of direct discrimination in European anti-discrimination law: theory, practice and limits*, iCourts Working Paper Series, no. 285, 2022, p. 9.

21 ECtHR (Grand Chamber), 5 September 2017, *Fábián v. Hungary*, appl. no. 78117/13), concurring opinion of judges O'Leary and Koskelo, par. 10.

recognizable 'truth') and are imbued with normative considerations and space for diverging interpretations. The case *Burden v. the United Kingdom*, decided by the ECtHR, provides a good example to explain what I mean to say.[22]

3.2.1.3 *Burden v. the United Kingdom*

The case *Burden v. the United Kingdom* concerned two sisters who had been living together all their lives and jointly owned the house they inherited from their parents some 30 years before. As they were now growing older, they feared that upon the death of one of them, the other would have to sell the house to pay the inheritance tax. Contrary to married couples and couples who had entered into a formal civil partnership under the Civil Partnership Act, no tax exemption existed for other relationships of long time and stable cohabitation. Being siblings, the Burden sisters could neither marry nor enter into a Civil Partnership, the latter being reserved for same-sex couples. The European Court of Human Rights had to decide whether this differential treatment violated Article 14 ECHR. After this question was assessed by a Chamber of the Court, the case was referred to the Grand Chamber for final judgment.

The Chamber judgment is interesting for the way in which the Chamber approached the comparability question as part of its justification review.[23] The Chamber simply left open whether the Burden sisters could claim to be in a similar position as married or civil partnership couples as in the Chamber's assessment the differentiation could be justified anyway.[24] The Chamber starts by pointing out the legitimacy of the goal pursued by the tax exemption, namely 'to promote stable, committed heterosexual and homosexual relationships by providing the survivor with a measure of financial security after the death of the spouse or partner'.[25] In assessing whether the means chosen are reasonable and objectively justified, the Chamber stresses the wide margin of appreciation applicable in the field of taxation. It acknowledges that '[a]ny system of taxation, to be workable, has to use broad categorisations to distinguish between different groups of tax payers' and that the 'implementation of any such scheme must, inevitably, create marginal situations and individual cases of apparent hardship or injustice'.[26] For this reason 'it is primarily for

22 ECtHR, (Grand Chamber), 29 April 2008, *Burden v. the United Kingdom*, appl. no. 13378/05.

23 ECtHR, (Chamber), 12 December 2006, *Burden and Burden v. the United Kingdom*, appl. no. 13378/05.

24 Idem, par. 58.

25 Idem, par. 59.

26 Idem, par. 60.

the State to decide how best to strike the balance between raising revenue and pursuing social objectives.'[27] In this respect, the Chamber considers that the legislature could indeed have granted the tax exemptions on a different basis, which would have included siblings living together in a long time relationship, but this is not what is determining. The question is whether the differential treatment 'exceeded any acceptable margin of appreciation', and the Chamber concludes this is not the case.[28]

All in all, the wide margin of appreciation left to the UK is a determining factor for the Chamber and for its acceptance of over- and underinclusion or 'misfit' between the means chosen and the goals pursued. One could also say that, by leaving the state this wide margin, the Chamber actually held that the UK *could justifiably regard* the Burden sisters as not being in a sufficiently similar position to claim inclusion in the tax exemption. In this context, it also takes into account the wider goals of the tax system as a whole ('raising revenue'), rather than just focusing on the inheritance tax law as such.

Though the Grand Chamber also concluded that Article 14 ECHR was not violated, it based its judgment squarely on a lack of comparability between the situation of the Burden sisters and married or civil partnership couples. It regards a relationship based on consanguinity as of a qualitatively and essentially different nature than the relationship between married couples or civil partners. The latter relationships stand out by being based on 'a public undertaking, carrying with it a body of rights and obligations of a contractual nature'; the absence of such a legally binding agreement makes the relationship between the Burden sisters, regardless the length or the supportive nature of their relationship, 'fundamentally different'.[29] For the Grand Chamber, this means the differential treatment is justified.

Concurring judge Björgvinsson does not agree with the Grand Chamber's analysis of the lack of similarity between the situation of the Burden sisters and married couples or civil partners. He rejects the idea that the sexual relationship which characterizes married couples and civil partners compared to the relationship between siblings is sufficiently relevant to justify the distinction made in the tax exemption scheme. In terms of the closeness of the personal attachment and practical aspects of their daily life and financial matters, the Burden sisters are comparable to the categories included. Nevertheless, he

27 Idem, par. 60.
28 Idem, par. 60–61.
29 ECtHR (Grand Chamber), 29 April 2008, *Burden v. the United Kingdom*, appl. no. 13378/05, par. 65.

considers the differential treatment justified for the reasons formulated in the Chamber judgment.

Dissenting judge Zupancic also regards the difference made by the majority between relationships based on blood ties and sexual relationship as unconvincing, as they may be equally important. He accepts that the Court gives special status to marriage, but as the tax exemption also applies to civil partnerships he considers the exclusion of other extramarital relationships characterised by similar close proximity as arbitrary and thus unjustified.

I discuss this case rather extensively, as it illustrates so clearly how equality analysis can indeed turn out to be muddled and elusive. The various assessments made by the Grand Chamber majority and the concurring and dissenting judges in this single case show how the analysis may shift depending on the perspective taken regarding the various elements in the review applied: the very goals of the inheritance tax exemption as such; the fit or proportionality between the means and ends of the regulation, including the (lack of) comparability of the various relationships of cohabitation involved; and the balancing of the inheritance tax exemption with wider rights and interests at stake in raising revenue through taxation. The position of the Burden sisters may be seen as similar or different depending on which elements of their relationship are perceived as most important or relevant in view of the goals of the tax exemption. The different assessments made in this case also show how this type of analysis may involve all sorts of normative considerations regarding similarity and difference and the wider interests served by the inheritance tax regulations and tax law more generally, on which reasonable people may reasonably differ. The Chamber judgment expresses this element of normative appreciation much more clearly than the Grand Chamber judgment by focusing on the question whether the UK legislature was overstepping its margin of appreciation or not by differentiating between relationships such as the Burden sisters were living in and other relationships of cohabitation. In this way the Chamber acknowledges that the question is not so much whether the Burden sisters *are* in a similar position as whether certain differences *may be regarded* as sufficiently relevant to justify unequal treatment by the competent state authorities. In my view, the Chamber's approach provides for a more transparent assessment by acknowledging the normative considerations involved in deciding whether differential treatment can be justified than a seemingly factual analysis of similarity.

As mentioned above, I will return to these issues when exploring the characteristics of discrimination review in Chapter 4.

3.2.2 *Presumption of Differences being Irrelevant – Grounds of Discrimination*

As already mentioned in Chapter 2, over time, all sorts of normative assessments justifying differential treatment based on the personal characteristics listed in equality and non-discrimination provisions such as Article 2 of the UDHR, Article 26 ICCPR or Article 14 ECHR have come to be questioned. Justifications used to treat people unfavourably on the basis of their race, sex, birth or other sensitive ground are to be approached with great suspicion. This has resulted in a strong presumption that differential treatment on these grounds can hardly ever be justified.[30]

Translating this presumption into the criteria used by courts in judicial review, this usually means that higher demands are placed on the various elements that play a role in this type of review, particularly regarding the legitimacy of the goal pursued by state authorities and/or on the degree of fit or proportionality between this goal and the means chosen. The US legal system provides an example of a jurisdiction which is very explicit in this respect by requiring a higher level of judicial scrutiny for several specific classifications. These include differentiations on the basis of sex and race. Sex-based distinctions can only be justified if the means chosen are 'substantially related' to an 'important' government interest; for race-based distinctions the means chosen must be 'narrowly tailored' to a 'compelling' state interest.[31] Similarly, the European Court of Human Rights applies a more stringent justification review by requiring state authorities to provide 'very weighty reasons' to justify differential treatment on those and several other sensitive grounds.[32]

In the past decades, in many jurisdictions other personal characteristics such as sexual orientation, disability and age have been added to the list of grounds that warrant stricter scrutiny than grounds of differentiation that are not perceived as sensitive or suspect, either by including them in more recent non-discrimination provisions, or by way of judicial interpretation of existing standards. This important development and its consequences for equality review will be discussed further in Chapter 4.

---

30 Cf. Fredman, *Discrimination Law*, 2022, p. 9.

31 See *Craig v. Boren*, 429 US 190 (1976) for sex-based classifications and *Korematsu v. United States*, 323 US 214 (1944) for race-based distinctions.

32 'Very weighty reasons' are generally also required to justify differentiations on the basis of sexual orientation, disability, and religion, though the Court's case law is not always as consistent regarding these grounds. See for an overview of the Court's approach J. Gerards, The Margin of Appreciation doctrine, the Very Weighty Reasons test and grounds of discrimination, in M. Balboni (ed), *The principle of discrimination and the European Convention of Human Rights*, Editoriale Scientifica, 2017, p. 27–61.

3.3 Difficulties and Limitations of a Formal Equality Approach

The focus of a formal equality approach on equality of treatment and treating likes alike, brings along a number of difficulties and limitations that have been pointed out extensively in academic literature.[33] These concern the possibility of 'equally bad' treatment resulting from a successful equality claim, its assimilationist outcome, its blindness to unequal effects as an equality issue, and its silence regarding the question how to treat unequal cases.

3.3.1 *Levelling Down Instead of Levelling Up*

Formal equality's focus on treating like cases alike does not preclude 'equally bad' treatment instead of equally favourable treatment resulting from a successful equality claim. Several examples may illustrate this.

Until the late 1980s, the Dutch social welfare system provided a survivor's benefit to widows only. Widowers were excluded because they were presumed to be the breadwinner and thus not in need of a survivor's benefit. In 1988 the Central Appeals Tribunal, the highest administrative court, held this to violate the equal protection and non-discrimination clause of Article 26 ICCPR. The Court considered that this arrangement could no longer be justified in view of the societal changes regarding gender relations.[34] As a direct result of this judgment, widowers became eligible to the same benefits as widows, but in response to the rising costs involved, the legislation concerned was subsequently amended. Since then it provides for an equal survivor's benefit for men and women at a much reduced level and under much more stringent conditions. Another example of levelling down as a way of achieving formally equal treatment may be derived from the successful desegregation campaigns in the USA. Instead of opening up its separate swimming pools for black and white people to all regardless the colour of their skin, a city in Mississippi responded to its obligation to desegregate these facilities by closing them all down.[35]

Given the separation of powers, Courts can be expected to be reluctant to consider levelling down unacceptable, as was explicitly held by the US Supreme Court in the Mississippi swimming pool case. In some jurisdictions, however, courts have sometimes clearly barred the possibility of levelling

33 Cf. the main points of critique formulated by Fredman, *Discrimination law*, 2022, p. 9–15.

34 *Centrale Raad van Beroep* (Central Appeals Tribunal), 14 May 1987, *Rechtspraak Sociale Verzekering* 1987, 246.

35 The US Supreme Court did not consider this to be a denial of the equal protection of the laws as guaranteed under the constitutional Equal Protection clause, *Palmer v. Thompson*, 403 US 217 (1971).

down. How courts operate in view of separation of powers principles may vary very well between countries and depend on the wider constitutional framework and legal practice of the judicial bodies concerned. Thus, for instance, the CJEU has held in several cases that equal treatment must be realized by levelling up, not levelling down.[36]

3.3.2 *Assimilation to the Existing 'Dominant Standard'*

A successful claim of formal equal treatment means a formerly excluded group may share in the benefits which the reference group already has. In many instances this assimilation to the existing 'dominant standard' is of crucial importance, as is, for example, the case with the equal right to vote, equal access to all public functions and equal employment rights for women.

At the same time, what the dominant standard has to offer may not fit very well with the actual position of the newly included group in social reality. To stick with the example of formal equal treatment of women and men: equal employment rights may mean women receive the same protection against dismissal and a right to equal pay. This is highly important in itself, but if protection against dismissal mainly covers full time workers on fixed contracts rather than part time workers or workers with flexible labour contracts, the protection provided will have considerably less meaning for women if it turns out they largely belong to the latter categories. Similarly, equal pay is crucial, but if job evaluation systems systematically value similar or even the same elements such as physical demands in 'women's jobs' (for example nursing or child care) much lower than in 'men's jobs' (for example construction), a lot of women may not really benefit from being granted equal treatment.[37]

The examples show that formal equality does not necessarily mean that the underlying, often implicit, dominant standard of reference of equal treatment comes into view as a (potential) equality issue itself. As MacKinnon put it: 'Under the sameness standard, women are measured according to our correspondence with man (...) Gender neutrality is thus simply the male standard'.[38]

36 See e.g. CJEU, 9 March 2017, *Petya Milkova*, C-406/15. The case concerned a difference in protection against dismissal for disabled civil servants compared to other disabled employees: 'the obligation to comply with EU law would require that the scope of the national rules protecting employees with a particular disability should be extended so that those protective rules also benefit civil servants with the same disability', par. 70. See for other examples Xenidis, Concept of direct discrimination, p. 11, footnote 36.

37 See for this and other examples of (potential) bias in the standard of reference of job evaluation schemes the ILO guide to job evaluation, *Promoting equity. Gender-neutral job evaluation for equal pay: a step-by-step guide*, 2009.

38 C. MacKinnon, *Feminism unmodified*, Boston, Harvard University Press, 1987, p. 34.

This hidden bias holds true for all sorts of other dominant standards affecting other groups:

> The application of standards that appear to be neutral, but which often embody the interests and experiences of socially privileged groups, means that a legal commitment to formal equality may exacerbate the inequality of socially or economically disadvantaged groups.[39]

On the other hand, it is important to realize how formal equality's assimilationist focus sometimes *does* change the dominant standard itself. A case in point is the successful equality claim before the South African Constitutional Court regarding access to marriage for same-sex couples. In the *Fourie* judgment the Court held that exclusion of same-sex couples from marriage violated the equality clause of the South African Constitution.[40] The Court ordered the state to make sure the legislation it was already considering to equalize the legal status of same-sex couples would not result in a remedy which would appear equal but would not be so in spirit. As the Court put it, it should not create a form of separation that may still reflect unwillingness to be as 'generous and accepting towards same sex couples as it is to heterosexual couples' in terms of both the material and financial elements associated with marriage as the more 'intangible' ones, such as the loyalty, care and affection associated with marriage.[41]

The Inter-American Court of Human Rights came to a similar outcome in its Advisory Opinion on gender identity and same sex marriage of 2017.[42] The Court goes even a step further by not leaving the States-Parties a choice of means to realize equal treatment of same-sex relationships: states are obliged to open marriage to same-sex couples. It does not consider it acceptable to create a separate civil union type of legal arrangement with the same rights; such a distinction cannot be justified. In this context the Court considers that marriage cannot be considered to be devoted to procreation, that the notion of 'family' has changed over time, and that having a separate institution for same-sex couples with otherwise the very same rights is belittling and stigmatizing.[43]

---

39 Albertyn and Goldblatt, Equality, 2007, p. 6.

40 Constitutional Court of South Africa, *Minister of Home Affairs and another v. Fourie and another*, [2005] ZACC 19.

41 Idem, par. 153 jo 51.

42 Inter-American Court of Human Rights, 24 November 2017, *Advisory Opinion OC-24/17 on Gender identity, and equality and non-discrimination of same-sex couples.*

43 Idem, par. 221–224.

3.3.3 *The Invisibility of Unequal Effects as an Equality Issue*

The focus of formal equality on unjustified unequal treatment makes it rather blind to unequal outcomes which may result from treating people the same; unequal results of equal treatment remain invisible as potential equality issues. As Anatole France famously put it, the 'majestic equality of the law forbids the rich and poor alike to sleep under the bridges, to beg in the streets, and to steal bread'.[44] Unequal results may flow in several ways from an equal treatment.

3.3.3.1 Facially Neutral Distinctions with Unequal Effects

Firstly, rules or measures based on seemingly neutral, that is non-sensitive classifications, may result in unequal effects for protected groups. If a Dutch educational institution advertising for a teaching job demands a high school diploma obtained at a Dutch school, this is unproblematic from a formal equality point of view as long as this requirement applies to all job applicants. No one is treated differently on the basis of sensitive criteria such as race or sex. However, given educational differences and disparities between people of Dutch descent and those belonging to ethnic minorities with a migration background, this requirement will affect the latter much more than the former. From the perspective of this detrimental outcome for a protected group of what is in itself equal treatment, a potential equality issue arises. Does this imply that the job requirement is unacceptable? This would seem to be too far reaching, as the question whether having a Dutch high school diploma can be justified depends very much on the nature of the teaching job concerned. It may be irrelevant for a teacher at an international school, but relevant for a teacher who is charged with preparing high school pupils for the particularities of the Dutch examination system.[45] In Chapter 5 will be discussed how this issue is approached under equality standards which include the concept of indirect discrimination. This concept does address disparities in the impact of seemingly neutral classification on protected groups as equality issues which are in need of closer scrutiny. For now it suffices to note that under a formal equality approach, requiring a Dutch high school diploma of all job applicants tends to remain invisible as an equality issue.

Similar issues of unequal effects flowing from equal treatment which remain invisible as equality issues from a formal equality perspective may arise

---

44 '[L]a majestueuse égalité des lois … interdit au riche comme au pauvre de coucher sous les ponts, de mendier dans les rues et de voler du pain.', A. France, *Le Lys Rouge*, 1894, ch. 7.

45 This example is based on an equal treatment case brought to the Netherlands Institute for Human Rights, see opinion 2021–110.

in the context of other protected categories. If part-time workers are granted worse labour conditions or pay than full-time workers, such differential treatment is in itself sex-neutral, but in view of the prevailing dominant division of labour regarding paid work and care in most countries, this will often result in many more women being negatively affected than men. If an unemployment benefit scheme sets the willingness to work on all days of the week, including Saturdays and Sundays, as a condition for receiving benefits, this in itself equal treatment may negatively affect Jewish and Christian workers who feel compelled to respect the day of rest prescribed by their faith.

3.3.3.2 Lack of Differentiation

A second way in which equal treatment may result in unequal outcomes is of a somewhat different nature. Unequal effects may also result from rules or measure which do not classify at all, that is from a lack of any differentiation as such. Here again an example may clarify how this can come about. In most countries, the government arranges for a system of public schools to ensure education for children. Suppose this educational system is geared exclusively to the educational needs of the 'average' child and does not provide for any specific facilities for blind or deaf children. It is self-evident blind and deaf children will not benefit much from this type of school system. The outcome of treating deaf or blind children and 'ordinary' children the same is indeed highly unequal. Under a formal equality approach, however, the state would still be considered to meet its obligation to treat all children equally as long as all children are treated the same and are not barred from attending a public school.

3.3.4 *Lack of Guidance in Dealing with Unalike Cases*

The invisibility of unequal effects as a potential equality issue means formal equality has no guidance to give in how to deal with 'unalike' cases. The above example of treating blind or deaf children the same in relation to their access to school is illustrative. Of course, under a formal equality approach differential treatment of deaf and blind children would be allowed (as unalike case may be treated unalike), but a formal equality approach does not *require* the state to take such differences into account and differentiate accordingly. Formal equality, then, does not provide much direction how to deal with groups of individuals who are not similarly situated as the reference group. This is indeed where the notion of substantive equality comes in, which takes on board the second part of the Aristotelian definition of equality, demanding unalike cases to be treated unalike in accordance with their unalikeness.

3.4 Substantive Equality: Like Cases Must Be Treated Alike *and* Unalike Cases Must Be Treated Unalike in Proportion to Their Unalikeness

The second part of the Aristotelian definition of equality is a crucial part of a substantive equality approach in law. The requirement of treating unalike cases unalike in accordance with their unalikeness, in addition to treating like cases alike, firmly renders it into a much broader notion than merely formal equality. If the notion of equality is limited to the first limb, it will only achieve substantive equality (that is an equal outcome), where cases are indeed alike. Where cases are unalike, it does not provide a guideline. This is exactly where the second limb comes in. Only by taking the two parts of the Aristotelian notion of equality together a fully and genuinely substantive approach to equality comes into view.

So far, a substantive equality approach is much less developed and much less clearly elaborated in legal doctrine than a formal equality approach. In fact, even in the two jurisdictions where a substantive equality approach has arguably been developed furthest in legal practice, that is in South Africa and Canada, the jurisprudence on substantive equality is characterized as unclear, up for diverging interpretations, or as inconsistent.[46] Nevertheless, sufficient examples of a substantive equality approach in legal practice exist to highlight some of its general features. These features include first and foremost a focus on 'unequal impact' as a trigger for equality review.[47] This is not to say, though, that unequal effects are sufficient to conclude equality standards have been violated. As with formal equality, substantive equality is about treatment which cannot be justified. Whereas formal equality is preoccupied with unjustified unequal treatment, substantive equality can be said to be also concerned with unjustified equal treatment. This means justification review is always part of equality review. Also similar to formal equality, in legal practice the major concern of substantive equality regards the treatment of protected groups such

46 For the South African jurisprudence see e.g. C. Albertyn, Contested substantive equality in the South African Constitution: beyond social inclusion towards systemic justice, *South African Journal on Human Rights*, 2018, p. 441–468. For the Canadian jurisprudence the dissenting opinion in *Fraser* is a case in point. According to the dissenters 'For 30 years, this Court has struggled to define the term "substantive equality." An intelligible and principled definition continues to be elusive'(par. 216) and 'the concept of "substantive equality" has become so vague that it is impossible for claimants or legislatures to anticipate its demands in advance. Legislatures are instead effectively expected to hit a moving target (…)' (par. 221), Supreme Court of Canada, *Fraser v. Canada* [2020] SCC 28.

47 Albertyn and Goldblatt, Equality, 2007, p. 6–7.

as ethnic minorities, women or disabled people, rather than non-sensitive or non-suspect categories of people such as car drivers or pedestrians.

In the following I will explore several core features of a substantive equality approach in more detail and then turn to the specific difficulties and limitations it brings along.

3.4.1 *Unequal Impact as Trigger for Substantive Equality Review*

To start with, let me repeat that if equal treatment results in an equal outcome, substantive equality has no issue with treating people the same. So granting women the equal right to vote satisfies both a formal and substantive equality approach. This is an important point to be aware of, as formal equality and substantive equality are often presented as opposites. This is not entirely correct. They only become opposites where equal treatment results in unequal outcomes. The latter is indeed where taking a substantive equality approach makes all the difference. To reach an equal outcome, differential instead of equal treatment may be necessary.[48]

3.4.1.1 The Classic Example: the 'Minority Schools in Albania' Case

A classic example of a substantive equality approach in legal practice can be found in an advisory opinion of the Permanent Court of International Justice (PCIJ) dating back to 1935.[49] It concerned a case regarding the treatment of religious and cultural minorities in Albania.[50] At stake was an amendment to the Albanian constitution, which provided for reserving the education of Albanian subjects to the state and for abolishing all private schools. It also stipulated that primary education was to be compulsory and provided for free in state schools. The Permanent Court was asked whether the abolishment of private schools was in conformity with Article 5 of the Albanian Declaration of 1921, which stipulated that Albanian nationals belonging to racial, religious or linguistic minorities 'will enjoy the same treatment and security in law and in fact' as other Albanian nationals. In addition it provided that '[i]n particular, they shall have an equal right to maintain, manage and control at their own expense or to establish in the future, charitable, religious and social

48 See for many examples M. Minow, *Making all the difference. Inclusion, exclusion, and American law*, Ithaca/London, Cornell University Press, 1990.

49 This Court was the precursor of the International Court of Justice.

50 Permanent Court of International Justice, *Minority Schools in Albania*, PCIJ Series A/B, no. 64 (1935).

institutions, schools and other educational establishments, with the right to use their own language and to exercise their religion freely therein'.[51]

From a formal equality approach, which was followed by the dissenting judges in this case, the new constitutional arrangement posed no problem in terms of the equality guarantees of the Albanian Declaration, as all Albanian nationals would receive the same treatment, regardless their membership of a minority or majority group.[52] The majority opinion, however, did not accept such a formal approach by interpreting Article 5 of the Albanian Declaration to require 'an effective, genuine equality' between the members of the majority and minority. According to the Court, having their own schools and other institutions mentioned in Article 5 is 'indispensable to enable the minority to enjoy the same treatment as the majority, not only in law but also in fact.'[53] It added that the replacement of their own institutions by those of the government 'would destroy this equality in treatment, for its *effect* would be to deprive the minority of the institutions appropriate to its needs, whereas the majority would continue to have them supplied in the institutions created by the State.'[54] [Emphasis added].

The emphasis on the unequal effect being decisive renders this interpretation into a clear instance of a substantive equality approach. This is further underlined by the additional remark, that granting the minorities the right to run their own schools is not to be regarded as a form of preferential treatment; it is indeed to prevent the majority being given a privileged position.[55] By adding this, the Court clarifies beyond any doubt how substantive equal treatment may not just allow differential treatment, but may indeed require it to achieve 'genuine' equality. Central in its approach is the outcome of the treatment provided, which may sometimes demand differential treatment instead of the same treatment.

The Albanian minority case remained a rather isolated instance of an expressly substantive equality approach until the eighties and nineties of the last century, when the development of a (more) substantive approach gained momentum in several jurisdictions.

---

51 Idem, par. 1.

52 Idem, par. 98.

53 Idem, par. 67.

54 Idem, par. 67.

55 'Far from creating a privilege in favour of the minority, as the Albanian Government avers, this stipulation ensures that the majority shall not be given a privileged situation as compared with the minority.' Idem, par. 67.

3.4.1.2 More Recent Examples of a Substantive Equality Approach

As mentioned before, in more recent times Canada and South Africa stand out as jurisdictions which have expressly adopted a substantive, outcome oriented equality approach under their constitutional arrangements. The Canadian Supreme Court and the South African Constitutional Court both emphasize that looking at the impact of a treatment is core to equality analysis. As the Canadian Court put it:

> (…) true equality does not necessarily result from identical treatment. Formal distinctions in treatment will be necessary in some contexts in order to accommodate differences between individuals and thus to produce equal treatment in a substantive sense (…) Correspondingly, a law which applies uniformly to all may still violate a claimant's equality rights. The main consideration … must be the *impact* of the law upon the individual or group. …[56] [Emphasis in original text].

Similarly, the South African Constitutional Court expressly holds that addressing disadvantage is central to a substantive equality approach, with dignity being its core value and purpose.[57]

The case *Eldridge v. British Columbia* provides a good illustration of what a substantive equality approach may mean in concrete cases.[58] This case concerned a deaf patient who complained about not being provided with a free sign language interpreter when he consulted his hospital doctor. He considered this to violate equality standards. The Supreme Court agrees with him. The Court holds that the principle of equality as enshrined in section 15 of the Canadian Charter of Rights and Freedoms[59] requires the government to consider the effects of the regulations it enacts and to take differences between people into account:

56 Supreme Court of Canada, *Law v. Canada* [1999] 1 SCR 497, par. 25.

57 Abertyn and Goldblatt, 2007, Equality, p. 13.

58 *Eldridge v. British Columbia* [1997] 3 SCR 624.

59 Section 15 reads as follows: '(1) Every individual is equal before and under the law and has the right to the equal protection and equal benefit of the law without discrimination and, in particular, without discrimination based on race, national or ethnic origin, colour, religion, sex, age or mental or physical disability.

(2) Subsection (1) does not preclude any law, program or activity that has as its object the amelioration of conditions of disadvantaged individuals or groups including those that are disadvantaged because of race, national or ethnic origin, colour, religion, sex, age or mental or physical disability.'

> Even in imposing generally applicable provisions, the government must take into account differences which in fact exist between individuals and so far as possible ensure that the provisions adopted will not have a greater impact on certain classes of persons due to irrelevant personal characteristics than on the public as a whole. In other words, to promote the objective of the more equal society, s. 15(1) acts as a bar to the executive enacting provisions without taking into account their possible impact on already disadvantaged classes of persons.[60]

Where proper communication between doctor and patient is crucial in the provision of medical care, a lack of effective communication due to the absence of an interpreter means that the deaf patient cannot be said to 'receive the same level of medical care as hearing persons'.[61] As the hospital could not show that a total denial of the interpretation service was nevertheless reasonable – no evidence was provided of an unduly strain on the financial resources – the Court concluded Section 15 had been violated.[62]

Similar to the Permanent Court of International Justice in the *Albanian Minority* case, the Canadian Court considers that the resulting differential treatment is not to be perceived as a more favourable treatment, but as a means to provide deaf persons with the same quality of treatment:

> Those who hear do not receive communication as a distinct service. For them, an effective means of communication is routinely available, free of charge, as part of every health care service. (…) Where it is necessary for effective communication, sign language interpretation should not therefore be viewed as an "ancillary" service. On the contrary, it is the means by which deaf persons may receive the same quality of medical care as the hearing population.[63]

In the European context, the judgment of the European Court of Human Rights in the case *Tlimmenos v. Greece* is a landmark decision.[64] Though the Court does not elaborate its substantive equality approach in any detail, the case is of particular interest for the way in which the Court explicitly refers to the second part of the Aristotelian formulation of equality. The case dealt with a Jehovah

60 *Eldridge v. British Columbia* [1997] 3 SCR 624, par. 64.
61 Idem, par. 71.
62 Idem, par. 94.
63 Idem, par. 71.
64 ECtHR (Grand Chamber), 6 April 2000, *Thlimmenos v. Greece*, appl. no. 34369/97.

Witness who was excluded from becoming a chartered accountant for having a criminal record. He objected to this exclusion, because his criminal record was the consequence of a sanction following his refusal to serve in the army on the basis of his religious convictions and not related to morally objectionable behaviour. The Court held that Thlimmenos should indeed not be equated with common criminals who were excluded from the job concerned for a lack of moral integrity. In more general terms, the Court considers that Article 14 ECHR may not only be violated when States treat persons in analogous situations differently without providing an objective and reasonable justification, but also 'when States without an objective and reasonable justification fail to treat differently persons whose situations are significantly different'.[65] So here again accommodation of difference is what equality standards may call for.[66]

3.4.2 *Accommodation of Difference: Duties of (Reasonable) Accommodation and Changing the Dominant Standard*

3.4.2.1 (Reasonable) Accommodation

The above cases show that substantive equality may bring along an obligation to accommodate difference and respond in a positive way to diversity and different needs to achieve an equal outcome. Difference should not lead to disadvantage and exclusion.

Particularly regarding people with disabilities, the Canadian example of applying a substantive equality approach is not an isolated one. The understanding of formal equal treatment being insufficient to guarantee genuine equality for this group seems quite self-evident. To participate on an equal basis in society, disabled people often need some form of accommodation. Someone who is dependent on a wheelchair may need a special desk at work and blind children will need other teaching materials than standard books to be able to profit from going to school.

65 Idem, par. 44.

66 The approach by the ECtHR in *Thlimmenos* did not come out of the blue. Already in 1968 the Court held in the *Belgian Linguistics* case that 'certain different situations call for different legal solutions and certain legal inequalities merely correct factual inequalities', ECtHR, 23 July 1968, *Belgian Linguistics*, appl. no. 2126/64, par. 10 (under 'Interpretation adopted by the Court). Tobler notes that the CJEU has formulated a similar understanding of equality under the general equality principle in EU law, according to which 'comparable situations must not be treated differently and [...] different situations must not be treated in the same way unless such treatment is objectively justified'. See C. Tobler, *Indirect discrimination under Directives 2000/43 and 2000/78*, Report European Network of legal experts in gender equality and non-discrimination, 2022, p. 47. For a recent case confirming this reading of equality see CJEU (Grand Chamber), 3 June 2021, *Hungary v. European Parliament*, Case C-650/18, par. 98.

In quite some jurisdictions this has been translated in equality provisions which demand 'reasonable accommodation' of disabled people to achieve (more) substantive equality. For the EU, for instance, Directive 2000/78/EC on equal treatment in employment provides that '[in] order to guarantee compliance with the principle of equal treatment in relation to persons with disabilities, reasonable accommodation shall be provided.' A lack of reasonable accommodation can only be justified if it would impose a 'disproportionate burden' on the employer.[67]

At the global level, the CRPD formulates a duty of reasonable accommodation for a much wider area than employment and requires the States Parties to this convention to 'take all appropriate steps to ensure that reasonable accommodation is provided' (Article 5 (3) CRPD). Here again, the reasonableness of what is required is measured by answering the question whether accommodation would impose 'a disproportionate or undue burden' (Article 2 CRPD). With 185 ratifications of the CRPD, this obligation is almost universally accepted. Of course, formal legal acceptance and actual implementation may be worlds apart, but the explicit inclusion of an obligation to provide for reasonable accommodation is conceptually of great importance. Interestingly, in Article 2 the CRPD defines a denial of reasonable accommodation as a distinct form of discrimination. I will return to this qualification in Chapter 6.

Though the concept of reasonable accommodation as such seems so far most frequently and explicitly accepted in the context of equality provisions regarding disabled people,[68] it is not necessarily limited to this group. The United States provide a good example. Title VII of the Civil Rights Act 1964, which prohibits discrimination in employment, requires employers to accommodate an employee's religious beliefs or practices, unless this creates an undue hardship.[69] This duty applies to practices such as wearing particular dress or head coverings (for example a headscarf or turban) or granting leave

67 Council Directive 2000/78/EC of 27 November 2000 establishing a general framework for equal treatment in employment and occupation (Framework Directive), Article 5.

68 See for an overview of developments regarding the concept of reasonable accommodation over the years Šárka Dušková, *Who should we accommodate? Opening the grounds for reasonable accommodation under the European Convention on Human Rights*, Doctoral Thesis, University of Essex, 2023.

69 A duty to accommodate religious manifestations often arises in a very similar way under freedom of religion provisions such as Article 9 ECHR. It often depends on the specific legal regulations in a particular jurisdiction whether claims for religious accommodation are pursued as equality/non-discrimination or freedom of religion claims.

for religious observance.[70] Pregnancy leave arrangements can also be seen as a form of accommodation of difference which flows from a substantive equality approach.[71]

Conceptually, then, (reasonable) accommodation is a notion which can be applied in relation to various groups protected by equality and non-discrimination standards to respond to their particular needs. Interestingly, in several jurisdictions, an obligation to provide (reasonable) accommodation has been formulated as part of a prohibition of indirect discrimination, whereas in others a lack of sufficient accommodation has been identified as a distinct, *sui generis* modality of discrimination. I will return to this in Chapter 5 and Chapter 6 respectively.

3.4.2.2 Changing the Dominant Standard or Standard of Reference: Universal Design

In addition to reasonable accommodation for individual persons with a disability, the CRPD calls for more structural and systemic forms of accommodation, including the promotion of 'universal design in the development of standards and guidelines'.[72] Thus, designing buildings, buses or trains from the start with the needs of wheel chair users in mind, avoids having to provide specific forms of reasonable accommodation for this group later. This type of systemic accommodation, which actually changes the dominant standard or point or reference itself, need not be limited to disabled people either. The equal needs of religious minorities to be free from work on their most important religious feast days, for instance, could be accommodated by including such days in the overall scheme of public holidays rather than providing religious minorities with a right to take a day off at their own expense. (See for further elaboration Chapter 6).

3.4.3 *Openness to Undoing Structural Disadvantage and Systemic Discrimination by Positive Discrimination or Positive Action*[73]

Substantive equality's preoccupation with equal outcomes rather than equal treatment as such, brings along a positive engagement with developing all sorts of policies and measures to improve the position of vulnerable or marginalized

---

70 See for an overview the information on the website of the US Equal Employment Opportunities Commission, https://www.eeoc.gov/religious-discrimination.

71 In the same vein see C. McCrudden and S. Prechal, *The concepts of equality and non-discrimination in Europe: a practical approach*, Report European Network of experts in the field of gender equality, 2009, p. 30.

72 Article 4(1)(f) CRPD).

73 For the way in which I use these terms in this study see Chapter 1.

groups that still face the consequences of historical or structural disadvantage and exclusion based on their race, sex, disability or other grounds specifically protected by equality and non-discrimination provisions. These policies may include all sorts of general measures to alleviate poverty, to expand employment opportunities, to improve access to affordable housing for the poor or quality education for all, but also more specific measures which are expressly directed at the groups concerned and differentiate on the very same grounds that are usually regarded as 'suspect'. From a formal equality perspective, the latter type of measures may be highly problematic as formal equality starts from the presumption that classifications on the basis of race, sex or other protected grounds can hardly ever be justified.

Under a substantive equality approach, however, such specific, remedial measures are not perceived as a derogation from equality standards, but as part and parcel of what these standards seek to protect and promote. As the South African Constitutional Court held in the case *Van Heerden*:

> [r]emedial measures are not a derogation from, but [are] a substantive and composite part of, the equality protection envisaged by the provisions of section 9 and of the Constitution as a whole. Their primary object is to promote the achievement of equality.[74]

To date, the South African Constitution may arguably be the most far reaching in this respect by expressly identifying as its overarching goal the dismantling of systematic under-privilege resulting from the past injustice of *Apartheid*:

> This substantive notion of equality recognises that besides uneven race, class and gender attributes of our society, there are other levels and forms of social differentiation and systematic under-privilege, which still persist. *The Constitution enjoins us to dismantle them* and to prevent the creation of new patterns of disadvantage. It is therefore incumbent on courts to scrutinise in each equality claim the situation of the complainants in society; their history and vulnerability; the history, nature and purpose of the discriminatory practice and whether it ameliorates or adds to group disadvantage in real life context, in order to determine its fairness or otherwise in the light of the values of our Constitution. [Emphasis added][75]

74 *Minister of Finance v. Van Heerden*, [2004] ZACC 3, par. 32.

75 Idem, par. 27.

The Inter-American Court of Human Rights is also very outspoken by regarding the more fundamental goal of undoing structural disadvantage and marginalization, which goes far beyond a formal equality approach, as core to the equality standards in the American Convention on Human rights. As it held in the *Fireworks Factory* case, the substantive dimension of equality as a Convention standard

> requires the adoption of positive measures of promotion in favor of groups that have historically been discriminated against or marginalized due to the factors referred to in Article 1(1) of the American Convention.[76] This means that the right to equality entails the obligation to adopt measures that ensure that the equality is real and effective; in other words, to correct existing inequalities, to promote the inclusion and participation of historically marginalized groups, and to guarantee to disadvantaged individuals or groups the effective enjoyment of their rights and, in short, to provide individuals with the real possibility of achieving material equality. To this end, States must actively combat situations of exclusion and marginalization.[77]

It may be clear that if this is perceived as what substantive equality as a legal standard is ultimately about, it takes on board an obligation to strive for a full and fundamental transformation of society as such. It is also clear that such an endeavour is closely linked to the realization of social rights and is implicitly or explicitly, imbued with some of the philosophical theories regarding distributive justice mentioned in Chapter 2.

Not many jurisdictions seem to go as far as South Africa or as the Inter-American Court of Human Rights, but many do acknowledge the need for some forms of remedial measures to improve the position of women, ethnic minorities or other disadvantaged groups in their societies, for instance by policies directed at redressing underrepresentation of these groups in employment, education or politics. I will return to this in Chapter 7.

---

76 This article mentions a familiar list of grounds, including, among others, sex, race and religion.

77 IACtHR, 15 July 2020, *Case of the workers of the fireworks factory in Santo Antônio de Jesus and their families v. Brazil* (preliminary objections, merits, reparations and costs), par. 199. The Court uses the terminology of 'material equality', '*de facto* equality' and 'substantive equality' interchangeably.

3.4.4 *Distinguishing Positive Discrimination or Positive Action and Accommodation of Difference*

Affirmative action measures and accommodation of difference can both be regarded as fitting the *adagium* that unalike cases are to be treated unalike in accordance with their unalikeness. Nevertheless, conceptually, it is important to distinguish the notion of positive discrimination or positive action from accommodation of difference as part of (substantive) equality standards.

Firstly, positive discrimination or positive action measures are temporary as a matter of principle. Even if it may take a long time for remedial measures to undo structural disadvantage and social and economic inequalities of marginalized groups, they are based on the idea that as soon as this is achieved, differentiation on sensitive or protected grounds will no longer be necessary; in this future situation, equal treatment will suffice again, as treatment will regard equal cases and thus result in equal outcomes. In contrast, accommodation of pregnant workers in employment by arranging for decent pregnancy and maternity leave is not a matter of temporary accommodation as long as it is women (or an occasional trans man), who give birth to the next generation and not machines. Similarly, accommodation of deaf and blind children in education, or of religious groups wishing to express their belief in the employment context, is not a matter of temporary special treatment to redress disadvantages which can be expected to become redundant over time, but will generally be needed on a more permanent basis as part of substantive equality standards. Both the Permanent Court of International Justice in the *Albanian Minority* case and the Canadian Supreme Court in the *Eldridge* case express this difference with remedial measures when they emphasize that the differential treatment required to accommodate the specific needs of the groups concerned is not to be regarded as providing a privilege or a more favourable treatment to those groups (see section 3.4.1).[78]

Secondly, so far, accommodation of difference has been accepted much more readily as a legal *obligation* which may flow from applying equality standards, particularly in the context of disability, than taking affirmative action measures. Even under the most far reaching substantive equality approach, represented by the South African constitution and the jurisprudence of its Constitutional Court, equality standards are interpreted as *allowing* remedial measures, not as imposing a positive duty to take them. For this Court, considerations regarding separation of powers principles seem to play a crucial role

78 Of course there may be overlap: lack of proper accommodation for certain groups may well be tied to historical and structural patterns of exclusion of these groups, or be the cause of structural disadvantage and inequalities.

in this respect.[79] I will return to the topic of accommodation of difference in Chapter 6 and to remedial measures in Chapter 7.

3.5 Difficulties and Limitations of a Substantive Equality Approach

Though the much broader focus of a substantive equality approach may provide an answer to some of the limitations attached to a merely formal equality approach (see section 3.3), in its application in legal practice it faces its own difficulties and dilemmas. Firstly, the question which differences are sufficiently relevant to warrant or require differential treatment becomes even more important and difficult to answer, if compared to a formal equality approach. Secondly, what I call the 'open-ended' nature of granting substantive equal treatment creates serious difficulties. For courts, in particular, it puts issues regarding the separation of powers squarely on the agenda of equality review. Thirdly, in its broadest understanding, a substantive equality approach runs into the limits of law as an instrument for social change.

3.5.1 *Which Differences Require Differential Treatment?*

Though compared to a formal equality inquiry questions regarding 'relevant' and 'irrelevant' differences are framed in a different way, they are also an important and difficult to answer part of substantive equality review. The question is not just which differences are, exceptionally, sufficiently relevant to justify unequal treatment, but which differences require some sort of accommodation or compensation to achieve a (more) equal outcome. As with formal equality review, the assessment of the relevance of differences between groups of people is much more than a factual exercise. It is intertwined with normative appreciations of what differences *are to be regarded* as *deserving* accommodation or compensation and which are not. Minow has aptly described this as the 'difference dilemma':

> (…) when does treating people differently emphasize their differences and stigmatize or hinder them on that basis? And when does treating people the same become insensitive to their difference and hinder them on *that* basis?[80]

---

79 C. Albertyn, Section 9 in a time of COVID: substantive equality, economic inclusion and positive duties, *South African Journal on Human Rights*, 2021, p. 205–229, p. 2019–2020.

80 Minow, Making all the difference, 1990, p. 20.

Taking a look at the development of notions of (reasonable) accommodation over the past decades, as mentioned before, the relevance of difference seems most easily and generally accepted where accommodation of disabled people is concerned. Disabled people are almost self-evidently perceived as deserving accommodation to meet equality standards.

Accommodation of religious groups is also quite common in many jurisdictions, but often more contested. European debates on prohibitions regarding headscarves or other religious attire in the workplace are but one example. In different jurisdictions, courts have come to different conclusions regarding the question whether equality standards require accommodation of such religious manifestations or allow for prohibitions. As the widely diverging regulations in France, the UK and the Netherlands regarding the wearing of religious dress and symbols in public functions show, ultimately, the balancing of equality rights with other public interests is at stake in justification review. Depending on different conceptualizations of state neutrality, for example, this balancing results in an almost absolute prohibition of religious attire in the public sector in France and a very high level of accommodation in the UK, with the Netherlands somewhere in between.[81]

In the Netherlands many more examples of the normative balancing involved in deciding about accommodation of difference can be derived from cases brought to the former Equal Treatment Commission and its successor, the Netherlands Institute for Human Rights. Thus, a public school was held to allow pupils to pray at school, but not to be bound to provide a dedicated space for doing so.[82] Similarly, schools are required to allow pupils to wear a (safe) headscarf during sports lessons for religious reasons, but refusing to attend sports lessons as such for these reasons need not be accommodated.[83] Another telling example regarding the difficult question whether differences are to be accommodated or not concerned a Muslim woman who received a Dutch welfare benefit. Welfare benefits are conditional on the willingness to actively work towards (re)integration in a paid job. When she repeatedly refused to participate in a job training programme to improve her employment opportunities because she was only allowed to wear a headscarf and not to wear a niqab, her welfare benefit was reduced. This reduction was upheld in court. The Court considered it justified as her wish to wear a niqab turned chances of

81 H. van Ooijen, *Religious symbols in public functions. A comparative analysis of Dutch, English and French justifications for limiting the freedom of public officials to display religious symbols*, Doctoral thesis Leiden University, Antwerpen, Intersentia, 2012.

82 Equal Treatment Commission, opinion 2000–51.

83 See, respectively, Equal Treatment Commission, opinion 1997–149 and opinion 1999–106.

her expeditiously finding work very small, which in turn would unneccesarily affect public expenditure.[84] Here again, normative considerations are inevitably involved in this type of assessment.

3.5.1.1 Accommodation and Competing or Conflicting Rights

Discussions on accommodation of difference as part of substantive equality standards become even more complex and normatively embedded where competing or conflicting rights may be involved. Such cases require a balancing of rights and are essentially normative in character. Many examples can be found in the sphere of religious accommodation and equal rights of women or sexual minorities.[85] In the Netherlands, several cases have come to court regarding men or women who refuse to shake hands with clients or colleagues of the opposite sex. Though after corona-experiences such cases seem overtaken by time, they raised quite heated debates and were met with different perspectives on which rights should prevail. The Dutch Equal Treatment Commission tended to give prevalence to the accommodation of religion over claims of sex equality, but was later overruled by Dutch courts.[86]

Another highly topical example of conflicting rights regards the question whether marriage officials who object to same-sex relationships for religious reasons must be accommodated for their refusal to officiate same-sex marriage. Here again, the balancing of the conflicting rights involved is inevitably a normative exercise and thus may result in quite different outcomes between jurisdictions. Thus, in the case of *Ladale*, the ECtHR held that the decision by a local authority in the UK to dismiss a registrar of marriages because she refused to register same-sex civil partnerships for religious objections to such unions did not violate the ECHR.[87] The South African Constitutional Court followed a different approach when it suggested in the *Fourie* case that it would accept

84 *Centrale Raad van Beroep* (Central Appeals Tribunal), 9 mei 2017, ECLI:NL:CRVB:2017:1639.

85 The tension between women's human rights and culture or religion figure prominently in human rights law more generally, see e.g. R. Holtmaat and J. Naber, *Women's human rights and culture: from deadlock to dialogue*, Antwerp, Intersentia, 2010; A. Timmer and R. Holtmaat, Article 5, in: P. Schultz, R. Halperin-Kaddari, B. Rudolf and M. Freeman (eds), *The UN Convention on the elimination of all forms of discrimination against women and its Optional Protocol: a commentary* (2nd ed), Oxford, Oxford University press 2022, p. 222–256.

86 See respectively Equal Treatment Commission, opinion 2006–221 and *Centrale Raad van Beroep* (Central Appeals Tribunal), 7 May 2009, ECLI:NL:CRVB:2009:BI2440.

87 The case of *Ladale* was one of four cases included in the joint judgment *Eweida a.o.*, see ECtHR, 15 January 2013, *Eweida a.o. v. UK*, application nos. 48420/10, 59842/10, 51671/10 and 36516/10.

legislation regarding same-sex marriage which would allow marriage registrars to invoke conscientious objections to officiating same-sex marriage.[88]

3.5.1.2 Positive Discrimination or Positive Action and Competing or Conflicting Equality Rights

Competing or conflicting rights are also involved where remedial measures are concerned, which differentiate on protected grounds like race or sex as such. Examples include reserving a certain percentage of places in educational institutions for black students, providing for specific management development programmes for women only or establishing quota for these groups in high level economic or political functions. In this type of conflicting rights cases, a substantive equality approach seems to be on a collision course with formal equality, as under a formal equality approach race or sex based distinctions are presumptively hard, if ever, to be justified. This issue will be explored further in Chapter 7.

3.5.2 *Open-Ended Nature of Substantive Equal Treatment*

A second major difficulty of applying a substantive equality approach concerns the often open-ended nature of providing substantive equal treatment in the form of (reasonable) accommodation. The question is *how far* differentiation has to extend, both in a qualitative and a quantitative sense.

To return to the example of providing substantive equality in education for disabled children: is it sufficient for a government to provide for a number of schools dedicated to blind children in which they receive some unspecified level of education, or should it provide for an educational package which resembles the curriculum of regular schools as closely as possible? If the latter, this means all regular educational materials used in 'normal' schools would have to be available for blind children in adjusted form, for example by being translated into Braille or put on tape. Similar questions arise if blind children are integrated in the regular educational system, as is the preferred option under the CRPD.[89] Generally speaking, the more facilities are provided to cater for the specific needs of blind children, the more 'substantive' the equal

---

88 Constitutional Court of South Africa, *Minister of Home Affairs and another v. Fourie and another*, [2005] ZACC 19, par. 159. Yet, one could read the judgment by the ECtHR regarding *Ladale* also in a different way which would be more similar to the South African decision. As the ECtHR emphasizes the wide margin of appreciation of the national authorities to regulate matters like this, the judgment could also imply that accommodating the conscientious objections of the marriage official would also have been acceptable under the Convention.

89 Article 25 CRPD calls for inclusive education at all levels.

treatment will be. Given scarce resources, however, there is a limit to what is feasible. If so, where to draw the line? And in terms of the CRPD: what is sufficient to be considered 'reasonable' accommodation?

A similar issue of open-endedness arises in a quantitative sense. Is it sufficient to accommodate the specific educational needs of blind and deaf children, or do children with ADHD or dyslexia have a similar right in view of their equal right to education? In welfare states with high educational levels this seems quite common, but even in this context at some point a limit to accommodation will be reached. In short: how far do state obligations to accommodate the needs of disabled children reach in view of each child's equal right to education? Can each child claim differential treatment which accommodates its individual, unique characteristics and needs? If this were the case, this would result in an 'absolute' form of substantive equal treatment as mentioned in section 3.1. To realize that degree or level of substantive equality is beyond the reach of any society, however wealthy it may be. So again the question that has to be answered is: where to draw the line?

The *Eldridge* case may serve as an illustration to show this issue indeed arises in legal practice, though the Canadian Supreme Court was not really facing it head-on. In *Eldridge*, the open-ended nature of substantive equality raises the question whether sign language interpretation has to be provided for each and every conversation between a deaf patient and hospital medical personnel, or can be limited in some way. And if deaf patients have to be accommodated by language support to have equal access to quality medical care, what about other categories of patients who may lack sufficient language skills, such as patients with a migration background?

To answer the first question, the *Eldridge* Court formulates a rather vague criterion for the scope of the language support to be provided. The state's duty does not extend to all medical situations, but has to guarantee 'effective communication':

> This is not to say that sign language interpretation will have to be provided in every medical situation. The "effective communication" standard is a flexible one, and will take into consideration such factors as the complexity and importance of the information to be communicated, the context in which the communications will take place and the number of people involved; (...) For deaf persons with limited literacy skills, however, it is probably fair to surmise that sign language interpretation will be required in most cases.[90]

90 *Eldridge v. British Columbia* [1997] 3 SCR 624, par. 82.

The second question raised by the open-ended nature of substantive equality – regarding other categories of people who may make similar claims for language support if the claim of the deaf patient is successful – were brushed aside by the Canadian Supreme Court. The Court regards this argument as 'purely speculative' and adds that deaf people face particular difficulties which renders it doubtful whether non-native speakers could claim to be in a similar or analogous situation regarding the language barriers they face.[91] The Court concludes that as the success of a potential equality claim of this nature cannot be predicted in advance, the 'possibility of such a claim cannot justify infringement of the constitutional rights of the deaf'.[92]

The problem of the open-ended character of substantive equal treatment is also present where the accommodation of other protected groups is at stake. Regarding accommodation of religion, the Dutch case on accommodation of prayer in public schools mentioned before is a good example. Is it sufficient to allow prayer in the school grounds, or should schools provide for a quiet corner to pray during breaks or for a dedicated room to do so?

Pregnancy leave arrangements are also very illustrative of the open-ended nature of substantive equality. The extent of the leave period before and after giving birth, but also the financial benefits attached to it, vary greatly between countries. From a substantive equality point of view, it is clear pregnancy has to be accommodated in view of women's equal right to work and to combine work with having a family, but how far should such accommodation reach? What level in terms of the period of the leave and the payment attached to it is necessary to meet substantive equality standards? This open-endedness may also explain why claims for pregnancy leave have often run along lines of a comparison with sick leave, as this type of arrangement may provide a concrete point of reference. A claim for pregnancy leave then turns into a claim of an unjustified difference in treatment between workers who are temporarily unable to do their job due to sickness and those who cannot do so because of pregnancy.[93] In this context it is illustrative how the EU Pregnant Workers Directive links the minimum standards for providing an income during the leave period to existing arrangements for sick leave.[94] The Directive does not guarantee pregnant workers and workers who have recently given birth a full salary, but they must be provided an income 'at least equivalent to that which

91 Idem, par. 89–90.

92 Idem, par. 90.

93 For a famous example see US Supreme Court, *Geduldig v. Aiello*, 417 US 484 (1974).

94 Council Directive 92/85/EEC of 19 October 1992 on the introduction of measures to encourage improvements in the safety and health at work of pregnant workers and workers who have recently given birth or are breastfeeding (tenth individual Directive within the meaning of Article 16(1) of Directive 89/391/EEC).

the worker concerned would receive in the event of a break in her activities on grounds connected with her state of health' (Article 11(3) Pregnant Workers Diective).[95]

All the above examples of the open-ended nature of a substantive equal treatment point to another crucial question: who decides where the lines are to be drawn? In this context, separation of powers issues present themselves as a hard nut to crack for courts faced with substantive equality claims.

3.5.3 *Open-Ended Nature of Substantive Equality and Separation of Powers*

For judicial bodies, the often open-ended character of substantive equality creates an additional dilemma in conducting substantive equality review, particularly where higher 'degrees' of substantive equal treatment involve significantly higher costs and resources, as is the case in the above examples regarding accommodation of disability and pregnancy. To what extent can courts tell governments how to spend their – inherently limited – budgets? In this regard, similar issues present themselves as in social rights adjudication.[96] Where realizing substantive equality has no fixed achievement level, as is also often the case with realizing social rights, the political powers are the first port of call for deciding where to draw the lines, particularly where the redistribution of scarce resources is involved. For courts, the crucial question then becomes how much leeway has to be left to the other branches of government.

Here again, as already pointed out in Chapter 2 (Section 2.4) the ways in which judicial bodies come to terms with this issue vary widely between jurisdictions and are closely linked to the competence granted under the applicable constitutional arrangements, including the scope of their remedial powers.[97] The resulting degree of deference will differ accordingly. Yet, even courts with very wide competence and remedial powers will face inherent limitations.[98] As the South African Court remarked, 'The inherited injustices at the macro level will inevitably make it difficult for the courts to ensure immediate present-day

95 See for further elaboration S. Burri, Protection and rights related to pregnancy and maternity in EU law, *Revue de droit comparé du travail et de la sécurité sociale*, 2019 (English Electronic Edition), p. 16–25.

96 For a discussion see e.g. H. Alviar García, K. Klare and L. Williams (eds), *Social and economic rights in theory and practice. Critical inquiries*, Abingdon/New York: Routledge 2015.

97 As mentioned in Chapter 1, the topic of remedies and enforcement of equality standards is beyond the scope of this study.

98 As is extensively discussed in a special issue of the *South African Journal of Human Rights*, 2020 no. 4, 'Separation of powers, the judiciary and the politics of constitutional adjudication'.

equity at the micro level. The judiciary cannot of itself correct all the systemic unfairness to be found in our society'.[99]

The often open-ended nature of substantive equal treatment may well explain why in legal practice a full-fledged substantive equality approach is not explicitly present in most jurisdictions. Substantive equality does manifest itself much more commonly in more limited fashion through the application by judicial bodies of closely related, but judicially more manageable legal concepts such as indirect discrimination, (reasonable) accommodation and positive discrimination or positive action, which are addressed in Chapters 5, 6 and 7.

3.5.4 *Limits of Law in Changing Dominant Standards and Addressing Systemic Disadvantage*

Some final words regarding the limits of law as such in achieving substantive equality. In its most far reaching conception as formulated by the South African Constitutional Court and the Inter-American Court of Human Rights, that is as requiring dismantling structural or systemic disadvantage and marginalization of vulnerable groups in society, it is not just courts who will have to face the limitations of their role as judicial bodies. Where structural disadvantage and marginalization are embedded not just in the dominant standards of law, but are often deeply engrained in the social, economic and cultural fabrics of societies, it is important to acknowledge that law itself is inherently a limited instrument for bringing about such profound and truly fundamental change.

3.6 Concluding Remarks

This chapter endeavoured to clarify how taking a formal or (more) substantive equality approach is of major importance for the visibility and outcome of equality claims. To sum up, a formal equality approach is preoccupied with the equality of the treatment. As long as people are treated the same, there is no violation of equality standards. Treating like cases unalike is the problem which may be successfully challenged. Under a formal equality approach, identifying equality problems is limited to looking for unjustified unequal treatment. A strong presumption of unequal treatment being unjustified is particularly acknowledged regarding sensitive or suspect categories or classifications, such as the protected grounds listed in non-discrimination provisions.

99 Constitutional Court of South Africa, *Port Elizabeth Municipality v. various Occupiers*, [2004] ZACC 7, par. 38.

In this context high(er) demands are placed on the justification of any differential treatment.

Substantive equality, on the other hand, is not preoccupied with the equality of the treatment itself, but with the equal outcome of a treatment. This different perspective means it may sometimes demand differential treatment to achieve a (more) equal result. It also means it is much more open to ameliorative measures directed at improving the position of socially and economically marginalized groups in society, such as disabled people, women, and racial, religious and sexual minorities. Though formal equality is the most common understanding of equality, approaches taking on board a more substantive, outcome oriented reading, are gaining ground in a wide range of jurisdictions.

This chapter also explored how application of the two approaches face their own difficulties and dilemma's. As both formal and substantive equality focus on unjustified treatment, be it unjustified unequal treatment or, in addition, also unjustified equal treatment, equality analysis inevitably involves all sorts of normative assessments and appreciation. Unsurprisingly, then, they can be up for a lot of discussion depending on the perspective taken.

In legal practice, the focus of equality claims is largely directed at distinctions based on sensitive or suspect criteria such as race, sex, religion, sexual orientation, gender identity, disability et cetera. This is where the concept of discrimination comes in, which will be the subject of following chapters.

CHAPTER 4

Discrimination – General Features

4.1 Introduction

A full-fledged development of legal standards expressly targeting discrimination does not have a very long history. It came about largely in the 20th century, particularly since World War II. According to the Stanford Encyclopedia of Philosophy, discrimination as a moral category did not become part of the vocabulary of social justice until the middle of the 19th century, and only gained momentum in the 20th century.[1] This seems to run parallel with the development of discrimination as a legal notion.

As a legal concept and standard, non-discrimination gained prominence in international law in the context of minority protection after the First World War. With the disintegration of the defeated Prussian kingdom and the Ottoman and Austro-Hungarian empires, the newly formed successor states were required to commit themselves to the protection of the ethnic and cultural minorities within their borders in return for international recognition as independent states. Under the auspices of the League of Nations many international treaties regulating the position of these minorities came into being, which usually included non-discrimination guarantees as well as particular rights for minorities to use their own language, have their own educational institutions and practice their religion.[2] After the Second World War, minority treaties were considered to have failed, and to be better replaced by the human rights principles adopted. It was not just minorities who were perceived as being in need of having their basic rights guaranteed, but all persons, without distinction.[3] This was reflected in the Charter of the newly founded United Nations. In addition to maintaining international peace and security, developing friendly relations among nations and achieving international co-operation in solving international problems, promoting and encouraging respect for human rights and for fundamental freedoms for all without distinction as to race, sex, language, or religion were formulated as one of the purposes of the United Nations in Article 1 of the UN Charter. The traumatic experiences

1 A. Altmann, Discrimination, in: *The Stanford Encyclopedia of Philosophy*, (version 20 April 2020), p. 16.
2 McKean, *Equality and discrimination*, 1983, p. 20–26.
3 Idem, p. 52.

DOI:10.1163/9789004538368_005

with Nazi rule and racist ideology were no doubt a major catalyst for this new emphasis on equal rights and protection against discrimination for all human beings.[4] The prominence of the latter is underscored by positioning a guarantee of equal entitlement to all rights and freedoms without distinction 'of any kind', including but not limited to race, colour, sex, language, religion, political or other opinion, national or social origin, property, birth or other status, at the beginning of the UDHR in Article 2, right after the proclamation of the inherent equality of all human beings in Article 1.[5]

Since then, non-discrimination provisions have become part and parcel of global and regional human rights conventions and national constitutions. In addition, in many jurisdictions they have been elaborated in more detailed non-discrimination law covering specific areas such as employment and access to goods and services. The latter type of elaboration is of particular importance for extending the reach of non-discrimination standards to horizontal relationships.

Over time, non-discrimination has shown itself to be a very dynamic legal concept and standard. Starting basically as a standard applicable with respect to a limited number of grounds such as race, sex and religion and being closely tied in with a notion of formal equality as discussed in Chapter 3, it developed both in terms of encompassing ever more grounds and of broadening its conceptual scope, thus significantly extending the protection non-discrimination standards may provide. As a result of this development, several distinct modalities of discrimination have come to play an increasingly important role in discrimination law.[6] In the application of non-discrimination standards by judicial bodies they often trigger specific forms of judicial review.

To start with, expanding the notion of discrimination by including the concept of indirect discrimination implies a potentially far reaching step beyond the original focus of non-discrimination standards on formal equality. Indirect discrimination problematizes rules or measures which are not expressly based on protected grounds such as race, sex, religion, sexual orientation et cetera,

---

4 See extensively on the influence of the Second World War on drafting the UDHR: J. Morsink, *The Universal Declaration of Human Rights: origins, drafting and intent*, Philadelphia, Univ. of Pennsylvania Press, 1999, Chapter 2: World War II as catalyst.

5 An important push for giving prominence to non-discrimination in the UDHR came from a strong women's lobby as far as sex discrimination was concerned, but more generally from the Soviet Union. The latter challenged Western powers for continuing colonialism and the US for its systemic racial segregation and the appalling levels of racial violence against black people. See for the role of colonialism and the issue of women's rights in the drafting process Morsink, *The Universal Declaration*, 1999, Chapter 3.

6 For the terminology I use for these different modalities see Chapter 1.

yet have a disparate, negative *effect* on the groups protected by the prohibition of discrimination on these grounds. Thus, for instance, exclusion of part-time workers from a pension scheme may also constitute discrimination on grounds of sex, even if 'part-time work' is in itself a sex-neutral distinction. As in social reality the far majority of part-time workers is usually female, women are much more negatively affected by such a policy than men. They are thus treated in a disadvantageous way, be it indirectly. Indirect discrimination's focus on the unequal outcome of a rule or measure, rather than on the sameness or difference of the treatment itself, links it to a more substantive approach to equality.

Another particular modality of discrimination, closely related to indirect discrimination or sometimes conceived as a particular part of this notion, is lack of (reasonable) accommodation. It has gained increasing attention in law. Its express inclusion as a distinct form of discrimination in the Convention on the Rights of Persons with Disabilities is a case in point.[7] Thus, for instance, in terms of the CRPD an employer will violate the prohibition of discrimination if he fails to accommodate the needs of a disabled worker, for instance by providing an employee with poor sight with a personal computer containing appropriate speech software, unless it would entail a disproportionate or undue burden to do so.[8] As briefly discussed in Chapter 3 (Section 3.4.2), a duty to provide accommodation entails differential treatment to reach a (more) equal outcome. As such it belongs to the realm of a substantive equality approach.

A third modality of discrimination which has been developed as a distinct legal concept is positive discrimination or positive action. In many jurisdictions, using distinctions such as race or sex as a basis for policies to ameliorate the position of racial groups or women is highly controversial, as it departs from the presumption of race or sex based differentiations being unjustified. At the same time, in most of these jurisdictions positive discrimination or positive action has been recognized as calling for a different, less strict kind of judicial review than 'ordinary' differential treatment on the grounds of race or sex with a negative effect on already disadvantaged group. As with the concepts of indirect discrimination and (reasonable) accommodation, the focus of positive discrimination or positive action on achieving a more equal outcome for certain groups links it to a substantive equality perspective.

---

7 Article 2 CRPD provides that '"Discrimination on the basis of disability" (…) includes all forms of discrimination, including denial of reasonable accommodation'.

8 Article 2 CRPD defines reasonable accommodation as 'necessary and appropriate modification and adjustments not imposing a disproportionate or undue burden, where needed in a particular case, to ensure to persons with disabilities the enjoyment or exercise on an equal basis with others of all human rights and fundamental freedoms'.

Last but not least, the notion of intersectional discrimination has come to the fore as an important modality of discrimination which seems hard to integrate into existing conceptual frameworks governing non-discrimination standards. Intersectional discrimination occurs when two sources of discrimination result in something 'qualitatively different' than just adding the two.[9] Thus, for example, a prohibition to wear a headscarf at work affects Muslim women who wish to wear it for religious reasons in a unique way. The way in which they experience disadvantage stems from the intersection of their sex and their religion and is quite different from the effects of such a policy on Muslim men or non-Muslim women.

As each of these modalities of discrimination and the way in which jurisdictions take them on board (or refrain from doing so) are of particular importance for the reach of equality standards, they will be elaborated in more detail in Chapters 5–8.

This chapter will focus on the general features of non-discrimination as a legal standard, from which the modalities mentioned branched off and developed into closely related, yet distinct legal concepts. It will start with a characterization of the prohibition of discrimination as a norm which forbids unjustified unequal treatment on the basis of protected grounds such as race, sex, religion, sexual orientation, disability and the like (Section 4.2), before exploring how grounds have been identified as sensitive or protected grounds (Section 4.3). Given the importance for judicial scrutiny of recognition as a protected ground, this section delves into the complexities involved in legally defining and delimitating grounds of discrimination. It also discusses the proliferation of discrimination grounds being included in non-discrimination law, which occurs in many jurisdictions. Section 4.4 turns to what is central to non-discrimination law: the way in which the use made of sensitive or suspect classifications in rules or policies – that is distinctions on the basis of a protected ground – translates into requirements of stronger justification to be acceptable. Stricter judicial review, then, is a fundamental feature of non-discrimination standards. The characteristics of this type of review show strong similarities across jurisdictions. To conclude the chapter, Section 4.5 discusses some of the difficulties and dilemmas of differentiating discrimination review according to the particular ground involved.

9 S. Fredman, *Intersectional discrimination in EU gender equality and discrimination law*, Report European Network of legal experts in gender equality and non-discrimination, 2016, p. 27–28.

4.2 Non-discrimination as a Specific Articulation of Equality

Discrimination often remains undefined in human rights treaties and national constitutions. The same holds true for its relationship with the concept of equality. No definition is provided in either the UDHR, ICCPR and ICESCR, the main regional human rights treaties or the constitutions of the countries figuring prominently in this study.[10] Nevertheless, the way in which non-discrimination provisions are almost always linked to a number of expressly enumerated grounds gives a quite clear indication of the distinct character of discrimination. Legal prohibitions of discrimination are a specific articulation of equality as a legal standard to protect (members of) groups deemed in need of particular protection. They are tied in closely with classifications on the basis of sensitive or suspect criteria and, as briefly discussed in Chapter 2 (Section 2.3.2) as such tend to require stronger justification to be acceptable than 'ordinary' differential treatment on the basis of non-sensitive criteria. The South African Constitutional Court is very explicit in this regard, by distinguishing 'mere differentiation' and 'differentiation that amounts to discrimination.[11]

Non-discrimination is usually part and parcel of equality standards codified in international and national law. Article 26 ICCPR is a typical example by mentioning a right to equality in one breath with a right to non-discrimination,[12] and subsequently specifying a number of grounds which warrant particular attention to avoid discrimination:

10 The two main treaties devoted to combatting discrimination, the ICERD and the CEDAW, do define discrimination. Article 1(1) ICERD: 'In this Convention, the term "racial discrimination" shall mean any distinction, exclusion, restriction or preference based on race, colour, descent, or national or ethnic origin which has the purpose or effect of nullifying or impairing the recognition, enjoyment or exercise, on an equal footing, of human rights and fundamental freedoms in the political, economic, social, cultural or any other field of public life'. The definition in Article 1 CEDAW is largely similar.

11 Albertyn and Goldblatt, Equality, 2007, p. 17–18.

12 The US Constitution and the ECHR present exceptions to expressly linking equality and non-discrimination in the text of their equality standards. The US constitutional equality principle does not mention discrimination in the Fourteenth Amendment, but uses 'equal protection' language and does not spell out specific grounds or groups which require particular protection in this respect. The ECHR, on the other hand, does not use equality terminology in Article 14, but is exclusively worded in terms of the enjoyment of the rights and freedoms of the ECHR being guaranteed 'without discrimination' on a number of specified grounds or on 'any other status'.

> All persons are equal before the law and are entitled without any discrimination to the equal protection of the law. In this respect, the law shall prohibit any discrimination and guarantee to all persons equal and effective protection against discrimination on any ground such as race, colour, sex, language, religion, political or other opinion, national or social origin, property, birth or other status.

Delving into the characteristics of legal prohibitions of discrimination of this kind, five closely related, interlinking features seem to stand out: discrimination has a pejorative meaning; it originates in group-based disadvantageous treatment; it concerns asymmetrical relations between groups; which particular groups suffer from disadvantageous treatment is context-specific; the disadvantageous treatment is of a structural, rather than incidental nature.

4.2.1 *Pejorative Meaning: Unjustified Treatment*

Generally speaking, discrimination has a negative ring to it. It is usually used in a pejorative sense, that is as some form of unfair, unjustifiable or 'wrong' treatment.[13] This is reflected in law. Discrimination is approached as being about *unjustified* differential treatment, it does not mean no differentiations whatsoever are allowed. In the wording of the ECtHR, only differentiations which have no 'objective and reasonable justification' amount to discrimination.[14] This pejorative meaning can explain why the non-discrimination provisions in the ECHR, ICCPR and other human rights conventions do not provide for a specific, express limitation clause, contrary to the specific standards formulated regarding the limitation of substantive rights such as the right to freedom of expression or freedom of association.[15]

---

13 McKean, *Equality and discrimination*, 1983, p. 10.

14 See e.g. ECtHR (Grand Chamber), 13 November 2007, *D.H. and others v. The Czech Republic*, appl. no. 57325/00, par. 175; See for the similar approach by the Human Rights Committee under the ICCPR its *General Comment No. 18: Non-discrimination*, 1989 and for the Committee on Economic, Social and Cultural Rights under the ICESCR ts General Comment No. 20 of 2012 on *Non-discrimination in economic, social and cultural rights (Art. 2, para. 2 of the ICESCR)*, E/C.12/GC/20.

15 Cf. e.g. Article 10(2) and 11(2) ECHR and Article 19(3) and 22(2) ICCPR. Canada seems to provide an exception by separating the justification review from the discrimination review under its Charter of Fundamental Rights. Justification review is conducted under the general limitation clause of Section 1, not under the non-discrimination provision in Section 15. Ultimately, however, as under the ECHR or the ICCPR, the acceptability of differential treatment depends on whether it can be justified. The South African Constitution has an even more complicated way of dividing its justification review between assessing the 'unfairness' of discrimination under Section 9 of the Constitution

4.2.2 *Origins in Group-Based Disadvantageous Treatment*

In the 19th century, discrimination became identified as a moral issue when it was increasingly recognized that 'large-scale injustices in history had a group-based structure'.[16] In Chapter 2, I already referred to how women were increasingly regarded as suffering from group-based oppression simply on account of their sex, resulting in calls for granting them equal rights as men. Acknowledging the group-based character of discrimination is not to say that the group as such is the wronged party and not (also) the individual members of the group,[17] or that all members of the group suffer from the discrimination or in the same way, but it is of great importance for understanding why the prohibition of discrimination came to be developed in many jurisdictions as moving beyond a demand of just formal equal treatment. As will be further explored in Chapter 5, the group-based character of discrimination is reflected in the development of the concept of indirect discrimination, which is triggered by the disparate effect of a neutral policy or measure on a protected group. Similarly, the notion of positive discrimination or positive action (see Chapter 7) is based on an endeavour to improve the overall position of a disadvantaged group, not of one or more individual persons belonging to the group as such. At the same time, this focus on the group is an important source of contestation regarding affirmative action measures. Though the source of disadvantage may be group-based, efforts to remedy this by a group-based rather than individual approach meets with objections in quite some jurisdictions.

4.2.3 *Asymmetrical Group Relations*

Legal prohibitions of discrimination are, implicitly or explicitly, concerned with asymmetrical group relations, which usually tie in with perceptions of the disadvantaged group being inferior or of lesser worth. Discrimination is not the same as 'mere' differential treatment of two groups. The South African Apartheid system differentiated in myriad ways between white and black people (and other people designated as coloured), but it would not make sense to say that white people were also discriminated under this system.[18] In a similar vein, differential treatment on the basis of sex, which is still pervasive all over the world, is mainly about discrimination against women, not men. Of course,

and an additional assessment under the general limitation clause applicable to fundamental rights undersection 36. Here again, however, together they provide a full justification review. Cf. Albertyn and Goldblatt, Equality, 2007, p. 81–82.

16 Altman, *Discrimination*, 2020, p. 16.

17 Idem, p. 13.

18 Idem, p. 3.

this is not to say men can never be discriminated against on the basis of their sex, but it suggests this is exceptional and not the core problem a prohibition of sex discrimination seeks to address. The CEDAW acknowledges this by being expressly directed at the elimination of discrimination against women, rather than discrimination on grounds of sex as such. Overall, women are in need of particular protection, not men. Similarly, the CRPD has an expressly asymmetrical focus by prohibiting discrimination on the basis of disability as such.[19]

This being said, positing asymmetrical group relations as the underlying rationale for non-discrimination provisions should be nuanced. An asymmetrical approach may be contested as a matter of principle. The US provide a clear example. Over the years, the jurisprudence of the Supreme Court has been moving from a more asymmetrical towards a symmetrical approach to equality and non-discrimination standards as is exemplified by its case law on affirmative action (see for further elaboration Chapter 7, Section 7.4.1). In addition, realities on the ground are often more complex than asymmetry at group level would suggest. Thus, for example, men may suffer as much from the negative effects of sex stereotypes as women, which sits uneasily with non-discrimination provisions being limited to protection of women as is the case in the CEDAW. More fundamentally, a focus on women in the latter convention may emphasize understanding gender as a binary, whereas it is increasingly acknowledged to be fluid.[20]

4.2.4 *Context-Specific*

Recognizing that discrimination is asymmetrical does not mean disadvantage is always suffered by the same groups. Context is determining here. Though for women and disabled people discrimination may be a worldwide experience, for racial or religious groups context matters much more. Catholics may

---

19 An interesting summing up of what are 'protected groups' rather than 'protected grounds' can be found in the Inter-American Convention on protecting the human rights of older persons, in force since 2017;

"Article 5 establishes the prohibition of discrimination based on the age of older persons and stipulates that 'States Parties shall develop specific approaches for older persons who are vulnerable and those who are victims of multiple discrimination, including women, persons with disabilities, persons of different sexual orientations and gender identities, migrants, persons living in poverty or social exclusion, people of African descent, and persons pertaining to indigenous peoples, the homeless, people deprived of their liberty, persons pertaining to traditional peoples, and persons who belong to ethnic, racial, national, linguistic, religious, and rural groups, among others."

20 See for an elaboration of this type of principled critique on the asymmetrical approach in the CEDAW D. Rosenblum, Unsex CEDAW, or what's wrong with women's rights, *Columbia Journal of Gender and Law*, 2011, p. 98–194.

face discrimination in one country, but not in another, or they may even be the main perpetrators of discrimination against other religious groups in yet another country. This contextuality may also explain why, contrary to the CEDAW and CRPD, the Convention regarding racial discrimination, ICERD, is not formulated in an asymmetrical way, but in terms of a prohibition of racial discrimination.

4.2.5 *Structural Rather Than Incidental: Patterns of Disadvantage*

Most importantly, perhaps, legal prohibitions of discrimination intend to target group-based disadvantageous treatment of some kind of structural, not incidental nature. It concerns groups who suffer from patterns of disadvantage rather than incidental and isolated instances of disadvantageous treatment. Though a dog-lover went all the way up to the Dutch Supreme Court with a claim of being discriminated in violation of Article 26 ICCPR because he had to pay a local tax for having a dog, whereas cat-lovers did not have to pay for their cat,[21] most people would probably not use the terminology of 'discrimination' for this type of differential treatment between owners of dogs and cats, regardless whether it is perceived as justified or not. The distinction does not reflect a more structural type of singling out dog-owners for disadvantageous treatment. To put it in another way, the distinction made between people possessing a dog or a cat for tax purposes is not in any way sensitive or suspect and does not affect a group which is more generally particularly disadvantaged.

The above characteristics of what legal prohibitions of discrimination are directed at are closely linked and intertwined. Together, they suggest that legal prohibitions of discrimination are primarily directed at differential treatment based on sensitive or suspect criteria, which negatively affect vulnerable groups facing patterns of disadvantage rather than incidental disadvantageous treatment.

Whatever the concrete legal terminology used in jurisdictions, this type of differential treatment usually invites stricter forms of judicial review when challenged before courts or other judicial bodies than differentiations based on non-sensitive or non-suspect criteria. Before turning to the various ways in which such stricter review may take shape, identifying which grounds are to be approached as protected grounds – and thus in need of stronger protection by heightened levels of scrutiny – is a crucial legal step.

21 *Hoge Raad* (Supreme Court), 19 September 1990, ECLI:NL:HR:1990:ZC4387.

4.3 Identifying Sensitive or Protected Grounds

As a start, it is important to distinguish conceptual understanding of what constitutes a sensitive or protected ground and legal identification of such grounds. Conceptual understanding regards the underlying rationale or foundations of identifying a ground as sensitive or protected, and thus deserving more protection by more stringent review. Legal identification as a protected ground is what ultimately matters legally for granting a high(er) level of protection under discrimination law.

4.3.1 *Conceptual Understanding of Sensitive or Protected Grounds*

Academic literature and case law from a variety of jurisdictions point to a number of underlying foundations or criteria used for identifying sensitive or protected grounds calling for the particular protection of non-discrimination standards.[22]

4.3.1.1 Immutable Personal Characteristics

The immutability of certain personal characteristics is a first rationale often mentioned for identifying a ground as deserving particular protection.[23] Characteristics such as race or sex are inherent characteristics beyond a person's choice and for this reason any distinctions based on such characteristics should meet with distrust and be perceived as hardly ever justified. Yet, 'immutability' as a foundation for identifying a ground as being hardly ever acceptable as a basis for differentiation cannot be the end of the story. On the one hand, it seems evident not all immutable characteristics are to be approached with distrust. If we only consider a characteristic like intelligence, it is obvious this is a fully accepted feature for distinguishing between persons in access to higher education or certain jobs. Immutability as such, then, is not a sufficiently decisive criterion for identifying a ground as sensitive. On the other hand, deciding which personal characteristics are indeed immutable is not as clear cut as it may seem. Biological sex has for a long time been perceived as an immutable characteristic, whereas current notions regarding sex and gender tend to emphasize their fluidity. Similarly, sexual orientation has met with different perceptions about being immutable or not. Whatever the merits of

22 The conceptual foundations identified show strong links with philosophical discussions on what makes discrimination 'wrong', see K. Lippert-Rasmussen, 'The philosophy of discrimination – an introduction', in: K. Lippert Rasmussen (ed), *The Routledge Handbook on the ethics of discrimination*, 2017.

23 Cf. Fredman, *Discrimination law*, 2022, p. 206–210.

either position, what seems to matter most is how this characteristic may be part of a person's core identity. For this reason, core identity-shaping characteristics are also often referred to as a basis for identifying a ground as sensitive and thus deserving strong protection.

4.3.1.2 Identity-Shaping Personal Characteristics

Core identity-shaping characteristics may be approached as effectively immutable, because they can only be abandoned, if at all, at (too) great cost to the individual person.[24] As the Canadian Supreme Court put it where sexual orientation is concerned:

> [W]hether or not sexual characteristics are based on biological or psychological factors, which may be a matter of some controversy, it is a deeply personal characteristic that is either unchangeable or changeable only at unacceptable personal costs, and so falls within the ambit of s. 15 protection.[25]

Other characteristics fitting this category include religion or belief and political opinion. These characteristics are often also core to personal identity and way of living and being. Of course, race and sex also belong to this type of characteristics, showing how different foundational criteria for identifying a protected ground may well overlap.

As holds true for the 'immutability' criterion, not all core identity-shaping characteristics will be regarded as deserving particular legal protection from non-discrimination standards. To give an example: for fervent soccer fans, personal identity and way of life may very well be profoundly shaped by and revolve around their favorite club in a way similar to how a particular religion may shape a person's life. Nevertheless, it is not likely that these soccer fans could call on non-discrimination law to be exempted by their employer from having to work on Sunday in order to attend the Sunday matches. This may well be due to a lack of connection with a third foundation often mentioned as a basis for regarding a ground as sensitive.

4.3.1.3 Structural Patterns of Disadvantage and Exclusion

This third rationale for identifying a ground as sensitive and calling for stricter scrutiny, turns the focus from personal characteristics or attributes to the

---

24 Cf Khaitan, *A theory of discrimination law*, 2015, p. 59.

25 Section 15 contains the Canadian constitutional equality and non-discrimination clause; Supreme Court of Canada, *Egan v. Canada* [1995] 2 SCR 513, p. 528.

characteristics of the groups which are negatively affected by the use made of the ground concerned: groups facing structural disadvantage or patterns of marginalization. This disadvantage can be political, social, and/or economic and usually has a historical dimension; structural patterns of disadvantage do not emerge overnight.[26] 'Grounds of discrimination are not purely legal constructs. They reflect a political and social reality to which law has, belatedly, given recognition. Discrimination was a fact of life long before the law decided that it should intervene to prohibit it.'[27]

A classic example of political disadvantage calling for closer scrutiny can be derived from US case law, which already in 1938 called for stricter judicial review when 'discrete and insular minorities' are affected.[28] Prominent examples of the role played by structural disadvantage as core to identifying differential treatment on certain grounds as requiring stricter inquiry are present in South-African jurisprudence. As described in Chapter 3, given the strong focus of South African constitutional law on substantive equality, identifying structural disadvantage as an important element in deciding which grounds deserve particular protection under non-discrimination standards, is not surprising. According to the South African Constitutional Court, the grounds explicitly protected in the Constitution, such as race, sex, sexual orientation, disability, religion and several other grounds, share the fact 'that they have been used (or misused) in the past (both in South Africa and elsewhere) to categorize, marginalize and often oppress persons who have had, or who have been associated with these attributes or characteristics'.[29] Though in Europe substantive equality does not play a similarly guiding role, the ECtHR has also identified historical and structural disadvantage as a very relevant rationale for heightening the protection offered by Article 14 ECHR.[30]

---

26 Cf. Khaitan, *A theory of discrimination law*, 2015, p. 51.

27 D. Pothier, Connecting grounds of discrimination to real people's real experiences, *Canadian Journal of Women and Law* 2001, p. 37–73, p. 41.

28 US Supreme Court, *United States v. Carolene products*, 304 US 144 (1938).

29 *Harksen v. Lane NO and others*, [1997] ZACC 12. The South African Constitution lists the following specific grounds in Art. 9(3): 'race, gender, sex, pregnancy, marital status, ethnic or social origin, colour, sexual orientation, age, disability, religion, conscience, belief, culture, language and birth'.

30 Thus regarding Roma, the ECtHR notes that 'as a result of their turbulent history and constant uprooting the Roma have become a specific type of disadvantaged and vulnerable minority (…) As the Court has noted in previous cases, they therefore require special protection'. ECtHR (Grand Chamber), 13 November 2007, *D.H. and others v. the Czech Republic*, appl. no. 57325/00, par. 182.

4.3.1.4 Prejudice, Stereotyping and Stigma

Closely related to the notion of structural disadvantage and exclusion, a fourth foundation for regarding differential treatment on certain grounds as worthy of higher protection levels is also connected to characteristics of the groups affected: groups suffering from prejudice, stigma and stereotyping deserve particular protection.[31] Thus, the US Supreme Court held that state laws prohibiting same sex marriage are unconstitutional because 'the necessary consequence is to put the imprematur of the State itself on an exclusion that soon demeans or stigmatizes those whose own liberty is then denied. Under the Constitution, same-sex couples seek in marriage the same legal treatment as opposite-sex couples, and it would disparage their choices and diminish their personhood to deny them this right'.[32] The ECtHR and IACtHR have also expressly recognized the relevance of stigma and stereotyping for applying a higher level of scrutiny, for instance regarding laws or measures affecting disabled people or people with HIV.[33]

4.3.1.5 From Protected Grounds to Protected Vulnerable Groups?

Different jurisdictions may put different emphasis on each of the four foundations identified above, may combine some or all of them, or remain rather silent about what is considered to be the underlying rationale.[34] From a legal point of view, what ultimately matters is not the underlying rationale, but the actual legal recognition of a ground as a protected ground, which will be discussed in the next section.

Nevertheless, it is important to point out that the implicit or explicit rationale for identifying the grounds of discrimination deserving particular protection may well influence the legal interpretation of non-discrimination

---

31 Solanke proposes to use stigma as the determining criterion, see I. Solanke, *Discrimination as stigma: a theory of anti-discrimination law*, Bloomsbury, 2017.

32 US Supreme Court, *Obergefell v. Hodges*, 576 US 644 (2015), p. 19.

33 ECtHR, 20 May 2010, *Alajos Kiss v. Hungary*, appl. no. 38832/06: where people with mental disabilities are concerned, 'very weighty reasons' must be present for restrictions of their rights. 'The reasons for this approach, which questions certain classifications per se, is that such groups were historically subject to prejudice with lasting consequences, resulting in their social exclusion. Such prejudice may entail legislative stereotyping which prohibits the individualized evaluation of their capacities and needs', par. 42. Regarding people with HIV see ECtHR,,10 March 2011, *Kiyutin v. Russia*, appl. no. 2700/10, par. 64. See for the IACtHR, 1 September 2015, *Gonzales Lluy v. Ecuador* (Preliminary objections, merits, reparations and costs).

34 Cf. Fredman, *Discrimination law*, 2022; she describes how Canadian jurisprudence puts more emphasis on immutability (p. 206) whereas South African jurisprudence gives a prominent role to a history of disadvantage (p. 217).

standards. In this respect, the third and fourth foundations mentioned show a clearly asymmetrical perspective on why grounds such as race, sex, disability and so on are to be considered protected grounds under non-discrimination law. Structurally disadvantaged groups and groups facing stereotyping and stigma deserve particular protection, not the socially dominant groups in society. In this way, these two foundations subtly turn attention away from the protected *ground* deserving more critical inquiry, to the protected *group* in need of stronger protection. As such, the third and fourth foundation seem closely connected to the notion of 'vulnerable groups' which is increasingly used in human rights law more generally, to identify groups in need of the particular protection of fundamental rights, including non-discrimination standards.[35] As the South African Constitutional Court considered: 'vulnerability … depends to a very significant extent on past patterns of disadvantage, stereotyping and the like'.[36] Similarly, the ECtHR is often referring to the vulnerability of groups as calling for particular protection, including under Article 14 ECHR.[37]

4.3.2 *Legal Identification of Protected Grounds*

4.3.2.1 Open and Closed Models of Protected Grounds

Regardless the underlying considerations for recognizing a particular ground as sensitive and thus deserving enhanced protection under discrimination law, legally speaking what matters is being accepted as a protected ground, either by express listing in equality or discrimination provisions or by judicial interpretation of these standards. In this regard the distinction between legally 'open' and 'closed' models of protected grounds is important.

Open models of protected grounds sometimes provide protection against discrimination by not mentioning any particular ground, the US 14th Amendment presenting a prime example,[38] but more commonly an open model

35 See for an analysis of the development of the concept of vulnerability in international human rights law e.g. A. Timmer, *Strengthening the equality analysis of the European Court of Human Rights: the potential of the concepts of stereotyping and vulnerability*, 2014; F. Ippolito, *Understanding vulnerability in international human rights law*, Editoriale Scientifica, 2020; A.Timmer, M. Baumgärtel, L. Kotzé and L. Slingenberg, The potential and pitfalls of the vulnerability concept for human rights, *Netherlands Quarterly of Human Rights*, 2021, p. 190–197.

36 *National Coalition for Gay and lesbian equality v. Minister of Home Affairs*, [1999] ZACC 17.

37 According to Dušková vulnerability 'serves a similar role as suspect grounds' in the case law of the ECtHR. S. Dušková, *Who should we accommodate? Opening the grounds for reasonable accommodation under the European Convention on Human Rights*, Doctoral Thesis, University of Essex, 2023, p. 169.

38 The 14th Amendment to the US Constitution provides simply that 'No state may deny to any person within its jurisdiction the equal protection of the laws'. This brief provision

enumerates a number of grounds without being exhaustive, thus leaving room for adding grounds. This is the main model adopted in international and regional human rights treaties and in many constitutional equality standards. Precise formulations may, of course, vary, but under this model, discrimination is prohibited on any grounds *such as* race, sex or a number of other specified grounds, or *on any other ground*.[39] An open formulation of grounds leaves room for adding grounds to the list by judicial bodies competent to interpret and apply these discrimination standards.

Closed models of protected grounds do not allow for such extension by judicial bodies, as they include an exhaustive list of protected grounds. This model seems common where focused, statutory discrimination laws are concerned, which apply to specific areas or fields of social and economic life and intend to regulate duties of non-discrimination in much more detail – often including duties for private parties. Prime examples include the EU equal treatment directives covering discrimination on the grounds of race and sex in *grosso modo* employment and access to goods and services, and the directive covering discrimination on the basis of religion or belief, age, disability and sexual orientation, which is limited to employment.[40] EU countries follow this model in implementing these directives in their national law.[41]

4.3.2.2 Importance of the Difference between Open or Closed Models

The distinction between an open or closed model of protected grounds is highly important because it provides different answers to the question who decides about extending the protection of non-discrimination standards to groups perceived in need of heightened protection. In an open model, judicial bodies having competence to interpret the standards can decide this and, as will become apparent in Section 4.3.3, they have often done so. This judicial role also gives open models more flexibility in acknowledging new or hidden grounds of discrimination, or intersectional discrimination. On the other

has given rise to an extensive jurisprudence covering a range of grounds including, but not limited to, race, sex, religion and sexual orientation.

39 Article 26 ICCPR '(…) the law shall prohibit any discrimination and guarantee to all persons equal and effective protection against discrimination on any ground such as …'; Article 14 ECHR: 'The enjoyment of the rights and freedoms set forth in [the] Convention shall be secured without discrimination on any ground such as …'; Article 21 EU Charter of Fundamental Rights: 'Any discrimination based on any ground such as. … shall be prohibited'.

40 Directive 2000/43/EC; Directive 2004/113/EC; Directive 2006/54/EC and Directive 2000/78/EC.

41 For an overview see S. Ganty and J.C. Benito Sanchez, Equinet report, *Expanding the list of protected grounds within antidiscrimination law in the EU*, 2021, p. 15.

hand, closed models of protected grounds may have greater democratic legitimacy by putting the legislative bodies in charge of deciding which particular forms of unequal treatment should demand more stringent justification to be acceptable. The difference between the two models may play out most clearly in situations where judicial bodies extend protection of non-discrimination standards to grounds which are particularly controversial, such as sexual orientation or gender identity.

4.3.2.3 Context-Specific and Dynamic Nature of Identifying Protected Grounds

Identifying which grounds deserve the extra protection discrimination standards have to offer is often context specific. In the US, for instance, the prohibition of discrimination on the basis of race was first to gain legal recognition, only later followed by the inclusion of discrimination on grounds of sex. Given its historical record of slavery and entrenched racial segregation, this may not be really surprising. In the EU, on the other hand, legal standards to eliminate sex discrimination preceded those on the basis of race by several decades. Again, this need not be surprising given the particular economic background and purpose of creating the European Community. As unequal pay of men and women was regarded as distorting competition, it was included in Community legislation from the start.[42] Notwithstanding this type of contextually informed variety, over time a number of grounds can be seen to have become universally recognized as deserving the protection of non-discrimination standards by being codified in international human rights treaties, which almost all nations in the world have ratified. Thus the ICCPR and ICESCR list race, colour, sex, language, religion, political or other opinion, national or social origin, property, birth or other status as protected grounds.[43]

4.3.3 *Expansion of Protected Grounds over Time*

The contextual and dynamic nature of identifying protected grounds is also manifest in the considerable expansion of protected grounds in many jurisdictions. This development seems particularly prominent in more recent times. Expansion may come about in two ways. Firstly, particular grounds can become included as distinct categories. This can be the result of identification by judicial bodies under open models of protected grounds described above, but also by the inclusion of a wider variety of grounds by legislative powers

42 E. Ellis and P. Watson, EU anti-discrimination law (2nd ed.), Oxford University Press, 2012, p. 23.

43 Article 26 ICCPR and Article 2(2) ICESCR.

in new or amended non-discrimination standards. Secondly, where judicial activity is concerned, expansion has not just happened through categorical inclusion, but also by (re)interpreting existing grounds in a broader way as including other grounds, that is through definitional inclusion.[44] The latter may actually also extend the list of protected categories in a closed model of protected grounds.

4.3.3.1 Expansion by Categorical Inclusion

Over time, the list of protected grounds has grown considerably. This trend can be traced back to the start of the codification of non-discrimination standards in international law. The Charter of the United Nations mentioned race, sex, language and religion; the UDHR added colour, political or other opinion, national or social origin, property and birth. All these grounds were subsequently included in the ICCPR and the ICESCR.[45] The main regional human rights treaties contain a quite similar list, with some minor variations stemming from specific regional preoccupations.[46]

For quite some time this 'classic' list formulated in international law seems to have formed the basis for the codification of many other discrimination standards, but more recently considerable further extensions are visible. In 2006 disability became prominently recognized by the adoption of a global Convention on the Rights of Persons with Disabilities (CRPD), in which non-discrimination figures as a focal point.[47] The rights of the elderly are also receiving increasing attention. In the Americas it already resulted in the very first human rights convention dealing with the equal rights of older persons, adopted in 2015.[48] At the UN level support for drafting a new human rights convention to protect this groups shows how the particular problems faced

44 The terminology of definitional and categorical inclusion is derived from A.J. Neuman Wipfler, Identity crisis: the limitations of expanding Government recognition of gender identity and the possibility of genderless identity documents, *Harvard Journal of Law and Gender* 2016, p. 491–554.

45 Article 1(3) UN Charter; Article 2 UDHR; Article 26 ICCPR; Article 2(2) ICESCR.

46 The European Convention on Human Rights additionally mentions 'association with a national minority' (Article 14); the American Convention on Human Rights does not include 'property', but added 'economic status, or any other social condition' (Article 1(1); the African Charter of Human and Peoples' Rights also omitted 'property', but added 'ethnic group' and 'fortune' to the UDHR list (Article 2).

47 Under the American human rights system a regional convention on the rights of disabled persons came into being in 1999, the Inter American Convention on the Elimination of all Forms of Discrimination against Persons with Disabilities.

48 Inter-American Convention on Protecting the Human Rights of Older Persons, 2015.

by the elderly resonate globally with ageing populations in various parts of the world.[49]

The EU Charter of Fundamental Rights of 2012 expanded the classic list of protected grounds by expressly including disability, age, sexual orientation and genetic features (Article 21(1)). The 2013 Inter-American Convention against all forms of Discrimination and Intolerance is even more extensive. On top of all the other grounds mentioned above, Article 1(1) specifically mentions nationality; gender identity and expression; cultural identity; socioeconomic status; educational level; migrant, refugee, repatriate, stateless or internally displaced status; mental or physical health condition, including infectious-contagious condition and debilitating psychological condition.

Inclusion of some of these more recently enumerated grounds seems to reflect judicial developments in a variety of jurisdictions. Of course, for judicial bodies the opportunities for identifying additional protected grounds depends on the type of cases brought to those bodies, so this may well vary between jurisdictions and be most prominent in jurisdictions dealing with a large number of diverse cases. Thus, over the years the ECtHR has come to recognize, among others, age, gender identity, sexual orientation, disability, marital status, and immigration status as being protected by the category of 'other status' under Article 14 ECHR.[50] Arguably two of the most important of these are sexual orientation and gender identity, as they are still very much contested categories in most parts of the world. Nevertheless, over the past decades, they have received increasing recognition and protection by semi-judicial and judicial human rights bodies and by constitutional courts.[51]

The expansion of identifying protected grounds continues, both globally and across jurisdictions. An example are calls to include socio-economic status or, as the UN Special Rapporteur on Extreme Poverty formulated it

---

49 For information on developments at the UN level see the website of the Open-ended Working Group on Ageing for the purpose of strengthening the protection of the human rights of older persons, https://social.un.org/ageing-working-group/.

50 See for an overview the Council of Europe/European Court of Human Rights, *Guide on Article 14 of the European Convention on Human Rights and on protocol No. 12 to the Convention. Prohibition of discrimination.* (Version 31 August 2023), par. 164–218.

51 For a general overview of developments see H. Lau, *Sexual orientation and gender identity discrimination*, Brill Research Perspectives in Comparative Discrimination Law, Brill 2018 and M. van den Brink and P. Dunne, *Trans and intersex equality rights in Europe – a comparative analysis*, report of the Network of experts in gender equality and non-discrimination, 2018.

deliberately asymmetrically, socio-economic disadvantage.[52] Quite some jurisdictions already have it included in some way or another and may recognize it as a factor under discrimination law, but so far it does not in and of itself seem to be a focal point of court cases dealing with discrimination.[53] This may well be due to the difficulties involved in defining and applying this ground in legal practice.

At the national level, an even larger variety of grounds seems to receive express protection, at least in the European context. A comparative overview of listed grounds in non-discrimination law in EU countries shows the list may expand far beyond the enumerated grounds in EU law. France is the most prolific by providing protection against discrimination on the basis of well over 20 grounds in the French Labour Code. In addition to grounds included in or obviously linked to the list in the EU Charter of Fundamental Rights, the enumeration in the Labour Code includes additional grounds such as morals, particular vulnerability resulting from economic hardship, trade union activities, last name, physical appearance, place of residence, bank domicile and being a whistle-blower.[54]

Extension of protected grounds meets with support as well as criticism.[55] Arguments in favour of expanding the list point to the importance of the symbolic message attached to naming social groups in need of protection and making this more visible for policy-makers and judicial bodies. Explicit

52 Report of the Special Rapporteur on extreme poverty and human rights, Olivier De Schutter, *Banning discrimination on grounds of socioeconomic disadvantage: an essential tool in the fight against poverty*, 15 July 2022.

53 Idem, section 21–23.

54 The full list includes 'discrimination (....) en raison de son origine, de son sexe, de ses mœurs, de son orientation sexuelle, de son identité de genre, de son âge, de sa situation de famille ou de sa grossesse, de ses caractéristiques génétiques, de la particulière vulnérabilité résultant de sa situation économique, apparente ou connue de son auteur, de son appartenance ou de sa non-appartenance, vraie ou supposée, à une ethnie, une nation ou une prétendue race, de ses opinions politiques, de ses activités syndicales ou mutualistes, de son exercice d'un mandat électif, de ses convictions religieuses, de son apparence physique, de son nom de famille, de son lieu de résidence ou de sa domiciliation bancaire, ou en raison de son état de santé, de sa perte d'autonomie ou de son handicap, de sa capacité à s'exprimer dans une langue autre que le français, de sa qualité de lanceur d'alerte, de facilitateur ou de personne en lien avec un lanceur d'alerte,origin', *Code du travail, Chapitre II: Principe de non-discrimination.* (Articles L1132–1 à L1132–4).

55 The following arguments for and against extension are largely derived from a report of the European Network of Equality Bodies by S. Ganty and J.C. Benito Sanchez, Equinet report, *Expanding the list of protected grounds within antidiscrimination law in the EU*, 2021, p. 25–28.

recognition also promotes data collection and research on behalf of improving the position of the groups concerned. Last but not least, identifying new grounds avoids having to look for more cumbersome or artificial ways to link a new ground to already protected grounds which could form the basis for a discrimination challenge. (For example, challenging discrimination of a socially disadvantaged group as a form of indirect discrimination on the basis of race or sex). As such it may also provide easier ways to address intersectional discrimination.[56] (see for further discussion Chapter 8). Arguments against expansion are concerned about extensions leading to 'ground inflation'. This may in fact detract from perceiving discrimination as something unacceptable. It may also become more difficult to distinguish non-discrimination standards from the main equality principle, which is also applicable to ordinary, non-sensitive classifications. In addition, critics argue, expansion of protected grounds may lead to populist backlash. Of course, other arguments for and against the extension of grounds can be ground specific.

4.3.3.2 Expansion by Definitional Inclusion

Expansion of protected grounds may also be the result of a broader reading of already protected grounds by judicial interpretation. Importantly, this type of extension can also operate in a closed model of protected grounds. Several examples can be found in a variety of jurisdictions.

A first example concerns discrimination on the basis of race. Racial discrimination is not always easy to pinpoint. For this reason the ICERD contains a broad definition. Racial discrimination is defined as any distinction, exclusion, restriction or preference 'based on race, colour, descent, or national or ethnic origin'.[57] Particularly in Europe, judicial bodies have also recognized several religious groups as being protected by a prohibition of racial discrimination, given the close and intertwined relationship which may exist between religion

56 The CESCR indicates that other prohibited grounds of discrimination than those explicitly listed in the ICESCR could be the result of intersectional discrimination on two or more grounds, see CESCR, General Comment No. 20: Non-discrimination in economic, social and cultural rights (Art. 2, para. 2 of the International Covenant on Economic, Social and Cultural Rights), UN Doc. E/C.12/GC/20, July 2, 2009, paras. 15 and 27 in particular. See for further discussion of intersectional discrimination Chapter 8.

57 Religion was deliberately not included in this list, even though the drafters were fully aware that racial and religious discrimination may be closely linked or intertwined – the Holocaust being still fresh in their minds. See D. Keane and A. Waughray, Introduction, in: D. Keane and A. Waughray (eds), *Fifty years of the International Convention on the Elimination of All Forms of Racial Discrimination. A living instrument*, Manchester, Manchester University Press 2017, p. 1–31.

and race or ethnic origin. Jewish and Sikh people are the prime examples. Some Muslim groups in Western Europe, who are mainly from non-European ethnic origin or descent, point to this precedent for claims to be similarly protected by legal standards banning racial discrimination.[58] As legal protection against racial discrimination is often stronger and covering broader areas of social life, inclusion under racial discrimination can indeed make a considerable difference.[59]

Caste-based discrimination is another example of a category that has become recognized as a form of racial discrimination, deserving protection under discrimination covering this ground. The supervisory body to the ICERD, the Committee on the Elimination of Racial Discrimination (CERD) has approached caste-based discrimination in this way by pointing out its close links with 'descent', which is explicitly mentioned in the definition of racial discrimination in the ICERD.[60] Though the interpretations of treaty bodies such as the CERD are authoritative, legally they have the (non-binding) status of soft-law. Interestingly, however, the CERD approach is also followed in some 'hard' case law from UK courts, which have come to deal with caste-based discrimination in Indian communities in their country.[61]

Defining 'sex' for purposes of non-discrimination law is another major example of how interpretation by judicial bodies may in fact extend the protection of non-discrimination law to other grounds. A seminal example bringing sexual orientation and gender identity under the protection of a prohibition on the basis of sex, can be derived from the jurisprudence of the US Supreme Court. In the *Bostock* case, the Supreme Court held that dismissing an employee for being homosexual or transgender amounts to sex discrimination

---

58 For a discussion on the legal possibilities of including Muslims under the protection of the CERD see S.E. Berry, Bringing Muslim minorities within the International Convention on the Elimination of All Forms of Racial Discrimination: square peg in a round hole?, *Human Rights Law Review* 2011, p. 423–450.

59 The EU equal treatment Directives are just one example. Directive 2000/43/EC on racial discrimination covers employment as well as goods and services, whereas Directive 2000/78/EC covering discrimination on the basis of religion is limited to employment.

60 The reading of caste-based discrimination as racial discrimination is not accepted by India, in which caste-based discrimination is still a major form of discrimination. See for an analysis of how caste-based discrimination is included under racial discrimination in the context of international human rights law A. Waughry and D. Keane, CERD and caste-based discrimination, in: A. Waughray and D. Keane (eds), *Fifty years of the International Convention on the Elimination of All Forms of Racial Discrimination: a living instrument*, Manchester University Press, 2017, Chapter 6, p. 121–149.

61 See for an example Waughry and Keane, CERD and caste-based discrimination, 2017, p. 121.

under Title VII of the Civil Rights Act.[62] Title VII operates under a closed model of protected grounds and does not list either sexual orientation or gender identity. In coming to its decision, the Court used what Lau terms the 'definitional rationale' for including the two grounds under sex-based discrimination: sexual orientation and gender identity are necessarily defined via a person's sex.[63] As the SC puts it:

> [I]t is impossible to discriminate against a person for being homosexual or transgender without discriminating against that individual based on sex. Consider, for example, an employer with two employees, both of whom are attracted to men. The two individuals are, to the employer's mind, materially identical in all respects, except that one is a man and the other is a woman. If the employer fires the male employee for no reason other than the fact he is attracted to men, the employer discriminates against him for traits or actions it tolerates in his female colleague.[64]

If this reasoning is followed throughout, the many international, constitutional and statutory non-discrimination standards covering sex discrimination could also protect against discrimination on the grounds of sexual orientation and gender identity without any need of express, separate inclusion as a protected ground. The higher protection this would provide for the groups concerned is obvious. So far, however, approaches in several other jurisdictions where judicial bodies explicitly dealt with this issue, are mixed. The CJEU, for example, did not consider discrimination on grounds of sexual orientation to fall under the protection provided against sex discrimination, but it did accept discrimination against transgender people to be covered by it.[65]

In Chapter 5 it will become clear how this type of expansion of protected grounds may also result from application of the concept of indirect discrimination. Thus, for example, discrimination against part-time or domestic workers may constitute indirect discrimination on the basis of sex and for this reason be reviewed with a high level of scrutiny, and be subsequently treated as a protected ground in itself.

---

62 *Bostock v. Clayton Country*, 590 US 644 (2020). The Supreme Court's reasoning regarding dismissal for being transgender constituting discrimination on the basis of sex is very similar.

63 Lau, Sexual orientation and gender identity, 2018, p. 8.

64 *Bostock v. Clayton Country*, 590 US 644 (2020), p. 9–10.

65 For sexual orientation see CJEU 17 February 1998, *Grant*, C-249/96, par. 27–28. For transgender see CJEU, 30 April 1996, *P v S*, C-13/94, par. 20–21.

In the above much attention was paid to identifying protected grounds, because of its importance for heightening the level of judicial scrutiny if differential treatment on the basis of protected grounds is at stake.

4.4 Discrimination Review – Justifying Difference in Treatment on the Basis of a Protected Ground

Generally speaking, discrimination is a particular form of unjustified unequal treatment. What stands out in discrimination review is its more stringent scrutiny of a difference in treatment on the basis of a protected ground compared to review of 'ordinary' classifications based on non-sensitive, non-protected grounds. Whether or not a jurisdiction uses the terminology of 'discrimination' also in relation to non-sensitive grounds, what ultimately matters is this raised standard of judicial review where protected grounds enter the scene.

This section explores discrimination review in more detail, particularly the ways in which more stringent scrutiny may be constructed. The focus is on differential treatment directly based on a protected ground; review of indirect discrimination and of unjustified lack of differential treatment (lack of reasonable accommodation) as a form of discrimination, are discussed in Chapter 5 and 6 respectively.

Models of review of a difference in treatment on a protected ground under general non-discrimination standards in national constitutions and under international human rights conventions show considerable similarities across jurisdictions. Again, this is not to say that the emphasis put on different elements of this review in different jurisdictions may not differ and lead to considerable variety in the outcome of a discrimination assessment.[66] Apart from such varieties within similar models of review, some important exceptions exist which do not follow these general models. The EU equality directives are a prime example. They have their own, specific approach to reviewing differential treatment based directly on a protected ground. This particular model of reviewing direct discrimination is closely linked to the much more detailed and focused nature of this type of regulation, covering an exhaustive, limited list of grounds and specific, distinct areas such as employment and/or access

66 Fredman notes, for example, how the problematic aspects of a heavy emphasis on a comparator analysis, as is characteristic of discrimination review in the UK, have been overcome in other jurisdictions such as Canada and the European human hights system by 'softening' or largely abandoning this approach. Fredman, *Discrimination law*, 2022, p. 256–257.

to goods and services. As the EU Member States have to transpose directives into their domestic legal systems, this approach is common in all EU countries. This particular review model will be dealt with separately in Section 4.4.3.

4.4.1 *Differential Treatment 'On the Basis of' a Protected Ground*

If a difference in treatment based on a protected ground leads to stricter forms of review, deciding when differential treatment is indeed 'on the basis of' such a ground is pertinent. Though at first sight it may seem clear when a difference in treatment is 'on the basis of' a protected ground, closer analysis reveals this is not always the case. Wider or narrower interpretation of 'on the basis of' may influence the protection provided by discrimination standards.

4.4.1.1 Intentional, Express Distinctions on the Basis of a Protected Ground

The most obvious case of a difference in treatment being 'on the basis of' a protected ground is when the protected ground is expressly and deliberately used. In this sense it is always 'intentional', which is not the same as being motivated by malice.[67] Excluding women from certain positions in the army or reserving marriage to different-sex couples are examples of using a protected ground as an express basis for differential treatment.

More difficult cases have presented themselves where views may differ whether a distinction is 'on the basis of' a protected ground. Jurisdictions may respond in different ways to such cases, but a generous rather than restrictive approach is visible in how some courts have included several distinct ways in which a difference in treatment or discrimination can be said to be 'based on' a protected ground: discrimination on a ground which is 'inextricably linked' to a protected ground, intra-group discrimination, 'but for' discrimination, what I would call 'ulterior motive' discrimination, and discrimination by association.

4.4.1.2 Discrimination 'Inextricably Linked' to a Protected Ground

Pregnancy discrimination is a famous example of the important difference it makes if discrimination 'on the basis of' a protected ground – in this case discrimination on the basis of sex – is read as including characteristics which are inextricably linked to or inseparable from a protected ground.

Discrimination on the basis of pregnancy, for example excluding pregnancy related health issues from a health benefit scheme, classifies between two groups which do not neatly coincide with the categories of men and

67 Khaitan, *Theory of discrimination law*, 2015, p. 70.

women: though the excluded group consists of women only (nowadays also a few exceptional trans men), the group of non-pregnant people consists of men and women. For this reason, the US Supreme Court held in the case of *Geduldig v. Aiello* that such an exclusion does not raise the question whether it constitutes discrimination on the basis of sex. As a result, the Court applied a very low level of judicial review under which classifications easily pass muster, unless they are clearly irrational.[68] The CJEU, on the other hand, held in the *Dekker* case that discrimination based on pregnancy is a form of sex discrimination, because it can only affect women. It is thus intrinsically, directly linked to sex.[69] As a consequence, any exclusion based on pregnancy must be measured against the same, stringent standard of review as discrimination on the basis of sex, which is not easily passed. Of course, if 'pregnancy' is included as a distinct ground in itself in a non-discrimination provision, this construction is not necessary to provide it the same level of protection.[70] To avoid any discussion, the South African Constitution expressly lists pregnancy as a protected ground, together with sex and gender.[71] The Canadian Supreme Court changed its position in this matter over time. In the 1979 case *Bliss v. Attorney General of Canada* the SC held that '[i]f section 46 treats unemployed pregnant women differently from other unemployed persons, be they male or female, it is ... because they are pregnant and not because they are women'.[72] In 1989 it expressly overturned this approach in *Brooks v. Canada Safeway Ltd.*: discrimination against pregnant women constitutes discrimination on the basis of sex.[73]

Whereas pregnancy has been identified as inextricably linked to sex because it is considered to be an inherent difference between men and women, in other situations certain criteria used as a basis for differential treatment may only be

68 US Supreme Court *Geduldig v. Aiello*, 417 US 484 (1974). In a more recent, similar vein, the Supreme Court does not approach abortion laws limiting decisions to terminate pregnancy as being based on sex and thus requiring more stringent review under Constitutional standards. Under the low scrutiny test applied, the Court overturned the precedent set in *Roe v. Wade* (410 US 113 (1973), allowing states to regulate abortion as they see fit. US Supreme Court, *Dobbs v. Jackson Women's Health Organization*, 597 US 215 (2022).

69 CJEU, 8 November 1990, *Dekker*, C 177/88, par. 17. The ECtHR follows the CJEU in this approach, see ECtHR *Napotnik a.o. v. Romania* (2020), sections 44–48.

70 This also avoids the complications in approaching pregnancy as 'inextricably linked' to sex in view of the contemporary realities of trans men who become pregnant and is responsive to the fluidity of the categories sex and gender.

71 Section 9(3).

72 Supreme Court, *Bliss v. Attorney General of Canada*, [1979] 1 SCR 183.

73 Supreme Court, *Brooks v. Canada Safeway Ltd.*, [1989] 1 SCR 1219.

inseparable from a protected ground in the specific circumstances of the case. Thus, the CJEU regarded a difference of treatment on the basis of marital status as (direct) discrimination on the basis of sexual orientation in a situation where marriage was only accessible for persons of different sexes.[74] Similarly, using pensionable age as a criterion for a difference in treatment, for instance if a redundancy scheme permits dismissal of employees who have acquired the right to draw a retirement pension, may be regarded as (direct) discrimination on the grounds of sex if the pension system provides for a different retirement age for men and women. In this particular situation, using pensionable age as the basis for a difference in treatment is inseparable from a difference in treatment on the basis of sex.[75] Again, whether or not a court regards this type of difference in treatment as being based on sex may result in quite different outcomes.

4.4.1.3 Intra-group Discrimination

Discrimination on a protected ground need not regard a protected group as such, but may be limited to a subgroup. Thus, for instance, in the former Dutch social security system married women were often excluded from unemployment or disability benefits, because they were presumed not to be the family breadwinner and thus not in need of such benefits. Here again, the excluded and included groups do not neatly divide along the lines of sex as such. Unmarried women can claim benefits on an equal basis with men. The CJEU had no difficulty, however, in regarding this type of exclusion as an unacceptable form of discrimination on the basis of sex as such. As this type of regulation expressly differentiates between married men and married women, this may not be surprising.[76] I will return to this way of dealing with intra-group discrimination in Chapter 8, as it also seems an interesting way to approach certain instances of intersectional discrimination.

Intra-group discrimination may also be regarded in a more general sense as discrimination 'on the basis of' a protected grounds, as is shown by a disability

---

74 CJEU (Grand Chamber), 1 April 2008, *Maruko*, C-267/06, par. 67–72.

75 Cf. CJEU, 18 November 2010, *Kleist*, C-356/09, par. 46. However, the CJEU does not always seem to be consistent, as is shown in the case *Schnorbus* (CJEU,7 December 2000, *Schnorbus*, C-79/99). The case concerned a preferential admittance scheme in Germany for people who had formerly been drafted into compulsory military service. As at the time the draft was limited to men, the preferred group consisted solely of men. Nevertheless, the CJEU was not willing to address this case as discrimination on the basis of sex as such, but only as a potential case of indirect discrimination on that ground, which allows for broader justification possibilities.

76 CJEU, 4 December 1986, *Federatie Nederlandse Vakbeweging* (FNV), C-71/85.

case decided by the CJEU. The case concerned the denial of an allowance to employees who had submitted a certain disability certificate before a particular date, reserving it to those who submitted this after that date. The Court held that discrimination on the basis of disability may not only arise when disabled persons are treated different from able bodied people, but also if unequal treatment is at stake between different categories of disabled persons.[77]

4.4.1.4 'But for' Discrimination

'But for' discrimination is also an important notion developed in the case law of some jurisdictions to decide whether a certain difference in treatment can be considered to be 'based on' a protected ground. It may have particular relevance in cases where a protected ground is not the sole criterion used as a basis for a difference in treatment, or not even as the core criterion. For the US Supreme Court, for instance, 'sex' being used as just one and not necessarily decisive element of a difference in treatment, is sufficient to address it as being based on sex as such. What counts is that discrimination would not have occurred 'but for' the use made of this criterion.[78] Similarly, in the Netherlands, using ethnic characteristics such as skin colour in identity checks as only one element among a range of other factors for purposes of establishing the legal or illegal residence status of foreigners entering the country, is sufficient to constitute discrimination on the basis of race or ethnic origin.[79]

4.4.1.5 'Ulterior Motive' Discrimination

If a difference in treatment is based on a neutral, non-sensitive criterion, but is in fact used to target a protected group, courts may still regard this as discrimination 'on the basis of' the protected ground. In this situation, the ulterior motive behind the difference in treatment is seen as the determining factor. The *Chez* case before the CJEU provides an example of this line of reasoning.[80] In this case, an electricity provider installed the electricity meters for the consumers of a certain district on concrete pylons at a height of about

---

77 CJEU, 26 January 2021, *Szpital Kliniczny*, C-16/19, par. 36. The CJEU explains its approach by holding this distinction to be inextricably linked to disability.

78 K. Eyer, The but-for theory of anti-discrimination law, *Virginia Law Review* 2021, p. 1621–1710, p. 1656.

79 *Gerechtshof Den Haag* (Court of Appeal The Hague), 14 February 2023, ECLI:NL:GHDHA:2023:173. The Court explicitly used the *but for* terminology. Referring to the jurisprudence of the ECtHR, it concludes that the fact that several, allegedly equally weighty factors were used to select people subject to identity checks, does not preclude the conclusion that the discrimination was 'but for' race or ethnic origin. (par. 8.14).

80 CJEU (Grand Chamber), 16 July 2015, *Chez*, C-83/14.

six metres, whereas in other districts the meters were usually placed at a height of 1.70 metres. The reason for high placement was prevention of tempering with the electricity meters. As the inhabitants of the district with the high-placed meters consisted primarily of people of Roma origin, this raised the question whether this particular placement constitutes discrimination (directly) based on race or ethnic origin. The CJEU answers this question in the affirmative, by holding that 'it is sufficient. … that that ethnic origin determined the decision to impose the treatment'.[81]

4.4.1.6 Discrimination 'by Association'

Another important way in which courts have interpreted discrimination to be 'on the basis of' a protected ground is by acknowledging discrimination 'by association'. This means that persons who do not belong to the protected group themselves can still be considered to suffer discrimination by being perceived as belonging to this group[82] or by being associated with it. The CJEU *Coleman* case shows how this notion provides enhanced protection against discrimination if it is recognized.[83] The case concerned a woman who was not treated unfavourably and harassed by her employer because she herself was disabled, but because she was the primary carer of a disabled child. The Court held that '[a]lthough, in a situation such as that in the present case, the person who is subject to direct discrimination on grounds of disability is not herself disabled, the fact remains that it is the disability which … is the ground for the less favourable treatment …'.[84]

4.4.2 *More Stringent Scrutiny of Justifying Differential Treatment Based on a Protected Ground*

As mentioned several times before, what makes non-discrimination stand out as a distinct part of equality as a legal standard is the more stringent scrutiny of the justification required to accept a difference in treatment on the basis

81 Idem, par. 76. If such ulterior motive is lacking, the treatment may still amount to indirect discrimination on grounds of ethnic origin given its disparate impact on people of Roma origin.

82 This form of discrimination by association may also be called discrimination by presumption.

83 CJEU (Grand Chamber), 17 July 2008, *Coleman*, C-303/06. In a similar way, the ECtHR included discrimination by association in ECtHR, 22 March 2016, *Guberina v. Croatia*, appl. no. 23682/13.

84 CJEU, *Coleman*, 2008, par. 50. As Tobler remarks, this case can also be interpreted as being concerned with the scope of the persons protected, rather than the ground as such. Tobler, Indirect discrimination Report 2022, p. 73.

of a protected ground, compared to unequal treatment on all sorts of other, non-sensitive or non-suspect grounds. As a result, it cannot be surprising that – apart from being applied with more rigour – the overall model of discrimination review is very similar to the general model for assessing justification of differential treatment discussed in the previous chapter in the context of a formal equality approach. It starts from the same, basic idea that equal treatment is the default position, whereas any difference in treatment requires the presence of an objective and reasonable justification. Differential treatment can only be allowed if it serves a legitimate aim and if a reasonable and objective relationship exists between this aim and the means employed. Assessing this involves inquiries into the actual goals of a rule, policy or measure, the degree of 'fit' between means and ends, including the element of the comparability of the cases, and consideration of other rights or interests involved. Overall, proportionality plays a central role in this assessment. I also discussed how assessments regarding all these elements of justification review are closely intertwined and inevitably involve normative considerations which may vary depending on the perspectives chosen.

As the overall model for discrimination review, that is for assessing differential treatment on protected grounds, is so similar, I do not repeat things here any further, but refer to what I discussed in Chapter 3, Section 3.2.1. Instead, this section explores how the more stringent level of scrutiny characteristic of discrimination analysis has taken shape in a variety of ways and by different legal constructions. Importantly, levels of scrutiny may differ depending on the protected ground at stake, but they may also be affected by other factors, such as the area of law or social life involved, or the presence of competing fundamental rights and interests.

4.4.2.1 Legal Constructions of More Stringent Scrutiny

The US model developed by the Supreme Court under the constitutional equality standards, which was already mentioned in Chapter 3 (Section 3.2.2) is probably the oldest example of how more stringent scrutiny can be constructed. The Supreme Court applies three distinct levels of scrutiny for classifications regarded as suspect, as semi-suspect or non-suspect: strict scrutiny, intermediate scrutiny and rational basis review.[85] For differences in treatment based on a suspect ground, such as race, and on semi-suspect grounds, such as sex, the scrutiny is heightened compared to other grounds not considered

85 For an overview see e.g. the information and further references on the website of the Legal Information Institute of Cornell University, https://www.law.cornell.edu/wex/equal_protection.

either suspect or semi-suspect. The stronger justification required concerns two elements. First of all, the scrutiny of the legitimacy of the goal of the rule or measure is raised from the requirement it must be 'legitimate' to a demand of serving an 'important' state interest (for semi-suspect classifications) or even 'compelling' state interest (for suspect categories). Secondly, the degree of 'fit' required between the goal and the means chosen differs. For ordinary classifications the means must be in some way 'rationally related' to the goal, but for semi-suspect classifications this standard is raised and must be 'substantially related' to the goal. Where suspect grounds are involved a third level of strictness requires the means to be 'narrowly tailored' to the goal. Overall, the lowest level of scrutiny leaves a high degree of discretion to the Government to classify as it sees fit.

The South African Constitutional Court distinguishes between two basic levels of scrutiny, one for 'mere classification' and one for discrimination. 'Mere classifications' are classifications which are not based on a prohibited ground mentioned in the South African Constitution (or included under it by judicial interpretation). The list of protected grounds include familiar categories such as race, sex, religion, et cetera. The review model applied to 'mere differentiation' strongly resembles the 'rational basis' test of the US Supreme Court.[86] Discrimination based on a prohibited ground, however, is presumed to be unfair and thus a violation of the non-discrimination clause.[87] This renders the possibility of justification highly exceptional.

Another way of constructing more stringent scrutiny can be found in the jurisprudence of the ECtHR. The Court uses the same overall model of review regardless the ground on which a difference of treatment is based, but raises the level of scrutiny for certain classifications by requiring the presence of 'very weighty reasons' for the differential treatment. So far, this more stringent justification requirement has been formulated regarding differences in treatment based on sex, race and ethnic origin, disability, sexual orientation, nationality, birth and religion.[88]

The Inter-American Court of Human Rights provides an example of yet another variety in constructing more stringent judicial review when a difference in treatment is based on a protected ground, by raising the level of scrutiny regarding all three elements of its justification test:

86 For an overview see Albertyn and Goldblatt, Equality, p. 18–26.

87 Section 9(5) of the SA Constitution explicitly provides for this.

88 For an overview see Gerards, The margin of appreciation doctrine, 2018. For race, the test has been formulated even more strictly, see further below in this section.

> the end pursued must not only be legitimate under the Convention, but also imperative. Also, the means chosen must not only be adequate and truly enabling, but also necessary; that is, that it could not be replaced by other less harmful means. In addition, there must be a strict proportionality analysis of the measure by which the benefits of adopting the measure in question must be clearly more advantageous than the restrictions it imposes on the treaty-based principles it affects.[89]

All these examples show how stricter scrutiny may regard several factors or a combination of factors as distinguished in Chapter 3 when discussing justification review of differential treatment under a formal equality approach: the legitimacy of the goal, the proportionality or 'fit' between means and ends including the comparability of the cases, and the balancing with other rights and interests which may be involved.

The important difference a more stringent review makes, can be illustrated with an example. Many countries exclude women from the armed forces. They may do so for several reasons. A country may be motivated by moral concerns, such as traditional notions regarding the proper role of women and men in society, but also by the physical requirements of the job. Nowadays, in most jurisdictions the former reason would probably not pass the requirement that the aim of this difference in treatment between men and women is legitimate. The exclusion would not pass discrimination review if only for that reason. The latter goal, however, is a functional one, and as such in itself a legitimate aim. The next step in the review would then turn to the proportionality or fit between means and ends. It is undeniable that as a matter of generalization men are physically stronger than women. In this respect, men and women differ and are as such not 'like cases'. It is also clear that this difference is based on a very broad generalization: a considerable number of men is physically weaker than a considerable number of women. This raises the question whether using the category 'women' as a proxy for lack of the required physical strength is sufficiently tailored to the end pursued to be justified, or considered to be overbroad and entailing an unacceptable level of overinclusion (men who are unfit physically for an army position) and underinclusion (women who would physically qualify). If only a low degree of fit is required, as

89 IACtHR, 24 November 2017, *Advisory Opinion OC-24/17 on Gender identity, and equality and non-discrimination of same-sex couples*, par. 81. For an overview of the jurisprudence of the IACtHR in this area see R. Celorio, Discrimination and the regional human rights protection systems: the enigma of effectiveness, *University of Pennsylvania Journal of International Law*, 2019, p. 781–837.

explicitly so in the 'rationally related' test of the US Supreme Court, the exclusion of women may be considered to pass muster, but if a stricter degree of fit is demanded, the exclusion will indeed fail to be acceptable.

If the country concerned would narrow the exclusion of women down to positions in the special commando forces, for which recruits have to meet extremely high physical requirements, it is again the degree of required fit or proportionality which would be a prominent part of the review. For a commando position, using the category 'women' as a proxy is certainly more narrowly tailored to the aim of their exclusion and as such more likely to pass discrimination review. Nevertheless, it does not constitute a 'perfect' fit. A perfect fit would only result from abandoning any use of a sex-based criterion and assessing each individual woman (like all applying men) for her physical ability to do the job. So here again, courts may differ in their appreciation whether a narrow fit needs to be 'perfect' or may still allow for some over- and under inclusion. In addition to this focus on the physical fitness requirement, other considerations may well play a role in the ultimate justification inquiry regarding the proportionality between means and ends. Thus, for instance, the authorities may argue that excluding women is more efficient and cost effective than wasting money and resources on recruits who will eventually not get through the training stage to become a commando. On the other side of the balance, the principled and symbolic importance of not excluding women from the most iconically 'male' functions in the army may be put forward as a wider societal interests at stake, even if it were true that no or hardly any woman would ever pass the physical test.[90]

All in all, this example intends to show how degrees of scrutiny regarding the various elements present in discrimination review influence the outcome of such review. At the same time, the example also shows how the many assessments to be made may depend on normative appreciation and particular perspectives taken. In this context, the more contested the subject matter of discrimination review, the more prominent the influence of normative appreciations. Approaches to discrimination on the basis of sexual orientation and gender identity are a case in point. Discrimination review is often up for discussion and, I would add, inevitably so.

4.4.2.2 Differing Degrees of Scrutiny between Protected Grounds

Degrees of scrutiny may not just differ between protected and non-protected grounds, but also between protected grounds as such. This can be very explicit,

90 I leave aside here the question to what extent the extremely high physical requirements may in themselves be questionable or gender biased.

or much more implicit in the actual application of a textually uniform review test for all grounds.

The US Supreme Court is very explicit in applying different levels of scrutiny between various protected grounds. Racial discrimination meets with the highest level of 'strict scrutiny', a level which is higher than applied to discrimination on the basis of sex or sexual orientation. Though this expressly differentiated review seems exceptional, other jurisdictions also show different degrees of rigour, be it often much more implicitly. Not all protected grounds are apparently equally sensitive and to be approached with the same level of suspicion. With the expanding number of protected grounds as discussed in Section 3.2.3, this seems inevitable.

The ECtHR has adopted a similar stance as the US Supreme Court by putting discrimination on grounds of racial or ethnic origin at the top of the pyramid: 'Where a difference in treatment is based on race or ethnicity, the notion of objective and reasonable justification must be interpreted as strictly as possible'.[91] This means that '[n]o difference in treatment which is based exclusively or to a decisive extent on a person's ethnic origin is capable of being objectively justified in a contemporary democratic society built on the principles of pluralism and respect for different cultures'.[92] In a 2022 Advisory Opinion the Court distinguishes more explicitly three different levels of scrutiny – in Strasbourg terminology three levels in the 'margin of appreciation' to be left to states – to evaluate whether a difference in treatment is acceptable in view of Article 14 ECHR.[93] The case concerned a difference in treatment between landowner associations in France set up before or after a particular date, that is on the basis of what is clearly a non-sensitive or non-suspect ground. The Court explains that the margin of appreciation may vary 'according to the nature of the status upon which the differential treatment. ... is based'.[94] The Court grants the national authorities a wide margin of appreciation in this particular case, but adds that this margin is much wider than 'if the distinction in question resulted from a ground regarded by the Court as unacceptable as a matter

91 ECtHR (Grand Chamber), 13 November 2007, *D.H. and others v. the Czech Republic*, par. 196.

92 Idem, par. 176.

93 ECtHR (Grand Chamber), 13 July 2022, *Advisory Opinion on the difference in treatment between landowners' associations "having a recognised existence on the date of the creation of an approved municipal hunters' association" and landowners' associations set up after that date.*

94 Idem, par. 98.

of principle, such as racial or ethnic origin, or as unacceptable in the absence of very weighty reasons, such as gender or sexual orientation'.[95]

In other jurisdictions differing levels of scrutiny for different grounds seem absent as they are not visible in the formulation of the justification test, but they may sometimes be implicitly present anyway. An example of a ground which is nowadays often included in lists of protected grounds, yet would seem to generally meet much less rigorous scrutiny than race or sex in judicial review, is age. As Lucy Vickers concludes on the basis of a comparison of age cases in the EU, US, UK, Canada and South Africa: 'Although most states are fairly strong in rejecting reliance on stereotypes to justify age discriminatory practices, the standard of review of justification in age cases is often lower than for other forms of discrimination.'[96] Sometimes this is quite explicit, as in the US, but it may also be only implicit, as in the EU.[97]

Several reasons may explain this difference. Firstly, age discrimination as such seems to have some distinct characteristics compared to discrimination on grounds such as race or sex. Disadvantages on grounds of age are often not suffered by all members of the age group (for example, poverty in western countries is very unequally divided for pensioners); different age groups may suffer very different forms of discrimination; age changes for each individual, so age is not a fixed category and everyone may experience some forms of age discrimination over time; and last but not least, age is often used as a convenient proxy for all sorts of issues, for example safe driving, right to vote, study support, old age pension, et cetera. As a consequence, the underlying notion that discrimination is about groups suffering from systemic or historical patterns of oppression or disadvantage does not similarly apply to age discrimination.[98] Secondly, as Vickers points out, the particular areas in which age discrimination occurs most frequently are employment, pensions, social security and other socioeconomic policy areas. As a consequence, 'there are

---

95 Idem, par. 100.

96 L. Vickers, *Comparative discrimination law: age as a protected ground*, Brill Research Perspectives in Comparative Discrimination Law, 2018, p. 87. The ECtHR seems to keep the issue whether age discrimination should meet with stringent review open when it remarks in *Carvalho Pinto de Sousa Morais* that 'it has not, to date, suggested that discrimination on grounds of age should be equated with other "suspect" grounds of discrimination', ECtHR, 25 July 2017, *Carvalho Pinto de Sousa Morais v. Portugal*, appl. no. 17484/15, par. 45.

97 Ibid.

98 Idem, p. 21.

strong economic and structural arguments in favour of aged based rules which counterbalance the strong social justice aspects to age equality'.[99]

This second point seems indeed highly important in influencing the degree of scrutiny applied by courts in reviewing discrimination on a protected ground, not just for age, but also where other grounds are concerned. In fact, several other factors than the particular protected ground as such may influence the level of judicial scrutiny in discrimination review.

4.4.2.3 Other Factors Influencing the Degree of Scrutiny

The higher scrutiny required when protected grounds are involved may be counter-balanced by other factors at stake in a particular case.[100] Without claiming to be exhaustive, some recurring factors are the area of law or social life involved and the presence of competing interests.[101]

Area of Law or Social Life Involved

Even if a protected ground is at stake, judicial review of differential treatment may become more lenient if the matter at hand involves a social policy area, budget allocations or some other field of law or social life perceived as being eminently a matter of political decision making. In such cases, division of powers principles often come to play a prominent role. European case law provides many examples of how such considerations may actually lower the level of scrutiny in discrimination review.[102] At the same time, as shown in the case law of the ECtHR, a protected ground such as disability being involved may also reduce the usually wide discretionary power left to the national authorities

99 Idem, p. 88.

100 See for a detailed analysis of how various factors pull in different directions in the case law of the ECtHR Gerards, The margin of appreciation doctrine, 2017.

101 For the ECtHR, the lack or presence of consensus or 'common ground' is also often an important factor, whereas this is expressly denied as being relevant by the IACtHR. For the former see Gerards, The margin of appreciation doctrine, 2017; for the latter see IACtHR, 24 November 2017, *Advisory Opinion OC-24/17 on Gender identity, and equality and non-discrimination of same-sex couples*, par. 83. For a comparative overview see Celorio, Discrimination and the regional human rights protection systems, 2019, p. 781–837.

102 See for example ECtHR, 11 December 2018, *Belli and Arquier-Martinez v. Switserland*, appl. no. 65550/13. In this case the continuation of a disability allowance for persons who moved abroad depended on whether they had paid social security contributions or not. The Court accepted a broad margin of appreciation, even if it affected disabled people, and found no violation of art. 8 jo 14 ECHR.

where social and economic policies are concerned.[103] As a result, different emphasis placed on either of these factors may pull in different directions.

Competing Rights and Interests

A different factor influencing the actual level of scrutiny applied may flow from competing rights or interests. Some well-known examples concern the competing rights of women and sexual minorities on the one hand and the rights of certain religious groups to freedom of religion on the other. Such competing interests may put extra weight into the balance for both sides. Clearly, competing rights and interests may pull in different directions and counterbalance the usually higher levels of scrutiny applied when protected grounds are involved.[104]

Positive Discrimination or Positive Action – Asymmetrical Review

A special type of competing rights which merits separate attention is present where affirmative action measures enter the picture. In such instances, the difference in treatment on a protected ground discriminates against a dominant rather than disadvantaged group. Positive discrimination or positive action usually meets with less stringent justification review than 'ordinary' discrimination negatively affecting a disadvantaged group. Lowering the degree of scrutiny when an otherwise advantaged group is affected demonstrates an asymmetrical approach to non-discrimination standards. I will revisit this issue in Chapter 7.

Non-sensitive Classifications Affecting a Fundamental Right

To complicate matters further, high(er) levels of scrutiny may also come into view when a classification on a non-sensitive ground affects a fundamental right. US jurisprudence is very explicit in this respect by demanding strict scrutiny not just when a suspect classification is at stake, but also when a fundamental right is affected.[105] Though less explicit, the actual practice of the ECtHR is quite similar. A difference in treatment which is not in itself based on a protected ground, may still have to meet a stringent standard of justification

---

103 See for example ECtHR, 22 March 2016, *Guberina v. Croatia*, appl. no. 23682/13, par. 73.The case concerned a tax reduction in relation to a disability.

104 Balancing seems to be the most prominent way of dealing with conflicting rights, see for approaches in a wide variety of jurisdictions the contributions in E. Brems (ed.), *Conflicts between fundamental rights*, Intersentia, Antwerp/Oxford/Portland, 2008.

105 See for an overview of when strict scrutiny is required the information and further references on the website of the Legal Information Institute of Cornell University, https://www.law.cornell.edu/wex/strict_scrutiny.

if a fundamental right is affected.[106] As both jurisdictions show, the lines between judicial review of equality and non-discrimination standards on the one hand, and general fundamental rights review on the other, may be quite fuzzy.

4.4.3 *The EU Model of Discrimination Review*

As mentioned in the introduction to this chapter, the EU model of review for justifying a difference in treatment on a protected ground has its own characteristics. This particular model may well be explained by the specific way in which EU non-discrimination law developed. It started with focused and often detailed legislation regarding sex discrimination, particularly in the area of employment and social security, before developing non-discrimination standards for several other grounds and including general equality and non-discrimination standards in the Charter of Fundamental Rights.[107]

This start may account for the important distinction made in the EU directives on equal treatment between direct and indirect discrimination and the particular justification review attached to each of these forms of discrimination. Differences in treatment on the basis of sex as such were considered to be unjustified as a matter of principle, except for some quite foreseeable and particular situations. As a result, the initial sex equality directives adopted a 'closed' model of justification review for direct discrimination.[108] They prohibit discrimination directly based on sex and do not allow for any justification review, unless the directive expressly allows for an exception. Thus, in the 1976 Directive regarding sex equality in employment, exceptions are limited to differences in treatment regarding the protection of women related to pregnancy and maternity; access to certain occupations for which sex may be considered a determining factor; and regarding certain positive action measures to promote equal opportunities for women.[109]

---

106 The margin of appreciation depends also on 'the nature and importance of the affected right or interest, in relation to the seriousness of the interference', Gerards, The margin of appreciation doctrine, 2017, p. 6.

107 I leave aside here the particular development of discrimination on the basis of nationality, which has played a crucial role in Community law from the start, but is less relevant for the subject matter of this section.

108 Council Directive 76/207/EEC of 9 February 1976 on the implementation of the principle of equal treatment for men and women as regards access to employment, vocational training and promotion, and working conditions; Council Directive 79/7/EEC of 19 December 1978 on the progressive implementation of the principle of equal treatment for men and women in matters of social security.

109 Directive 76/207/EEC, Article 2(2), 2(3) and 2(4). In 2006 this directive was replaced by and integrated into the so called Recast Directive, Directive 2006/54/EC of the European

Where indirect discrimination may be at stake the possibilities for justification are not limited to a number of express exceptions, but are open to whatever objective and reasonable justification may be present: indirect discrimination occurs 'where an apparently neutral provision, criterion or practice would put persons of one sex at a particular disadvantage compared with persons of the other sex, unless that provision, criterion or practice is objectively justified by a legitimate aim, and the means of achieving that aim are appropriate and necessary'.[110] This possibility of 'open' justification makes sense, as the number and variety of apparently neutral provisions or measures which can have a disparate effect on women is potentially large and hardly foreseeable.[111]

As will be discussed further in Chapter 5, the inquiry under EU indirect discrimination review whether an objective and reasonable justification exists is quite similar to the justification review described above in Section 4.4 under general non-discrimination standards prevalent in international human rights treaties and national constitutions. For now, it suffices to point out the important difference between the limited possibility for justification review of direct discrimination under important parts of EU law compared to discrimination review under the 'open' justification model usually applicable to discrimination standards in human rights treaties and national constitutions discussed in Section 4.4. To give an example: under the closed justification model of EU law, the dismissal of a pregnant employee is a form of direct discrimination on the basis of sex. As the applicable directive does not allow for an exception to this difference in treatment, it violates the prohibition of discrimination on the basis of sex, whatever the reasons put forward by the employer.[112] If this difference in treatment were to be reviewed under Article 14 ECHR or

Parliament and of the Council of 5 July 2006 on the implementation of the principle of equal opportunities and equal treatment of men and women in matters of employment and occupation (Recast). The model of justification review is similarly 'closed' where direct discrimination is concerned.

110 Directive 2006/54/EC, Article 2(1)(b).

111 This may also explain why the EU sex equality directive regarding the broad area of goods and services has an open model of justification review for both direct and indirect discrimination; Council Directive 2004/113/EC of 13 December 2004 implementing the principle of equal treatment between men and women in the access to and supply of goods and services.

112 The case *Webb* is a pertinent example. It concerned a woman who was hired to replace a pregnant worker. After a few weeks she found out she was pregnant herself and was subsequently dismissed by the employer. As the Directive does not allow for any exceptions to the protection against dismissal of pregnant workers, these circumstances could not provide a justification. CJEU, 14 July 1994, *Webb*, C-32/93.

Article 26 ICCPR, the relevant inquiry would be if an objective and reasonable justification exists for this differential treatment. Though this may lead to the same outcome, this is not necessarily so as it depends on the appreciation of the supervising judicial body.

The 'closed justification model' for direct discrimination review and 'open' justification review for indirect discrimination was also adopted in subsequent EU directives covering grounds other than sex, but not throughout. It was fully adopted in Directive 2000/43 regarding discrimination on the basis of race or ethnic origin. For direct discrimination on this ground, the Directive only allows for two exceptions: when race or ethnic origin constitutes a genuine and determining occupational requirement (for instance, hiring an actor to play the role of John F. Kennedy) or for purposes of positive action.[113] Here again, the difference with an open justification model as is applied under the ECHR or ICCPR is significant: it is not up to the judicial supervisory body to assess any other forms of different treatment directly based on race or ethnic origin. The legislator has decided what is acceptable or not. For alleged indirect discrimination, the justification review is fully open and follows the model for indirect sex discrimination mentioned above.

The Directive covering discrimination on the basis of religion or belief, disability, age or sexual orientation in employment allows for a much more open justification review, not just regarding indirect discrimination, but also regarding direct discrimination.[114] For age discrimination this is explicitly formulated in Article 6, which specifies that differences of treatment directly based on age are allowed if they are objectively and reasonably justified. Given the many instances in which age figures as a convenient and pragmatic classification, providing for wider possibilities of justifying the use made of this criterion makes sense.[115]

113 Directive 2000/43, Article 4 and Article 5.

114 Council Directive 2000/78/EC of 27 November 2000 establishing a general framework for equal treatment in employment and occupation (Framework directive).

115 Council Directive 2004/113/EC of 13 December 2004 implementing the principle of equal treatment between men and women in the access to and supply of goods and services does not follow the closed model either. In the context of access to and supply of goods and services too many legitimate exceptions to a prohibition of direct discrimination on the basis of sex are possible. Article 5 provides for a general justification possibility even in cases of direct discrimination on the basis of sex. Examples mentioned in the Preamble that would fall under this exception include e.g. the establishment of single-sex shelters for victims of sex-related violence or the organisation of single-sex sporting activities.

Although this open model of direct discrimination review does not apply to the other grounds covered in this Directive, Article 2(5) contains a general provision applicable to all grounds which may perform a similar role. It provides that the Directive 'shall be without prejudice to measures laid down by national law which, in a democratic society, are necessary for public security, for the maintenance of public order and the prevention of criminal offences, for the protection of health and for the protection of the rights and freedoms of others'. This provision is unique to this Directive; it is not part of the directives regarding sex or race and ethnic origin. Article 2(5) provides in fact for a general limitation clause, which seems clearly inspired by the formulation of the provisions allowing for fundamental rights limitations in the ECHR. Though Article 2(5) has not figured prominently yet in the case law of the CJEU, it may potentially blur the distinction between review of direct and indirect discrimination under the Framework Directive.

4.5 Difficulties and Dilemmas of Ground-Depending Differentiated Review

To start with, discrimination review runs into similar difficulties as already discussed in the previous chapter in the context of how unequal treatment is to be justified under a formal equality approach, with its focus on the *adagium* that like cases must be treated alike (Section 3.2.1). In both instances, justification review is far from a mathematical exercise. Different perspectives and normative appreciation may figure in many ways, be it regarding the identification and legitimacy of the goal(s) pursued, the required fit between means and ends and the related questions concerning the comparability of the cases involved, or the balancing with other rights and interests.

The way in which discrimination review differentiates levels of scrutiny depending on the ground involved adds an additional layer of complexity, particularly in view of the proliferation of grounds identified as protected grounds. In the first place, difficulties arise from the fact that no unambiguous answer seems possible to the question which grounds deserve higher protection and which do not – as seems evident from the broad range of grounds identified as protected grounds in different jurisdictions. Secondly, a higher protection level for protected grounds leads to pressure to expand protected grounds and in many jurisdictions this is indeed happening. At the same time, the more grounds are identified as a protected ground, the greater the need will be for differentiating between grounds in discrimination review. As Fredman remarks, an extension of grounds is usually counterbalanced by differing levels of scrutiny, as apparently not all protected grounds are equally invidious.[116] All this leads to a third way in which complexity of discrimination review may be enhanced. It establishes an explicit or implicit hierarchy between protected grounds. This in turn may result in competition between grounds in terms of being regarded as deserving the highest level of scrutiny, for example by emphasizing the vulnerabilities or relative disadvantage of one group compared to another. The latter is not just problematic for the risk of pitting one protected group against another, but also for the risk of ignoring the differences which may exist within protected groups; not all members of a protected group are as vulnerable or marginalized. Intersectional approaches try to find a way out of this type of dilemma, but create their own difficulties as I will explore further in Chapter 8.

Of course, competition between protected grounds against the backdrop of an ever-expanding number of grounds identified as deserving the protection of non-discrimination standards could also have a different effect. It could also lead to a trivialisation of what these standards seek to address and detract from the idea that discrimination is a particularly serious matter requiring stringent inquiry.

4.6 Concluding Remarks

This Chapter analyzed the general features of non-discrimination as a legal standard as deriving from the understanding that it requires more stringent scrutiny to assess whether a difference in treatment on a protected grounds can be justified. When protected grounds are involved, differential treatment should meet with suspicion.

No single, foundational rationale exists for legally identifying protected grounds, but a 'classic' list has been formulated in the UDHR and the two foundational global human rights covenants, the ICCPR and the ICESCR. These include race, colour, sex, language, religion, political or other opinion, national or social origin, property and birth. Since then, the number of protected grounds has expanded considerably, particularly since the turn of the century. Under non-discrimination standards containing an open, non-exhaustive list of grounds, judicial bodies may play a leading role in bringing additional grounds under the protection of non-discrimination law and many have indeed done so. As shown, under 'closed' models of listed grounds, some important

116 Fredman, Discrimination law, 2022, p. 197–198.

expansions by judicial intervention are also possible by extensive interpretation of the scope of an already protected ground. In fact, having a closed list of protected grounds may increase pressure to include other grounds under already covered grounds. Overall, expansion of protected grounds has occurred in many jurisdictions and has resulted in the inclusion of, among others, sexual orientation, gender identity, disability and age.

The ways in which higher scrutiny is constructed varies between jurisdictions, but shows quite some parallels. It may concern one or more elements of discrimination review, be it the identification and legitimacy of the goal(s) pursued, the required fit between means and ends and the related questions concerning the comparability of cases involved, or the balancing with other rights and interests. If anything, the above has highlighted the increased complexity of discrimination review flowing from the expansion of and increasing differentiation between protected grounds. Generally speaking, in most jurisdictions the strictest scrutiny is usually reserved for discrimination on the basis of race and sex, but degrees of scrutiny in discrimination review are also informed by other factors than a protected ground being involved, such as the area of law or social life at stake and/or the presence of competing rights and interests.

All in all, discrimination review is complicated, highly contextual and rife with normative appreciation. It is not a value-free, mathematical exercise and as such it is not surprising that the outcome of review by judicial bodies can be perceived as unpredictable or up for discussion. In my understanding, this is in a way inevitable.

The above exploration of the general features of discrimination as a legal concept started from the understanding of discrimination as closely linked with a formal equality approach and being focused on unequal treatment on the basis of a protected ground. This understanding of discrimination started to change when the limitations of a formal equality approach became increasingly apparent, and legal willingness grew in several jurisdictions to expand the notion of discrimination to include modalities linked to a more substantive equality approach, such as the concepts of indirect discrimination, (reasonable) accommodation and positive discrimination or positive action, to be discussed in the next three chapters.

CHAPTER 5

Indirect Discrimination

5.1 Introduction

Over the years, important modalities of discrimination developed as distinct legal concepts. Two of these are closely related and are the subject of this and the next chapter: indirect discrimination and lack of (reasonable) accommodation.[1] Both concepts take the disparate impact of a certain treatment on a protected group as a starting point for investigating whether this negative outcome violates equality and non-discrimination standards or not, but their more exact relationship is not as clear. In some legal settings a lack of (reasonable) accommodation is approached as being included under the notion of indirect discrimination, in others it is perceived as a form of discrimination *sui generis*. This second approach will be explored in Chapter 6. So far, no common approach has developed across jurisdictions.

This chapter will first address the development and general features of the concept of indirect discrimination (Section 5.2).[2] Over the past decades it developed simultaneously across a wide variety of jurisdictions as a concept with distinct, general features, including very similar models for judicial review. Judicial review has in fact been a major driving force behind its development.

By problematizing the unequal effects of seemingly neutral rules, policies or practices as equality issues, the development of the concept of indirect discrimination represents an important step away from a merely formal towards a more substantive approach of equality. How important and how far away, however, is up for a lot of discussion. In academic literature assessments of the potential of the concept in addressing more structural and systemic levels of discrimination have been mixed, ranging from regarding its usefulness in achieving real structural change as very limited to perceiving it as a powerful instrument for addressing institutionalised forms of discrimination.[3] As for my own position, from its initial development in the case law of the CJEU in

1 For an explanation of how I use these and other core terms in this study see Chapter 1.

2 This chapter includes several parts of one of my earlier publications on indirect discrimination: T. Loenen, Indirect discrimination as a vehicle for change, *Australian Journal of Human Rights* 2000, p. 77–96, http://classic.austlii.edu.au/au/journals/AUJlHRights/2000/21.html.

3 For the first position see e.g. S. Fredman, *Discrimination Law*, Oxford 2011 (2nd ed), p. 182. Fredman moved to a less sceptical assessment in the 3rd edition of this book published in 2022, p. 280–306. For a brief discussion of the latter position see e.g. M. Gijzen, *Selected*

© TITIA LOENEN, 2025 | DOI:10.1163/9789004538368_006

the eighties of the last century, I have regarded the concept of indirect discrimination as a potentially revolutionary concept, while at the same time acknowledging that the realisation of this potential depends to a large extent on how indirect discrimination review is actually shaped and applied in legal practice.[4] In addition, the concept has some inherent limits in being capable of fully addressing the dominant standards prevalent in law and society, that is in addressing systemic discrimination. I still hold on to this understanding, though over the years I have become ever more convinced that realising the potential of the concept of indirect discrimination is not primarily a matter of courts willing to apply the concept, but of legislative and administrative powers taking it on board proactively when designing and implementing legislation and policies.

As by now a considerable body of case law on indirect discrimination has developed in a variety of jurisdictions, all this can be very well illustrated by examples from actual legal practice. Using these examples, Section 5.3 will discuss the far-reaching potential of the concept of indirect discrimination in addressing structural disadvantage and systemic discrimination, whereas Section 5.4 will focus on how the realization of this potential depends to a large extent on the way in which indirect discrimination review is shaped and applied in more detail in legal practice. Application is often very complex and meets with its own difficulties and dilemmas. The way in which these are handled in a jurisdiction is of major importance for its actual reach. In addition, judicial practice illustrates some inherent limitations of the concept in addressing systemic discrimination through discrimination law, which will be discussed in Section 5.5.

5.2 Development and General Features of Indirect Discrimination

5.2.1 *Development and General Acceptance of the Concept over Time*

Judicial interpretation has been the driving force behind the development of the concept of indirect discrimination.

Issues in Equal Treatment Law: A multi-layered comparison of European, English and Dutch law, Antwerp/Oxford, Intersentia, 2006, p. 64–67.

4 T. Loenen, Rethinking sex equality as a human right, *Netherlands Quarterly of Human Rights*, 1994, p. 253–270; T. Loenen, Indirect discrimination: oscillating between containment and revolution, in: P. Rodrigues and T. Loenen (eds), *Non-discrimination law: comparative perspectives*, The Hague/London/Boston, Kluwer Law International, 1999, p. 195–211; Loenen, Indirect discrimination as a vehicle for change, 2000.

The United States can very probably claim to be the 'founding fathers' of the concept of indirect discrimination, or in the American terminology: disparate or adverse impact. The roots of disparate impact analysis can be traced to the famous *Griggs* case.[5] In this case the US Supreme Court had to decide whether having a high school diploma as a condition for promotion constituted discrimination on the basis of race, as black employees would have much greater difficulty in meeting such a requirement than white workers. The applicable federal legislation, Title VII of the Civil Rights Act, prohibits discrimination on the basis of race, colour, religion, sex and national origin in employment. It does not, however, explicitly cover both direct and indirect discrimination. The Supreme Court ruled that an employer's facially neutral employment practice, which is not based on race as such, but which can be shown to have a disparate impact on black employees, establishes a *prima facie* case of race discrimination. To save the practice the employer will have to show the practice is job related or otherwise constitutes a 'business necessity'. In *Griggs* the Supreme Court concluded that the high school completion requirement did not bear a demonstrable relationship to successful job performance and thus did not serve a business necessity. This approach was later extended to sex discrimination cases.[6]

In Europe, a very similar concept was developed in the case law of the CJEU in the area of sex discrimination. It did not come out of the blue.[7] To start with, the CJEU was already familiar with the notion of indirect discrimination on the basis of nationality. Given the importance of eradicating discrimination on this ground in view of the primary goals of the European Community (free flow of workers, goods and services) it is not surprising that the CJEU was keen to address all kinds of more subtle and hidden forms of discrimination on the basis of nationality, and not just outright exclusions. Thus already in 1973 it held in the case *Sotgiu* that 'the rules regarding equal treatment forbid not only overt discrimination by reason of nationality, but also covert forms of discrimination which, by application of other criteria of differentiation, lead in fact to the same result'.[8] The second influence on the development of the concept of indirect discrimination in the context of sex discrimination cases seems to have been influenced by developments in the United States. In the first

5 *Griggs v. Duke Power Co*, 401 US 424 (1971).

6 US Supreme Court, *Dothard v. Rawlinson*, 433 US 321 (1977).

7 See for a detailed historical analysis of the emergence and development of the concept of indirect discrimination in the EU legal framework C. Tobler, *Indirect discrimination. A case study into the development of the legal concept of indirect discrimination under EC law*, Antwerpen/Oxford, Intersentia, 2005.

8 CJEU, 12 February 1974, *Sotgiu*, C-152/73.

indirect sex discrimination case to reach the CJEU in 1980, Advocate General Warner drew explicitly on *Griggs* to convince the Court that paying part-time workers less than full-time workers indeed amounts to indirect discrimination on the basis of sex, in contravention of the principle of equal pay enshrined in Community Law.[9] In the subsequent landmark case *Bilka*, the CJEU embraced this concept more fully and articulated the test to be applied in indirect discrimination cases.[10] At stake was the exclusion of part-time workers from an occupational pension scheme. Though this practice was in itself sex neutral, in its practical effects it excluded much more women than men, given the overrepresentation of women in part-time work. The European Court of Justice ruled that this violated the prohibition of sex discrimination, unless the employer could come up with a convincing justification. As the Court formulated it, the right to equal pay

> is infringed by a department store company which excludes part-time employees from its occupational pension scheme, where that exclusion affects a far greater number of women than men, unless the undertaking shows that the exclusion is based on objectively justified factors unrelated to any discrimination on grounds of sex.[11]

The Court subsequently elaborated what this 'objective justification' requirement entails. The measure or practice has to meet 'a real need of the enterprise' and to be 'appropriate and necessary' to that end.[12] In later cases, where indirect discrimination by the state was at stake, the 'real need of the enterprise' requirement was replaced by the more general notion of 'legitimate aim'.[13] In the directives covering discrimination on additional grounds to sex, adopted after the turn of the century, largely similar definitions have been included which have become leading in the EU context. Indirect discrimination is taken to occur where an apparently neutral provision, criterion or practice would put persons having a particular sex, racial or ethnic origin, religion or belief,

9 CJEU, 31 March 1981, *Jenkins*, C-97/80. Though in the meantime the 1976 Directive on equal treatment had come to include a prohibition of both direct and indirect discrimination, indirect discrimination was not defined. The latter came about only much later.

10 CJEU, 13 May 1986, *Bilka*, C-170/84.

11 Idem, par. 31.

12 Idem, par. 34.

13 Initially, many of these cases concerned indirect discrimination on the basis of sex in state regulated social security schemes. For an overview see e.g. J. Steiner, The principle of equal treatment for men and women in social security, in: T. Hervey and D. O'Keefe (eds), *Sex equality law in the European Union*, Chichester, Wiley, 1996, p. 111–136.

disability, age or sexual orientation 'at a particular disadvantage' compared with other persons 'unless that provision, criterion or practice is objectively justified by a legitimate aim and the means of achieving that aim are appropriate and necessary'.[14]

Conceptually speaking, the likeness between the European and American concepts of indirect discrimination and disparate impact is striking. Differences stem from the different context in which the concepts are operating, but do not affect their basic similarity. The American notion of disparate impact under Title VII of the Civil Rights Act is clearly tailored to the employment context, whereas the European notion of indirect discrimination is formulated in a more general way and can thus rather easily be applied in a broader area and to a broader range of grounds of discrimination, but for both the core idea is the same: an apparently neutral distinction, practice or policy, which does not differentiate expressly on a protected ground of discrimination, yet has a discriminatory or disparate impact on a group protected against such discrimination, may also violate the prohibition of discrimination unless an objective justification can be shown to exist.

The notion of indirect discrimination has subsequently been taken on board in a wide range of jurisdictions beyond the United States and the EU. Though taking quite some time to follow the lead of the CJEU in this respect,[15] the ECtHR fully embraced the concept of indirect discrimination in 2007 in the Grand Chamber judgment *D.H. and others v. The Czech Republic* regarding a case of indirect discrimination of Roma children in the educational system. In doing so, the Court expressly referred to EU law and the case law of the CJEU.[16]

The Strasbourg Court's American counterpart had less opportunities to address the issue of indirect discrimination, but had no qualms in using the concept in its judgment on a ban on *in vitro* fertilisation in Costa Rica. The Court considered that although infertility can affect both men and women 'it is especially related to a woman's body. (…) Even if the ban on IVF is not expressly addressed at women, and thus appears neutral, it has a disproportionately

14 Directive 2000/43/EC Article 2(2)(b); Directive 2000/78/EC Article 2(2)(b); Directive 2006/54/EC Article 2(1)(b).

15 Cf. J. Gerards, Non-discrimination, the European Court of Justice and the European Court of Human Rights: who takes the lead? In T. Giegerich (ed), *The European Union as the protector of equality*, 2020, p. 135–163, p. 141.

16 ECtHR (Grand Chamber), 13 November 2007, *D.H. and others v. the Czech Republic*, appl. no. 57325/00: '… a general policy or measure that has disproportionately prejudicial effects on a particular group may be considered discriminatory notwithstanding that it is not specifically aimed at that group', par. 175.

negative impact on women'.[17] The youngest regional human rights court, the African Court of Human and Peoples' Rights, adopted the concept of indirect discrimination in 2020.[18] In several more recent regional human rights treaties covering discrimination it has been expressly included.[19]

Turning to the national level, the Canadian Supreme Court used the notion of adverse impact early on.[20] It links it expressly to its substantive equality approach:

> Adverse impact discrimination occurs when a seemingly neutral law has a disproportionate impact on members of groups protected on the basis of an enumerated or analogous ground. There is no doubt that adverse impact discrimination violates the norm of substantive equality which underpins the Court's equality jurisprudence.[21]

More recently, the Indian Supreme Court followed suit. In the case *Nitisha*, it referred with approval to the approach taken by the Canadian Supreme Court, as well as to case law from several other jurisdictions, including the US, the UK and South Africa.[22] For the South African Constitutional Court Article 9(3) of the Constitution provides in itself a legal basis for application of the concept of indirect discrimination, as it expressly prohibits both direct and indirect discrimination.[23]

To finish this *tour d'horizon* of how the concept of indirect discrimination has become widely accepted as part of legal equality and non-discrimination

---

17 IACtHR, 28 November 2012, *Artavia Murillo e.a. ('In vitro fertilization'), v. Costa Rica* (Preliminary objections, merits, reparations and costs), par. 299 .

18 ACtHPR 15 July 2020, *Kambole v. United Republic of Tanzania*, appl. no. 018/2018. The Court refers to the ICERD and CEDAW to corroborate its interpretation that the non-discrimination provision in Art. 2 of the African Charter includes both direct and indirect discrimination, par. 69–70.

19 See Inter-American Convention against all forms of discrimination and intolerance (2013), Article 2 and the Inter-American Convention against racism, racial discrimination and related forms of intolerance (2013), Article 2.

20 See Supreme Court of Canada, *Eldridge v. British Columbia* [1997] 3 SCR 624, par. 77.

21 Supreme Court of Canada, *Fraser v. Canada* [2020] SCR 113, quote from summary at the beginning of the judgment. The Court uses the terminology of adverse impact, disproportional impact and indirect discrimination interchangeably.

22 Supreme Court of India, 25 March 2021, *Lt Col Nitisha v. Union of India*. The case concerned a selection process for officers in the Indian army applying for permanent service. For a fuller discussion see V. Khanna, Indirect discrimination and substantive equality in *Nitisha*: easier said than done under Indian constitutional jurisprudence, *International Journal of Discrimination and the Law*, 2022, p. 74–86.

23 The first judgment by the Constitutional Court in which indirect discrimination figured prominently was *City Council of Pretoria v. Walker* [1998] ZACC 1.

standards, it is worth mentioning that it has also become part and parcel of the conceptualization of discrimination at the global level as is reflected in the work of the UN human rights treaty bodies. Already in 2005 Vandenhole concludes that though the concept of indirect discrimination is not expressly mentioned in the text of the ICCPR, ICESCR, ICERD, CEDAW and CRC, all supervisory bodies to these conventions have used the concept.[24] As the Canadian Supreme Court remarked in its 2019 landmark case *Fraser* on indirect discrimination, in which it referred extensively to academic research regarding this concept, awareness of adverse impact discrimination is indeed a 'central trend' in the development of discrimination law.[25]

This broad acceptance of the notion of indirect discrimination is arguably one of the most important developments in the conceptualization of equality and non-discrimination as a legal standard in the past decades. With its focus on the outcome of a treatment and problematizing unequal impact or effects as an equality issue, it signifies a major step away from a merely formal, towards a more substantive equality approach.

5.2.2 *General Characteristics of Indirect Discrimination Analysis*

As with the review of differences in treatment which are expressly based on a protected ground (see Chapter 4.4), notwithstanding all sorts of varieties, indirect discrimination analysis has a common structure across jurisdictions. It is triggered by the adverse or disparate impact of an apparently neutral rule, measure or practice on a group protected by non-discrimination law. Disparate impact, however, is not sufficient to conclude it constitutes a form of (unacceptable) discrimination. Whether this is the case depends on the question whether a convincing justification can be put forward. Differently put, a disparate or detrimental effect on a protected group results in a *prima facie* claim of indirect discrimination, which can be rebutted by an objective justification. Through this construction, indirect discrimination is related to a prohibited discrimination ground in substance, rather than in form, as is the case with direct discrimination.[26] Generally speaking, then, indirect discrimination review consists of two main elements: establishing disparate impact and, if this is indeed shown to be present, assessing whether a justification exists.

Establishing disparate impact requires a contextual analysis as it has to map empirical or social realities to identify how these are related to the groups

---

24 W. Vandenhole, *Non-discrimination and equality in the view of the UN human rights treaty bodies*, Antwerpen/Oxford, Intersentia 2005, p. 36.

25 Supreme Court of Canada, *Fraser v. Canada* [2020] SCR 113, par. 31.

26 Cf. C. Tobler, *Indirect discrimination under Directives 2000/43 and 2000/78*, Report European Network of legal experts in gender equality and non-discrimination, 2022, p. 37.

protected by non-discrimination law. Treatment resulting in disparate effects in one context or situation may not have the same consequences in another. Thus, for instance, whereas in the current social realities in Europe the exclusion of part-time workers from an occupational pension scheme will have a disparate impact on women given the gendered division of labour market participation, this need not be the case in the future, if at some point this division will have become balanced. Of course, if in that future time part-time workers are still excluded from certain benefits reserved to full-time employees this may be unfair, but it would have ceased to be an issue of indirect discrimination on the basis of sex.

In addition to linking the disadvantage suffered to a protected group, disparate impact analysis will have to answer the question what degree of disadvantage is sufficient to trigger application of the concept of indirect discrimination. In both respects, methods considered appropriate or valid for establishing disparate impact may vary between jurisdictions. A method which is commonly used regards statistical information. Other methods used for establishing disparate impact include more qualitative approaches. The choice of methods allowed is of great significance in terms of how difficult or easy it is to make a claim of disparate impact in a legal procedure and thus on the actual reach of the concept of indirect discrimination in a particular jurisdiction. I will return to this in Section 5.4. For now, it is important to note that once the claimant has shown a *prima facie* case of disparate impact to exist, the burden of proof usually turns to the respondent to provide a justification for using a certain criterion or taking a particular measure, notwithstanding its disparate effects.

Except for EU law, with its equality directives operating on the basis of a rather sharp distinction between direct and indirect discrimination (see Chapter 4.4.3), the structure or model of justification review of indirect discrimination is usually very much similar to justification review conducted if direct discrimination is at stake, that is if a distinction in a rule, measure or policy is expressly based on a protected ground (see for an elaboration of this review Chapter 4.4.2).

The Canadian Supreme Court and the South African Constitutional Court in fact have explicitly expressed that the presence of direct and indirect discrimination is to be assessed in the same way. The Canadian Court held in the *Eldridge* case that 'the same two-step approach to s. 15(1) applies regardless of whether the discrimination alleged is direct or indirect'.[27] For the South African Constitutional Court following the same approach means that a finding of

27 Supreme Court of Canada, *Fraser v. Canada* [2020] 3 SCR 113, par. 49.

both direct and indirect discrimination results in a (rebuttable) presumption of such discrimination being 'unfair' and thus unjustified.[28]

Similarly, the ECtHR applies the same model of justification review regardless the type of discrimination involved. A rule or measure with a discriminatory effect on a protected group violates Article 14 ECHR, unless it can be objectively and reasonably justified, that is unless it serves a legitimate aim and the means employed are proportional. In this setting it applies more stringent scrutiny if suspect grounds are involved.[29] As may be apparent from the *Bilka* test mentioned above, review of indirect discrimination under the EU equality directives is also very similar to this type of justification test, as opposed to the review of the CJEU of direct discrimination.

Notwithstanding this commonly shared structure of justification review in indirect discrimination analysis, the way in which it is applied in actual legal practice, particularly in terms of the strictness of the review, may vary significantly between jurisdictions and lead to very different outcomes. Indeed, the degree of scrutiny seems often not as strict as scrutiny of discrimination which is expressly based on a protected ground. This difference may well flow from indirect discrimination having a weaker link with the protected ground than direct discrimination: the group affected is heterogenous.[30] As with establishing disparate impact, I will return to this topic in Section 5.4.

5.3 Potential Reach of the Concept of Indirect Discrimination – Addressing Structural and Systemic Discrimination

In its more modest legal role, the concept of indirect discrimination is helpful in detecting hidden forms of discrimination based on seemingly neutral criteria, which may have been used as a cover to circumvent a prohibition of unequal treatment expressly based on a protected ground. The case *Jenkins*

28 *City Council of Pretoria v. Walker*, [1998] ZACC 1, par. 35–36.

29 Thus in in the *D.H.* case, the Court held that if 'the difference in treatment is based on race, colour or ethnic origin, the notion of objective and reasonable justification must be interpreted as strictly as possible', ECtHR (Grand Chamber), 13 November 2007, *D.H. and others v. the Czech Republic*, appl. no. 57325/00, par. 196.

30 Cf. Tobler, Indirect discrimination, Report, 2022, p. 10; Collins and Khaitan also note that the 'wrong' of indirect and direct discrimination may not run fully parallel, see H. Collins and T. Khaitan, Indirect discrimination law: controversies and critical questions, in: H. Collins and T. Khaitan (eds), *Foundations of indirect discrimination law*, Bloomsbury 2018, p. 1–30, p. 7–9.

already mentioned above is a good example.[31] The employer did not provide equal pay for equal work to his male and female employees, but when he was required to do so by equal pay legislation he reverted to paying his part-time workers less than his full-time workers. The CJEU made short shrift with this cover up. As discussed in Chapter 4 (Section 4.4.1), in some jurisdictions such intentional indirect discrimination may actually be identified as a form of 'direct' discrimination for this very reason and be subjected to the same strict review.

A much more far-reaching role of the notion of indirect discrimination, which is also much more debated, regards the ways in which it is capable of unveiling and addressing all sorts of discrimination of a structural and systemic nature, which – often unconsciously – may lie hidden behind many seemingly neutral standards organizing law and society. In the following, my focus is on the latter.

5.3.1 *Identifying and Addressing Structural Disadvantage and Systemic Discrimination*

To start with, the role of the concept of indirect discrimination in unveiling and addressing structural disadvantage and systemic discrimination has not sufficiently crystallized yet in legal practice to allow for a fully developed conceptual analysis of this role. In many respects, it is still a puzzling concept in discrimination law.[32] Nevertheless, with an increasing amount of available case law from a wide variety of jurisdictions it is possible to paint a broad picture of some of the emerging features of its instrumentality in this respect.

In several jurisdictions judicial bodies have taken a very robust stance in identifying the notion of indirect discrimination as an expression of substantive instead of merely formal equality and as a particularly useful instrument to address structural disadvantage and root causes of discrimination. The Canadian and Indian Supreme Courts are very explicit in this respect and have characterized the concept of indirect discrimination in express terms as a way to address systemic discrimination. In its judgment in *Fraser*, the Canadian Supreme Court emphasizes how application of the concept of adverse impact discrimination can also address systemic and institutional discrimination.[33]

31 CJEU, 31 March 1981, *Jenkins*, C-97/80.

32 Cf. Collins and Khaitan, Indirect discrimination law: controversies and critical questions, 2018.

33 Supreme Court of Canada, *Fraser v. Canada* [2020] 3 SCR 113, par. 36. The Court also uses 'adverse impact discrimination' as interchangeably with 'systemic discrimination', see par. 29.

The extensive indirect discrimination analysis of the Indian Supreme Court in the case *Nitisha* is particularly interesting in this respect for the way in which it grounds its full embracement of the notion of indirect discrimination in the doctrinal development of the concept elsewhere. Significantly to start with, the Supreme Court's considerations regarding the 'theoretical foundations of indirect discrimination' belong to a part of the judgment carrying the heading 'systemic discrimination'.[34] The Court squarely regards adoption of the notion of indirect discrimination as a choice for substantive equality instead of formal equality.[35] After providing an overview of how the concept has been applied in the US, the UK, South Africa and Canada in a series of landmark cases, including the cases *Griggs* and *Fraser* (discussed in Section 5.2) and *Mahlangu* (to be discussed below), it links these developments to the evolving analytical framework of indirect discrimination in India, which it characterizes as 'still at a nascent stage'.[36] According to the Court, the focus of discrimination review 'has switched from looking at the intentions or motive of the discriminator to examining whether a rule, formally or substantively, "contributes to the subordination of a disadvantaged group of individuals"'.[37] The Court ends this part of the judgment by considering that 'an analysis of discrimination, with a view towards its systemic manifestations (direct and indirect), would be best suited for achieving our constitutional vision of equality and non-discrimination'.[38]

In applying this far-reaching notion of the functional reach of indirect discrimination to the case at hand, the Court acknowledges how the disparate effect on women of the facially neutral selection criteria used for granting permanent service in the Indian army reflect that the 'structures of our society have been created by males and for males' and flow from 'the insidious patriarchal system'.[39] In this context, an analysis in terms of indirect discrimination is necessary as '[a] facially equal application of laws to unequal parties is a farce, when the law is structured to cater to a male standpoint'.[40] To remedy the indirect discrimination, the selection criteria have to be adjusted.

In the European context, the CJEU and ECtHR tend to be much less clear in what they perceive to be the overall goal or function of the concept of indirect discrimination (and of equality and non-discrimination standards more generally) in terms of how this may relate to systemic discrimination, though

34 Supreme Court of India, 25 March 2021, *Lt Col Nitisha v. Union of India*, Part F.
35 Nitisha, par. 42–45.
36 Nitisha, par. 46.
37 Nitisha, par. 46.
38 Nitisha, par. 77.
39 Nitisha, par. 100.
40 Nitisha, par. 100.

particularly the ECtHR seems to share a heightened sensitivity to the role of these standards in combatting more structural forms of disadvantage faced by groups such as Roma.[41]

However this may be, the links between the concept of indirect discrimination and the type of robust substantive equality approach as expressed by the Indian Supreme Court can be corroborated by examples from case law in a variety of jurisdictions. The way the concept has been applied in legal practice shows it has indeed a far-reaching potential in addressing structural inequalities and disadvantage faced by protected groups.

In the following I will illustrate this by providing a number of telling examples regarding indirect discrimination on the basis of sex, race and religion. The available case law concerning these grounds is quite abundant, particularly regarding sex and religion. In the Netherlands, already since the early eighties of the last century, the Equal Treatment Commission (ETC) and its successor, the Netherlands Institute for Human Rights (NIHR), have developed an elaborate line of jurisprudence from which a substantial number of the following examples are drawn. Though soft-law only, this character does not make its conceptual value less significant than examples derived from binding court decisions.[42]

By highlighting jurisprudence in which application of the concept of indirect discrimination has had considerable structural effects, I do not intend to ignore that this sample is not representative of the bulk of the case law on indirect discrimination. Ultimately, its reach depends on the strictness or leniency with which judicial bodies are willing to apply it. (See for further elaboration Section 5.3.5 and 5.4.)

---

41 See the robust stance of the ECtHR in this regard in the line of cases on educational segregation of Roma, a.o. ECtHR (Grand Chamber), 13 November 2007, *D.H. and others v. the Czech Republic*, appl. no. 57325/00 and ECtHR (Grand Chamber), 16 March 2010, *Oršuš and Others v. Croatia*, appl. no. 15766/03.

42 The ETC was a semi-judicial body. Its main task was supervision of the General Equal Treatment Act, which came into force in 1994. This task was passed on to the NIHR in 2012. Complaints can be heard and opinions given, which are not legally binding. The General Equal Treatment Act covers discrimination on the basis of religion, belief, political opinion, race, sex, nationality, sexual orientation and civil status in all major areas of social and economic life like employment, the liberal professions, insurance, banking, housing, welfare, education and healthcare. The indirect discrimination review applied follows the EU model. With over 100 opinions rendered each year, the ETC/NIHR have covered a particularly wide range of cases enabling them to build up an extensive jurisprudence.

5.3.2 *Examples of the Potential Reach of Indirect Discrimination Analysis Regarding Discrimination on the Basis of Sex*

The case law regarding indirect discrimination on the basis of sex is particularly rich in Europe, where protection of sex discrimination became from early on a prominent element in the case law of the CJEU and exerted a lot of influence on European countries, including the Netherlands.[43] In a way, the CJEU's case law on indirect sex discrimination set the stage for application of the concept regarding other grounds such as race and religion. As already mentioned, in adopting the notion of indirect discrimination at a much later stage, the ECtHR followed the CJEU's lead.

The probably most well-known line of CJEU cases regarding indirect discrimination on the basis of sex regards part-time workers. Starting with the cases *Jenkins* and *Bilka* mentioned before in Section 5.2.1, the CJEU built up a considerable jurisprudence, in which disadvantageous treatment of part-time workers compared to full-time workers is critically examined for its disparate impact on women; if such differentiation cannot be justified by being appropriate and necessary to achieve a legitimate aim, it violates the prohibition of indirect discrimination. Applying this indirect discrimination review, the position of part-time workers has been structurally improved in several ways, for example by prohibiting this group of workers being paid less than full-time employees, by prohibiting their exclusion from pension schemes or from social security benefits such as allowances in event of illness or invalidity payments.[44] Interestingly, following up on increasing awareness of the widespread practice of treating part-time workers less favourable than full-time workers, a separate Directive was adopted which prohibits discrimination on the basis of part-time work as such.[45] In this way an instance of indirect discrimination is transformed into direct discrimination on a different ground. The Directive allows for broad possibilities of justifying differential treatment

43 In most European national jurisdictions, the concept of indirect discrimination was introduced as a result of EU law, see Tobler, Indirect discrimination, 2005, p. 59.

44 See, respectively, CJEU, 31 March 1981, *Jenkins*, C-97/80; CJEU, 13 May 1986, *Bilka*, C-170/84; CJEU, 13 July 1989, *Rinner-Kühn*, C-171/88 and 13 December 1989, *Ruzius-Wilbrink*, C-102/88. Of course, I am aware that not all decisions of the CJEU are necessarily followed up to the full in the Member-States, in particular when the duty bearers are private companies, but they definitely provide an important incentive for changing realities on the ground.

45 Council Directive 97/81/EC of 15 December 1997 concerning the Framework Agreement on part-time work concluded by UNICE, CEEP and the ETUC. (The abbreviations stand for the Union of Industrial and Employer's Confederations of Europe (UNICE), the European Centre of Enterprises with Public Participation (CEEP) and the European Trade Union Confederation (ETUC).

of part-time and fulltime workers, as would be the case under the openly formulated 'objective justification' possibility applicable when indirect discrimination is at stake, but it renders the step of establishing 'disparate impact' on women superfluous.[46]

Less well-known examples of CJEU case law regard (sex neutral) breadwinner benefits in social security arrangements, which tend to advantage men rather than women, as men are more frequently the breadwinner of a family. In addition, such benefits usually provide a disincentive for the breadwinner's partner (so usually women) to earn an income, as this income may result in reduction or loss of the breadwinner benefit. The Court regards such benefits to constitute indirect sex discrimination, unless an objective justification can be put forward. In the leading, (Dutch) case *Teuling*, the Court held that withholding a supplement to an invalidity benefit because of the presence in the household of a spouse with an income was objectively justified, because the supplement was intended to guarantee a minimum subsistence income for the family concerned.[47] This outcome meant that breadwinner benefits could remain in place in a variety of social security schemes directed at guaranteeing a subsistence family income, yet in other instances where this was not the case the concept of indirect discrimination was subsequently used in the Netherlands to challenge bread winner benefits.[48] Thus, in the Dutch setting, the notion of indirect discrimination was very functional in raising awareness regarding the structural disadvantage faced by non-breadwinners in social security and quite helpful in significantly reducing the number of such benefits.

The abundance of cases brought to the Dutch ETC provide several other interesting examples of the potential reach of indirect discrimination in addressing structural forms of disadvantage experienced by women. In applying the concept of indirect discrimination, the ETC has shown from early on how it can be used to successfully challenge all sorts of subtle and structural forms of discrimination against women. In this respect it often drew much inspiration from the (legally binding) case law of the CJEU, yet it has taken the concept at some points a major step further. A first example concerns

46 Clause 4 reads: 'Principle of non-discrimination. 1. In respect of employment conditions, part-time workers shall not be treated in a less favourable manner than comparable full-time workers solely because they work part time unless different treatment is justified on objective grounds.'

47 CJEU, 11 June 1987, *Teuling-Worms*, C-30/85.

48 For an overview see M. Driessen and A. Veldman, *Inkomenszekerheid* (Income security), in: R. Holtmaat en T. Loenen (red.), *Vrouw en Recht* (Woman and law), Nijmegen, 1997, p. 181–223.

discrimination in pay practices. The ETC acknowledges the detrimental effects on women of basing salaries on experience in gainful employment only and on the last earned pay. As women leave the labour market for some time to take care of their children far more often than men, such a policy has a disparate impact on women re-entering the labour market. Drawing on the decision of the European Court of Justice in *Nimz*,[49] the ETC does not consider such policies objectively justified. It demands that *all* relevant experience, including relevant experience from unpaid work, is taken into account and assessed on an individual basis. As far as the last earned pay provides a proper indication of relevant experience it is justified to use this as a starting point, but the employer should periodically reconsider whether, compared to a man doing work of equal value, a lower salary on the basis of lesser experience at the start of the employment is still warranted.[50]

Exclusionary pay practices deriving from a segregated labour market have also been quite successfully challenged through claims of indirect discrimination. Many occupational pension schemes, for instance, exclude typically 'female' jobs like administrative functions or cleaning from coverage. Likewise, other financial arrangements are sometimes reserved for technical, that is mainly male, personnel only. As such exclusions affect women much more than men, the ETC closely scrutinises the justifications advanced. On the whole, it does not consider such practices objectively justified. Financial considerations of the employer are not accepted in themselves as a justification and even if the scheme is part of a collective labour agreement this cannot necessarily save it.[51]

The last example in the area of pay concerns a job evaluation scheme which was widely used in the healthcare sector, covering some 150,000 persons. On the basis of an extensive and thorough examination of the system, the ETC concluded that it harboured several subtle mechanisms which led to a lower appraisal of (elements of) typically 'female' functions like nursing compared to

49 In this case the CJEU held that the connection between seniority and experience must be established for every individual case and may not be taken for granted as a valid generalisation. Seniority does not imply by definition a better job performance and thus cannot be the basis for a higher salary just in itself. As linking conditions of labour like pay to seniority is likely to have a disparate impact on women, this may amount to indirect discrimination on the basis of sex prohibited by then article 119 of the EC Treaty. CJEU, 7 February 1991, *Nimz*, C-184/89.

50 See ETC opinions 98–27, 98–28, 98–102, 98–138 and 98–142.

51 See, for example, opinions 97–71, 97–139, 98–16 and 98–22. See for the issue of costs being an insufficient justification in themselves also CJEU, 17 June 1998, *Hill/Stapleton*, C-243/95, par. 40.

(elements of) typically 'male' functions like management.[52] To start with, the different elements of nursing activities were much less extensively identified and described than elements of managing, which were laid down in detail. Besides, descriptions of male functions were often formulated more weighty than female functions. Thus aspects of management in the total score for functions was given far more weight than aspects of care taking. Further, similar elements were valued less in female functions than in male functions. In this way, unattractive elements in the latter were compensated for to a larger extent than in the former. And to give a last remarkable example of gender bias in the system: the regular and sensitive contacts of nursing personnel on a ward for premature babies with the babies' parents was valued hardly any higher than the contacts some categories of technical personnel could incidentally have with patients.

Another remarkable line of cases deals with a 'right' to a part-time job instead of a full-time one, to facilitate combining paid work and care taking activities. The ETC regards the refusal of an employer to make a job available part-time as a policy which has a disparate impact on women, as women much more than men are in need of and looking for part-time work as they still bear the larger part of caretaking activities. This means the employer has to advance an objective justification for his practice of making a job full-time or nearly full-time available only. Similarly, the request of a worker to reduce her number of working hours may not be refused unless the employer can show the refusal is objectively justified, that is, is both appropriate and necessary to achieve a real need of his enterprise. The ETC is not inclined to be very lenient towards the employer.[53]

Other salient examples of the structural reach of indirect sex discrimination review can be drawn from several more recent judgments of the South African Constitutional Court. In the *Mahlangu* case the Court held that exclusion of domestic workers from a social security benefit, which is a common practice in many countries, constitutes a form of indirect discrimination. As the Court notes, in the South African setting mainly black women bear the brunt, which

52 Opinion 98–55.

53 Opinion 98–56. In 2000 legislation has come into force in the Netherlands (*Wet aanpassing arbeidsduur*; Adjustment of working hours Act), which gives workers a right to reduce their working hours, unless the employer can advance a compelling business interest (*zwaarwegend bedrijfsbelang*) for refusing it. This means a (conditional) right to part-time work need not be constructed through indirect discrimination claims.

renders the indirect discrimination to be intersectionally based on sex, gender and race.[54] In the European context, in a similar challenge to the exclusion of domestic workers from a social security scheme, the CJEU held the exclusion of this group to constitute indirect discrimination on the basis of sex for which no objective justification exists.[55]

Two other landmark judgments are worth mentioning, which affect millions of people in South Arica. In the 2021 *Sithole* case the Constitutional Court was confronted with differential treatment regarding matrimonial regimes, a legacy of the past Apartheid system.[56] For black couples, the default regime was not community of property, as it was for other couples. Arranging for community of property was possible, but cumbersome to realize and many black people would not even know it to be a possibility. The Court held that this differentiation between black and other couples constitutes a violation of the prohibition of discrimination on the basis of race as such, but in addition expressly considers it to be indirect discrimination on the basis of sex and gender as evidence shows that black women are disproportionately hard hit compared to their husbands.[57]

A year later the Court decided another major case concerning marriage law. Under the applicable Marriage Act and Divorce Act, Muslim marriages, that is marriages solemnized under *Sharia* law, were not recognized. As a consequence, all sorts of protections offered under these acts to married people during marriage and after its dissolution were not offered to persons married according to Muslim rites. The Court held this to constitute direct discrimination on the basis of religion and marital status, as civil law marriages are protected, but again added specific considerations regarding the particular disadvantage suffered by Muslim women rather than Muslim men under this arrangement: 'the differentiation caused by the Marriage Act strikes particularly at women, and "works to the detriment of Muslim women and not Muslim men" [reference omitted]'.[58]

54 Constitutional Court of South Africa, *Mahlangu and Another v. Minister of Labour and Others*, [2020] ZACC 24.

55 CJEU, 24 February 2022, *TGSS*, C-389/20.

56 Constitutional Court of South Africa, *Sithole and Another v. Sithole and Another*, [2021] ZACC 7.

57 Idem, par. 27.

58 Constitutional Court of South Africa, *Women's Legal Centre Trust v. President of the Republic of South Africa and Others*, [2022] ZACC 23, par. 49.

5.3.3 *Examples of the Potential Reach of Indirect Discrimination Analysis Regarding Discrimination on the Basis of Race or Ethnic Origin*

In addition to the landmark cases of *Griggs* and *Mahlangu* already discussed above, the far-reaching potential of the concept of indirect discrimination in tackling structural inequalities faced by racial minority groups can be illustrated with several landmark cases from the ECtHR and some interesting cases from the Netherlands.

The ECtHR used the concept in a line of cases regarding educational segregation of Roma, which is a particularly pressing issue in European countries with a significant Roma population. The Court's judgments have identified the disproportionate number of Roma children being placed in special schools for children with mental disabilities as a form of indirect racial discrimination.[59] Relegating Roma children from time to time to separate classes because of their lack of sufficient command of the language commonly used in the educational system[60] or assigning them to physically separate school buildings[61] have met with the same verdict. In all these cases, no convincing reasons could be put forward to justify the resulting segregation. Interestingly, in the case *X and Others v. Albania*, the Court held expressly that a failure to implement appropriate desegregation measures 'to correct the applicants' factual inequality and avoid the perpetuation of the discrimination that resulted from their over-representation in the school' and 'thereby breaking their cycle of marginalization', also constitutes a violation of the non-discrimination standards of the ECHR.[62] Apparently, in the Court's approach remedying a situation of indirect discrimination may imply a duty to take remedial measures.

The concept of indirect racial discrimination has also been used to bring the politically sensitive issue of national immigration policies up for assessment by the ECtHR under Article 14 ECHR. In the *Biao* case the Court acknowledged that a requirement of having Danish nationality for at last 28 years for purposes of certain types of family reunion, 'had the indirect effect of favouring Danish nationals of Danish ethnic origin, and placing at a disadvantage, or having a disproportionately prejudicial effect on persons who, ..., acquired Danish nationality later in life and who were of an ethnic origin other than Danish'.[63]

---

59 ECtHR (Grand Chamber), 13 November 2007, *D.H. and others v. the Czech Republic*, appl. no. 57325/00.

60 ECtHR (Grand Chamber), 16 March 2010, *Oršuš and Others v. Croatia*, appl. no. 15766/03.

61 ECtHR, 11 December 2012, *Sampani and others v. Greece*, appl. no. 59608/09.

62 ECtHR, 31 May 2022, *X and others v. Albania*, appl. no. 73548/17 and 45521/19, par. 84. The case was decided under the 12th Protocol.

63 ECtHR (Grand Chamber), 24 May 2016, *Biao v. Denmark*, appl. no. 38590/10, par. 112–113.

In the Netherlands, the Dutch ETC and its successor, the NIHR have time and again identified disadvantageous treatment of people of non-Dutch origin as a form of indirect racial discrimination. Requirements to speak Dutch fluently or without any accent have been identified as constituting a presumption of indirect discrimination on the basis of race, because such requirements disproportionately affect persons of non-Dutch origin, which can only be rebutted if the respondent has serious and genuinely functional reasons for setting this condition.[64] Similarly, a housing corporation cannot refuse to rent a house to someone just because this person does not speak Dutch.[65] A final example to illustrate the wide variety of cases within reach of indirect racial discrimination analysis, concerned the requirement of four years of residence in the Netherlands as a condition for being eligible to emergency shelter for homeless families; this was also regarded as a violation of the prohibition of indirect discrimination on the grounds of race.[66]

Another interesting case to mention in this selection of cases addressing indirect racial discrimination is the South African case *Walker*.[67] It dealt with a more exceptional claim of indirect discrimination against a structurally advantaged, not disadvantaged, group. The case concerned a municipal policy of charging a flat rate per household for water and electricity in formerly black areas (still composed of a mainly black population) and a metered rate for formerly white areas (still mainly populated by white people), resulting in higher rates paid in the latter. The fact that in this situation the disparate impact affects white people is no impediment for the Court to identify it as an instance of indirect discrimination on the basis of race, but it does play an important role in deciding whether it can be justified: 'The more vulnerable the group adversely affected by the discrimination, the more likely the discrimination will be held to be unfair'.[68] Considering that the white claimant 'belongs to a group that has not been disadvantaged by the racial policies and practices of the past', and that in a period of transition flat rates for black areas are acceptable for lack of other available solutions, the Court concludes that the policy can pass muster and does not violate the Constitutional non-discrimination standards.[69] The way in which the Court lowers the degree of scrutiny of its

64 E.g. ETC opinion 2007–127 and NIHR opinion 2015–32.

65 E.g. NIHR opinion 2016–14.

66 NIHR opinion 2023–97.

67 Constitutional Court of South Africa, *City Council of Pretoria v. Walker*, [1998] ZACC 1.

68 Idem, par. 45.

69 Idem, par. 47–49.

justification review is a clear example of an asymmetrical approach to the concept of discrimination (see Chapter 4, Section 4.4.2).

5.3.4 *Examples of the Potential Reach of Indirect Discrimination Analysis Regarding Discrimination on the Basis of Religion*

As a preliminary remark, it is important to be aware that many of the cases to be discussed below as instances of indirect discrimination on the basis of religion may also be approached as cases regarding a limitation of freedom of religion. The focus chosen varies between jurisdictions. In the case law of the ECtHR and the Canadian Supreme Court, for example, this type of cases is usually approached as an interference with freedom of religion, though as far as the ECtHR is concerned, the *Thlimmenos* case provides an important exception by being analysed under Article 14 ECHR.[70] Given my focus on indirect discrimination analysis, in the following I only use examples in which this concept played a central role.[71]

Abundant jurisprudence from a variety of jurisdictions may illustrate the potential reach of indirect discrimination analysis regarding religion. Neutral dress codes resulting in a limitation of religious expressions belong to the most prominent examples.

Here again, from the start a large number of cases reached the Dutch ETC regarding 'new' religious expressions brought along by people with a migrant background, which enabled it to develop a detailed line of jurisprudence. Many of the cases dealt with employers who would not allow Muslim employees to wear a headscarf as part of their dress policies. As in the far majority of cases these dress codes were formulated in a neutral way, without expressly referring to religious expressions (for example by prohibiting any type of head gear or requiring an overall 'neutral' appearance) the ETC used the concept of

---

70 ECtHR (Grand Chamber), 6 April 2000, *Thlimmenos v. Greece*, appl. no. 34369/97.

71 Notwithstanding this difference in framing, the way in which it is assessed whether the infringement can be justified closely resembles the justification test under discrimination review. See McCrudden; 'the same approach to justification generally will be applied to Article 9 claims and Article 14 indirect discrimination claims', C. McCrudden, Indirect religious discrimination: resisting the temptations of premature normative theorization, *Harvard Human Rights Journal*, 2021, p. 249–280, at p. 257. See for an extensive comparison between the approach to claims for religious accommodation by the CJEU (starting from equality/non-discrimination) and the ECtHR (starting from freedom of religion) S. Haverkort-Speekenbrink, *European non-discrimination law. A comparison of EU Law and the ECHR in the field of non-discrimination and freedom of religion in public employment with an emphasis on the Islamic Headscarf issue*, Antwerp, Intersentia, 2012.

indirect discrimination to assess their validity under Dutch non-discrimination standards.

Overall, in assessing the objective justifications put forward the ETC and its successor, the NIHR, tend to give priority to employees to manifest their religion by wearing a headscarf, a turban or other religious sign or symbol at work. Arguments that a headscarf is not representative, may negatively affect a company's image or result in a loss of customers or clients, are not accepted.[72] Only functional reasons, for example considerations of safety or hygiene are considered valid.[73] This accommodationist application of the notion of indirect discrimination by the ETC/NIHR covers both private and public employment, providing largely the same protection to civil servants, public school teachers and other people employed by the state as to privately employed workers. So far, the only exceptions concern public functionaries exercising core state authority, such as members of the judiciary and the police. For this category arguments regarding state neutrality have been accepted as a justification to limit the wearing of religious garments or symbols at work.[74]

On the basis of its jurisprudence, the ETC published detailed guidelines regarding religious expressions in employment and in education.[75] The latter covers personnel as well as pupils. Both guidelines apply to private as well as public employment and education and have been largely accepted as part of Government policy.

Similar use has been made of the concept of indirect discrimination by the South African Constitutional Court in the case *Pillay*, its leading case regarding neutral dress codes resulting in a limitation of religious expressions.[76]

---

72 See for an overview of the jurisprudential lines developed by the ETC its *Advies 2004/06 inzake arbeid, religie en gelijke behandeling* (Advice on employment, religion and equal treatment).

73 See e.g. ETC, opinion 2011–95.

74 The ETC/NIHR has not explicitly dealt with a case concerning a judge, but it did deal with a case of a law clerk who refused to refrain from wearing her headscarf during court sessions (opinion 2001–53 and more recently confirmed in opinion 2016–45). The ETC/NIHR considered this to be a violation of the applicable equality standards, considering that a law clerk is not a member of the judiciary as such. From this it can be inferred that the ETC/NIHR will probably accept the argument if a judge is concerned.

75 *Advies 2004/06 inzake Arbeid, religie en gelijke behandeling* (Advice 2004/06 concerning Employment, religion and equal treatment) and *Advies 2008/03 inzake gelijke behandeling in het onderwijs: 'Naar een discriminatie vrije school'* (Advice 2008/03 concerning equal treatment in education: 'Towards a discrimination-free school'. Both are available on the website of the NIHR, http://www.mensenrechten.nl/publicaties/zoek.

76 Constitutional Court of South Africa, *MEC for Education: Kwazulu-Natal and Others v. Pillay*, [2007] ZACC 21.

The case concerned school regulations prohibiting the wearing of jewellery with the school uniform. As a consequence the complainant, Sunali Pillay, was not allowed to wear a nose stud to give expression to her Hindu religion and culture. The Constitutional Court considered this to amount to indirect discrimination for its disparate impact and the lack of a convincing justification. Interestingly, drawing on the concept of (reasonable) accommodation used in the context of freedom of religion and disability law, the Court construed the lack of justification expressly in terms of a lack of accommodation.[77] As the Court put it:

> While the extent of this exclusion [from the mainstream of society] is most powerfully felt by the disabled, the same exclusion is inflicted on all those who are excluded by rules that fail to accommodate those who depart from the norm. Our society which values dignity, equality, and freedom must therefore require people to act positively to accommodate diversity. Those steps might be as simple as granting and regulating an exemption from a general rule or they may require that the rules or practices be changed (…).[78]

In this way the Court integrated a lack of accommodation into its indirect discrimination review.

Other examples of indirect discrimination cases worth mentioning here concern the assessment of the highly contested issues of face-covering veils and of marriage officials who refuse to officiate same-sex marriage or civil partnership for religious reasons.

Where prohibitions on the wearing of a niqab or burqa are concerned, the need for good communication is usually the main argument put forward to justify such prohibitions. The ETC assesses this argument on the basis of a contextual analysis. It generally accepts it as a justification in the context of education, so not allowing a pupil to wear it in school is objectively justified.[79] However, for parents coming to school the situation is different. When a school director refused to talk to a parent of a potential future pupil because she was wearing a face-covering veil, which she refused to remove during an interview with a male person, the ETC held this to violate the prohibition of indirect discrimination. The ETC considered that the director could have received the

---

77 Idem, par. 71–74.

78 Idem, par. 75.

79 ETC, opinion 2003–40.

necessary information he needed regardless the woman wearing a full veil. Alternatively, he could also have asked a female colleague to talk to the woman instead.[80]

The ETC came to a similar conclusion in a case regarding an organisation providing advice on financial and other issues to socially vulnerable people.[81] The organisation had adopted a policy of not servicing clients wearing a face-covering veil, unless they would remove their veil during the interview with the social counselor, be this a man or a woman. The argument for the policy was the need of effective communication, facial expressions being deemed crucial for making sure the client had understood everything. The ETC did not accept this argument, pointing to the possibility of allocating the veil-wearing woman to a female counselor, with whom she would not feel required to wear the veil.

The position of the marriage official who refuses to officiate same-sex marriage or civil partnership is also a topic of much debate.[82] In the Netherlands, over the years the ETC shifted its position from considering this acceptable to unacceptable under non-discrimination standards. Same-sex marriage became possible under Dutch law in 2001. Already in 2002 the ETC was confronted with the first complaint of a job applicant for the function of marriage official who was refused for not being willing to service same-sex couples for religious objections. The municipality concerned held this objection to be an unacceptable infringement of the prohibition of discrimination on the basis of sexual orientation. The ETC did not agree. It considered the job-refusal to constitute indirect discrimination on the basis of religion, which was not justified as long as homosexual couples would not be barred from getting married because of a lack of officials willing to perform the service.[83] After several years of intense societal and political debates, however, this position changed. Confronted with a new complaint in 2008, the Commission took the opportunity to overrule its former opinion as a pragmatic solution rather than a principled balancing of the interests at stake. It now emphasised that in acting as a state representative, a marriage official cannot be allowed to discriminate on the basis of sexual orientation, even if this stems from his

80 ETC, opinion 2004–95.

81 ETC, opinion 2005–86.

82 See for an overview of developments in the Netherlands regarding this issue B. MacDougall, E. Bonthuys, K. Norrie and M. van den Brink, Conscientious objection to creating same-sex unions: an international analysis, *Canadian Journal of Human Rights*, 2012, p. 127–164.

83 ETC oordeel 2002–25 and 2002–26.

religious convictions.[84] In 2014 this soft-law view was rendered into a hard-law regulation.[85]

5.3.5 *Preliminary Findings Regarding the Application of the Concept of Indirect Discrimination*

In providing the examples above, I included quite some detail to show several important features of the potential reach of indirect discrimination analysis, which bring me to some (tentative) conclusions about the ways in which it works as a concept in legal practice. If anything, indirect discrimination review is often highly complex.

First of all, the examples show how the concept can indeed reach a very broad range of situations in which the unequal outcome of a rule, policy of measure can be problematized as an equality issue, instead of remaining invisible because it is not expressly based on race, sex or religion. As many of these situations are not foreseeable, an open system of justification review is inevitable; even where race and sex based discrimination is at stake, a broader range of justifications may come into view compared to instances of direct discrimination on these grounds.

Secondly, the examples show that with the possibility of justification taking centre stage, indirect discrimination analysis is bound to be rife with many normative considerations and assessments, again even more so than where direct discrimination is concerned. The outcome of indirect discrimination review in judicial procedures can be even more unpredictable, particularly in controversial cases where perspectives may differ widely.

Thirdly, and conceptually of great significance, the examples show that not all forms of disadvantage addressed through indirect discrimination analysis have the same character. Some are based on a *challenge to differential treatment* on the basis of a neutral criterion that is closely linked to a protected ground and causes the disparate impact by this very link, others *challenge an equal treatment* on the basis of a neutral criterion with a disparate effect.

5.3.5.1 Challenging Differential Treatment with a Disparate Impact on a Protected Group

The cases regarding part-time and domestic workers are a prime example of indirect discrimination cases challenging a difference in treatment. As these

---

84 ETC oordeel 2008–40. The ETC explained its change of position more fully in an advice on the subject: *Advies 2008/04 inzake gewetensbezwaarde ambtenaren van de burgerlijke stand: 'Trouwen? Geen bezwaar!'* (Advice 2008/04 on conscientious objections of civil registrars: 'Marriage? No objection!').

85 *Wet van 4 juli 2014, Staatsblad* 2014, 260 (Law of 4 July 2014, Government Gazette 2014.260).

group are overwhelmingly composed of women, a detrimental treatment of these groups has a disparate effect on women. Interestingly, as the disadvantageous treatment of the part-time workers was so prevalent in the employment context, in EU law it has become recognized as a protected ground in its own right by the adoption of a directive regulating equal treatment of part-time and other workers. In this way it receives stronger protection than genuinely neutral (or rather non-sensitive) grounds. In addition, this recognition makes the first step of indirect discrimination analysis (establishing disparate impact) superfluous.

Another feature of this type of indirect discrimination is worth mentioning. As the disadvantageous treatment complained of results from a difference in treatment between two groups, the claim of the excluded group is one of inclusion by being treated the same as the included group. Confusingly, then, this is a claim of formal equal treatment (in the examples: of part-time and fulltime workers, respectively domestic workers and other workers), but this equal treatment does not regard the underlying groups for whom the protected ground 'sex' was formulated (women and men). All in all, this type of cases show how close links may exist between indirect and direct discrimination analysis and how the distinguishing lines between the two may become blurred.

The two South African cases which regarded the difference in treatment of black marriages compared to other marriages and of Muslim marriages compared to other marriages as a form of indirect sex discrimination are also claims for formal equal treatment: black marriages must have the same access to the marital regime of communal property, Muslim marriages must have access to the same types of protection during marriage and after divorce. Contrary to the part-time and domestic workers cases, however, the difference in treatment between the marriage types at stake were not aligned with the categories of men and women as such (women are as a matter of logic not overrepresented in black marriages or Muslim marriages). The disparate impact on women is even more indirect: it derives from the difference in protection they receive compared to their husbands within the applicable marriage regime.

5.3.5.2 Challenging Equal Treatment with a Disparate Impact on a Protected Group

Some other cases discussed above are not challenging forms of differential treatment with a disparate effect, but challenge an equal treatment based on a neutral criterion having a detrimental effect on protected group.

This type of case can take two quite different forms. Sometimes, these cases boil down to a claim for adjusting the criteria which are applied equally to all, because the criteria in themselves are biased and responsible for the disparate impac. They are as such unacceptable and should be replaced by truly neutral criteria. The case *Nitisha*, regarding the criteria for granting permanent service in the Indian army being more difficult to meet for women than men, and the Dutch case on excluding experience outside paid work as part of the criteria for deciding about the salary level of a new employee, are examples of this type of unjustified equal treatment amounting to indirect discrimination.

A second form which challenges to equal treatment in indirect discrimination cases can take is of a *conceptually different* nature. In some of the above cases of this type, the indirect discrimination does not derive from the criteria or rules themselves being unacceptable, but from a lack of creating exceptions to do justice to the different situation and needs of the claimant. These cases are in fact about the duty to 'treat unalike cases unalike' and to provide (reasonable) accommodation. All the cases regarding (potential) indirect discrimination on the basis of religion discussed above belong to this type. They all call for accommodation of religious manifestations such as wearing a headscarf, face-covering veil or nose-stud, or allowing for objections to officiate same-sex marriage. A case of this nature regarding indirect sex discrimination is provided by the opinions of the Dutch ETC regarding a 'right' to part-time work, to accommodate the particular needs of workers who combine paid work and care-taking responsibilities. The indirect discrimination in this type of case results from insufficient (that is unjustified lack of) accommodation. Here again the claim is one of inclusion by differential treatment.

Other examples of indirect discrimination analysis discussed in the preceding sections are much more hybrid and (even) more complicated. The quite complex Dutch job evaluation scheme was considered to constitute indirect discrimination because of a mixture of unjustified differentiation between categories of workers clearly being aligned to female and male workers (administrative versus technical personnel), and unjustified lack of differential treatment or accommodation (not properly valuing job elements in typically female functions such as nursing compared to elements of more typically male functions such as management). It seems clear that redressing such complicated forms of indirect discrimination requires a complete, sophisticated make-over of the scheme as such in order to structurally change the hidden, male standards for job evaluation.

5.3.6 *Conclusions Regarding the Potential Reach of the Concept of Indirect Discrimination*

On the basis of the examples presented above, my conclusion would be that the concept of indirect discrimination has indeed a far-reaching potential in identifying and addressing many forms of structural disadvantage and systemic discrimination. How far-reaching may perhaps be best illustrated by the way in which the US Supreme Court curtailed its reach under Constitutional equality review.

In *Washington v. Davis*, a case concerning racial discrimination, the US Supreme Court was confronted with the question whether the disparate impact analysis developed in cases like *Griggs* under Title VII of the Civil Rights Act would equally apply under the constitutional equality standards. As affluence and poverty in the US run along racial lines and the scope of constitutional protection against discrimination is very broad indeed, the Court judgment showed a clear awareness of the far-reaching implications of fully adopting the disparate impact approach:

> A rule that a statute designed to serve neutral ends is nevertheless invalid, absent compelling justification, if in practice it benefits or burdens one race more than another, would be far-reaching and would raise serious questions about, and perhaps invalidate, a whole range of tax, welfare, public service, regulatory, and licensing statutes that may be more burdensome to the poor and to the average black than to the more affluent white.[86]

The Supreme Court was apparently not willing to take this risk of having to invalidate all kinds of federal and state statutes because of their disparate impact on black people. To block this, the Court in *Washington v. Davis* ruled that discriminatory *intent* is required to bring an effective claim of discrimination under the Constitution. It held that to be constitutionally valid '(…) the invidious quality of a law claimed to be racially discriminatory must ultimately be traced to a racially discriminatory purpose'.[87] In this way, the Supreme Court reduced the use of disparate impact analysis in its initial form to specific and limited areas like the employment sphere covered by Title VII.

A requirement of 'intent' to bring a successful claim is a very effective means of curtailing the scope of the notion of indirect discrimination. It significantly reduces its potential bite. The decision of the Supreme Court in *Feeney* provides a good example.[88] In this case a woman challenged a statute of the State of Massachusetts which gave absolute preference to army veterans applying for state civil service jobs. As this group was almost exclusively male (98%) and constituted more than 25% of the entire state population, women were in fact

86 US Supreme Court, *Washington v. Davis*, 426 US 229 (1976), p. 248.

87 Idem, p. 240.

88 US Supreme Court, *Personnel Administrator of Massachusetts v. Feeney*, 442 US 256 (1979).

almost completely excluded from the state civil service, except for traditionally female jobs, for which male workers would not apply. A clear example of a case raising an issue of disparate impact and calling for an inquiry into the presence of a justification for this policy.

The Supreme Court, however, never reached any balancing of interests as would be required under a justification test. It precluded the claim of discrimination from the start by holding that the contested provisions did not infringe the constitutional equality clause, as they did not intend to discriminate against women. Their purpose was to reward the services rendered by the army veterans, not to prefer men over women. Not just women were affected, some men were disadvantaged as well. The disproportionately large number of women affected does not make any difference to the Court:

> "Discriminatory purpose", however, implies more than intent as volition or intent as awareness of consequences. ... It implies that the decision maker, in this case a state legislature, selected or reaffirmed a particular course of action at least in part "because of", not merely "in spite of", its adverse effects upon an identifiable group.[89]

This intent requirement seriouslyly reduces the potential reach of the concept of indirect discrimination. As a result, it only plays a very limited role in constitutional discrimination review by the Supreme Court.[90]

This type of back-tracking approach has not been followed in any of the other jurisdictions I have drawn on in this study, where establishing disparate impact of a rule, policy or measure is sufficient to trigger the question whether it can be objectively justified. Though this may sound straightforward, also in jurisdictions in which 'intent' is not a prerequisite for accepting a claim of indirect discrimination, the actual potential and 'bite' of the concept also depends very much on how the difficulties and dilemmas it brings along in its application are approached in legal practice.

---

89 Idem, p. 279.

90 In addition, under the Trump Administration the use of disparate impact claims under statutory non-discrimination law has come under increasing attack as part of a wider roll-back of the protection provided by civil rights law to historically disadvantaged groups, see A. Agathocleous, K. Conway and R. Moore, *Trump on DEI and anti-discrimination law. Rolling back the clock of racial justice*, American Civil Liberties Union, 2 July 2022.

5.4 Difficulties and Dilemmas of Indirect Discrimination Review

The examples of indirect discrimination analysis in the previous section show that it can be very complicated and will inevitably include many normative considerations and assessments. As a consequence, the outcome of indirect discrimination review may differ considerably depending on the perspectives taken. In addition, outcomes may also depend on the way the various elements of discrimination review are applied by judicial bodies. In legal practice, courts face a number of difficulties and dilemmas which allow for widely diverging approaches.

5.4.1 *Distinguishing Indirect from Direct Discrimination – Fuzzy Demarcations*

A first difficulty of indirect discrimination analysis may regard the distinction between direct and indirect discrimination as such, which is crucial in jurisdictions where justification review of the two modes of discrimination significantly differ, as is the case in EU law. This may explain why the preoccupation with this distinction is most prominent in this type of context. As discussed in Chapter 4.4.1, in some jurisdictions specific forms of indirect discrimination may turn into direct discrimination if an apparently neutral rule or measure is in fact intentionally targeting a protected group, or if it is inextricably linked to a protected ground. In addition, as mentioned above in the previous section, distinctions on the basis of an apparently neutral criterion which give very frequently rise to indirect discrimination may be 'promoted' into becoming a prohibited ground in their own right, as happened to part-time work in the EU context.

In many other instances, the lines between direct and indirect discrimination may remain much more fuzzy and invite discussion. The different readings of the prohibition of wearing a headscarf in the case *Achbita* is but one prominent example. The CJEU qualified the employer's underlying policy of neutrality as a potential instance of indirect discrimination on the basis of religion,[91] which was criticized by academic scholars who identified it as direct discrimination on this ground.[92] In this respect, I would not be surprised if

91 CJEU (Grand Chamber), 14 March 2017, *Achbita*, C-157/15. The CJEU confirmed this understanding in the subsequent joint cases CJEU (Grand Chamber), *Wabe* and *Müller*, 15 July 2021, C-804/18 and C-341/19.

92 See e.g. S. Ouald-Chaib and V. David, *European Court of Justice keeps the door to religious discrimination in the private workplace opened. The European Court of Human Rights could close it*, Blog Strasbourg Observers, 27 March 2017.

in fuzzy instances such as at stake in *Achbita*, the choice for addressing such cases as a cases of indirect discrimination rather than direct discrimination may also be influenced by the broader possibilities of balancing the rights and interests involved under the objective justification test.[93] Anyway, the case law of the CJEU includes many more examples of the fuzzy lines between direct and indirect discrimination. The demarcation seems overall rather unclear.[94]

In other jurisdictions, distinguishing the two is often far less important, as indirect discrimination is reviewed in the same or largely similar way as direct discrimination, rendering identification as the one or the other superfluous. Thus, for example, the Indian Supreme Court did not pay any attention to the concept of indirect discrimination when it held that the criminalisation of 'carnal intercourse against the order of nature' is a violation of, among others, the constitutional equality standards insofar as it applies to the consensual sexual conduct of adults of the same sex.[95] Though the penal law formulation suggests this case concerns indirect discrimination on grounds of sexual orientation rather than direct, as it also applies to, for example, having sex with animals, the issue of whether this was direct or indirect discrimination on the basis of sexual orientation did not play any role in the judgment. The law was considered to violate the right to equality by targeting a specific part of the population for their sexual orientation.

As mentioned before, the Constitutional Court of South Africa and the Canadian Supreme Court also accord less importance to the difference, as both direct and indirect discrimination meet with a similar level of strict scrutiny (see Section 5.2.2). As the South African court puts it, there is 'no qualitative difference between discrimination that occurs directly or indirectly'.[96] Any justification for either of these two forms of discrimination meets with stringent judicial review.

Nevertheless, the notion of indirect discrimination is relevant in all jurisdictions also for different reason, as it helps identifying all sorts of more hidden forms of discrimination and usually triggers more stringent scrutiny wherever disparate impact affects protected groups.

---

93 See for further elaboration T. Loenen, In search of an EU approach to headscarf bans: where to go after *Achbita* and *Bougnaoui*? *Review of European Administrative Law*, 2017, p. 47–73.

94 See for an extensive discussion Tobler, Indirect discrimination, 2005, p. 307–370.

95 Supreme Court of India, 6 September 2018, *Navtej Singh Johar v. Union Of India*.

96 Constitutional Court of South Africa, *City Council of Pretoria v. Walker* [1998] ZACC 1, par. 95.

5.4.2 *Establishing Disproportionate or Disparate Impact*

A second difficulty in applying the notion of indirect discrimination regards the way in which disparate impact can be demonstrated. Establishing disparate impact on a protected group in fact involves two steps itself. A practice or policy must be shown first of all to have a detrimental effect, and secondly, to affect a protected group disproportionately. Both steps bring along their own difficulties and dilemmas.

Though the first step seems quite easy, in practice it sometimes turns out to be pretty complicated. In the European context, especially cases concerning part-time work have proven to pose difficult problems. An example may be derived from the diverging ways in which the Dutch ETC and the CJEU considered a claim of unequal pay between part-time and full-time workers. The case before the CJEU concerned a German pay practice of paying a bonus for overtime work only if the hours worked surpassed the normal full-time standard.[97] Thus, a part-time worker with an individual labour contract of 20 hours would not receive any extra pay for overtime work unless (s)he worked more than 40 hours. Though it seemed evident to the Dutch ETC in a very similar case that such a pay practice disadvantages part-time workers, the CJEU had a different view. Instead of taking the individually contracted hours as a starting point for defining overtime work, and comparing the pay of full-time and part-time workers in respect of the hours worked on top of that contract, the Court compared the overall wage received by part-time workers and full-time workers for the same number of hours worked. This comparison leads to an entirely different conclusion: as both part-time and full-time workers receive the same pay for each hour worked (a part-time worker with a labour contract of 20 hours receives the same pay for the 24th hour worked as the full-time worker) no differential treatment exists, and thus no disadvantage, to start with. In this way, the claim did not pass the requirement of establishing a disparate impact right from the beginning. The CJEU did not reach the stage of having to decide whether an objective justification was present, a justification which the Dutch ETC thought was absent.[98]

---

97 CJEU, 15 December 1994, *Helmig*, C-399/92.

98 As the case law of the CJEU is leading for the applicable Dutch equality standards, the ETC had to (and did) align its approach in a subsequent case to the CJEU jurisprudence, see ETC opinion 1997–72. Other examples may also illustrate the sorts of difficulties involved in assessing whether differing conditions of labour for full-time and part-time workers create a particular disadvanatge. Is it a disadvantage for part-time workers if they receive a *pro rata* compensation only for time spent on further education or union activities, or are full-time workers disadvantaged if they only receive the same compensation as part-time workers? And what about having full-time and part-time workers pay the same

The second step of establishing a disparate impact claim concerns linking the adverse impact once identified to a group protected by the applicable non-discrimination clause. Issues connected to this step regard the degree of disparate impact required and the nature and amount of proof to substantiate this. How hard or lenient it is for claimants to establish a *prima facie* case of disparate impact will greatly influence the actual reach of indirect discrimination claims in a particular jurisdiction.

In the early days of the development of indirect discrimination review in the European context of sex discrimination, a lot of emphasis was placed on providing statistical proof. This was already rife with difficulties, even if regarding the position of women a lot of data are usually available.[99] When application of the concept is extended to other grounds of discrimination such as race or religion, lack of statistical information easily becomes an unsurmountable hurdle. Since then, and possibly due to this broadening application, more open approaches to the requirements of proving disparate impact have developed.

The use of statistics may still be relevant, but is usually approached as one among other ways of establishing disparate impact. Other ways may include using common sense reasoning or referring to 'facts of common knowledge or understanding', for instance by assuming that disadvantageous treatment of part-time workers will usually entail disparate effects for women, or that dress codes requiring a neutral appearance will generally have a detrimental effect on persons wishing to express their religious convictions by wearing certain attire.[100]

Overall, several courts expressly accept a rather open approach to the admissibility of evidence. As the ECtHR held in the case *D.H. v. the Czech Republic*: 'there are no procedural barriers to the admissibility of evidence

amount of money for private use of a company car. Is that a practice which disadvantages full-time workers, as they have less time off work than part-time workers to use it privately in the first place? The answers given will decide whether there is any basis for an indirect discrimination claim to start with.

99 For example, problems exist regarding the ways in which to use the data or which comparisons to make. See C. Tobler, *Indirect discrimination under Directives 2000/43 and 2000/78*, Report European Network of legal experts in gender equality and non-discrimination, 2022, p. 99.

100 See for examples of such types of reasoning in different jurisdictions e.g. McCrudden, Indirect religious discrimination, 2021, p. 263; Gerards, Non-discrimination, who takes the lead? 2020, at p. 144.

or predetermined formulae for its assessment'.[101] The CJEU takes a similar position,[102] as does the Canadian Supreme Court.[103]

The South African Constitutional Court is interesting to mention in this context for its principled emphasis on qualitative and contextual rather than quantitative analysis. The position of the complainant is carefully considered in terms of elements such as the group (s)he belongs to and its position in society; whether this position is characterized by historical patterns of group disadvantage, systemic inequality, stigmatization or other forms of vulnerability or marginalisation. In assessing these elements, all sorts of secondary sources may be relied on, such as books, articles or reports regarding the position of disadvantaged groups.[104]

Of course, whether an assessment of disparate impact is qualitative, quantitative or a combination, it is bound to include normative considerations and allow for different perspectives resulting in different appreciations of disparate impact. The South African case *Jordan* provides an interesting illustration.[105] In this case the Constitutional Court was faced with a challenge to heavier criminal law sanctions being applicable to sex workers, who were made the primary offender, compared to their clients, who were only liable as an accomplice. The dissenting judges in this case regarded this distinction to constitute indirect discrimination on the basis of sex given the overrepresentation of women in the category of sex workers and the detrimental effects of the criminal law provisions in terms of reinforcing sexual double standards and perpetuating gender stereotypes.[106] The majority did not approach the distinction through this lens and regarded it as a 'gender neutral' distinction between dealer and customer, which is a common distinction in a number of statutes.[107] It could

101 ECtHR (Grand Chamber), 13 November 2007, *D.H. and others v. the Czech Republic*, appl. no. 57325/00, par. 178. In this case the assessment was based on statistical evidence: a much higher percentage of Roma children was placed in special schools than other children. In the case *Oršuš* the Court accepted the proof of indirect discrimination being provided without statistical evidence, ECtHR (Grand Chamber), 16 March 2010, *Oršuš and Others v. Croatia*, appl. no. 15766/03, par. 153.

102 See e.g. CJEU, 8 May 2019, *Villar Láiz*, C-161/18, par. 47.

103 Cf. Supreme Court of Canada, *Fraser v. Canada* [2020] 3 SCR 113: 'In sum, both evidence of statistical disparity and of broader group disadvantage may demonstrate disproportionate impact, but neither is mandatory and their significance will vary depending on the case.' (See summary at the beginning of the judgment).

104 Albertyn and Goldblatt, Chapter 35, Equality, 2007, p. 76–77.

105 Constitutional Court of South Africa, *S. v. Jordan and Others*, [2002] ZACC 22.

106 Idem, par. 64–66.

107 Idem, par. 10.

not 'be said to be discriminating on the basis of gender, simply because the majority of those who violate such a statute happen to be women'.[108] As a consequence, the distinction was considered a 'mere' distinction between the two types of offenders and under the lenient justification test applicable to such (non-sensitive) classifications it was considered justified by the goal of outlawing commercial sex.

5.4.3 *Varying Degrees of Scrutiny*

Once a claimant has established a *prima facie* claim of disparate impact, the burden of proof usually shifts to the defendant to provide a convincing justification.[109] This shift makes it significantly easier for the claimant to make an indirect discrimination claim succeed in a legal procedure.

Justification analysis is core to indirect discrimination analysis. The possibility of justification as part of indirect discrimination analysis may turn out to seriously limit its reach if justifications are easily accepted, but it is also an indispensable component of the concept of indirect discrimination. The possibility of justification is necessary, as it would be untenable to strike down any classification with a disparate effect on a group protected by discrimination law. To give some examples: requiring a high level of proficiency in Dutch for a teaching job in a Dutch school can be justified, even if it may have a disparate impact on persons with an ethnic minority background; regulating economic life and regular working hours around the prevalent days of rest (in Western societies around Sunday, in countries with a Muslim majority around Friday) can be justified, even if it may have a disparate effect on persons of a minority religion. This is not to deny, of course, that for indirect discrimination analysis to have any real 'bite', much depends on how strict this test is applied in actual legal practice.[110] In this respect, degrees of scrutiny may indeed differ significantly between jurisdictions, but also within jurisdictions, depending on several factors.

In fact, degrees of strictness in legal practice may well differ in similar ways as where a difference in treatment is directly based on a protected ground. Thus, the particular ground at stake may play a prominent role also in this setting. Regarding the European context, for example, McCrudden concludes that indirect discrimination on the basis of sex and race are treated much more

---

108 Idem, par. 18.

109 Again, in this respect the US Supreme Court developed a more restrictive approach in the case *Wards Cove Packing Co. v. Atonio*, 490 US 642 (1989).

110 Cf. Fredman, Discrimination law, 2022, p. 295–298.

strictly than religion.[111] Other factors affecting the degree of scrutiny mentioned in Chapter 4.4.2 may be equally relevant for justification review as part of indirect discrimination analysis: the area of law involved (for example, more leeway regarding social policy areas), the presence of competing rights (for example, less leeway for accommodation of religion if it interferes with gender equality) and the affected persons or group not being structurally disadvantaged, but belonging to a dominant group (for example, less strict review of measures indirectly affecting white people in South Africa).[112]

In addition, and more particular to indirect discrimination analysis compared to direct discrimination, as the link between an indirectly discriminatory, neutral rule, and a protected ground is less strong than if a rule or measure is expressly based on a protected ground, in legal practice justification review could very well turn out to be less strict in a more general sense, even if this is not visible in the structure or wording of the applicable justification test.[113]

5.5 Inherent Limitations of the Concept of Indirect Discrimination in Addressing Structural Disadvantage and Systemic Discrimination

A fundamental limit to the potential reach of the concept of indirect discrimination to address structural disadvantage and systemic discrimination is of a much more inherent nature. Application of the concept does not necessarily change the underlying dominant standards in law or society which are often responsible for disparate effects of facially neutral rules or policies on protected groups. In addition, its use in a court of law may easily find its limits in separation of powers principles.

5.5.1 *Dominant Standards in Law and Society*

Indirect discrimination analysis does not necessarily address or modify the underlying dominant standards having a detrimental effect on a protected group. For example, successfully challenging differences in treatment between

111 C. McCrudden, Indirect Religious Discrimination, 2021, p. 277.

112 According to Neumann, generally speaking the justification test may also be more easily met where horizontal relations are at stake. G. Neuman, Questions of indirect discrimination on the basis of religion, *Harvard Human Rights Journal*, 2021, p. 177–194, at p. 193.

113 As Tobler remarks, 'It is characteristic for indirect discrimination that the disadvantaged group consists not exclusively, but only predominantly, of persons who are protected by the discrimination ground in question. Accordingly, they are 'merely' disproportionately represented in the disadvantaged group.', Tobler, Indirect discrimination, report, 2022, p. 10.

part-time and full-time workers for its detrimental impact on women is in itself very important and redressing this by providing equal treatment significantly improves their position on the labour market, but this in itself will not necessarily change the underlying, gendered division of labour grounded in a breadwinner-homemaker model. A non-discrimination claim cannot in itself reach that fundamental level. As the CJEU expressly considered in the *Bilka* case: a demand of equal pay may prohibit the exclusion of part-time workers from an occupational pension scheme, but it 'does not have the effect of requiring an employer to organize its occupational pension scheme in such a manner as to take into account the particular difficulties faced by persons with family responsibilities in meeting the conditions for entitlement to such a pension'.[114]

The case law regarding educational segregation of Roma provides another example in the area of racial discrimination. Indirect discrimination analysis may unveil the structural disadvantage and systemic discrimination experienced by Roma children in the educational system, but it does not in itself undo it. Much more is needed to achieve structural and systemic change. This points to a second, inherent limitation of the use that can be made of the concept of indirect discrimination in a court of law: the division of powers between the branches of government.

5.5.2 *Division of Powers – Limits to the Role of Courts*

In indirect discrimination cases boiling down to claims of equal treatment to what another group already has (for example, equal treatment of part-time workers and full-time workers) a point of reference exists for the treatment due if the objective justification test is not met. Where such a point of reference does not exist, that is when an indirect discrimination claim regards an omission to accommodate differences, this is much more complex. As the examples of indirect discrimination cases of this type show, deciding about the treatment due is much more open-ended: how far should accommodation go, what level of accommodation is 'sufficient' to meet the objective justification test not being met? That is, where should judicial bodies draw the line, and where should they leave this matter to the other branches of Government? Similar to the problems linked to what I discussed in Chapter 3 in general terms regarding the often open-ended character of realising substantive equality, this seems a prominent feature in indirect discrimination cases. Let me illustrate the dilemma with yet another example from the Netherlands.

114 CJEU, 13 May 1986, *Bilka*, C-170/84, par. 60.

In the eighties the Dutch Unemployment Act was amended. During discussions in Parliament, concerns were raised about the discriminatory effect of the notion of 'work history', which was a central feature of the statute. The draft regulation provided that the length of time for receiving unemployment benefits would vary with the number of years a claimant would have been gainfully employed, that is with someone's work history. As Dutch women discontinue paid work much more often than men to look after children, the question was raised whether this would result in indirect discrimination. As a majority considered this to be the case, the statute was modified. In the adjusted provisions, it made room for also taking into account the time spent on taking care of children. The period spent on taking care of children under six years of age was to count in the same way as time spent in gainful employment, care taking for children between six and twelve years old would count for half. As the provisions were formulated in a sex neutral way, it included caring fathers as well as caring mothers. In this way, a significant social gender difference in labour market participation and care taking activities was incorporated in an accommodating way.[115]

But what if this care provision had not been introduced. Could the same result have been achieved by a legal procedure? This is not very likely. Of course, a Court could have applied the concept of indirect discrimination to conclude, as did the legislator in this case, that a criterion such as 'work history' has a disparate impact on women and thus raises an issue of indirect discrimination. But what should be the next step? Concluding that this criterion may not be used at all would entail far-reaching financial consequences, which even activist judicial bodies may be very hesitant to impose given division of power principles. A solution sometimes used by courts is to allow the state a certain period of time to adjust the challenged legislation. Crucially, however, lacking a clear point of reference, a court cannot design a care provision as was included in the unemployment benefit provisions by the Dutch legislator. Division of powers issues, then, are a particularly prominent feature of indirect discrimination cases dealing with claims for (reasonable) accommodation.

5.6 Concluding Remarks

Indirect discrimination has developed into a widely accepted concept with quite commonly shared, general features. It problematizes the disparate effect

115 Loenen, Verschil in gelijkheid (Difference in equality), 1992, p. 256–257.

of ostensibly neutral rules, measures or policies on a group protected by equality and non-discrimination standards as an issue of equality. If no objective justification can be put forward, such rules or policies violate equality standards.

Across jurisdictions, judicial review of indirect discrimination runs along very similar lines. With its focus on the outcome of a treatment as the trigger for an inquiry, the notion of indirect discrimination belongs to the realm of a substantive equality approach. For this reason the concept has been applauded as a potentially far-reaching instrument for addressing the structural disadvantage and systemic discrimination suffered by groups protected by equality standards, though more sceptical views regard it as not capable of doing so. With the availability of an increasingly extensive body of case law from across jurisdictions it has become apparent that both types of evaluation can be supported. Much depends on the strictness of judicial assessment of the objective justification test, which is core to indirect discrimination review. In addition, application of the concept comes with its own set of difficulties and dilemmas and usually involves – as is the case with (direct) discrimination review more generally – a wide variety of normative considerations and assessments to be made. In such a setting, different perspectives may lead to vary different outcomes, even if the overall model of indirect discrimination analysis is similar across jurisdictions.

CHAPTER 6

Lack of (Reasonable) Accommodation as a Modality of Discrimination

6.1 Introduction

Lack of (reasonable) accommodation is coming increasingly to the fore as a distinct legal concept and modality of discrimination, but it is much less crystallized than indirect discrimination. Whereas the latter has established itself as a broadly accepted, distinct concept and manifestation of discrimination with very similar general features across jurisdictions, this is not the case in respect of the former.

In this Chapter I reserve the term 'reasonable accommodation' for the specific way in which it is used in the CRPD as a form of individual accommodation due to disabled persons. To denote the more general notion of accommodation which is present in several jurisdictions, I use (reasonable) accommodation (with brackets) as a generic term.[1]

The notion of (reasonable) accommodation as part of discrimination analysis has gained considerable traction with the adoption of the CPRD in 2006, in which it occupies a prominent place.

Generalizing the definition in the CRPD beyond the particular context of disability, (reasonable) accommodation can be broadly described as appropriate modifications and adjustments to ensure persons the enjoyment or exercise on an equal basis with others of all human rights and fundamental freedoms, which can be provided without imposing a disproportionate burden.[2] Key to this notion is that it concerns *differential* treatment to redress a disadvantageous impact on people who do not fit the standard model or point of reference of rules, measures or practices.[3]

1 For further explanation of the complications regarding the use of terminology see Chapter 1.

2 The CRPD defines reasonable accommodation in Article 2 as 'necessary and appropriate modification and adjustments not imposing a disproportionate or undue burden, where needed in a particular case, to ensure to persons with disabilities the enjoyment or exercise on an equal basis with others of all human rights and fundamental freedoms'.

3 Cf. Š. Dušková, *Who should we accommodate? Opening the grounds for reasonable accommodation under the European Convention on Human Rights*, Doctoral Thesis, University of Essex, 2023, https://repository.essex.ac.uk/35695/, who identifies as key to reasonable

The CRPD has become very influential globally. The Convention is widely ratified and its approach to (reasonable) accommodation has been followed in many national jurisdictions.[4] At the same time, the particular context and focus of the notion of reasonable accommodation in the CRPD as a form of accommodation which is limited to individual adjustments and to persons with disabilities, seems to contribute to confusion about (reasonable) accommodation as a much broader concept in equality and non-discrimination law. Anyway, manifestations of notions of (reasonable) accommodation in legal practice are quite fragmented and not fully aligned. (Reasonable) accommodation is in many respects an underdeveloped concept in the legal practice of jurisdictions.

The idea that a lack of accommodation of certain individuals or groups may constitute a form of discrimination was present in legal practice before the terminology of (reasonable) accommodation was used and long before the CRPD-model of reasonable accommodation gained prominence. Examples of this were already discussed in Chapter 3 (see the *Minority Schools in Albania* case, Section 3.4.1) and in Chapter 5 (see several of the indirect discrimination cases regarding religious accommodation, in Section 5.3.4). In addition to confusion which may be attributed to the very specific articulation of reasonable accommodation in the CRPD, the lack of clarity surrounding the concept of (reasonable) accommodation is further enhanced in two ways: approaches are not always consistent even within jurisdictions, and a variety of terminology is used. Sometimes the concept of reasonable accommodation is expressly employed, but in many other instances the basic notion of what it stands for is clearly visible in the application of equality standards in legal procedures, without the terminology being utilised at all. Fitting the notion of (reasonable) accommodation within equality and non-discrimination standards does not appear easy.[5]

This chapter aims to bring some more clarity in this confusing picture. It will try to do so by first paying attention to the overarching notion which can be considered to encompass the various legal manifestations of (reasonable) accommodation (Section 6.2). In my view the best way to understand a lack of (reasonable) accommodation as a modality of discrimination is to approach it as an expression of the second limb of the Aristotelian formulation of equality: unalike cases must be treated unalike in accordance with their unalikeness.

---

accommodation 'a differential treatment to redress the unintended disadvantageous impact of structures on those who diverge from the norm', p. 117.

4 Dušková, Who should we accommodate, 2023, p. 46–50.

5 Cf. the conclusions of Dušková, Who should we accommodate, 2023, p. 198–209.

This overarching notion seems to encompass three different manifestations of (reasonable) accommodation analysis in different jurisdictions, which are addressed in the subsequent sections.

To start with, as became apparent in Chapter 5, in several jurisdictions (reasonable) accommodation appears as part of indirect discrimination review. I will briefly revisit this connection in Section 6.3, before turning to lack of (reasonable) accommodation as a distinct, *sui generis* modality of discrimination. Interestingly, in several jurisdictions an approach in terms of indirect discrimination is present simultaneously with a *sui generis* notion; apparently, Courts do not necessarily view the two ways of integrating a lack of (reasonable) accommodation into equality and non-discrimination analysis as mutually exclusive.

As a *sui generis* notion, it is important to distinguish two ways in which lack of (reasonable) accommodation has materialized in equality and non-discrimination analysis. On the one hand, it appears as a broad and general modality of discrimination, applicable to a number of protected grounds or more generally to all such grounds, and covering both individual and group-based accommodations (Section 6.4). On the other hand, the CRPD established a more particular conception of lack of reasonable accommodation as a *sui generis* form of discrimination, which is articulated in a more limited way as a specific form of individual or personalized accommodation for disabled persons (Section 6.5). As mentioned, this model is highly influential in legally shaping the notion of (reasonable) accommodation in many jurisdictions, but it does not neatly fit with the other approaches to (reasonable) accommodation discussed in Sections 6.3 and 6.4. All in all, as will become apparent, the boundaries between these three ways of approaching (reasonable) accommodation under equality and non-discrimination standards are fuzzy and may overlap.

Different approaches to how (reasonable) accommodation fits into equality and non-discrimination analysis translate into a variety of – again sometimes confusing – models for (reasonable accommodation) review in legal practice. Nevertheless, this type of review meets with several common difficulties and dilemmas which seem to be largely shared between jurisdictions and are explored in Section 6.6.

6.2 Grounding (Reasonable) Accommodation: Treating Unalike Cases Unalike in Accordance with Their Unalikeness

Conceptually, (reasonable) accommodation can be grounded in the second limb of the Aristotelian *adagium* that like cases must be treated alike, and unalike case unalike in proportion to their unalikeness.[6] It recognizes that differential treatment instead of the same treatment may sometimes be needed to achieve an equal outcome. The *Minority Schools in Albania* case of 1935 provides an early example in legal practice. As discussed in Chapter 3 (Section 3.4.1), in this case the PCIJ held that the cultural and religious minorities should be treated differently from the majority to guarantee 'genuine' equality; their right to equal treatment meant that they should be allowed to establish their own schools instead of being assimilated into the majority public school system. Chapter 3 also explained that 'treating unalike cases unalike in accordance to their unalikeness' in addition to 'treating like cases alike', is core to a substantive equality approach with its orientation on the unequal outcome of a treatment rather than being preoccupied with the sameness or difference of the treatment as such. Difference should not lead to exclusion; difference must be taken into account and be accommodated to achieve a (more) equal outcome. From this perspective, a lack of (reasonable) accommodation is an issue covered by equality and non-discrimination standards. The concept problematizes all sorts of disadvantage which may flow from the prevailing standards of reference not being geared to (members of) protected groups as equality or non-discrimination issues.

(Reasonable) accommodation is not to be confused with preferential treatment or positive discrimination, as was emphasized by the PCIJ in the *Minority Schools in Albania* case and the Canadian Supreme Court in its judgment in *Eldridge*.[7] Another illustrative example of the importance of this conceptual distinction can be derived from the case law of the US Supreme Court. As this Court is well known for its critical stance towards affirmative action, it is all the more telling that it clearly identifies reasonable accommodation as a very different concept. The Court holds that preferences in the form of reasonable accommodation as required by the Americans with Disabilities Act are not to be equated with preferential treatment as such, despite the treatment due indeed being 'special' and 'different':

6 Cf. C. McCrudden and S. Prechal, *The Concepts of Equality and Non-discrimination in Europe: A Practical Approach* (Report European Network of experts in the field of gender equality), 2009, p. 30. As Henrard puts it: 'Duties of reasonable accommodation fit the scheme of duties of differential treatment perfectly', see K. Henrard, Duties of reasonable accommodation in relation to religion and the European Court of Human Rights, *Erasmus Law Review*, 2012, p. 59–77, at p. 68.

7 See Chapter 3, Section 3.4.1.

> The Act requires preferences in the form of "reasonable accommodations" that are needed for those with disabilities to obtain the *same* workplace opportunities that those without disabilities automatically enjoy [emphasis in original text]. By definition any special "accommodation" requires the employer to treat an employee with a disability differently, i.e., preferentially. And the fact that the difference in treatment violates an employer's disability-neutral rule cannot by itself place the accommodation beyond the Act's potential reach. Were that not so, the "reasonable accommodation" provision could not accomplish its intended objective.[8]

As will be further explored in Chapter 7, positive discrimination or positive action may also be perceived as a manifestation of 'treating unalike cases unalike in accordance with their unalikeness', but is to be distinguished from (reasonable) accommodation by being about *temporary* measures, which have the express purpose to *undo* or at least reduce the difference or 'unalikeness' itself. Thus, establishing quota for women or minorities in politics is directed at achieving more equal representation of these groups. Once this is achieved, such measures are no longer necessary.

6.2.1 *Levels and Types of Accommodation*

It is useful to distinguish different levels and types of accommodation. As will become apparent in Section 6.5, this distinction is of particular importance under the CRPD.

First of all, individual or personalized accommodation caters for the particular needs of an individual person in need of accommodation. Many examples can be given: providing an employee in a wheelchair with an adjusted desk, temporarily relocating a pregnant woman to another position if her job poses potential risks to her unborn child,[9] or exempting *Thlimmenos* from the condition of not having a criminal record to become a registered accountant.[10]

Accommodation can also be provided at a group-based or collective level and thus be directed at accommodation of difference of a more structural nature. For example, arranging for an exemption for all Sikh persons wearing a turban from being obliged to wear a helmet on a motorbike or at a construction site; providing a building with ramps that make it accessible to anyone

8 US Supreme Court, *Airways v. Barnett*, 535 US 391 (2002), par. 397.

9 This example from Canadian case law is mentioned in Dušková, Who should we accommodate, 2023, p. 54.

10 ECtHR (Grand Chamber), 6 April 2000, *Thlimmenos v. Greece*, appl. no. 34369/97.

using a wheelchair; providing pregnancy and maternity leave for all workers to ensure women can combine paid work and having a child. Providing civil partnership for same-sex couples to legally arrange their relationship.

A third, more systemic level of accommodation regards changing the dominant standards which are responsible for the disadvantage suffered by those who do not fit those standards. Accommodation of this kind makes the standards as such more inclusive. In the context of disability, the CRPD uses the term 'universal design' (Article 2 CRPD). If buildings, trains or buses are designed from the start with disabled people in mind, they will be accessible to wheelchair users and make differential treatment for this group redundant. Similarly, taking the combination of paid work and care as the starting point in employment law instead of the breadwinner-homemaker model will make it easier for mothers and all other parents to share family responsibilities with gainful employment. Adopting a wide notion of 'the family' in family or personal law, including non-traditional families, allows for including same-sex couples in marriage law, instead of creating a separate accommodation through a civil partnership regime.

The above levels and types of accommodation cannot be separated into watertight compartments. As the examples show, they are often matters of degree and the boundaries between them can be very fuzzy. Providing a ramp for an individual worker in a wheelchair may benefit a much wider group of disabled persons; similarly, providing an individual exemption for a Sikh person to wear a helmet at a construction site easily becomes a collective arrangement if a large number of Sikh workers is employed.[11] The latter example also illustrates that changing the dominant standard itself (allowing everyone to refrain from the wearing of a safety helmet) is not by definition always the best solution.

Indeed, the examples also show that the particular types of accommodation can come in a wide variety of ways: as exemptions to a rule, measure or policy; as an adjustment regarding a factual situation; as a more structural adaptation of rules, policies or a factual situation; or as an even more systemic change of the underlying dominant standards themselves, which makes them more inclusive as such. What is in fact needed or possible to accommodate difference to achieve a (more) equal outcome is thus highly context specific.

In different jurisdictions different ways exist to link an obligation to provide one or more of the various levels and types of accommodation sketched above to equality and non-discrimination standards.

---

11 Cf. Henrard, Duties of reasonable accommodation, 2012, p. 64.

6.3 Lack of Accommodation as a Form of Indirect Discrimination

In Chapter 5 (Section 5.3.5) some clear links between the concepts of (reasonable) accommodation and indirect discrimination have become visible. Lack of (reasonable) accommodation and indirect discrimination are partly overlapping modalities of discrimination. This is due to the overall focus of both concepts on the outcome of a treatment, regardless it being seemingly neutral.[12]

Cases such as *Pillay* and the other cases discussed regarding indirect discrimination on the basis of religion show how, in several jurisdictions, a disparate impact on a protected group or an individual member of such a group becomes questioned as a potential case of discrimination. If the disparate impact results from insufficient accommodation, the treatment will not be considered to pass the objective justification test under indirect discrimination analysis. In this way, application of the latter concept may include the former.

Disparate effects as the shared trigger for both indirect discrimination and (reasonable) accommodation review is expressly acknowledged in Canadian jurisprudence. The Canadian Supreme Court is very explicit in approaching a duty of accommodation as part and parcel of indirect discrimination analysis under the Constitutional equality standards. According to this Court, it does not matter whether the disproportionate impact flows from a law which includes 'seemingly neutral rules, restrictions or criteria that operate in practice as "built-in headwinds" for members of a protected group',[13] or from 'the *absence* of accommodation for members of a protected group' [emphasis in original text].[14]

At this point it may be interesting to note that, in addition to being included under the notion of indirect discrimination, a duty of (reasonable) accommodation has occasionally been identified as part of direct discrimination analysis in the context of pregnancy and maternity. Conceptually this makes sense if discrimination on the basis of pregnancy/maternity is approached as direct discrimination on grounds of sex or discrimination in its own right. Thus, in

---

12 Cf. E. Bribosia and I. Rorive, *Reasonable accommodation beyond disability in Europe?* Report European Network of legal experts in the non-discrimination field, 2013, p. 5.

13 Supreme Court of Canada, *Fraser v. Canada* [2020] 3 SCR 113, par. 53 (pointing to the US *Griggs*-case as a good example, US Supreme Court, *Griggs v. Duke Power Co*, 401 US 424 (1971).

14 Supreme Court of Canada, *Fraser v. Canada* [2020] 3 SCR 113, par. 54, emphasis in original text, referring to the case *Eldridge* as a good example, Supreme Court of Canada, *Eldridge v. British Columbia* [1997] 3 SCR 624.

the US claims for accommodation of needs attached to pregnancy, for example adjusted break or work schedules, can be based on the prohibition of discrimination under the Pregnancy Discrimination Act.[15] Similarly, a lack of proper accommodation of the needs of breastfeeding workers can be challenged as an instance of direct sex discrimination under EU Directive 2006/54.[16] Of course, regulating these types of accommodation in more detail in specific statutory law renders claims under non-discrimination provisions redundant.

The selection of indirect discrimination cases explored in Chapter 5, Section 5.3.5 shows that the overlap between indirect discrimination analysis and lack of (reasonable) accommodation is partial; many cases of indirect discrimination are not about a lack of accommodation. Conceptually, a duty of (reasonable) accommodation stands out in its own right because it concerns an obligation of differential treatment, of treating unalike cases unalike in accordance with their unalikeness. It is this particular element of a substantive approach to equality which is in several jurisdictions coming more prominently to the fore as a distinct concept and modality of discrimination analysis in its own right, that is as a *sui generis* form of discrimination. In this respect, two varieties of this approach merit attention. An approach which regards lack of (reasonable) accommodation as a *general, sui generis* modality of discrimination, and an approach which regards it as a much more *particular, sui generis* form of discrimination, limited to individual accommodation in the context of disability (the CRPD-model).

6.4 Lack of Accommodation as a General, *sui generis* Modality of Discrimination

In the seventies and eighties of the past century, lack of (reasonable) accommodation as a general and distinct, *sui generis* modality of discrimination started to appear in several jurisdictions in the context of prohibitions of discrimination on grounds of religion and was subsequently applied to other grounds. In this type of setting the terminology of 'reasonable accommodation' became more often used.[17] This general approach to lack of (reasonable)

15 See for an overview of the protection afforded by this Act in terms of accommodation 'Legal rights of pregnant workers under Federal Law' on the website of the US Equal Employment Opportunities Commission, https://www.eeoc.gov/laws/guidance/legal-rights-pregnant-workers-under-federal-law.

16 CJEU, 19 October 2017, *Otero Ramos*, C-531/15, par. 63.

17 For an overview of this development see Dušková, Who should we accommodate, 2023, Chapter 2.

accommodation as a distinct modality of discrimination emerged first of all in the USA and in Canada. It seems most broadly developed so far in the context of the ECHR, but has also been taken on board by the South African Constitutional Court as part of its expressly substantive understanding of equality. As each of these jurisdictions show some interesting varieties in their approach to (reasonable) accommodation, they merit separate attention.

6.4.1 *(Reasonable) Accommodation in the USA and Canada*

6.4.1.1 The United States

In 1977, the US Supreme Court first interpreted the prohibition of discrimination in Title VII of the Civil Rights Act to include an obligation for employers to provide reasonable accommodation regarding religious expressions of their employees, unless this would pose an 'undue hardship'.[18] This obligation 'to reasonably accommodate' all aspects of religious observance and practice of an employee's or prospective employee's religion was subsequently incorporated expressly into Title VII, including the condition it would not impose an 'undue hardship' on the employer. The latter is for the employer to establish.[19] The review test for what would constitute 'undue hardship' was formulated rather leniently for the employer. The obligation to provide reasonable accommodation applies if it does not require more than 'a *de minimus* cost'.[20]

Subsequent case law extended an obligation of reasonable accommodation to disabled persons in several particular areas before being incorporated more broadly in the Americans with Disabilities Act of 1990. This Act covers private employers, schools, transportation and other areas of public life, including the provision of services.[21] It defines denial of reasonable accommodation as a distinct form of discrimination and replaced the 'undue hardship' criterion applicable to religious accommodation by a more stringent condition. The obligation to provide reasonable accommodation is present unless this would impose a 'significant difficulty or expense'. According to Dušková, this higher standard of review was deliberately chosen because of the particular importance attached to the inclusion of disabled persons in economic life.[22]

18 US Supreme Court, *Trans World Airlines v. Hardison*, 432 US 63 (1977).

19 Section 701(j) and 703(a)1 of Title VII of the Civil Rights Act.

20 US Supreme Court, *Trans World Airlines v. Hardison*, 432 US 63 (1977), par. 84.

21 Dušková, Who should we accommodate, 2023, p. 40.

22 Accommodation will bring significant costs, but may also create economic benefits if disabled persons are included in the workforce, Dušková, Who should we accommodate, 2023, p. 41–42. For a more detailed overview of developments in the US regarding accommodation of pregnancy related needs and religious practices see W.R. Corbett, Reasonably accommodating employment discrimination law, *Penn State Law Review* 2024, p. 535–568.

As already mentioned in Chapter 5, Section 5.3.4, in several jurisdictions an obligation to provide religious accommodation may also be derived from the constitutional protection of freedom of religion, showing its overlap with non-discrimination review. In both instances, the limits of the obligation to accommodate religious expressions depend on some form of justification test, but under constitutional review this test is usually much more open and not formulated in terms of 'undue hardship'. As the constitutional provisions have a much broader reach than statutory non-discrimination law regulating reasonable accommodation in particular areas and for particular groups, this need not be surprising.[23]

6.4.1.2 Canada

Canada also embraced the notion of reasonable accommodation as part of the general norm of non-discrimination first of all regarding religion.[24] In 1985, in a case involving application of the Ontario Human Rights Code, the Canadian Supreme Court had to decide whether the refusal of an employer to accommodate the wish of an employee not to be required to work on Saturdays for religious reasons amounted to discrimination. The Court concluded that this was indeed at hand. Approaching the case as an issue of 'adverse effect discrimination', it held that the adverse impact of the requirement on the employee could have been reasonably resolved by providing the accommodation asked for. As the Court considered in more general terms:

> In a case of adverse effect discrimination, the employer has a duty to take reasonable steps to accommodate short of undue hardship in the operation of the employer's business.[25]

This approach ties in with the general, substantive reading of equality taken in the first case dealing with the equality standards included in Section 15 of the Canadian Charter of Fundamental Rights and Freedoms, *Andrews v. Law Society of British Columbia*. In this case the Supreme Court of Canada considered in very general yet principled terms that these standards may also include an obligation to accommodate difference by treating people differently:

---

23 This also means there is more room for balancing all interests involved, Dušková, Who should we accommodate, 2023, p. 34.

24 L.B. Waddington, Reasonable accommodation – time to extend the duty to accommodate beyond disability? *Nederlands Tijdschrift voor de Mensenrechten*, 2011, p. 186–198, p. 189.

25 Supreme Court of Canada, *Ontario Human Rights Commission v. Simpson-Sears* [1985] 2 SCR 536, at p. 537.

> (…) for the accommodation of differences, *which is the essence of true equality*, it will be frequently necessary to make distinctions [emphasis added].[26]

So as already remarked in Chapter 5 (Section 5.2.1) in the context of indirect discrimination analysis, the Canadian Supreme Court regards the various modalities of discrimination – be it direct or indirect discrimination, or lack of (reasonable) accommodation – as being part and parcel of a single overarching notion of equality and non-discrimination, which takes the disadvantageous *effect* of a treatment as the starting point for discrimination review.[27] As a result, lack of (reasonable) accommodation can be submitted to scrutiny under general equality standards as included in the Charter of Fundamental Rights and Freedoms. The *Eldridge* case regarding reasonable accommodation of a deaf patient, discussed in Chapter 5, Section 5.4.1) is a case in point. Interestingly, as Dušková notes, in addition to linking (reasonable) accommodation to cases of indirect discrimination, a duty of accommodation has sometimes also been read into cases that could otherwise be regarded as constituting direct discrimination. Thus, for instance, the Canadian Supreme Court held that accommodation was required for a pregnant woman whose work posed risks for her unborn child by adjusting her duties.[28] If reasonable accommodation is an integral part of discrimination analysis, this is a logical conceptual corollary.

Under statutory law, in 1998 an obligation to provide reasonable accommodation – unless it imposes undue hardship – was expressly included in the Canadian Human Rights Act. It covers all grounds protected by this Act, which include race, national or ethnic origin, colour, religion, age, sex, sexual orientation, gender identity or expression, marital status, family status, genetic characteristics and disability.[29] This type of regulation provides a firm stamp of approval by the legislature of judicial interpretation of equality standards.

26 Supreme Court of Canada, *Andrews v. Law Society of British Columbia* [1989] 1 SCR 143, p. 169.

27 This is referred to as a 'unified' approach to non-discrimination, see Waddington, Reasonable accommodation 2011, p. 189 and Dušková, Who should we accommodate, 2023, p. 52.

28 Dušková, Who should we accommodate, 2023, p. 54. Waddington and Hendriks also noted this already in 2002 in relation to the EU context, see L. Waddington and A. Hendriks, The expanding concept of employment discrimination in Europe: from direct and indirect discrimination to reasonable accommodation discrimination, *International Journal of Comparative Labour Law and Industrial Relations*, 2002, p. 403–427, at p. 424.

29 Section 2 Human Rights Act; an additional, more unusual ground included is 'conviction for an offence for which a pardon has been granted or in respect of which a record suspension has been ordered'.

6.4.2 *(Reasonable) Accommodation and 'Treating Unalike Cases Unalike' in the Case Law of the European Court of Human Rights*

Tracing the development of the notion of (reasonable) accommodation in the jurisprudence of the ECtHR, Dušková shows how the Court grappled with this notion and how it has endeavoured to incrementally integrate it into its case law. If anything, her analysis shows that the jurisprudence of the Court regarding this concept has not crystallized yet into a clear and consistent approach and is often quite confusing.[30]

Interestingly, Dušková's analysis points to three distinct ways in which (reasonable) accommodation figures in the Court's case law. Firstly, before the Court explicitly tied a duty of accommodation to the prohibition of discrimination in *Thlimmenos*, such a duty was sometimes already implicitly present in judgments assessing the violation of other fundamental rights, such as Article 8 (the right to private and family life) and Article 9 (the right to freedom of religion). Secondly, the notion of (reasonable) accommodation as a distinct form of discrimination was developed by the Court under Article 14 ECHR, *Thlimmenos* representing the first landmark case.[31] In this context, the Court approaches the notion in a general way as a demand to treat unalike cases unalike, which implies it is (potentially) applicable to all protected grounds of discrimination. The first and second way of addressing (reasonable) accommodation still run parallel in the case law of the Court. A third distinct way in which duties of accommodation have come to figure in the case law of the Court regards disability. In this context the Court has started to reference the CRPD as a leading model for approaching accommodation of disabled people. In doing so, the Court has linked this approach to its broader notion of accommodation as part of discrimination review (that is to the second way identified above). So far, the Court reserves the specific terminology of 'reasonable accommodation' to cases regarding disability.[32]

---

30 Dušková, Who should we accommodate, 2023.The often muddled character of the case law is a recurring theme in her book.

31 In some cases the Court also used Article 1 Protocol no. 12, which provides for a non-accessory right to non-discrimination. So far, this protocol is only ratified by a minority of states parties to the ECHR.

32 Dušková, Who should we accommodate, 2023, p. 150.

6.4.2.1 Lack of Differential Treatment or Accommodation as a (Potential) Violation of Human Rights Other Than the Prohibition of Discrimination

Similar to the way in which (reasonable) accommodation of religion has come to figure in the US and Canadian context as part of an inquiry regarding the right to freedom of religion, the ECtHR and its predecessor, the European Commission on Human Rights, have dealt with this type of issue under Article 9 ECHR.

In this line of cases, a lack of accommodation of religious observance or practices may constitute a violation of the freedom of religion. If a rule or measure interferes with the freedom of religion, the question is raised whether it can be justified under the applicable limitation clause. Central to this analysis is the proportionality between the aims pursued and the means chosen.[33] In this appraisal, the possibilities of providing accommodation may be part of the balancing exercise: if accommodation could have prevented the interference without constituting a disproportionate burden, the proportionality test is not met.[34]

Examples of cases in which complaints about lack of (reasonable) accommodation were brought to the Strasbourg bodies under Article 9 ECHR show they may regard a wide variety of issues. They include claims by Sikh persons to be exempted from the obligation to wear a helmet or the obligation to remove their turban for purposes of a security check;[35] claims to have adjusted working hours to be able to comply with religious observance or practice;[36] and a claim by a marriage official to be exempted from the duty to officiate same-sex marriage or civil partnership for reasons of conscientious objection.[37] Though such claims are not discussed by the Strasbourg bodies in terms of (reasonable) accommodation (and in the examples mentioned the lack of exemption or adjustments asked for were not held to violate Article 9 ECHR), the underlying issues are clearly about claims of (reasonable) accommodation.

---

33 Cf. Henrard, Duties of reasonable accommodation, 2012, p. 74–75.

34 Cf. Dušková, Who should we accommodate, 2023, p. 82.

35 EComHR, 12 July 1978, *X. v. United Kingdom*, appl. no. 7992/77 for exemption to wear a helmet on a motorbike; ECtHR, 11 January 2005, *Phull v. France*, appl. no. 35753/03 for removal of a turban for a security check.

36 EComHR, 12 March 1981, *X. v. United Kingdom*, appl. no. 8160/78 and EComHR, 3 December 1996, *Konttinen v Finland*, appl. no. 24949/94.

37 ECtHR, ECtHR, 15 January 2013, *Eweida and others v. the United Kingdom*, appl. nos. 48420/10, 59842/10, 51671/10 and 36516/10.

Several other types of cases can be identified as dealing *de facto* with claims of (reasonable) accommodation under general human rights review rather than non-discrimination standards. These regard, among others, claims for accommodation of transgender persons in view of Article 8 ECHR by being registered differently than others, that is according to their actual gender, rather than the sex assigned to them at birth;[38] claims of accommodation of the specific housing needs and way of living of Roma, also in view of Article 8 ECHR, by being allowed to stay on sites where they had settled in violation of the applicable regulations;[39] and claims of accommodation of persons with disabilities, again on the basis of Article 8 ECHR, by being provided with wheelchair accessibility of private beaches or of public buildings.[40] As my focus in this study is on duties of (reasonable) accommodation as part of equality and non-discrimination standards, I do not explore this way of addressing accommodation issues in the case law of the ECtHR any further.[41]

6.4.2.2 Lack of Differential Treatment or Accommodation as a General, *sui generis* Form of Discrimination Covering All Protected Grounds

As mentioned before, though it did not use the terminology of accommodation as such, in *Thlimmenos* the Court for the first time linked the prohibition of discrimination articulated in Article 14 ECHR to a *de facto* duty of (reasonable) accommodation, when it held in very express terms that discrimination may also occur if '[s]tates without providing an objective and reasonable justification fail to treat differently persons whose situations are significantly

38 Dušková, Who should we accommodate, 2023, p. 119–121, discussing several trans rights cases.

39 Dušková, Who should we accommodate, 2023, p. 147–148, discussing the cases ECtHR, 24 April 2012, *Yordanova and others v. Bulgaria*, appl. no. 25446/06 and ECtHR, 17 October 2013, *Winterstein and others v. France*, appl. no. 27013/07.

40 K. Henrard, Duties of reasonable accommodation on grounds of religion in the jurisprudence of the European Court of Human Rights: A tale of (baby) steps forward and missed opportunities, *International Journal of Constitutional Law* (I·CON), 2016, p. 961–98, at p. 968, discussing the cases ECtHR, 24 February 1998, *Botta v. Italy*, appl. no. 21439/93 and ECtHR, 14 May 2002, *Zehnalova and Zehnal v. Czech Republic*, appl. no. 38621/97.

41 For the same reason I do not explore other types of general legal obligations which may include duties for an employer to accommodate the needs of workers. In the Netherlands, for instance, employers are bound by duties of 'good employership' towards their employees. See for a brief discussion of such obligations to accommodate the needs of workers more generally Waddington and Hendriks, The expanding concept of employment discrimination, 20112002, p. 416–417.

different'.[42] For *Thlimmenos* this meant that Greece had to make an exception on his behalf to the applicable regulations, so he could become a registered accountant even if he had a criminal record.

So far, the ECtHR has availed itself explicitly of this line of thinking beyond the sphere of religious accommodation in several other cases worth mentioning here. They cover claims of discrimination on the basis of sexual orientation, sex or gender, disability and language. As the reasoning of the Court regarding the conceptual scope of the right not to be discriminated against by a lack of differential treatment is principled and of a general character, it could be applied to any other protected ground.

The Court's approach to this modality of discrimination is nicely recapitulated in *Adám and others v. Romania*.[43] In this case students belonging to the Hungarian minority in Romania complained, among others, about the language in which they had to sit some of their exams. Though they had the opportunity to have their education in their native language, they had to take additional exams on Romanian language and literature, which made it more difficult for them to obtain their diploma.

The Court approaches this complaint as a potential violation of the prohibition of discrimination in terms of an unjustified failure 'to treat differently persons whose situations are significantly different'.[44] In its recapitulation of the applicable principles, the Court provides an overview of its review standards regarding this modality of discrimination and of the grounds of discrimination to which it has been applied in the Court's case law.[45]

As a failure 'to treat differently situated persons differently' may amount to discrimination, Article 14 entails a positive obligation for the State 'to make necessary distinctions between persons or groups whose circumstances are relevantly and significantly different'.[46] Regarding the latter a 'certain threshold' must be reached, which the Court subsequently formulates as the requirement that the measure at stake 'must produce a *particularly prejudicial impact* on certain persons as a result of a protected ground' [emphasis added].[47]

---

42 ECtHR, *Thlimmenos*, 2000, par. 44.

43 ECtHR, 13 October 2020, *Adám and others v. Romania*, appl. nos. 8114/17 and five others.

44 ECtHR, *Adám and others*, par. 87.

45 The case was reviewed under non-discrimination provisions included in Article 1 of Protocol No. 12, which have a broader scope than Article 14 ECHR, but as the Court holds, the meaning and scope of the notion of 'discrimination' are the same. ECtHR, *Adám and others*, 2020, par. 82.

46 ECtHR, *Adám and others*, 2020, par. 87.

47 ECtHR, *Adám and others*, 2020, par. 87.

In addition to references to its Grand Chamber judgment in *Thlimmenos* covering discrimination on the basis of religion, the Court refers to several cases dealing with other protected grounds: the cases *J.D. and A. v. UK* and *Taddeuci and McCall v. Italy*.[48]

J.D. and A. v. UK concerned two claims of discrimination, one on the basis of gender,[49] and one on the basis of disability, deriving from the same housing benefits scheme.[50] The scheme provided for a generally applicable reduction in housing benefits to stimulate tenants with 'extra' bedrooms to leave their homes for smaller ones. The reduction was challenged by a female tenant who lived in a home included in a 'sanctuary scheme' designed to provide protection against the risk of serious domestic violence and by a tenant whose home had been specifically adapted to the needs of her severely disabled child. Both claimed an exception should be made for them in view of their particular need to be able to stay in their specifically adapted homes. The Court acknowledges that they are indeed in a 'significantly different' situation and 'particularly prejudiced' by the policy.[51] Turning to the question whether the policy is nevertheless objectively and reasonably justified, the Court considers that, given the protected grounds of gender and disability being involved, only 'very weighty reasons' can provide a justification.[52] After balancing all the interests at stake it holds in favour of the female tenant faced with the risk of violence, but not of the tenant with the disabled child.[53]

Taddeuci and McCall v. Italy concerned a claim of discrimination on the basis of sexual orientation.[54] The applicants were a same-sex couple who wished to live in Italy. One was Italian, the other a non-EU national. They challenged the Italian rules applicable to obtaining a residence permit for family reasons. They could not comply with the conditions for obtaining a permit, as this was only possible for a 'spouse' recognized as such under Italian law. The latter was only accessible for heterosexual married couples. Though this requirement was also applicable to unmarried heterosexual couples, the Court considered that Tadeucci and McCall were in a significantly different

48 ECtHR, *Adám and others*, 2020, par. 88.

49 Gender is the terminology used in this judgment itself, not sex discrimination.

50 ECtHR, 24 October 2019, *J.D. and A v. the United Kingdom*, appl. nos. 32949/17 and 34614/17.

51 ECtHR, *J.D. and A.*, 2019, par. 92.

52 Idem, par. 97.

53 Regarding the latter, the Court considers that the difficulties attached to moving could be mitigated by other applicable policy measures, whereas this would not be a solution for the tenant facing the risk of domestic violence. ECtHR, *J.D. and A.*, 2020, par. 101–105.

54 ECtHR, 30 June 2016, *Taddeucci and McCall v. Italy*, appl. no. 51362/09.

situation, as contrary to unmarried heterosexual couples, under the applicable rules they could not get married in Italy to obtain the required status of 'spouse'.[55] As Italy could not provide an objective and reasonable justification for this arrangement, the Court held that Article 14 in conjunction with Article 8 ECHR was violated by failing to treat them differently from heterosexual unmarried couples.[56]

After referencing this guiding case law, the ECtHR applies the principle that 'significantly different situations' have to be treated differently to the complaints raised in *Adám and others*, but its conclusion is not in favour of the complainants. The Court accepts the aim of the policy as designed to provide education in the minority language while at the same time ensuring sufficient knowledge of the official language. It regards the way in which the authorities test that knowledge to fall within their margin of appreciation. The Court also considers that the additional exams are the consequence of the voluntary choice of the students to study in their native language rather than the official language and do not impose an excessive burden on the applicants. It also considers that nothing in the case shows that they were deprived in practice of this real choice or that the authorities had the intention to forcefully assimilate the Hungarian minority.[57] In conclusion, the Court considers that the Romanian policy 'did not place them in a different situation that was sufficiently significant' for the purposes of applying the Convention standards regarding non-discrimination.[58] As a result, the Court considers it is not necessary to assess the justification provide by the state.[59]

6.4.2.3 Overlap with Indirect Discrimination

Even if the Court identifies in the cases discussed an unjustified lack of differential treatment as a distinct form of discrimination, the Court seems to simultaneously perceive it as closely related to or overlapping with the concept of indirect discrimination. This becomes apparent by taking a closer look at its consideration in *J.D. and A.* Before investigating whether there has been a discriminatory failure to make a distinction on behalf of the applicants, the Court considers that the issues raised in the case are about indirect discrimination:

55 Idem, par. 85.
56 Idem, par. 96.
57 ECtHR, *Adám and others*, 2020, par. 99–106.
58 Idem, par. 107.
59 Idem, par. 107.

> In the present case, the applicants have been treated in the same way as other recipients of the Housing Benefit (…) Thus, the issue arising in this case is one of alleged indirect discrimination.[60]

A close parallel with indirect discrimination analysis is also visible in the way in which the requirement of a 'significant difference' being present is to be measured. Demanding that the challenged measure produces 'a particularly prejudicial impact' seems very similar to the 'disproportionately prejudicial effects' identified in *D.H. v. the Czech Republic* as the trigger for reviewing alleged indirect discrimination.[61] Similar to what was discussed in Chapter 5 (Section 5.3.5), this shows that lack of differential treatment as a form of discrimination and indirect discrimination are overlapping concepts.

6.4.2.4 Reasonable Accommodation of Disabled People as Part of Discrimination Review: Connecting to the CRPD-Model

The ECtHR has developed a considerable body of case law on disability issues, including implied accommodation claims, using the two approaches discussed above to answer the question whether a lack of such accommodation violates the ECHR.[62] With the CRPD gaining increasing prominence, the ECtHR has started to connect its broad approach to a duty to accommodate as part of discrimination analysis – in Strasbourg terminology a positive obligation to treat significantly different cases differently – explicitly to the CRPD-model of reasonable accommodation.[63] In doing so, it reserves the specific terminology of 'reasonable accommodation' to disability cases, whereas in cases covering other protected groups it adheres to the terminology developed in *Thlimmenos*.[64]

The case *Arnar Helgi Lárusson v. Iceland* of 2022 is a good example of how the ECtHR connects the CRPD-model with the ECHR and tries to integrate the former into the latter.[65] At issue was a complaint by a wheelchair user about a lack of access to two local public buildings with a social and cultural function.

---

60 ECtHR, *J.D. and A.*, 2019, par. 90.

61 ECtHR (Grand Chamber), 13 November 2007, *D.H. and others v. the Czech Republic*, appl. no. 57325/00, par. 175.

62 For a comprehensive overview of its disability case law see *Factsheet – Persons with disabilities* on the Court's website.

63 According to Dušková, the Court expressly connected a duty of reasonable accommodation (using this particular terminology) to an obligation to treat different situations differently for the first time in ECtHR, 23 February 2016, *Çam v. Turkey*, appl. no. 51500/08. Dušková, Who should we accommodate, 2023, p. 149.

64 Dušková, Who should we accommodate, 2023, p. 150.

65 ECtHR, 31 May 2022, *Arnar Helgi Lárusson v. Iceland*, appl. no. 23077/19.

In its judgment the Court first refers to its general approach to the notion of discrimination as including both 'treating differently, without an objective and reasonable justification, people in relevantly similar situations' and 'without an objective and reasonable justification, fail[ing] to treat differently people whose situations are significantly different'.[66]

The Court subsequently considers that the ECHR 'should, as far as possible, be interpreted in harmony with other rules of international law of which it forms part' and refers to the CRPD standards, including the interpretation and elaboration of these standards by the CRPD-Committee in General Comments No. 2 and No. 6 (see Section 6.5 below for further elaboration of the CRPD-standards).[67] In this context the Court notes that under the CRPD issues of accommodation and accessibility 'should be viewed within the context of discrimination'.[68]

Turning back to its own jurisprudence, the Court emphasizes that the States 'enjoy a certain margin of appreciation in assessing whether and to what extent differences in otherwise similar situations justify different treatment' and that this margin is usually wide when general measures of economic or social strategy are involved.[69] The Court considers that 'a similarly wide margin 'should be afforded to the State when a claim is made concerning a lack of access to public buildings within the context of the right to respect for private and family life'.[70]

Looking once more to the CRPD, to live up to the need of a harmonious interpretation of the ECHR and the CRPD, the Court considers that Article 14 ECHR

> has to be read in the light of the requirements of those texts regarding "reasonable accommodation" – understood as "necessary and appropriate modification and adjustments not imposing a disproportionate or undue burden, where needed in a particular case (...) Such reasonable accommodation helps to correct factual inequalities which are unjustified and which therefore amount to discrimination.[71]

According to the Court, these considerations apply equally to the participation of people with disabilities in social and cultural life.[72]

66 ECtHR, *Arnar Helgi Lárusson*, 2022, par. 55 and 56.
67 ECtHR, 31 May 2022, *Arnar Helgi Lárusson*, 2022, par. 57.
68 Idem, par. 57.
69 Idem, par. 58.
70 Idem, par. 58.
71 Idem, par. 59.
72 Idem, par. 59.

Applying these general principles to the case at hand the Court concludes that the lack of access to the buildings does not amount to 'a discriminatory failure by the respondent State to take sufficient measures'.[73] In this regard the Courts considers that the municipal authorities demonstrated a general commitment to improve gradual access, but had decided for the time being to prioritize accessibility to educational and sports facilities over cultural facilities.[74] For these reasons, the Court holds that imposing a duty on the State to adopt further measures

> would have amounted to imposing a "disproportionate or undue burden" on it within the context of its positive obligations, as established by the Court's case-law (...), to reasonably accommodate the applicant.[75]

The way in which the Court comes to its conclusion clearly shows how the Court tries to combine the CRPD-model of approaching a denial of reasonable accommodation as a distinct form of discrimination with its own model of regarding a lack of different treatment of significantly different situations as a violation of Article 14 ECHR. The case also shows how the inquiry into the presence of an objective and reasonable justification is central and boils down to an evaluation of proportionality.

At the same time, the Court does not fully align its approach to reasonable accommodation with the CRPD. As will be elaborated in Section 6.5, whereas the CRPD makes an important distinction between 'reasonable accommodation' as an individual or personalized accommodation, and 'accessibility' as a collective, group-focused form of accommodation, the ECtHR puts the two in the same basket.[76] In fact, the case law of the Court shows how the lines between individual and collective accommodation are quite thin and fuzzy and may well be a matter of the actual number of persons benefitting from a particular form of accommodation rather than a matter of principled difference. The case *Toplak and Mrak v. Slovenia* may serve as an example.[77]

This case concerned a complaint of insufficient accommodation of disabled persons with muscular dystrophy regarding the right to vote. It was part of a line of cases brought to Slovenian courts in order to improve access to the

---

73 Idem, par. 63.
74 Idem, par. 63.
75 Idem, par. 63.
76 This is indeed a major part of the criticism of Broderick regarding this judgment, A. Broderick, *Arnar Helgi Lárusson v. Iceland: muddying the waters on inaccessibility of public buildings*, Blog Strasbourg Observers, 30 August 2022.
77 ECtHR, 26 October 2021, *Toplak and Mrak v. Slovenia*, appl. no. 34591/19 and 42545/19.

voting process.[78] For my purpose here, the particularly relevant aspect of this case concerned the inability of one of the complainants to hold a pen, so he would not be able to personally mark his ballot paper. The accommodation offered by the local electoral body consisted of being allowed to bring along a personal assistant of his own choice. As this would jeopardize the secrecy of his vote, the complainant did not accept this solution and instead required the installation of a voting machine.

It seems evident that contrary to the provision of a personal assistant, the latter is not an individual form of accommodation – it lies much more in the realm of 'accessibility' as distinguished under the CRPD from 'reasonable accommodation'. Nevertheless, the Court reviews both forms of accommodation in the same way under the Convention's non-discrimination standards to decide whether there is, without an objective and reasonable justification, a failure to treat people in a significantly different situation differently. The Court considers that installing a voting machine would involve considerable financial investments, that their operation poses potential problems of its own for guaranteeing the secrecy of the vote, and that they are not widely available in the member states.[79] For these reasons, and because accommodation of people with disabilities may take a variety of forms, the Court holds that the decision to use voting machines or not 'is to be made primarily by the national authorities'.[80] Given the other options available, especially the possibility of being assisted by a person of his own choice, Slovenia 'could not be said to have failed to strike a fair balance between the protection of the interests of the community and respect for the first applicant's rights and freedoms, as safeguarded by the Convention.[81]

All in all, then, the ECtHR connects its own broad approach regarding non-discrimination as including an obligation to accommodate 'significantly different situations' to the specific articulation of the duty of reasonable accommodation in the CRPD, without fully following the CRPD-model.

6.4.3 *South Africa*

What stands out in South African jurisprudence is the principled substantive approach to equality and non-discrimination standards as core to the overall constitutional goal of undoing structural and systemic disadvantage. This translates into the Constitutional Court's conceptualization of (reasonable)

78 Idem, par. 6.
79 Idem, par. 128.
80 Idem, par. 129.
81 Idem, par. 131.

accommodation as part and parcel of equality standards. The Court often uses the express terminology of 'reasonable accommodation' and understands it as a general obligation to positively accommodate difference. As the Court put it, core to the principle of reasonable accommodation is the endeavour to include those who are marginalized because they do not fit the dominant standards:

> At its core is the notion that sometimes the community, whether it is the State, an employer or a school, must take positive measures and possibly incur additional hardship or expense in order to allow all people to participate and enjoy all their rights equally. It ensures that we do not relegate people to the margins of society because they do not or cannot conform to certain social norms.[82]

As a corollary to this broad notion of the need for accommodation, the Court perceives of reasonable accommodation as coming in different shapes and types, be it at the individual or more collective and structural level.[83]

The jurisprudence also shows how the Constitutional Court uses several ways to conclude a duty of reasonable accommodation exists. To start with, similar to the US, Canada and under the ECHR, such a duty may figure as part of the constitutional right to freedom of religion where religious accommodation is concerned.[84] More importantly for this study, as part of an assessment under equality standards, reasonable accommodation appears in two ways. The Constitutional Court has addressed a lack of accommodation both as constituting indirect discrimination and as constituting a violation of the prohibition of discrimination in its own right, that is as a *sui generis* modality of discrimination. The Court's judgment in the case *Pillay* discussed in Chapter 5 (Section 5.3.4) is the prime example of an approach under indirect discrimination analysis. In this case the Court held that indirect discrimination occurred for the very reason that the school did not accommodate Pillay's wish to wear a

---

82 Constitutional Court of South Africa, *MEC for Education: Kwazulu-Natal and Others v Pillay*, [2007] ZACC 21, par. 73.

83 Idem, par. 75: 'Our society which values dignity, equality, and freedom must therefore require people to act positively to accommodate diversity. Those steps might be as simple as granting and regulating an exemption from a general rule or they may require that the rules or practices be changed or even that buildings be altered or monetary loss incurred.'

84 See e.g. Constitutional Court of South Africa, *Christian Education South Africa v. Minister of Education*, [2000] ZACC 11. In this case a school based on a particular religious ethos claimed it should be exempted from the prohibition of corporal punishment in educational institutions. The Court considered the refusal of the exemption justified.

nose stud for religious and cultural reasons. Indirect discrimination was established, because the school's policy failed to treat those pupils who wish to wear jewellery for religious or cultural reasons differently from others.

In a landmark judgment regarding accommodation of persons with visual impairments, the case *Blind SA*, the Court links the concepts of indirect discrimination and reasonable accommodation even more closely together.[85] The case concerned a claim by a public interest organisation, Blind SA, regarding the unconstitutionality of the Copy Right Act in view of the severe limitations this Act imposed on making works under copyright available in accessible formats for visually impaired people. The Court presents two ways of reasoning that both lead it to the conclusion that the regulations in the Copy Right Act violate the prohibition of discrimination on the grounds of disability in Article 9(3) of the Constitution.

The first reasoning is along lines of indirect discrimination analysis, when the Court emphasizes that the disparate effect of the regulation goes to the heart of the constitutional challenge: 'The protection that the Copyright Act affords owners of copyright in literary works gives rise to a sharp disparity between those with print and visual disabilities, and those who do not suffer these impairments' and this is considered to amount to a violation of the prohibition of discrimination on the grounds of disability.[86]

The Court subsequently explains that 'the same conclusion is reached' in another way.[87] This other way of reasoning clearly reflects the second limb of the Aristotelian formula, that unalike cases must be treated unalike. The Court considers that given the particular hardship suffered by those with visual impairments, the regulation 'cannot be applied as if all persons who need access to literary works are similarly situated, when they are not'.[88] It points out that this idea reflects the broader principle that to avoid discrimination, sometimes the state 'must treat people in the same way or make available the same entitlements', and sometimes it 'is required … to recognize the differences between persons and to provide different or more favourable treatment to some, so as to secure non-discriminatory outcomes for all'.[89]

---

85 Constitutional Court of South Africa, *Blind SA v. Minister of Trade, Industry and Competition and others* [2022] ZACC 33.

86 Idem, par. 66.

87 Idem, par. 67.

88 Idem, par. 67.

89 Idem, par. 68.

Being thus understood as an integral part of equality and non-discrimination standards, it cannot be surprising that the notion of a lack of reasonable accommodation as a form of discrimination may also be applicable to other grounds.[90]

6.5 Lack of Accommodation as a Particular, *sui generis* Modality of Non-discrimination: the CRPD-Model

After denial of reasonable accommodation was included in the CRPD as a distinct form of discrimination in 2006, the concept of reasonable accommodation has taken up a prominent role on the legal stage of many jurisdictions.[91] Article 2 of the CRPD defines 'discrimination on the basis of disability' as including a denial of reasonable accommodation. The same provision subsequently defines 'reasonable accommodation' as

> necessary and appropriate modification and adjustments not imposing a disproportionate or undue burden, where needed *in a particular case*, to ensure to persons with disabilities the enjoyment or exercise on an equal basis with others of all human rights and fundamental freedoms. [emphasis added]

This particular formulation of a denial of reasonable accommodation as a form of discrimination has an individual focus. It ties in with the specific character of the notion of reasonable accommodation in the context of disability, as has been pointed out in academic literature.[92] The crucial importance of this individual focus of a duty of accommodation for disabled persons is emphasised in view of the wide diversity of needs of disabled people. To properly respond to this diversity, the accommodation needed may take myriad

---

90 An example is a case regarding accommodation of gender identity decided under statutory non-discrimination legislation, the Promotion of Equality and Prevention of Discrimination Act, by the Equality Court. In this Act an express duty of reasonable accommodation was included regarding the prohibition of discrimination on the grounds of race, gender and disability (Section 7, 8 and 9). In the case *Subramoney* the Court held that a denial of accommodation of a trans person in a male prison who wished to express her preferred gender by wearing female clothing and makeup violated the prohibition of discrimination on grounds of gender. It could not be justified by safety concerns. Equality Court, *September v. Subramoney NO and Others* (EC10/2016) [2019] ZAEQC 4.

91 Dušková, Who should we accommodate, 2023, p. 46–50.

92 See e.g. Waddington, Reasonable accommodation 2011, p. 188.

forms and be unique to the individual persons concerned.[93] The supervisory body to the CRPD confirmed this reading of the CRPD in its General Comments No. 2 on accessibility and No. 6 on equality and non-discrimination.[94] The duty to provide reasonable accommodation creates an individual entitlement to such accommodation, unless this would impose a 'disproportionate or undue burden'.

In the CRPD, the duty of reasonable accommodation is distinguished from two other types of obligations directed at better adjusting law and society to the needs of disabled people, and thus to accommodation in a broader sense.

The first type of adjustment beyond reasonable accommodation regards the duty of States parties to take appropriate measures to ensure persons with disabilities access to a wide variety of aspects of public and private life on an equal basis with others, including access 'to the physical environment, to transportation, to information and communication, including information and communication technologies and systems, and to other facilities and services open or provided to the public' (Article 9(1)). The CRPD-Committee distinguishes this type of obligation from reasonable accommodation in two ways. Contrary to the duty of reasonable accommodation, this 'accessibility' obligation is not individualized and not of an immediate character. It relates to groups and is subject to gradual implementation.[95] This is not to say that accessibility duties come with no strings attached. The CRPD stipulates in Article 9(2)(a) that States parties have to take concrete action and 'develop, promulgate and monitor the implementation of minimum standards and guidelines for the accessibility of facilities and services open or provided to the public'. The CRPD-Committee regards the obligation to ensure accessibility as a proactive, systemic duty.[96]

The second type of obligation requiring adjustments beyond reasonable accommodation is directed at promoting 'universal design' wherever this is possible, that is designing products, environments, programmes and services from the start in such a way that they are usable to all people, without the need for adaptation or specialized design (Article 9(2)(h) juncto Article 2). Thus for example, designing trains in such a way that wheelchair users can access them from the train platform, without the need of particular devices.

---

93 Waddington, Reasonable accommodation 2011, p. 197, Henrard, Duties of reasonable accommodation, 2012, p. 64.

94 CRPD-Committee, *General Comment No. 2 (2014), Article 9, Accessibility*; CRPD-Committee, *General Comment No. 6 (2018) on equality and non-discrimination.*

95 GC no. 6 on equality and non-discrimination, par. 41 and GC no. 2 on accessibility, par. 25–27.

96 GC No. 6 on equality and non-discrimination, par. 24 sub (a).

The CRPD-Committee explains in its General Comment No. 2 on accessibility and General Comment No. 6 on equality and discrimination how it understands the relationship between the obligations to provide reasonable accommodation, to realize accessibility and to promote universal design. First of all, it regards all three to be part of the overarching goal of the CRPD to realize substantive, inclusive equality, not just formal equality. Though formal equality is helpful in combatting direct discrimination and negative stereotyping and prejudice, it is not sufficient as it does not consider and embrace differences among human beings.[97] Secondly, in a more concrete way, the Committee regards the duty of reasonable accommodation as complementing the obligations regarding accessibility and universal design. Individual reasonable accommodation is necessary where the other two obligations have not been realized yet or are not sufficient to accommodate the more unique needs of the individual concerned.[98]

Though the CRPD and the CRPD-Committee use the terminology of 'accommodation' exclusively in relation to 'reasonable accommodation' and not in relation to promoting or ensuring accessibility and universal design, conceptually they can be regarded as belonging to this category. As discussed in Section 6.2.1, they represent different levels and types of accommodation.

The CRPD only defines denial of individual accommodation as a distinct form of discrimination. The obligations regarding accessibility and universal design are not cloaked in that language, even if their connection with equality and non-discrimination standards is quite obvious.[99] On the one hand, the CRPD-Committee is quite aware of this link when it notes that accessibility duties should also be framed as equality and non-discrimination issues, but on the other hand it does not elaborate this much further in its General Comment No. 2 on accessibility. It limits itself to remarking that the duties of States parties to ensure access 'should be seen from the perspective of equality and non-discrimination' and that denial of access 'constitutes an act of disability-based discrimination that is prohibited by Article 5 of the Convention'.[100] This point is not elaborated either in General Comment no. 6 on equality and non-discrimination, which repeats the distinction to be made

97 GC No. 6, par. 10–11.

98 GC No. 2, par. 25.

99 And as the CRPD Committee remarks, equality and non-discrimination are core to the CRPD as a whole: 'Equality and non-discrimination are at the heart of the Convention and evoked consistently throughout its substantive articles with the repeated use of the wording "on an equal basis with others", which links all substantive rights of the Convention to the nondiscrimination principle.' CRPD Committee, General Comment no. 6, par. 7.

100 General Comment No. 2, par. 34.

between duties regarding reasonable accommodation and accessibility without exploring their relationship with the overarching concepts of equality and non-discrimination.[101]

Another point that remains unclear is the relationship between indirect discrimination and a duty of reasonable accommodation. General Comment No. 6 on equality and non-discrimination provides definitions of indirect discrimination and reasonable accommodation without making any remarks on their potential overlap or links.[102] This is all the more surprising, as the General Comment does expressly distinguish reasonable accommodation from 'specific measures' including 'affirmative action measures' by emphasising the temporary and preferential nature of the latter as compared to the former:

> While both concepts aim at achieving de facto equality, reasonable accommodation is a non-discrimination duty, whereas specific measures imply a preferential treatment of persons with disabilities over others to address historic and/or systematic/systemic exclusion from the benefits of exercising rights. Examples of specific measures include temporary measures for countering the low numbers of women with disabilities employed in the private sector and support programmes to increase the number of students with disabilities in tertiary education.[103]

6.5.1 *Global Influence of the CRPD-Model of Reasonable Accommodation*

The conceptualization of reasonable accommodation in the CRPD as confined to accommodation at an individual level and being particularly designed to address discrimination on grounds of disability, seems to be an influential model worldwide. According to Dušková, a right to reasonable accommodation is now common in many jurisdictions around the world, yet '[c]ountries typically legislate it for persons with disabilities and do not explicitly extend the right to anyone else'.[104] In Europe, for example, a duty of reasonable accommodation in the employment setting was included in the EU Directive 2000/78/EC regarding discrimination on the grounds of religion or belief, disability, age or sexual orientation, but it was expressly limited to disability.[105] At the same time, calls for extending it beyond disability grow louder as is borne out by the Network of European equality bodies which

101 General Comment No. 6, par. 24.

102 General Comment No. 6, par. 18.

103 General Comment No. 6, Equality and non-discrimination, par. 25 sub (c).

104 Dušková, Who should we accommodate, 2023, p. 27.

105 Directive 2000/78/EC, Article 5.

regards this 'crucial to any ambition for substantive equality across all the discrimination grounds'.[106] Broadening duties of reasonable accommodation to other protected grounds would indeed tie in with the approach to (reasonable) accommodation as developed by the ECtHR and in the other jurisdictions discussed in Section 6.4.

6.6 Difficulties and Dilemmas of Applying the Concept of (Reasonable) Accommodation

As Section 6.4 has shown, no common approach to (reasonable) accommodation exists across jurisdictions. It has also become apparent that the boundaries between the legal concepts of indirect discrimination and (reasonable) accommodation are fluid. So far, contrary to indirect discrimination, regarding duties of (reasonable) accommodation no more or less common approach to analysing it as part of discrimination review has developed. A variety of models of judicial review exist. Nevertheless, across such difference, several common elements in this type of analysis can be discerned as well as some shared difficulties and dilemmas in applying the concept of (reasonable) accommodation in legal practice.

6.6.1 *Variety of Models of Review*

Generally speaking, the model of judicial review of (reasonable) accommodation will vary depending on the particular modality of discrimination it is regarded to be or belong to.

When a lack of accommodation is addressed as a form of indirect discrimination, assessing whether it violates the prohibition of discrimination will proceed along the lines of first establishing disparate impact and, if so, investigating whether an objective and reasonable justification exists. (See Chapter 5, Section 5.2.1).

In jurisdictions where it is addressed as a distinct modality of general discrimination analysis, judicial review models are not aligned. As has become apparent in Section 6.4. Canada can be said to have adopted a unified approach to all modalities of discrimination. The South African Constitutional Court seems to emphasize, at least it did so in *Blind SA*, that reasoning along the lines of indirect discrimination or reasonable accommodation will lead to the

106 N. Crowley, *Equality bodies and reasonable accommodation beyond the ground of disability*, Equinet report 2022, p. 7.

same conclusion.[107] For both Courts, the inquiry whether a lack of reasonable accommodation violates the equality and non-discrimination standards is triggered by the disparate effect of neutrally formulated rules or policies on a protected group or member of such a group.

The ECtHR has taken a somewhat different approach, by developing a distinct model of review for establishing whether a lack of (reasonable) accommodation violates Article 14 ECHR. The added value of a distinct approach to (reasonable) accommodation review compared to an approach in terms of indirect discrimination could be that it would skip the step of a showing of disparate impact, before turning to the justification stage. However, this is not the case. In the Strasbourg case law, the actual review seems to closely resemble analysis in terms of indirect discrimination. The 'disproportionately prejudicial effects' criterion of indirect discrimination review reappears in another form as an inquiry into the question whether the 'different situation' which would give rise to a duty of accommodation, is 'sufficiently significant'. To establish this, 'a measure must produce a particularly prejudicial impact on certain persons as a result of a protected ground'.[108] Though not using exactly the same wording as in indirect discrimination cases, this review model closely resembles indirect discrimination analysis. (See Chapter 5, Section 5.4).

Under the CRPD, the Committee has formulated its own, distinct model of reasonable accommodation review, which is geared to its particular conceptualization of reasonable accommodation as directed at accommodation at the individual level. This review consists of two steps. The first step regards an assessment of the reasonableness of the accommodation in terms of its relevance, appropriateness and effectiveness for the person concerned, whereas the second step subsequently addresses the question whether the required accommodations constitute a disproportionate or undue burden.[109] Assessing the duty of accessibility is less clearly defined, as the CRPD allows for gradual implementation, but the Committee emphasizes that States parties have to develop and monitor national accessibility standards and undertake a comprehensive review of their laws on accessibility to identify and address gaps in legislation and implementation.[110]

107 Constitutional Court of South Africa, *Blind SA v. Minister of Trade, Industry and Competition and others*, [2022] ZACC 33, par. 67.

108 ECtHR , Adám and others, par. 87 (with reference to J.D. and A. v. UK, 2019, par. 85).

109 CRPD-Committee, General Comment No. 6, par. 25.

110 CRPD-Committee, General Comment No. 2, par. 27–28.

6.6.2 *Justification and Proportionality – Levels of Scrutiny*

Whatever the precise formulation of the review model, as with the other modalities of discrimination discussed before, in (reasonable) accommodation cases the possibility of an objective and reasonable justification is a central feature of assessing whether equality and non-discrimination standards have been violated. This means that the actual bite of (reasonable) accommodation review will depend on the degree of strictness with which the presence of a justification is assessed.

Here again, as with direct and indirect discrimination, the level of scrutiny applied may well differ depending on the protected grounds involved. In the US, for example, religious accommodation in employment leaves more leeway for the employer under the '*de minimus* standard' than accommodation for disabled persons, which is assessed under the standard of 'significant difficulty or expense' (see Section 6.4.1). The case law of the ECtHR also shows how the protected ground involved may influence the degree of scrutiny by referring to the 'very weighty reasons' standards applicable where the accommodation claimed regards gender or sexual orientation (see Section 6.4.2).

Similarly, where accommodation requires the development of social or economic policies, or has serious budgetary consequences, the level of scrutiny may well be lower. As the ECtHR considered in *Arnar Helgi Lárusson* 'when it comes to measures of economic or social strategy' the states usually enjoy a wide margin of appreciation'.[111]

6.6.3 *Lack of a Point of Reference and Open-Endedness – What Role for Judicial Bodies?*

Where a difference in treatment is claimed to violate equality standards, a point of reference exists to answer the question whether it can be justified or not. Where an absence of different treatment is claimed to violate equality standards, such a point of reference is lacking. For judicial bodies, this open-ended character of (reasonable) accommodation may pose particular problems in view of separation of powers principles. As the South African Constitutional Court remarked in the case *Pillay*, accommodation of difference may come in many forms. It 'might be as simple as granting and regulating an exemption from a general rule, or they may require that the rules or practices be changed, or even that buildings be altered or monetary loss incurred'.[112] The more far-reaching the accommodation needed, the more judicial bodies

111 ECtHR, *Arnar Helgi Lárusson*, 2022, par. 58.

112 Constitutional Court of South Africa, *MEC for Education: Kwazulu-Natal and Others v. Pillay* (CCT 51/06) [2007] ZACC 21, par. 75.

will have to negotiate the tensions between their own role and the role of the other branches of government as guarantors of equality standards, or, in case of international courts, the role of the national authorities.

The open-ended nature of accommodating difference may explain why the CRPD distinguishes obligations regarding accessibility and universal design from the duty of reasonable accommodation as an entitlement to individual accommodation. The former two will usually require the development of regulations and policies with a broad reach and may implicate substantial budget allocations. Governmental action is indispensable. In this context, the CRPD-Committee emphasizes the need to establish minimum standards for the accessibility of different services provided by public and private enterprises and for persons with different types of impairments. This implies developing a broad range of policies and action plans.[113] If anything, then, accommodation of difference requires a proactive approach.

6.6.3.1 The Need for a Proactive Approach to Accommodation of Difference

The need for a proactive approach to (reasonable) accommodation to fulfil equality standards is perhaps most clearly recognized and embraced where accommodation of disabled persons is concerned, but another example of this would be the regulation of pregnancy and maternity leave (pregnancy leave for short). Even if this type of taking differences into account is not cloaked in the specific terminology of (reasonable) accommodation, conceptually it belongs to the notion that 'unalike cases must be treated unalike in accordance with their unalikeness'.

Pregnancy leave arrangements are indeed a very good illustration of the difficulties and dilemmas involved in applying the notion of (reasonable) accommodation and the need for pro-active regulation. Recognition of pregnancy as a relevant difference which needs to be accommodated is widely accepted. As it is not of an incidental nature, most jurisdictions have regulated it on a collective basis. Importantly, contrary to 'individual' reasonable accommodation, in this situation granting pregnancy leave does not depend on the question whether it puts a 'disproportionate burden' on an individual employer. Rather, the regulation decides that question for all employers covered. At the same time, how far a decent pregnancy arrangement should extend in terms of the period of leave granted before and after birth and the level of financial compensation guaranteed, is open-ended. It may vary significantly between

113 CRPD-Committee, General Comment No. 2, par. 30–33.

jurisdictions. Even within the EU this is the case, particularly where the financial component of regulation is concerned.[114]

The open-endedness of a decent pregnancy leave arrangement explains why it may be difficult for judicial bodies to intervene and decide when accommodation is sufficient or not. It also explains why in the past in several jurisdictions legal proceedings focused on linking claims for (better) pregnancy leave to existing arrangements regarding sick leave. Claiming unjustified unequal treatment is easier to construe than a much more indeterminate claim of (reasonable) accommodation in its own right. In the EU Directive 92/85/EEC on pregnancy leave, a link with sick leave is still present where the level of pay to be granted to a pregnant worker is concerned: financial compensation must at least be of the same level as the benefits attached to sick leave.[115]

Though courts may still play an important role where accommodation does not meet some minimum level, it is ultimately up to the legislature and not to judicial bodies to regulate pregnancy leave in more detail. In this respect, judicial review of lack of (reasonable) accommodation as a violation of equality standards is very similar to adjudication of social rights and faces the same sort of difficulties and dilemmas.[116]

6.7 Concluding Remarks

An inquiry into a lack of (reasonable) accommodation as a potential violation of equality and non-discrimination standards is triggered by the disparate effect of a rule, measure or policy on a group protected by these standards. Similar to the concept of indirect discrimination, by being focused on the outcome of a treatment, embracing the notion of (reasonable) accommodation implies an important step towards a more substantive equality approach.

---

114 For an overview see the Infogrraphic Maternity and Paternity leave in the EU, https://www.europarl.europa.eu/RegData/etudes/ATAG/2023/739346/EPRS_ATA(2023)739346_EN.pdf.

115 Directive 92/85/EEC, Article 11(3).

116 See a.o. J. King, *Judging social rights*, Cambridge, Cambridge University Press, 2012; S. Fredman, Review article: Coming of age: socio-economic rights as human rights, in: S. Fredman and M. Campbell (eds), *Social and economic rights and constitutional law*, Cheltenham, Elgar Publ., 2016; E. Cameron, A South African perspective on the judicial development of socio-economic rights, in: L. Lazarus, C. McCrudden and N. Bowles (eds.), *Reasoning rights. Comparative judicial engagement*, Oxford, Hart Publ., 2014, p. 319–338.

Fundamental to the concept of (reasonable) accommodation is the idea that 'difference' may require differential treatment. As such it is an expression of the second limb of the Aristotelian notion of equality that 'unalike cases must be treated unalike in accordance with their unalikeness'.

In legal practice, no common understanding or approach to (reasonable) accommodation exists across jurisdictions. The basic notion of the obligation to treat unalike cases differently and to regard a lack of accommodating unalike cases as a form of discrimination has appeared in mainly three ways: as a form of indirect discrimination, as a generally applicable, *sui generis* form of discrimination, and as a particular *sui generis form* of discrimination, specifically applicable to disability and with some specific features. The latter approach has become very prominent under the influence of the CRPD, which seems to have been a driving force for jurisdictions worldwide to take the concept on board. At the same time, increased attention to reasonable accommodation in the context of disability has resulted in calls for extending its application to grounds beyond disability. In this respect, its close link with a more substantive approach to equality is seen as a major reason for doing so. As the network of European equality bodies put it 'a wider understanding of reasonable accommodation, beyond the ground of disability, is (..) crucial to any ambition for substantive equality across all the discrimination grounds'.[117]

The analysis of the various approaches taken to (reasonable) accommodation as part of equality standards has also explored some of the main difficulties and dilemmas involved in applying the concept in legal practice. Particularly the open-endedness of what constitutes sufficient accommodation to meet equality standards raises issues of separation of powers principles, which are very similar to the application of social rights and equally complex.

---

117 N. Crowley, *Equality bodies and reasonable accommodation beyond the ground of disability*, Equinet report 2022, p. 7.

CHAPTER 7

Positive Discrimination or Positive Action

7.1 Introduction

Of all the concepts discussed in this study, positive discrimination or positive action stands out by meeting with particularly strong controversy and contestation in both public and legal debates.[1] This has been so from the very time when affirmative action gained prominence in a variety of jurisdictions in the last decades of the past century, particularly in the US and Europe, as a tool to improve the position of structurally disadvantaged groups such as women and racial minorities. Discussions have not abated since then.

As discussed in Chapter 3 and Chapter 6, positive discrimination or positive action is not to be confused or equated with (reasonable) accommodation. Several courts have expressly explained that providing accommodation for disabled people or religious minorities is not to be put on a par with preferential treatment or privileging these groups. (See Chapter 3, Section 3.4.2 and Chapter 6, Section 6.2.) In the words of the CRPD-Committee, '[w]'hile both concepts aim at achieving de facto equality, reasonable accommodation is a non-discrimination duty, whereas specific measures imply a preferential treatment of persons with disabilities over others to address historic and/or systematic/systemic exclusion from the benefits of exercising rights'.[2]

Controversies surrounding positive discrimination or positive action start with the very terminology used to describe the phenomenon. In fact, it comes in a wide variety of terms, such as positive, benign or reverse discrimination, remedial, ameliorative or special measures, affirmative or positive action and preferential treatment. 'Discrimination' has a pejorative ring. For those who regard positive discrimination or positive action as a perfectly acceptable and legitimate means to undo the effects of past discrimination and improve the position of structurally disadvantaged groups, using the term 'discrimination' sends the wrong message, even if it is combined with the adjective 'positive'. It is not to be regarded as discrimination at all. For those who perceive positive discrimination or positive action as highly problematic for the way in which it differentiates between groups on the basis of what is generally to be

1 Cf. Fredman, Discrimination law, 2022, p. 366.

2 CRPD-Committee, *General Comment No. 6 (2018) on equality and non-discrimination*, par. 25(c).

considered a suspect ground of discrimination, the terminology of 'discrimination' conveys precisely why it is so controversial and why it sits uneasily with equality standards. As also further explained in Chapter 1, as neutral terminology is not possible in this context I use all these terms interchangeably.[3]

Legally, positive discrimination or positive action meets with a variety of responses to its acceptability as a tool to improve the position of disadvantaged groups. In this chapter I will explore the way in which this has taken shape. As with the other concepts discussed in the previous chapters, judicial interpretation and review have exerted a profound influence. The relevant case law which has shaped legal approaches to positive discrimination and positive action deals in the far majority of cases with affirmative action regarding women and racial minorities. Remedial measures regarding these groups have created the frame of reference for special measures regarding other groups and will figure most prominently in this chapter.

Section 7.2 starts with an exploration of the general features of positive discrimination or positive action measures or policies, pointing out the important difference between remedial measures which are expressly based on a protected ground of discrimination such as race or sex, and other policies directed at improving the position of women or racial groups, which do not use race or sex as the basis of differential treatment. My focus in this chapter is on the former, as this is the type of affirmative action which is central to the controversies surrounding it. Section 7.3 briefly discusses three different types of arguments which play a prominent role in debates on the acceptability of positive discrimination or positive action, yet are often not properly distinguished: arguments regarding the instrumentality, the legitimacy and the legality of affirmative action. Though the former two will often feed into legal approaches to remedial measures, the absence or presence of a legal basis for positive discrimination or positive action is the starting point for any legal inquiry and as such merits closer attention. As is the case with the other concepts explored in this study, judicial interpretation and review have ultimately proven crucial for delimitating the acceptability of affirmative action. Section 7.4 will discuss the similarities and differences in the ways in which this has taken shape in different jurisdictions. Section 7.5 is subsequently devoted to an analysis of several distinct difficulties and dilemmas to be faced in positive discrimination or positive action review. An important concern in this context is how to deal with intersectionality. On the one hand, intersectional perspectives call for taking into account the distinct disadvantages which may result from

3 See more extensively on how I use the various terms in this book Chapter 1.

the intersection of two or more protected grounds of discrimination. On the other hand, taking this on board in the setting of remedial measures may result in uncalled for competition between various disadvantaged groups in laying claims to scarce resources. In addition, difficulties seem to be posed by the existence of blurred lines between remedial measures, 'ordinary' social policies, (reasonable) accommodation and 'ordinary' discrimination.

7.2 General Features

In his comparative study, Oppenheimer traces affirmative action as an issue that arises when societies are confronted with 'the question of how to remedy past discrimination and structural disadvantage'.[4] As such it has come to the fore across jurisdictions, particularly regarding groups in society facing a history of discrimination and exclusion on the basis of their race, sex or religion. More recently, attention for remedial measures regarding disabled people has become more prominent.[5] What stands out is its remedial purpose.

The most commonly discussed positive discrimination or positive action measures concern affirmative action directed at remedying the underrepresentation of certain groups in the area of employment, access to education and political representation.[6] Worldwide, the groups perceived as in need of and favoured by such measures usually consist of women and/or racial or religious/cultural minorities; again, more recently disabled people are also more often included. Of course, country specific remedial measures may derive from the particular historical and social context shaping structural disadvantage and inequality. Thus, for example, India has developed extensive affirmative action policies on behalf of scheduled castes and tribes, and other backward classes, whereas South Africa is unique for its remedial measures on behalf of racial groups which make up the majority in this country.

It is important to note that remedial measures may come in a wide variety of forms and shapes, not all of which are as controversial. They constitute

4 D.B. Oppenheimer, *The Ubiquity of positive measures for addressing systemic discrimination and inequality. A comparative global perspective*, Brill Research Perspectives in Comparative Discrimination Law, 2019, p. 2.

5 Idem, p. 2. Oppenheimer points out that affirmative action is not common regarding groups suffering from discrimination on the basis of sexual orientation, gender identity or age, p. 2.

6 These are the areas most extensively discussed by Oppenheimer, Ubiquity of positive measures, 2019. Regarding the latter he notes that quite some countries in Africa and Asia (including China) and most countries in Latin America have set-asides for women in national legislative bodies, p. 84–85.

a continuum from 'soft voluntary inclusion programmes' to 'hard quota systems', and '[a]long this continuum, the closer we get to the hard quota laws, the greater the opposition'.[7] The latter may include, for example, reserving a number or percentage of places in higher functions, education or political bodies for women or racial or religious/cultural minorities. In other instances affirmative action does not involve quota as such, but provides for some other form of preferential treatment of these groups, for example by giving them priority if they are equally qualified. More indirect remedial measures seek to lower the barriers disadvantaged groups face to access higher functions, education or political representation. This may include the provision of special management development training for women or special coaching and support for students who belong to racial minority groups.

Whereas in the above examples the affirmative action measures differentiate on the grounds of race or sex as such, other remedial measures may be race- or sex-neutral. Job application trainings for people re-entering the labour market do not differentiate between men and women, but will be particularly beneficial to the latter as they are over-represented in this category. Providing for sufficient and affordable child care facilities will equally tend to benefit the labour market participation of women more than the gainful employment of men. Similarly, providing for extra financial resources for schools or for social counselling in poor neighbourhoods will often benefit disadvantaged racial minorities rather than more well-off groups. And using outreach programmes to find a larger pool of potential job applicants or students, including more women and persons belonging to racial minorities, are also ways of shaping affirmative action without resorting to race- or sex-based distinctions.

In public debates, controversies usually focus on remedial measures which distinguish on the basis of race, sex or another protected ground as such. This is reflected in legal realities. Legally speaking, the difference between remedial measures which make deliberate or express use of a protected ground such as race or sex to remedy disadvantage and those which do not, is also very important. The former are typically the kind of measures that meet with legal contestation and discussion. They are often perceived as particularly controversial because the ground for differentiation used is otherwise a suspect ground. As such, they are not in line with the *presumption* of such categories being irrelevant as a basis for differentiation and with the ultimate goal of a society in which such categories are irrelevant for the position human beings are able to occupy in society.

7 Oppenheimer, Ubiquity of positive measures, 2019, p. 7.

This focus on affirmative action which expressly differentiates on the basis of a suspect ground is reflected in the body of case law which has developed across jurisdictions. It is also the focus of the following sections. Judicial review of the compatibility of positive discrimination or positive action with equality standards revolves around remedial measures expressly using race or sex as a ground for differentiation.

7.2.1 *Characteristics of Affirmative Action Expressly Based on a Protected Ground*

Positive discrimination or positive action measures or policies taking centre stage in legal debates on their compatibility with equality standards can be characterized by three elements. Firstly, they are special measures directed at the improvement of the position of structurally disadvantaged groups to reduce existing gaps with more advantaged ones. They aim to correct factual or *de facto* inequalities.[8] Secondly, these measures are based on a protected, suspect ground, which is precisely why they raise so much controversy. Affirmative action, then, is not to be put on a par with general social policies directed at improving the position of structurally disadvantaged groups, which do not use a protected ground as the basis for differential treatment.[9] Thirdly, the purpose of affirmative action implies that remedial measures are of a temporary nature: if the goals they seek to achieve have been reached, they are no longer necessary and should be abandoned.[10] Of course, where structural disadvantage is ingrained in society, effectively reducing inequalities may take quite a long period, but affirmative action is in a principled way time bound. Its temporary character also suggests the need of monitoring mechanisms to measure the progress made.

Its temporary nature is an element of what sets affirmative action apart from (reasonable) accommodation. The CEDAW Committee clearly points out

---

8 Cf. e.g. ECtHR (Grand Chamber), 13 November 2007, *D.H. and others v. the Czech Republic*, appl. no. 57325/00, par. 175: 'Article 14 does not prohibit a member State from treating groups differently in order to correct "factual inequalities" between them'. In a very similar way the CJEU speaks about the purpose of 'reducing de facto inequalities', linking this goal expressly to a substantive quality approach, see CJEU, 30 September 2004, *Briheche*, C-319/03, par. 25.

9 The CEDAW Committee clearly distinguishes the two, see *General Recommendation No. 25, on article 4. paragraph 1, on temporary special measures*, 2004, par. 19.

10 Both the ICERD and the CEDAW are explicit about the temporary nature of special measures, see Article 2(2) ICERD and Article 4(1) CEDAW. The CRPD-Committee has also expressed this in *General Comment No. 6 (2018) on equality and non-discrimination*, par. 25(c).

the difference between the two, when it discusses the different character of Article 4(1) CEDAW on temporary special measures and Article 4(2), regarding 'special measures aimed at protecting maternity'. The first are aimed at accelerating the improvement of the position of women 'to achieve their de facto or substantive equality with men, and to effect the structural, social and cultural changes necessary to correct past and current forms and effects of discrimination against women'.[11] They have as such a temporary nature and should be abolished after their goals have been reached. The latter, however, are of a permanent nature, as they provide for a difference in treatment between women and men due to their biological differences.[12]

7.2.2 *Relationship with Substantive Equality*

With its goal of achieving a more equal outcome, positive discrimination or positive action belongs conceptually to the realm of substantive equality. It starts from the second limb of the Aristotelian *adagium*, which calls for treating unalike cases unalike in accordance with their unalikeness. The 'unalikeness' in this respect being the factual inequalities in terms of access to employment, education or political representation et cetera.

For jurisdictions following a substantive approach to equality, remedial measures fit smoothly, whereas from a formal equality perspective, they are highly problematic. As will be elaborated in Section 7.3.3 remedial measures are often expressly linked to a substantive equality approach.

7.3 Legitimacy, Instrumentality and Legality

In public debates regarding positive discrimination or positive action several types of arguments play a central role, which are often conflated: arguments regarding its legitimacy, its instrumentality and its legality.[13] Distinguishing them is important, as they play different roles in deciding about the legal acceptability of affirmative action. From a legal point of view, how jurisdictions approach the legality of remedial measures in view of equality standards is the primary concern. It is the focus of this chapter. This is not to say that questions

---

11 CEDAW, *General Recommendation No. 25, on Article 4, paragraph 1, on temporary special measures*, 2004, par. 15.

12 Idem, par. 16. The Committee adds this will be the case 'at least until such time as the scientific and technological knowledge. ... would warrant review', par. 19.

13 L. Mulder, Voorkeursbehandeling van vrouwen en de betekenis van gelijkheidsbeginselen (Preferential treatment of women and the meaning of equality principles), *Nederlands Juristenblad* 1984, p. 1391–1397.

of legitimacy and instrumentality do not provide an important background for legal approaches. They feed into all sorts of considerations involved in legally assessing the permissibility of affirmative action.

7.3.1 *Legitimacy*

Legitimacy is arguably the core concern in public debates on positive discrimination or positive action. Discussions regarding legitimacy are closely related to political and philosophical views and theories regarding equality and justice as meta-juridical idea(l)s. Argumentations supporting the legitimacy of affirmative action usually take either a retrospective or prospective point of departure, or a combination of both.[14]

7.3.1.1 Retrospective Theories

Retrospective theories generally start from the idea that (continuing) injustice caused by past discrimination against particular groups in society has to be compensated. Some sort of collective restitution or reparation is needed, which can be achieved by affirmative action.

A crucial objection to this type of reasoning centres around the question whether collective redress is a proper way of dealing with the consequences of past injustice. To begin with, a discrepancy exists between individual members of the groups who suffered from discrimination in the past and those who benefit from remedial measures in the present. Not all women or members of disadvantaged racial groups have personally suffered discrimination. In addition, not all men or all members of racially more advantaged groups have been guilty of discrimination and some may be actually disadvantaged themselves. If so, why should they suffer? Why would 'the African American son of a successful neurosurgeon' get preference over 'the white son of coal miner's family'?[15] Put differently, there is a *misfit* between those who benefit or suffer from positive discrimination or positive action and those who are past victims or

14 This brief overview of the main types of reasoning for and against affirmative action in terms of its legitimacy is largely based on two Dutch dissertations on this topic unless otherwise indicated, see B.P. Sloot, *Positieve discriminatie. Maatschappelijke ongelijkheid en rechtsontwikkeling in de Verenigde Staten en Nederland* (Positive discrimination. Social inequality and legal development in the US and the Netherlands), Zwolle, Tjeenk Willink, 1986; J.H. Wiggers, *Recht doen naan gelijkheid. Een beschouwing over voorkeursbehandeling en de betekenis van het gelijkheidsbeginsel in het grensgebied van recht en sociaal-politieke ethiek* (Doing justice to equality. A reflection on preferential treatment in the border area between law and socio-political ethics), Nijmegen, Ars Aequi Libri, 1991.

15 R. Fullinwider, *Affirmative action*, in: *The Stanford Encyclopedia of Philosophy*, 2018, p. 16.

perpetrators of discrimination. Related to this, opponents to affirmative action point out that those who profit most from remedial measures are often those who are already better off within the group concerned rather than belonging to its weakest members. (See Section 7.5.1 for further elaboration how this surfaces in case law.) In this situation remedial measure benefit people who are not really in need of special support.

Supporters of compensation theories will often argue against this line of thinking by stressing the systemic character of past discrimination. Where discrimination has become ingrained in the fabrics and structures of society, it cannot be traced back to concrete individual acts. Systemic and institutionalized discrimination is often invisible. Selection criteria for jobs or educational places and attributing the required qualifications to individuals, for example, may be marred by unconscious bias. In this type of context, questions of guilt are irrelevant, or rather not relevant at the individual level. Society can be held to have a collective guilt towards groups disadvantaged by structural forms of past discrimination. Women and racial minorities have suffered as a group from discrimination; men and racial majorities have profited from it as a group. Collective redress is a logical corollary. It may be clear that this collective focus will not resonate with people who adhere to a fundamentally individual view of the human person.

7.3.1.2 Prospective Theories

Prospective theories approach the legitimacy of affirmative action from a future-based perspective. They are often part of redistributive theories of justice. Positive discrimination or positive action may figure as an instrument to achieve a more equal distribution of scarce goods, such as jobs or places in higher education. Prospective theories regard redressing disadvantage and realizing more equal distribution as a valuable goal in itself, regardless the origins of the disadvantage and inequality.

Within this type of reasoning supporting remedial measures, many varieties exist. A common approach takes the creation of equal opportunities as its central concern. Effective equality of opportunities presupposes the absence of barriers to participate on an equal basis in society and to develop one's talents to the full. Where such barriers exist, affirmative action may be justified. This line of thinking usually starts from the presumption that – given an equal distribution of talents and capacities across human beings – genuine equality of opportunity will result in a more or less equal distribution of jobs, wealth and income and the like between men and women or between racial minority and majority groups. Serious inequalities suggest that real equality of opportunities has not been achieved. This may well be due to power imbalances between dominant and non-dominant groups.[16] Affirmative action may be a helpful instrument to address this.

Critiques of this type of reasoning often call into question the supposedly causal link between equality of opportunity and equal distributive outcomes. Differences in talent and individual preferences of individual people are highlighted as playing an important role in the ultimate distribution of social goods. Women, for example, may well be more inclined to prefer other than technical schooling and jobs, which may be unrelated to a lack of equal opportunities. If this is the case, it becomes questionable why unequal distribution of jobs in this sector should be redressed by affirmative action policies.

Prospective reasonings which regard remedial measures legitimate are not always focused on redistributive justice. Other considerations of justice or of promoting greater welfare for society as a whole may play their part. These utilitarian approaches to remedial measures point, for example, to the expected benefits of increasing the social and economic integration of certain groups or the positive influence of having more role models for persons belonging to socially disadvantaged groups. In addition, the merits of diversity for the functioning of all sorts of organisations and institutions have gained increasing traction to support affirmative action measures, particularly in the US and Europe.[17] More generally, the beneficial effects of diversity and inclusion for the performance of businesses, economies and societies at large due to the variety of perspectives people bring in, is more globally emphasized.[18] These presumed beneficial effects tie in closely with discussions on the instrumentality of affirmative action: can and does it really achieve what it intends to?

7.3.2 *Instrumentality*

To start with, two aspects of the instrumentality of positive discrimination or positive action measures should be distinguished: the instrumentality of using quotas, set-asides or other remedial measures to provide better access to

16 See e.g. J.E. Goldschmidt, Staats- en bestuursrechtelijke aspecten van positieve actie (Constitutional and administrative aspects of positive action), in: W.P. Fase, J.E. Goldschmidt en B. P. Sloot, *Positieve discriminatie* (Positive discrimination), *preadviezen NJV*, 1989, p. 57–117.

17 See Fullinwider, Affirmative action, 2018, for a discussion of diversity arguments (p. 9–11) and integration arguments (p. 13–15) in the US context. Diversity arguments have also gained increasing attention in Europe, see e.g. the overview of diversity policies in the EU on its website https://commission.europa.eu/strategy-and-policy/policies/justice-and-fundamental-rights/combatting-discrimination/tackling-discrimination/diversity-and-inclusion-initiatives_en.

18 Cf. ILO Report *Transforming enterprises through diversity and inclusion*, 6 April 2022.

valuable, yet scarce resources, and the instrumentality of this better access – if realized – for achieving the underlying goals of affirmative action, that is in terms of the retrospective or prospective theories discussed above.

Instrumentality of the first kind seems to be the very reason why affirmative action policies would resort to using classifications directly based on a suspect ground such as race or sex rather than choosing race- or sex-neutral measures. Targeted policies using quotas or set-asides respond to scarcity of resources. If the number of coveted jobs, places in education or political bodies, and financial resources were unlimited, using this instrument would not be necessary at all. When they are, the more specific the focus on a particular underrepresented group, the more instrumental this will be in reducing underrepresentation. For example, setting concrete and compulsory quota for women in corporate boards provides quicker results than waiting for the effects of better management training and coaching policies. Similarly, given the prevailing gendered division of paid work and care in most countries, an employment policy giving priority to female workers in access to scarce child care facilities is more instrumental in helping them to stay on the labour market when they get children than providing equal access to male and female employees alike. In fact, without prioritizing female workers, the more employed fathers outnumber employed mothers, the more difficult it will be for the latter to access child care at all if the availability of this facility is a core problem. Scarcity of resources is thus in many instances the driving force behind remedial measures distinguishing directly on the basis of a protected ground of discrimination. Neutral measures are often much less instrumental. At the same time, targeted measures such as prioritising women for access to child care may well reproduce stereotypes about gender roles.

Regarding the US context, Fullinwider points out how neutral steps were often considered ineffective by US Courts in the seventies of the last century, when the use of preferential hiring was commonly used as a remedy for past racial discrimination. Courts sometimes ordered institutions to adopt quotas or take in a specified number of formerly excluded groups to comply with the prohibition of discrimination under Title VII of the Civil Rights Act. Such measures aimed at changing the organizations and institutions themselves, which was considered necessary to prevent ongoing and future discrimination. 'The dilemma was this: courts could impose racial preferences to change foot-dragging or inept defendants … or they could order less onerous steps they knew would be ineffective, thus letting discrimination continue'.[19]

19 Fullinwider, Affirmative action, 2018, p. 5.

The second aspect of instrumentality – achieving the underlying goals of affirmative action – is usually the focus of discussions between opponents and supporters of remedial measures. Critics may either doubt whether the underlying goals are reached at all, or they may regard any positive impact to be counterbalanced by adverse effects.[20] Affirmative action can create a lot of resentment if it is perceived as unfair and result in backlash against the very groups who are supposed to benefit from these measures. In addition, remedial measures may risk to enhance stigmatization and prejudice by reinforcing the idea that the disadvantaged groups lack the capacities to improve their position under their own steam. And as mentioned above regarding the example of preferential treatment in access to child care facilities, it may enhance the very stereotypes which the measures seek to modify. Of course, as affirmative action measures aim for future effects, it is often hard to assess their instrumentality *ex ante*.

Concerns about the adverse effects of affirmative action may also lead to strategic rather than principled arguments against the use of this type of instrument to achieve more de facto equality.[21]

7.3.3 *Legality*

The legality of positive discrimination or positive action depends on the applicable equality standards, which may vary significantly between jurisdictions. To start with, important differences may exist in the legal basis for remedial measures. Some jurisdictions provide for an express mandate by the legislator, whereas in others its legality is entirely shaped by judicial bodies under general equality standards.

In the first respect, an early, express mandate for affirmative action can be found in the 1965 convention on racial discrimination. It is formulated in a particularly strong way. Article 2(2) ICERD requires States parties 'when the circumstances so warrant' to take special measures 'to ensure the adequate development and protection of certain racial groups or individuals belonging to them, for the purpose of guaranteeing them the full and equal enjoyment of human rights and fundamental freedoms'. It adds that such special measures must be temporary. They 'shall in no case entail as a consequence the

20 See for examples of this type of discussion in the US Fullinwider, Affirmative action, 2018, p. 9–15.

21 J.E. Goldschmidt, 'Ms Goldschmidt, is it true you are deaf? That would really help us to meet our quota!'. Positive discrimination revisited ..., In: M. van den Brink, S. Burri and J.Goldschmidt (eds), (2015) *Equality and human rights: nothing but trouble? Liber amicorum Titia Loenen* (SIM *Special*), SIM/Utrecht University, 2015, p. 345–357, at. p. 349.

maintenance of unequal or separate rights for different racial groups after the objectives for which they were taken have been achieved'. Under these conditions, special measures of this kind 'shall not be deemed racial discrimination' (Article 1(4) ICERD).

As this type of provision was not included in the general human rights conventions dating from around the same time, the ICCPR and ICESCR of 1966, this suggests affirmative action was considered of particular significance in the context of eliminating racial discrimination.[22] It also turned out to be regarded as of specific importance for women. A provision on 'temporary special measures aimed at accelerating de facto equality between men and women' was in 1979 included in Article 4(1) CEDAW. Similar to the ICERD, such measures are to be abolished after they have achieved their objectives and are not to be regarded as discrimination as defined in the convention (Article 4(1) CEDAW). Last but not least, 'specific measures which are necessary to accelerate or achieve de facto equality of persons with disabilities' are also expressly allowed under the more recent CRPD and not to be regarded as discrimination (Article 5(4) CRPD).

Specific provisions on affirmative action may of course also be found in constitutional equality standards. Canada and South Africa are prime examples. Section 15(2) of the Canadian Charter of Rights and Freedoms allows for measures aimed at 'the amelioration of conditions of disadvantaged individuals or groups', in particular groups 'disadvantaged because of race, national or ethnic origin, colour, religion, sex, age or mental or physical disability'. The Constitution of South Africa also includes a very general mandate in Section 9(2) to take 'legislative and other measures designed to protect or advance persons, or categories of persons, disadvantaged by unfair discrimination' to promote the achievement of the full and equal enjoyment of all rights and freedoms. In their case law, the apex courts in both countries have stressed that this type of measure is part and parcel of a substantive approach to equality and not to be regarded as discrimination.[23]

---

22 In their general comments, the supervisory bodies to the ICCPR and ICESCR have subsequently interpreted the equality standards in their respective covenants as including a mandate to take affirmative action to correct or redress discrimination, without limiting this to any particular groups. See for the Human Rights Committee, *General Comment No. 18: Discrimination*, 1989, par. 10 and for the Committee on Economic, Social and Cultural Rights, General Comment No. 20 of 2012 on *Non-discrimination in economic, social and cultural rights (Art. 2, para. 2 of the ICESCR)*, E/C.12/GC/20, par. 9.

23 According to the Canadian Supreme Court, Section 15(2) of the Charter of Fundamental Rights and Freedoms regarding ameliorative measures and the general equality provision contained in Section 15(1) 'work together to promote the vision of substantive equality

In addition to constitutional arrangements, jurisdictions may provide for a legal mandate for remedial measures in statutory laws and regulations covering particular areas such as employment, education or political representation. The EU equality directives, for example, have such a more focused approach, allowing for positive action in particular fields as an exception to the requirement of equal treatment. The directives covering discrimination on the grounds of race and sex include *grosso modo* employment and access to and supply of goods and services. For discrimination on the basis of religion or belief, disability, age or sexual orientation, positive action is limited to employment. All these directives allow for 'maintaining or adopting specific measures to prevent or compensate for disadvantages linked to' the particular ground(s) covered in these directives, with a view to achieving 'full equality in practice'.[24] In line with this, the CJEU formulates the goal of positive action as achieving 'substantive, rather than formal equality by reducing de facto inequalities, which may arise in society'.[25]

Where no express mandate to take affirmative action measures is included in equality standards, as is the case in the majority of general human rights conventions at both the global and regional level, such as the ICCPR, ICESCR, ACHR, ACHPR and ECHR, the legality of such measures depends on the interpretation of equality and non-discrimination standards by the relevant supervisory bodies. All of these have indeed accepted the permissibility of special measures to correct inequalities under their equality mandates as a matter of principle.[26] As will be explored in Section 7.4, this does not mean they are equally lenient in assessing the legality of concrete affirmative action measures. More generally, judicial interpretation and the degree of stringency in reviewing remedial measures varies significantly between jurisdictions.

---

that underlies s.15 as a whole'. Supreme Court of Canada, 27 June 2008, *R. v. Kapp*, [2008] 2 SCR 483 par. 16. The South African Constitutional Court held that remedial measures are not a deviation from the right to equality. They 'are not "reverse discrimination" or "positive discrimination"... and integral to the reach of our equality protection', Constitutional Court of South Africa, *Minister of Finance v. Van Heerden*, [2004] ZACC 3, par. 30.

24 Article 5 Directive 2000/43; Article 7(1) Directive 2000/78; Article 6 Directive 2000/113; Article 3 Directive 2006/54.

25 CJEU, 30 September 2004, *Briheche*, C-319/03, par. 25.

26 For an overview of equality standards in the main global and regional human rights conventions see M. Mwakagali, *International human rights law and discrimination protections. A comparison of regional and national responses*, Brill Research Perspectives in Comparative Discrimination Law, Brill, 2019.

7.3.3.1 Legal Obligation versus Legal Competence

The prohibitions of direct and indirect discrimination create a legal obligation for the duty bearer, be it a state or non-state actor, and a legal entitlement for the rights holder. Similarly, providing (reasonable) accommodation may constitute a legal obligation. The legal status of positive discrimination or positive action in terms of being permissive or compulsory seems less clear.[27]

Several courts have expressly held that affirmative action is not an obligation, but part of the discretionary powers of state authorities. Thus, the Canadian Supreme Court regards Section 15(2) of the Charter of Rights and Freedoms as a permissive mandate to protect ameliorative measures against challenges of 'reverse discrimination'. Similarly, the Indian Supreme Court and the Constitutional Court of South Africa approach remedial action as a type of measure allowed and encouraged by Constitutional equality standards, but not as an enforceable obligation.[28]

As far as I am aware, where courts have sometimes formulated a duty to take measures to reduce factual inequalities in general terms, they do so without actually specifying the precise nature of such measures. This leaves state authorities discretionary space for choosing between positive action directly based on a protected ground, or choosing much less controversial, neutral measures. The case law of the ECtHR regarding the segregation of Roma in education provides an example. As the Court has held this segregation to be discriminatory, states have 'to take steps to correct the applicants' factual inequality and avoid the perpetuation of the discrimination (...) thereby breaking their circle of marginalization'.[29] It does not, however, prescribe the specific type of action to be taken. Indeed, the Court time and again emphasizes that is up to the national authorities to choose the particular measures to end segregation.[30]

---

27 Cf. Fredman, Discrimination law, 2022, p. 431–432.

28 See the conclusions drawn by Fredman, Discrimination law, 2022, p. 431–432 and Albertyn and Goldblatt, Equality, 2007, p. 222–223. Tobler notes the same for EU law, Tobler, Indirect discrimination, Report 2022, p. 75.

29 ECtHR, 31 May 2022, *X and others v. Albania*, appl. no. 73548/17 and 45521/19, par. 84. The IACtHR also formulates a duty to take affirmative action in general terms, which it ties expressly to a substantive reading of equality: 'States are obliged to take affirmative action to reverse or change discriminatory situations that exist in their societies to the detriment of a specific group of persons', IACtHR, 17 September 2003, *Advisory Opinion OC-18/03 on Juridical condition and rights of the undocumented migrants*, par. 104.

30 This is repeated in ECtHR, 31 May 2022, *X and others v. Albania*, appl. no. 73548/17 and 45521/19, par. 86.

Even if an express legal basis is present, discussions on the legal acceptability of positive discrimination or positive action continue. A crucial question remains how far affirmative action measures may go. It may make quite a difference whether a preferential hiring policy is limited to giving priority to women or persons belonging to a racial minority group if they are 'equally qualified', or if these categories are given absolute preference for a period of twenty years. The combination of a far reaching type of preferential treatment with a long time period would seem to be clearly disproportionate, even if affirmative action is allowed as a matter of legal principle. As is the case regarding any of the modalities of discrimination discussed in the previous chapters, remedial measures are subject to justification review.

7.4 Positive Discrimination or Positive Action Review

Affirmative action review mirrors 'ordinary' discrimination review by requiring an objective and reasonable justification for adopting remedial measures. Yet, as its purpose is benign, the crucial question to be answered in any jurisdiction is whether it has to be reviewed with the same degree of strictness or in a much more lenient way.

7.4.1 *Symmetrical or Asymmetrical Equality Approaches – Strict or Lenient Scrutiny*

As Chapter 4 discussed, to justify a classification on a protected ground it has to serve a legitimate aim and the means chosen to achieve this aim have to meet requirements of proportionality. Ultimately, the level of scrutiny to be applied in this assessment is crucial.

Approaches to the degree of stringency to be applied where remedial measures are concerned may diverge significantly between jurisdictions. This has considerable consequences for the actual use that can be made of affirmative action measures by governmental bodies, employers, educational institutions or other organisations. A central question in this respect is whether equality and non-discrimination standards are approached in a symmetrical or asymmetrical way.

A symmetrical reading regards distinctions based on a protected ground as always suspect and hard to justify, regardless whether it is to the detriment of an already disadvantaged group, or intended to improve their position. It ties in with a formal equality approach. Judicial scrutiny of remedial measures can be expected to be very strict as it is to be viewed with as much suspicion as 'ordinary' discrimination directly based on a protected ground. Several legal ways of constructing more stringent scrutiny were explored in Chapter 4 (Section 4.4.2) which may affect all elements of justification review: the legitimacy of the aim of the challenged rule or policy, the proportionality or 'fit' between means and ends, and the balancing with other rights and interests that may be involved.

Understandings of equality and non-discrimination standards in terms of substantive equality have a very different take on remedial measures as they are not preoccupied with the sameness or difference of the treatment as such. They look at the outcome of the treatment, be the latter the same or different. If affirmative action is aimed at a positive effect for a structurally disadvantage groups, it is not to be viewed with suspicion. Judicial review can be expected to be much more lenient. It will allow for much more leeway for the state or private actors to design remedial measures. A more lenient assessment will be less demanding regarding the various elements of the justification review mentioned above.

The crucial difference of taking a symmetrical or asymmetrical approach for assessing the compatibility of affirmative action measures with equality standards can be illustrated with a landmark case decided by the US Supreme Court, in which the majority and the dissenting opinions broke down along this dividing line.

7.4.1.1 Symmetrical Approach – the US Supreme Court

The 1995 judgment of the US Supreme Court in the case *Adarand Constructors* is very illuminating.[31] In this case the Court was faced with a federal affirmative action policy concerning federal agency contracts. The policy provided for financial compensation if the prime contractor hired subcontractors certified as small businesses controlled by socially and economically disadvantaged individuals. Racial minorities were presumed to fall into this category. Adarand Constructors was not a certified business. Because of this policy, it missed out on a contract. Adarand claimed the race-based presumption in the affirmative action policy violated the constitutional equality clause.

The 5–4 majority of the Supreme Court agreed. What is important to notice here is the level of scrutiny it applied to reach this decision. The Court decided the long standing question whether 'benign' discrimination, intended to improve the position of racial minorities, should be considered in the same way as 'invidious' discrimination against them. It answered this question in the affirmative: the level of review in both cases should be strict scrutiny.[32]

31 United States Supreme Court, *Adarand Constructors v. Federico Pena*, 515 US 200 (1995).

32 Idem, p. 227. For the characteristics of the strict scrutiny test see Chapter 4, Section 4.4.2.

In this context the Court stressed the personal character of the right to equal protection: it has the same meaning for everyone, as the equality clause 'protects persons, not groups'. Thus, the Supreme Court clearly took a symmetrical approach to the equality clause. Distinctions based on race are always highly suspect and subject to strict scrutiny. This leaves very little room for affirmative action.

The repeated emphasis by the Court on the personal character of the right to equal treatment aligns closely with views questioning the legitimacy of affirmative action because of the lack of fit between the individual persons who suffer from it and those who benefit. Preferential treatment cannot be justified by the social realities and consequences of past discrimination. At bottom, any misfit between the victims/perpetrators of discrimination on the one hand, and those who profit/suffer from affirmative action on the other, is unacceptable to the Court. Only very narrowly tailored measures serving a compelling state interest, that is measures which fit seamlessly with concrete instances of discrimination, seem to be able to survive such an individualized interpretation of the constitutional equality standards.

The dissenters profoundly disagreed with this approach. They adopted an asymmetrical reading of equality by stressing the need to differentiate between benign and invidious discrimination in the level of scrutiny to be applied, as '[t]here is no moral or constitutional equivalent between a policy that is designed to perpetuate a caste system and one that seeks to eradicate racial subordination'.[33] In their eyes the majority approach is flawed because it ignores the decisive relevance of the social and historical context of discrimination on the basis of race. A proper, contextual approach means that only classifications which exclude racial minorities should be subject to strict scrutiny, not those meant to be inclusionary. 'No sensible conception of the Government's constitutional obligation to "govern impartially", (…) should ignore this distinction'.[34]

The approach by the dissenters resonates with views supporting the legitimacy of affirmative action by pointing to the need of collective redress for past discrimination. For them, this should result in much more lenient justification review. By giving centre stage to the (historical) context of race discrimination the dissenters take an expressly asymmetrical approach. The differing results of both approaches are evident: under strict scrutiny hardly any classification will survive.

33 Idem, dissenting opinion, p. 243.
34 Idem, p. 243.

More recently, a fully symmetrical approach to affirmative action has also been adopted by the Supreme Court regarding affirmative action policies in higher education. In 2023 the Court struck down the admissions policies of Harvard College (a private institution) and of the University of North Carolina (a public institution), which took into account the racial background of potential students as one among a range of other factors to promote diversity of the student body.[35] The Supreme Court held that all the qualities or characteristics of a prospective student may be taken into account, but each student 'must be treated based on his or her experiences as an individual – not on the basis of race'.[36] As a consequence, diversity may still be a goal in higher education, but it has to be reached by race neutral policies and practices, such as targeted outreach or pathway programmes.[37]

In the US context, taking a symmetrical approach has a peculiar effect if we compare affirmative action for racial minorities with remedial measures for women. As 'ordinary' discrimination on the basis of sex meets with a more lenient review standard than discrimination on the basis of race (see Chapter 4, Section 4.4.2), it would follow that affirmative action for women is also to be assessed under a less stringent test.[38]

7.4.1.2 Asymmetrical Approach – Canada and South Africa

Contrary to the US Supreme Court, in Canada and South Africa the highest courts have adopted an asymmetrical line of reasoning. As explained in Chapter 3, Section 3.4.3, in view of their substantive approach to equality the amelioration of the position of disadvantaged groups in society is considered to be a major purpose of the equality and non-discrimination standards in the Canadian Charter of Fundamental Rights and Freedoms and in the South African Constitution. In the leading case *Kapp*, the Supreme Court of Canada emphasizes the independent role of the provision on 'ameliorative measures' in Section 15(2) of the Charter as part of this substantive equality goal. This section is not to be read as an exception to the prohibition of discrimination in

35 United States Supreme Court, *SFFA v. President and fellows of Harvard College*, and joined case *SFFA v. University of North Carolina*, 600 US 181 (2023).

36 Idem, p. 40.

37 Cf. Department of Justice and Department of Education, *Questions and answers regarding the Supreme Court's decision in Students for Fair Admissions v. Harvard College*, 14 August 2023, p. 3. https://www.justice.gov/d9/2023-08/post-sffa_resource_faq_final_508.pdf.

38 In *Mississippi University for Women v. Hogan*, 458 US 718 (1982), the US Supreme Court indeed applied the 'substantially related' test to assess an affirmative action measure. The majority held that it did not pass that test. This case is still the leading precedent for affirmative action regarding women.

Section 15(1), but as enabling governments to pro-actively combat discrimination by designing programs directed at improving the situation of disadvantaged groups.[39] As a consequence, ameliorative policies will not be subject to scrutiny under Section 15(1) if the government can demonstrate they fit the criteria mentioned in Section 15(2): they have an ameliorative or remedial purpose and target a disadvantaged group protected by Section 15.[40]

The South African Constitutional Court also emphasizes that remedial measures as envisaged in Section 9(2) of the Constitution, that is measures designed to protect or advance persons or categories of persons who have been disadvantaged by unfair discrimination, are not a deviation from the right to equality and non-discrimination: 'They are not "reverse discrimination" or "positive discrimination"'.[41] For this reason they meet with significantly less stringent judicial review. As the Court formulates it, 'the remedial measure must be reasonably capable of attaining the desired outcome'.[42] This boils down to a quite lenient test, which 'does not seem to be much more onerous than a rationality test'.[43]

7.4.2 *Grey Areas: Varying Levels of Scrutiny Depending on Subject Matter*

If an express legal mandate exists for positive discrimination or positive action, an asymmetrical and thus more lenient review may be likely, but this is not always the case. In fact, the type of measure and subject matter seem also very important for the degree of strictness. As so often, the particular context may considerably influence the degree of stringency of justification review. The jurisprudence of the ECtHR provides some clear examples of varying levels of scrutiny depending on the type and subject matter of the remedial measure involved.

The standard of review for remedial measures set out in the Grand Chamber judgment in *Stec* seems quite straightforward.[44] The case concerned different pensionable age for men and women, which was originally intended to correct the disadvantaged economic position of women, due to the traditional, gendered division of paid labour and unpaid care. The Court reiterates in general terms that Article 14 ECHR does not prohibit treating men and women

39 Supreme Court of Canada, *R. v. Kapp*, [2008] 2 SCR 483, par. 35–38.

40 Idem, par. 40–41.

41 Constitutional Court of South Africa, *Minister of Finance v. Van Heerden*, [2004] ZACC 3, par. 30.

42 Idem, par. 41.

43 Albertyn and Goldblatt, Equality, 2007, p. 39.

44 ECtHR (Grand Chamber), 12 April 2006, *Stec and Others v. the United Kingdom*, appl. no. 65900/01 and 65731/01.

differently in order to correct factual inequalities. In this context it allows the States parties a wide margin of appreciation, also in view of the socio-economic nature of the arrangements at stake. In the case at hand, the Court accepts that the difference in pensionable age is not 'manifestly unreasonable' in view of their origin and of the steps taken by the UK to end this inequality in the future, when social and economic changes will have removed the need for this type of special treatment of women. Until that time the UK enjoys a wide margin of appreciation in choosing the time frame and steps to take towards this end.[45] This review standard is a far cry from the 'very weighty reasons' test usually applied in sex discrimination cases.

In other types of cases regarding remedial measures for women the ECtHR is much less lenient in its review. According to Sjöholm a clear line can be drawn between affirmative action measures to correct economic inequalities and remedial measures intended to compensate inequalities resulting from unequal child-rearing and parenting roles.[46] In the latter context, remedial measures which are actually designed to or have the effect of enhancing traditional and stereotypical gender roles are assessed on the basis of the 'very weighty reasons' test. Thus, the Court is not inclined to easily accept different treatment of men and women regarding parental leave or other benefits connected to child-rearing, regardless their alleged remedial purpose.[47] In fact, the Court seems to reject the idea that this type of measure can be seen (any longer) as remedial at all.

The judgment in *Beeler* can illustrate this reasoning.[48] The Court had to deal with a difference in treatment between widows and widowers regarding pension benefits. Before 1997, Swiss survivor's pensions were limited to widows. When widower's pensions were introduced, they were limited to widowers taking care of children under eighteen. A similar reduction of the entitlements of widows was not considered appropriate yet in view of the still continuing unequal division of gender roles. In the case at hand, the complainant, who had given up his job to raise his children after he became a widower, was faced with a lack of income when his youngest child came of age.

In its assessment of the compatibility of this regulation with the equality standards under the ECHR, the Court does not inquire whether the

---

45 Idem, par. 66.

46 M. Sjöholm, *Gender-sensitive norm interpretation by regional human rights law systems*, Leiden/Boston, Brill, 2018, p. 200–207.

47 See e.g. ECtHR (Grand Chamber), 22 March 2012, *Konstantin Markin v. Russia*, appl. no. 30078/06.

48 ECtHR (Grand Chamber), 11 October 2022, *Beeler v. Switzerland*, appl. no. 78630/12.

arrangement is 'not manifestly unreasonable', but applies the 'very weighty reasons' test.[49] It rejects the argument of the government, that the difference can still be seen as intended 'to compensate for the less favourable situation of women in the labour market and the persisting unequal distribution of household tasks'.[50] Instead, it considers that 'the old "factual inequalities" between men and women have become less marked' and that accordingly such assumptions cannot justify the difference in treatment anymore. The Court adds that the legislation rather contributes 'to perpetuating prejudices and stereotypes regarding the nature or role of women in society and is disadvantageous both to women's careers and to men's family life'.[51]

What becomes apparent in this type of case is the dependence of the acceptability of remedial measures on the factual circumstances in which inequalities figure, which may change over time. It seems to imply that governments have to monitor and adjust them if developments warrant it. It also seem to suggest that at some point, the remedial nature itself of such measures may become questioned.

Another case regarding remedial measure in which the Court applied much more stringent scrutiny than a 'not manifestly unreasonable' test concerned political representation of particular ethnic groups in Bosnia and Herzegovina after the war in the former Yugoslavia.[52] As agreed in the 1995 peace arrangements, the constitution of Bosnia and Herzegovina provided for a system of power-sharing which limited eligibility to several political bodies to the so-called 'constituent peoples'. These included Bosniacs, Croats and Serbs, but excluded members of other groups such as citizens of Roma or Jewish origin.

In this case the ECtHR reiterates that the applicable standard of review for any difference of treatment on the basis of race or ethnic origin must be very strict, the starting point being that discrimination based solely or to a decisive extent on a person's ethnic origin cannot be objectively justified in today's democratic society.[53] The Court acknowledges the exceptionality of the case and the importance of the power-sharing system as an important element in endeavours to end a brutal conflict. This context 'could explain, without necessarily justifying' the arrangements made at the time, but the Court considers the maintenance of this system in any event to violate the requirements

49 Idem, par. 95.

50 Idem, par. 91.

51 Idem, par. 113.

52 ECtHR (Grand Chamber), 22 December 2009, *Sejdić and Finci v. Bosnia and Herzegovina*, appl. nos. 27996/06 and 34836/06.

53 Idem, par. 44.

of proportionality. In coming to this conclusion the Court points to the positive developments which have taken place since 1995 and to the availability of alternative ways of power-sharing, which do not exclude other vulnerable groups.[54]

Significant varieties in the actual stringency of assessing affirmative action measures are also visible in the case law of the CJEU. In the cases *Kalanke* and *Marschall*, the CJEU almost closed the door to any preferential treatment policy regarding access to jobs.[55] At issue were affirmative action policies to redress the under-representation of women in certain functions. The measures gave priority to women in the selection process if they were 'equally qualified'. This is quite a weak form of preferential treatment. The CJEU takes an almost fully symmetrical approach to this type of remedial measure by rejecting any policy which gives 'absolute and unconditional' priority to women when women and men are equally qualified.[56] Ultimately, an individual assessment of the qualities of the candidates must be included in the selection process, which takes account of the specific personal situations of all candidates.[57] The judgments clearly preclude any more far-reaching preferential treatment measures, such as giving preference to 'sufficiently qualified' female candidates.[58]

Regarding other types of preferential measures, however, the CJEU has taken a much more lenient approach. In the case *Badeck* a quite comprehensive remedial programme was at stake regarding access and promotion of women to eliminate their under-representation in the public service.[59] The Court reiterates its very restrictive approach to preferential treatment in access to certain functions, but takes a far more lenient perspective on some other, binding targets included in the programme. One of these consists of allocating at least half of certain training places to prepare for higher functions to women. The Court considers this an acceptable measure to improve the ability of women to compete on the labour market and to pursue a career on an equal footing with men. The CJEU explains the difference in the strictness of its assessment standard by regarding the first type of preferential treatment as directed at an (unacceptable) goal of equality of result, and the latter as one of (acceptable) equality of opportunity: 'The provision at issue ... forms part of a restricted concept of equality of opportunity. It is not places in employment

54 Idem, par. 46–48.
55 CJEU, 17 October 1995, *Kalanke*, C-450/93; CJEU, 11 November 1997, *Marschall*, C-409/95.
56 CJEU, 17 October 1995, *Kalanke*, C-450/93, par. 22.
57 CJEU, 11 November 1997, *Marschall*, C-409/95, par. 35.
58 CJEU, 6 July 2000, *Abrahamsson*, C-407/98, par.56.
59 CJEU, 28 March 2000, *Badeck*, C-158/97.

which are reserved for women but places in training with a view to obtaining qualifications with the prospect of subsequent access to trained occupations in the public service'.[60]

A similar, more asymmetrical approach in cases dealing with remedial measures other than access to jobs is confirmed in the decision of the Court in *Lommers*.[61] This case concerned a policy by a Dutch ministry, which reserved very scarce childcare facilities for female staff. An exception was made for male staff in exceptional circumstances, like single fathers. Interestingly, Advocate General Alber identifies this preferential treatment measure as an expression of the principle of equal treatment, as this principle seeks to create a substantive equality and not just a formal one.[62] The CJEU considers this particular affirmative action policy justified. In view of the extreme scarcity of available nursery places, it does not exceed the requirements of proportionality.[63] Both *Badeck* and *Lommers* suggest the CJEU leaves more leeway for remedial policies, as long as these do not focus on direct access to jobs.

The above examples of ambivalences and inconsistencies in the strictness of judicial review may well be related to several specific difficulties and dilemmas which judicial bodies have to respond to in assessing remedial measures.

7.5 Difficulties and Dilemmas of Positive Discrimination or Positive Action Review

7.5.1 *Demarcation of the Beneficiary Group*

As Fredman notes, delineating the beneficiaries of affirmative action is a 'particularly controversial issue' courts have to deal with.[64] This issue appears in different shapes. In judicial review it often translates into the question how much or what kinds of over- and underinclusion, or misfit, between the means and ends of a concrete remedial measure is acceptable. If judicial review is lenient it allows for much more misfit than if it is strict, but both over- and underinclusion of affirmative action policies may create their own dilemmas.

60 Idem, par. 52.
61 CJEU, 19 March 2002, *Lommers*, C-476/99.
62 Opinion of Advocate General S. Alber, 6 November 2001, case *Lommers*, C-476/99.
63 Idem, par. 43–47.
64 Fredman, Discrimination law, 2022, p. 419.

7.5.1.1 Overinclusion

Overinclusion may be at stake if the beneficiary group of a remedial measure is itself diverse and also consists of people who are quite privileged rather than being disadvantaged. Though this may mean they are not really in need of affirmative action to help them along, they may benefit most from such measures precisely by their privileged position within the group. A prime example may be derived from experiences in India with affirmative action programmes, where it has become known as the 'creamy layer' problem.[65] Many wealthy members of the target groups – scheduled castes and tribes, and 'backward classes' – profited from the reservations for these categories in public employment and higher education. In response, the Indian Supreme Court held in 1993 that the reservations should be linked to actual economic disadvantage to exclude the creamy layer.[66] In this way, the Supreme Court in fact acknowledges the importance of the often compounded nature of structural disadvantage, flowing from multiple or intersectional discrimination. At the same time, using economic disadvantage as an additional criterion requires the development of indicators to decide about the in-group and the out-group. This may give rise to new contestation and make remedial measures more complicated to properly implement.[67]

A special instance of overinclusion may arise when a remedial measure is not based on a protected ground as such, but on a proxy, that is a neutral criterion that is very closely aligned to the disadvantaged group.[68] As a result, the beneficiaries of the measure may also include persons belonging to the dominant, advantaged group. The South African case *Van Heerden* is an interesting example. At stake was a remedial financial measure to diminish the pension gap between post-Apartheid parliamentarians and those from the Apartheid era. The far majority of the former group had previously been excluded from political representation, but not all of them. Some beneficiaries belonged to a formerly advantaged group of white parliamentarians. According to the Constitutional Court, this overinclusion does not affect the validity of the

65 Fredman, Discrimination law, 2022, p. 419.

66 Supreme Court of India, 16 November 1992, *Indra Sawhney v. Union of India*, discussed in Fredman, Discrimination law, 2022, p. 386–387 and Oppenheimer, The ubiquity of positive measures, 2019, p. 30–31.

67 As Oppenheimer remarks: 'Determining who precisely should benefit, is an ongoing point of contention', Oppenheimer, The ubiquity of positive measures, 2019, p. 32.

68 This type of remedial measure could be termed 'indirect affirmative action', cf. Fredman, Discrimination law, 2022, p. 299–300.

remedial scheme. It should be judged 'by whether an overwhelming majority of members of the favoured class are persons designated as disadvantaged by unfair exclusion'.[69] A certain degree of misfit is allowed.

7.5.1.2 Underinclusion

A degree of misfit between the remedial measure and the beneficiary group may also arise by the underinclusion of certain groups in concrete affirmative action measures. In India, for example, Muslim and Christian Dalits are not covered by the reservations for the scheduled castes and tribe due to the identification of the caste system with the Hindu religion. Currently, a challenge to this exclusion is pending for the Supreme Court.[70]

Other examples of underinclusion of remedial measures can be derived from Canada and South Africa. So far, these cases show how both Courts apply a rather lenient review and accept the leeway of the relevant authorities to limit ameliorative measures to particular disadvantaged groups, even if this excludes others. In *Alberta v. Cunningham*, the Supreme Court of Canada had to deal with ameliorative measures on behalf of a distinct aboriginal community, the Métis, which excluded members of other aboriginal groups with a similar history of disadvantage. According to the Court, this does not render such measures unacceptable under the constitutional equality standards. The Court accepts these measures to benefit some groups only:

> Ameliorative programs, by their nature, confer benefits on one group that are not conferred on others. These distinctions are generally protected if they serve or advance the object of the program, thus promoting substantive equality. This is so even where the included and excluded groups are aboriginals who share a similar history of disadvantage and marginalization.[71]

The Court adds that it is not necessary to go into the question of the precise considerations for the distinctions made in ameliorative programmes, as '[t]he law is best left to develop on an incremental basis.'[72] The formulations used by the Court clearly imply a rather lenient review of the permissibility of the

---

69 Van Heerden, par. 40.

70 '"Won't wait for panel", SC to rule on quota for Dalit Muslims, Christians', *Times of India*, 13 April 2023. At the time of writing it was still pending.

71 Supreme Court of Canada, *Alberta v. Cunningham*, [2011] 2 SCR 670, par. 53.

72 Idem, par. 55.

challenged measure and a willingness to leave a wide margin of appreciation to the government in developing its ameliorative policies.

A similar leniency is visible in South Africa. A leading case in this respect is *Motala v. University of Natal.*[73] The case regarded an Indian student with excellent credentials. She was nevertheless denied admission to the university as a consequence of an affirmative action policy on behalf of African applicants. Because of the poor educational record of this group under *Apartheid*, the admissions criteria they had to meet were lower than for other applicants. This remedial policy was not considered to violate the constitutional equality standards. Though it was acknowledged that both Indian and African pupils had been disadvantaged by the *Apartheid* system, the measure was justified because the degree of disadvantage suffered by African pupils had been significantly greater.

As the above decisions show, applying more lenient review to classifications based on a protected ground if they are designed for remedial purposes, allows for leeway to differentiate between disadvantaged groups in providing affirmative action. This points to another difficulty or dilemma in designing and reviewing ameliorative programmes: they may involve or lead to competition between vulnerable groups regarding access to scarce resources.[74]

7.5.1.3 Competition between Vulnerable Groups for Scarce Resources

Affirmative action policies may regard a variety of vulnerable and disadvantaged groups, be it women, persons belonging to racial groups, disabled people or religious and cultural minorities. Which groups would deserve support by remedial measures is context-specific, but where available resources are scarce, deciding which groups are to be included in remedial programmes will always involve drawing lines of a more or less painful nature.

The South African case law provides several examples to illustrate the dilemmas and complexities this may result in when designing remedial policies. The example of the competition between African and Indian students regarding access to higher education in the case *Motala* was already discussed in the previous section. In *Solidarity v. Department of correctional services* the Constitutional Court was faced with an affirmative action policy designed to achieve a more representational workforce in the Department of correctional

73 This case was not decided by the Constitutional Court, but by the (then) Supreme Court, *Motala and another v. University of Natal*, 1995 (3) BCLR 374.

74 Cf. Fredman, Discrimination law, 2023, p. 427.

services.[75] The numerical targets formulated were based on the overall population in South Africa, which roughly amounted to almost 80% African, 9% coloured, 2.5% Indian, and 9% white people. The remedial measure was challenged by coloured applicants, who were denied a job because coloured workers were already over-represented. The Constitutional Court held that using this type of ceiling for various groups did not violate the equality clause, even if it did affect in this case persons of a disadvantaged group. It agreed with the government that the 'level of representation of each group must broadly accord with its representation among the people of South Africa'.[76] As a consequence, denying 'an African, Coloured person or Indian person appointment to a certain occupational level' on the basis that they are 'already overrepresented or adequately represented in that level' is allowed.[77] The applicants were nevertheless successful in their claim for a different reason: the numbers relied on should have been more specific than the national statistics, as the Western Cape region has a significantly different demographic composition. As a result of *Apartheid* policies, coloured people are concentrated in this region so make up a much larger part of the population. This should have been reflected in setting the targets.[78] This judgment again shows the importance of the degree of scrutiny applied by courts in assessing the acceptability of remedial measures under equality standards. If the review would have been very strict, as is the case in the American approach to affirmative action, this type of remedial measure would not survive judicial scrutiny.

An even more complicated affirmative action policy was at stake in a case regarding the appointment process of – still predominantly white and male – insolvency practitioners.[79] The remedial programme included an intersectional approach by combining the various racial categories relevant to remedial measures in South Africa with gender. The scheme operated on the basis of four categories of beneficiaries who were given different degrees of preference in a ratio of 4:3:2:1. Category A consisted of African, Coloured, Indian and Chinese women who had become citizens before democracy was established in 1994. Category B comprised of African, Coloured, Indian and Chinese men who became citizens before that date and category C of white

75 Constitutional Court of South Africa, *Solidarity and others v. Department of correctional services and others*, [2016] ZACC 18.

76 Idem, par. 40.

77 Idem, par. 49.

78 Idem, par. 78–79.

79 Constitutional Court of South Africa, *Minister of Constitutional Development and another v. South African Restructuring and Insolvency Practitioners Association and others*, [2018] ZACC 20.

women who were already citizens in 1994. Category D consisted of white men and all persons who became citizens after the *Apartheid* period, whatever their gender or regardless their racial affiliation. The Court does not consider this an acceptable form of remedial action. This is not caused by the first three categories, but by the fourth one, which it holds to be arbitrary.[80] Category D lumps together white men with groups which were also disadvantaged under *Apartheid*[81] and with young people belonging to these disadvantaged groups, who also still suffer the consequences of that period. As such, the policy is not 'reasonably likely to achieve equality'.[82]

7.5.2 *Thin or Blurred lines between Remedial Measures and 'Ordinary' Social Policies*

In social welfare states, all sorts of policies are developed to improve the position of specific groups facing particular problems or hardship. These may range from targeted skills training for unemployed youth or women re-entering the labour market, providing additional language courses for pupils with a migrant or ethnic minority background and tax reductions for single parents or the elderly, to providing social counselling services in poor neighbourhoods, financing women's shelters or setting up specific campaigns to combat hate speech against LGBTIQ+ people.

Though public views regarding the desirability of these types of policies may self-evidently differ, generally speaking their legitimacy or legality are not very likely to be fundamentally challenged. Two things merit attention in this context. First of all, in the examples mentioned, considerable degrees of over- or underinclusion are commonly accepted. Though not all single parents or the elderly need extra financial support, tax reductions do not seem to raise considerable protest as long as the majority of these groups need them and assessing need on an individual basis may be too cumbersome or expensive to operationalize. Similarly, subsidizing women's shelters may be underinclusive as victims of domestic violence are not always female, but this underinclusion does not render such subsidies invalid. Governments have a large leeway to develop social policies and limit the beneficiary groups, if only because financial resources are inherently limited. Not all needs of all people can be satisfied at the same time. Secondly, the types of policies mentioned are

80 Idem, par. 51.

81 In this context the Court recalls that under the Apartheid system millions of black people living in the 'so-called independent homelands' were stripped of South African citizenship, par. 50.

82 Idem, par. 58.

usually not framed in terms of positive discrimination or affirmative action, even if they use classifications based on a protected ground. Rather, this type of treating different groups of people differently to respond to their specific needs are indeed part and parcel of what can be considered 'ordinary' social policy making.

If this is the case, why then do some social policies become identified as 'affirmative action' and raise so much more controversy? As I understand it, remedial measures are hardly contested as long as those who do not benefit from these measures do not face concrete negative effects at a *personal*, individual level or do not feel *individually* wronged. The latter seems closely linked to the expectations people have of being entitled to a fully individualized or personalized treatment or not. Let me clarify this.

The types of positive discrimination or positive action generating the fiercest controversies usually focus on preferential treatment of women or racial minorities regarding access to jobs and education to reduce underrepresentation. An explanation for this particularly strong opposition can be found in two characteristics of such measures. To start with, those who bear the burden of the preferential treatment are identifiable individuals. This group consists of all the other (potential) applicants who do not belong to the categories receiving preferential treatment. For them the pain of affirmative action is concrete and directly felt. In addition, where access to employment and education is at stake, preferential treatment in the selection process runs counter to widely shared convictions that individual merit should be the one and only determining criterion for allocating such valuable yet scarce goods: the best candidate is entitled to a particular job or place in education.[83] This requires a fully personalized assessment.[84]

These two characteristics are much less prominent or absent in the other types of social policy mentioned above, which may also use classifications based directly on race or sex. Money spent on language support for ethnic minority pupils or skills training for unemployed youth or women re-entering the labour market cannot be spent on other policies, but this effect is very diffuse and remains largely invisible. It does not translate into an identifiable group of individuals bearing the costs. In addition, allocation of this type of

83 I might add that in these dominant perceptions awareness of the unconscious bias which may be present in what is 'best' and who is 'best' is usually absent.

84 As Fredman explains in her analysis of the case law of the CJEU, this emphasis on individual merit is crucial for the approach taken by the Luxemburg Court and its principled rejection of giving 'automatic' priority to women, even if the preferential treatment is limited to situations in which women and men are equally qualified. Fredman, Discrimination law, 2022, p. 398–402.

resources seems more easily accepted as being group-based. It is not closely linked to strong expectations of being based on an exclusively individualized assessment of need.

7.5.3 *Thin or Blurred Lines between Remedial Measures, 'Ordinary' Discrimination and (Reasonable) Accommodation*

The lines between remedial measures and 'ordinary' discrimination may sometimes be quite fuzzy. Examples can be particularly derived from affirmative action on behalf of women responding to their – still predominant – role as the primary caretaker. Hard to classify cases may come in several shapes.

Sometimes the adverse effects of ameliorative measures may challenge the remedial nature of a policy as such. The judgment of the ECtHR in the case *Beeler*, discussed in Section 7.4.2, may provide an example. The more favourable pension benefit accorded to mothers to acknowledge the disadvantage they experience on the labour market due to the continuing unequal distribution of parental roles was not accepted by the Court, because it considered the legislation to perpetuate stereotypes of the role of women in society and thus being 'disadvantageous to both women's careers and men's family life'.[85]

In other instances, policies may be presented as having a remedial purpose, whereas their ulterior motive is directed at protecting and enhancing traditional parental roles. The Strasbourg case *Konstantin Markin* is an illustrative example.[86] Though the Russian government tried to save a policy providing for a three year period of parental leave exclusively for female military personnel by arguing, among others, that it constituted positive discrimination, the ECtHR did not buy this argument. It considered it 'misconceived', as the arrangement was 'clearly not intended to correct the disadvantaged position of women in society or "factual inequalities" between men and women'.[87]

Other examples of cases belonging to grey areas in between affirmative action and 'ordinary' discrimination regard favourable treatment of mothers because of considerations of the 'best interests of the child'. The judgment of the Constitutional Court of South Africa in *Hugo* is a case in point.[88] At stake was a presidential pardon for certain categories of prisoners, including young people, disabled people and all mothers with minor children under the age of

85 ECtHR (Grand Chamber), 11 October 2022, *Beeler v. Switzerland*, appl. no. 78630/12, par. 113.

86 ECtHR (Grand Chamber), 22 March 2012, *Konstantin Markin v. Russia*, appl. no. 30078/06.

87 Idem, par. 141.

88 Constitutional Court of South Africa, *President of the Republic of South Africa and Another v. Hugo*, [1997] ZACC 4.

twelve. Excluding fathers with young children was based on several reasons. Releasing all fathers in the same position would not only mean a very high number of prisoners would be released, as the male prison population was fiftyfold the number of women, but given the realities of women shouldering the primary burden of care taking, it would be much less effective in serving the interests of children. The Court accepts these arguments. In doing so it expressly considers that the difference in treatment does not affect a historically disadvantaged group.[89] Though this does not render an inquiry into the justification for the measure redundant, it affects the strictness of the Court's review.[90] The judgment again shows the relevance of taking an asymmetrical rather than symmetrical approach to discrimination.

Thin or blurred lines may also exist between remedial measures and (reasonable) accommodation as becomes apparent in the context of maternity leave and parental leave. Providing maternity leave is a form of (reasonable) accommodation to recover from giving birth to a child and physically and mentally adjusting to the new situation before returning to work. When maternity leave turns into parental leave for mothers only to overcome the particular difficulties they face compared to men to retain their job and taking care of children, it enters the realm of affirmative action.

This raises two difficulties. Firstly, as maternity leave may differ widely between countries, both in terms of the period of leave and the financial compensation provided, where is the line to be drawn between maternity leave and parental leave for women only? What is a 'reasonable' maternity leave, and when does such leave stop being an arrangement to do justice to the specific needs of the parent who gives birth to a child? Extending maternity leave to a long period may well provide a barrier against more equal sharing of family responsibilities between men and women.[91] To answer such questions, in the

---

89 Idem, par. 41.

90 A case of a quite similar nature decided by the ECtHR regarded the possibility of staying the execution of a prison sentence for women with a child below one year of age, also in view of the best interest of the child. The ECtHR upholds this measure by considering both the 'best interest' argument and the special bonds between mother and child during this period as relevant factors. In considering all the elements of this case, the Court applies a more lenient test than the 'very weighty reasons' standard. It accepts that the arguments put forward by the Romanian government 'can constitute a sufficient basis for justifying the difference in treatment'. ECtHR, 3 October 2017, *Alexandru Eneche v. Romania*, appl. no. 16986/12, par. 76.

91 S. Burri, Parents who want to reconcile work and care: which equality under EU law? In: M. van den Brink, S. Burri and J.Goldschmidt (eds.), (2015) *Equality and human rights: nothing but trouble? Liber amicorum Titia Loenen* (*SIM Special*), SIM/Utrecht University, 2015, p. 261–277, at p.276.

European context the EU legislator has developed legal standards harmonizing maternity leave and parental leave arrangements.[92]

A second difficulty concerns the question to what extent parental leave exclusively provided to women can be regarded as an acceptable form of remedial action to support them in combining paid work and family responsibilities. Limiting parental leave to women for this reason was quite commonly accepted in European countries in the seventies and eighties of the past century. The cases *Hofmann* decided by the CJEU and *Petrovic* assessed by the ECtHR attest to this. Both courts accepted a (partly paid) parental leave arrangement for mothers after expiry of the maternity leave period from which fathers were excluded to support them in combining paid work and care.[93] Since then, traditional divisions of gender roles have shifted much further. As a result, limiting parental leave to mothers is not considered acceptable anymore, as is apparent, for example, from the judgment of the ECtHR in *Konstantin Markin* and reaffirmed in *Gruba*.[94] In fact, the emphasis the Court puts on the detrimental effects of reserving parental leave to women on both mothers and fathers by reproducing stereotypical gender roles, suggests it regards it as 'ordinary' discrimination and cannot be regarded anymore as a remedial measure at all.[95] Social developments have rendered such perceptions as outdated.

7.6 Concluding Remarks

Positive discrimination or positive action to correct or reduce factual inequalities between structurally disadvantaged and advantaged groups in society remains a controversial and contested issue. Though it is generally allowed in most jurisdictions as a matter of legal principle, to what degree it is actually

92 Council Directive 92/85/EEC of 19 October 1992 on the introduction of measures to encourage improvements in the safety and health at work of pregnant workers and workers who have recently given birth or are breastfeeding (tenth individual Directive within the meaning of Article 16(1) of Directive 89/391/EEC); ; Directive (EU) 2019/1158 of the European Parliament and of the Council of 20 June 2019 on work-life balance for parents and carers and repealing Council Directive 2010/18/EU.

93 CJEU, 12 July 1984, *Hofmann*, C-184/83; ECtHR, 27 March 1998, *Petrovic v. Austria*, appl. no. 20458/92.

94 ECtHR (Grand Chamber), 22 March 2007, *Konstantin Markin v. Russia*, appl. no. 30078/06; ECtHR, 6 July 2021, *Gruba and others v. Russia*, appl. no. 66180/09.

95 See ECtHR, *Gruba*, 2021, par. 80. For the EU see CJEU, 30 September 2010, *Roca Álvarez*, C-104/09. In this case the CJEU held that a regulation denying fathers the same rights as mothers to time off for taking care of his children violated equal treatment standards.

accepted may differ widely. Judicial bodies play a crucial role in demarcating the boundaries.

Where remedial measures are at stake, the level of scrutiny applied in judicial review is usually lower than the standard applicable to 'ordinary' discrimination, the US being an exception. More lenient review indicates an asymmetrical and more substantive rather than formal approach to equality. Nevertheless, within asymmetrical approaches, degrees of scrutiny may still differ considerably depending on the type of measure and other factors involved, such as the policy area and other rights or interests involved. As with justification review regarding the modalities of discrimination discussed in the preceding chapters, the stringency of assessing the acceptability of remedial measures is influenced by a variety of other factors.

Affirmative action to reduce underrepresentation of women or persons belonging to racial groups in employment and education seems to be the most contested type of remedial measure. In this context, identifiable, individual people often bear the burden of the policy. Feelings of being personally wronged are exacerbated by the expectation that selection for a job or a coveted place in education will be based on a fully personalized treatment on the basis of individual merit.

The increasing experience with remedial policies, particularly in India and South Africa, show how affirmative action policies come with their own distinct problems. Particularly the demarcation between and within disadvantaged groups profiting from remedial measures may pose complex questions for judicial bodies called on to review their acceptability under the prevalent equality standards. In addition, the boundaries between affirmative action, (reasonable) accommodation and 'ordinary' discrimination may be quite fuzzy, as is the boundary between remedial measures and other types of social policy common in social welfare states. Such complexities seem particularly present when measures are called for to improve the position of a variety of disadvantaged groups. In this context, multiple and intersectional discrimination may be at stake, which is the topic of the next chapter.

CHAPTER 8

Intersectional Discrimination

8.1 Introduction

Attention for intersectional discrimination gained momentum with the seminal publication by Crenshaw on this topic in 1989.[1] The notion derives from the understanding that structural disadvantage is often compounded instead of being shaped along a single axis of social identity or group membership such as sex or gender, race, class, sexual orientation, disability or age.[2] The concept tries to capture how disadvantage may take a distinct form at the intersection of these and other categories protected by non-discrimination standards. As Crenshaw famously put it regarding intersectional discrimination suffered by black women, 'the intersectional experience is greater than the sum of racism and sexism'.[3]

To give some examples: in many western countries, black or ethnic minority women may suffer much more than either white women or ethnic minority men from poor employment conditions for precarious or domestic work as they are usually overrepresented in this category of work; dress codes prohibiting religious attire may have a distinct negative effect for Muslim women who wish to wear a headscarf for religious reasons, which is not comparable to their impact on Christian women or Muslim men; elderly women may be much more at risk of being poor than young women or elderly men due to pension gaps; disabled women may not be regarded as potential mothers and as a consequence be denied all sorts of specific reproductive help or benefits which able bodied women have easy access to and disabled men may not need.[4]

Intersectional discrimination has been much discussed in theory and academic literature, but has not much crystallized yet in legal practice. As has been remarked, a large discrepancy exists between progress in scholarship on

1 K. Crenshaw, Demarginalising the intersection of race and sex: a Black feminist critique of antidiscrimination doctrine, feminist theory and antiracist politics, *University of Chicago Legal Forum*, 1989, Article 8, p. 139–167.

2 N. Stoljar, Discrimination and intersectionality, in: K. Lippert-Rasmussen (ed), *The Routledge Handbook of the Ethics of Discrimination*, Routledge 2018, Chapter 5, p. 68–79, p. 70.

3 Crenshaw, Demarginalising the intersection of race and sex, 1989, p. 140.

4 The latter example is derived from B. Smith, Intersectional discrimination and substantive equality: a comparative and theoretical perspective, *The Equal Rights Review*, 2016, p. 73–102, p. 85.

 | DOI:10.1163/9789004538368_009

intersectionality on the one hand and in legal doctrine and discrimination law more generally on the other: '(…) intersectionality has been engaged with, but never quite translated into mainstream antidiscrimination law'.[5] Case law in which the notion is expressly used is scarce. It does not provide clearly defined and more or less consistently applied models for judicial review yet.

Against the background of intersectional discrimination as a legal concept being largely uncharted territory in most jurisdictions, this Chapter has a modest goal. It endeavours first of all to map some of the main emerging features of intersectional discrimination as a legally relevant, distinct notion. This will include a brief explanation of the meaning and importance of using an intersectional perspective, as well as discussing some of the main difficulties and dilemmas that using the concept may entail (Section 8.2). I subsequently provide a *tour d'horizon* of approaches to addressing intersectional discrimination in judicial analysis which seem to have come to the fore so far in several jurisdictions. In doing so, I tentatively try to explain how they seem to fit into the existing conceptual frameworks regarding equality and non-discrimination analysis, particularly along lines of direct and indirect discrimination (Section 8.3).

8.2 General Features

8.2.1 *Defining Intersectional Discrimination*

The terminology of intersectional discrimination, multiple discrimination and compound or aggravating discrimination is sometimes used as interchangeably, sometime to denote distinct forms of discrimination.[6] In this study I prefer to use the terminology 'intersectional discrimination' as coined by Crenshaw. Following Fredman, I regard it as a particular form of multiple discrimination; intersectional discrimination is to be distinguished from multiple discrimination of a sequential and of an additive nature.[7] Sequential multiple discrimination occurs over time. It involves separate occasions of discrimination on

5 S. Atrey, *Intersectionality and comparative antidiscrimination law. The tale of two citadels*, Brill Research Perspectives in Comparative Discrimination Law, Brill, 2020, p. 43.

6 See for some of the terminological controversies R. Xenidis, Multiple discrimination in EU anti-discrimination law. Towards redressing complex inequality?, in: U. Belavusau, and K. Henrard (eds), *EU anti-discrimination law beyond gender*, Oxford, Hart Publishing, 2018, p. 41–74, at p. 6–8.

7 S. Fredman, Intersectional discrimination in EU gender equality and non-discrimination law, Report EU Network of legal experts in gender equality and non-discrimination, 2016, p. 27–28.

different grounds. For legal purposes, each occasion is not presenting anything different from instances of 'ordinary' discrimination based on a single ground.[8] Additive discrimination regards discrimination on two or more grounds happening at the same occasion. Fredman gives the example of a woman being harassed because she is a woman and because she is gay.[9] Intersectional discrimination is closely linked to this type of multiple discrimination, but what sets it apart is the way in which discrimination on the basis of a combination of two or more protected grounds results in a distinct, qualitatively different type of disadvantage.[10] The classic example given by Crenshaw concerned a US case regarding black women who suffered much more from a 'first in last out' dismissal policy than either white women or black men, due to the fact that the company concerned had not started to employ black women at all until a few years before the lay-off. Their discrimination claim was rejected as the Court which reviewed the case refused to regard 'black women' as a special class covered by either the prohibition of sex discrimination or discrimination on the basis of race.[11]

As the example illustrates, particular manifestations of intersectional discrimination are contextually shaped. In the US case discussed by Crenshaw, the continuing effects of racial segregation and discrimination materialized in the distinctly adverse effects of the lay-off policy for black women. In other contexts different intersectionalities may play out in their own distinct ways. Since the initial focus of intersectional discrimination on issues figuring on the agenda of black feminism and critical race theories, it has been embraced as a much wider concept applicable to the intersection of all grounds protected under non-discrimination standards.[12]

8.2.2 *Importance of an Intersectional Perspective*

An intersectional perspective is important for several reasons. To start with, it makes clear that the groups protected by discrimination law are not internally homogenous. They may consist of all sorts of subgroups with their own particular needs. This implies an anti-essentialist view of these groups.[13]

In addition, by emphasizing the often compound nature of disadvantage suffered by groups at the intersection of two or more protected grounds of

8 Idem, p. 27.
9 Idem, p. 27.
10 Idem, p. 28.
11 Crenshaw, Demarginalising the intersection of race and sex, 1989, p. 141–143.
12 Cf. Xenidis, Multiple discrimination in EU anti-discrimination law, 2020, p. 47.
13 Stoljar, Discrimination and intersectionality, 2018, p. 74–76.

discrimination, an intersectional perspective calls for more targeted attention to combat discrimination. General policies for improving the position of women, racial minority groups or disabled people may not be adequate as the forms, causes and extent of the disadvantage suffered may differ considerably within these groups depending on their intersection with categories such as class, age, sexual orientation or gender identity. In the South African context, for example, it has been averred that the category of 'women' does not exist at all because of its profound interaction with race, class and religion: 'In South Africa, there are no "women". There are only black women, Muslim women, white women, women living in poverty, women subject to customary law, and so on'.[14]

A third reason why taking an intersectional perspective is important points to the hierarchies existing within groups protected by discrimination law. Intersectionality is not just about recognizing the heterogenous nature of these group, it makes visible relationships of superiority and inferiority, of dominance and subordination within them. This was also an import element in Crenshaw's analysis. Though feminism was perceived to fight for the equality of all women, Crenshaw showed how it in fact takes the experiences of white women as the frame of reference for doing so. Similarly, in the fight against racism, the experiences of black men were taken as the starting point. This dominant perspective 'contributes to the marginalization of Black women in feminist theory and antiracist politics'.[15]

I could add that in western societies more generally the dominant standard of reference for women's emancipation is often still implicitly white middle class women, whereas women with a migration background and/or working class women may experience quite different problems. In India, the dominant perspective for sex/gender equality may be implicitly shaped by the perspectives of Hindu women, which may not serve Muslim women well as they face quite distinct forms of disadvantage. In China, research suggests dividing lines within the female population run along a rural/urban axis, with rural women often becoming marginalized as migrant domestic workers.[16] In short, though the dominant frames of reference may differ depending on the particular context, everywhere in the world hierarchies are present also within the

14 E. Bonthuys, Institutional openness and resistance to feminist arguments: the example of the South African Constitutional Court, *Canadian Journal of Women and the Law*, 2008, p. 1–36, at p. 26.

15 Crenshaw, Demarginalizing the intersection of race and sex, 1989, p. 140.

16 Qinxuan Peng, No country for the low-end? – An intersectional analysis of the status of migrant women workers as domestic helpers and relevant laws in China, *International Journal on Minority and Groups Rights*, 2019, p. 575–599.

disadvantaged groups protected by discrimination law. Intersectional perspectives help making such important differences visible.[17]

8.2.3 *Problematic Aspects of Taking an Intersectional Perspective*

Though the importance of including an intersectional perspective in discrimination analysis seems clear, it also comes with its own problems and risks. First of all, the risk of essentialism in approaching distinct groups may repeat itself. This may be a particular danger if intersectionality is focused on identity and does not pay sufficient attention to class.[18] The notion of intersectionality itself may presuppose that some 'essential' identities exist before they intersect.[19] It may also entail the danger of assuming that all members of intersectionally formed sub-groups share a fixed identity or are perceived to do so.[20] This focus may obscure economic and distributive issues. It may also reinforce stereotyping.[21]

Another risk of intersectional approaches mentioned in academic literature points to losing sight of what binds or may bind disadvantaged groups rather than what sets them apart. In political and legal struggles it may be more effective to collaborate in combatting discrimination along shared lines of experiences of oppression than stressing in-group, internal differences.[22] More generally, simplifying categories may also be needed to recognize common experiences of discrimination, even if this inevitably involves a reduction of fuller and more complicated realities.

Some sort of reduction is all the more important in view of concerns that an intersectional perspective may lead to an ever expanding fragmentation of identifying groups suffering from intersectional discrimination.[23] The number of subgroups can easily proliferate if an intersectional approach is not somehow checked.[24] If taken to its utmost extreme, an intersectional perspective

17 As Stoljar puts it, an intersectional perspective 'makes the invisible visible', Stoljar, Discrimination and intersectionality, 2018, p. 75.

18 See discussion of this in Atrey, Intersectionality and comparative antidiscrimination law, 2020, p. 35–36; in a similar vein Fredman, Intersectional discrimination, Report EU network, 2016, p. 31.

19 Atrey, Intersectionality and comparative antidiscrimination law, 2020, p. 36.

20 Fredman, Intersectional discrimination, Report EU network, 2016, p. 31.

21 Idem, p. 32.

22 See Smith, Intersectional discrimination and substantive equality, 2016, at p. 82. He refers to the work of Spivak, who has called this 'strategic essentialism' and to Butler as acknowledging this may indeed be useful.

23 Fredman, Intersectional discrimination, Report EU network, 2016, p. 31.

24 An example of the problem of extreme proliferation would be to identify and approach the position of elderly, disabled, lesbian black women with a migrant background as

would result in a fully individualized substantive equality approach as discussed in Chapter 3 (Section 3.1), as each person's position in society is the outcome of an intricate combination of myriad characteristics and experiences, making for a unique identity and socio-economic position. As I explained there, such a fully personalized approach is not feasible in an absolute way. To be manageable, law and policies have to use classifications on the basis of generalizations as their point of departure. Fully individualized treatment is the exception, not the rule. The real challenge, then, is the proper level of generalization or particularity to be chosen. How broad or narrowly tailored should classifications be? This leads us back to some of the general features and concerns of discrimination analysis explored in Chapter 4. I will return to this in Section 8.3.

These problematic aspects of an intersectional approach feed into another particular problem for developing policies to combat discrimination which was also encountered before. Attention for intersectional discrimination, no matter how necessary, may lead to competition and even polarization between subgroups protected by non-discrimination law. Where financial and other resources are limited, allocating resources to some groups rather than others will imply making difficult choices. This may be perceived as creating a hierarchy of 'more deserving' and 'less deserving' disadvantaged (sub)groups. Chapter 7 illustrated that this is not a hypothetical issue. In the context of remedial measures, the South African Constitutional Court has been confronted with this issue several times. It accepted treating groups which have suffered most under the *Apartheid* system (African people) more favourably than other groups (such as Indian or coloured people), which were also disadvantaged by this system, yet to a lesser extent. (See Chapter 7, Section 7.5.1.2). The more intersecting grounds are involved in designing remedial measures, the greater the complexities of drawing proper lines between who deserves what.[25]

---

distinct from either younger women or able bodied women sharing all these other characteristics, or from elderly men sharing all the other features. To overcome the problems of fragmentation Schiek suggests to limit an intersectional approach to discrimination to three nodes: race, gender and disability. D. Schiek, On uses, misuses and non-uses of intersectionality before the Court of Justice (EU), *International Journal of Discrimination and the Law*, 2018, p. 82–103, at p. 87.

25 The empirical research by Cruells and Coll-Pleans regarding the complexities and dilemma's raised by intersectional considerations in several Spanish public policy programmes directed at improving the position of LGBT people are very informative of the type of problems involved. They investigate the advantages and disadvantages of combining a single axis approach focusing on LGBT people with a multiple and intersectional discrimination model taking into account the links with gender identity and women/men

The difficulties sketched above pose a variety of problems for adopting an intersectional perspective in the application of equality and non-discrimination standards. The limited recognition of this perspective seems to stem particularly from the ground-based focus of discrimination law. Protected grounds, that is grounds identified as deserving the particular protection of non-discrimination standards, are central to it. Identification as a protected ground usually leads to special protection. Classifications based on protected grounds constitute categories that have to be met with suspicion. They are usually subject to stricter judicial review, both where potential direct or indirect discrimination is at stake (see Chapter 4 and 5). Identification as discrimination may be much more problematic if an intersectionally shaped disadvantage is not expressly aligned with or identified (yet) as a protected ground. I explore this further in the next section.

8.3 Intersectional Discrimination Review

8.3.1 *Growing Recognition of Intersectional Discrimination as a Legally Relevant Concept*

Increasing acknowledgment of intersectional discrimination as a legally relevant concept has been identified as a general trend in global human rights law. Particularly since the turn of the century efforts have been made to include the notion in the conceptual framework of human rights.[26]

The first traces of paying attention to intersectional discrimination, be it implicitly and without using the terminology, predate this development. At the global level it is already an important element in the CEDAW.[27] Several provisions deal with intersectional discrimination. The most prominent are those addressing the intersection of sex/gender and marital status.[28] Article 16 includes an extensive list of common forms of intersectional discrimination

---

equality. M. Cruells and G. Coll-Planas, Challenging equality policies: the emerging LGBT perspective, *European Journal of Women's Studies*, 2013, p. 122–137.

26 For an overview see J. Bond, *Global intersectionality and contemporary human rights*, Oxford, Oxford University Press, 2021.

27 Traces of an intersectional approach are absent in the ICERD, but the CERD Committee recognized its relevance in its *General Recommendation No. 25 (2000) on the gender related dimensions of racial discrimination*, which elaborates how racial discrimination affects women in a different way or to a different degree than men.

28 In addition, the preamble refers to the particular predicament of women in poverty and Article 14 specifically regards a quite elaborate list of particular problems faced by rural women.

on these grounds faced by women within marriage and after divorce. As in quite some parts of the world family or personal law is regulated according to religious affiliation, religion may be a third intersecting ground creating its own distinct forms of discrimination against women.[29] In addition to Article 16, Articles 9 and 11 CEDAW address two other equality issues flowing from the intersection of sex and marital status. Article 9 prohibits discrimination of married women under nationality laws and Article 11(2)(a) prohibits dismissal of women on the basis of marital status.

Where women's rights are concerned, addressing this type of intersectional discrimination seemed obvious from the start. Perhaps too obvious to articulate it as anything special. It was not framed as intersectional or multiple discrimination. At the same time, the text of the Women's Convention shows the selectiveness of the kinds of intersectionality addressed in it at the time. Whereas in the contemporary world intersections between gender and race, ethnic origin and/or migration background are of central concern, particular attention for this is lacking in the CEDAW. The CEDAW Committee has taken some efforts to make up for this in its work. In General Recommendation No. 28 on the core obligations of the States parties, the Committee expressly mentions the importance of the notion of intersectionality as 'a basic concept'. It regards discrimination on the basis of sex and gender as 'inextricably linked with other factors that affect women, such as race, ethnicity, religion or belief, health status, age, class, caste and sexual orientation and gender identity'.[30] Several other General Recommendations regard intersectionally formed groups, such as older women and indigenous women and girls.[31]

The CRPD attests to the growing attention to intersectional discrimination by including in its preamble an express reference to multiple and aggravating forms of discrimination faced by disabled people 'on the basis of race, colour, sex, language, religion, political or other opinion, national, ethnic, indigenous or social origin, property, birth, age or other status.[32] Sensitivity to intersectional issues also surfaces in several provisions, such as provisions requiring

29 The many reservations to Article 16 CEDAW are often linked to religious objections.

30 Committee on the Elimination of Discrimination Against Women, *General Recommendation No. 28 (2010) on the core obligations of States Parties under Article 2 of the Convention on the Elimination of All Forms of Discrimination against Women*, par. 18.

31 *General recommendation No. 27 (2010) on older women and protection of their human rights*; *General recommendation No. 39 (2022) on the rights of indigenous women and girls.*

32 CRPD Preamble, under (p). In addition, it points several times to the intersection with gender under (q) and (s), and to poverty under (t). At the regional level, intersectional discrimination is also surfacing more visibly in recent conventions addressing discrimination, such as the Inter-American Convention against all forms of discrimination and

particular attention for disabled women and girls (Article 6), disabled children (Article 7) and for the gender-specific and age-specific needs of disabled persons faced with violence (Article 16). The concept of intersectionality itself, however, is not used or defined in the CRPD. Similar to the CEDAW Committee, the CRPD Committee has now included the concept of intersectional discrimination in its General Comments.[33]

As Bond shows more generally, attention to intersectionality has increased over time in the 'soft law' work of all treaty bodies and is now commonly recognized as an important concept.[34] At the same time, she concludes that intersectional analysis has remained 'spotty, inconsistent, and underdeveloped'.[35]

Inclusion of intersectional perspectives in 'hard law' judicial analysis of equality and non-discrimination standards is also quite patchy and underdeveloped. In several jurisdictions, however, express efforts are under way to conceptually integrate intersectional discrimination in the overarching equality and non-discrimination framework. South Africa stands out in this respect. I will give it particular attention in the sections to come. In addition, I will discuss how judicial review of intersectional discrimination has also been present in potentially significant ways in the jurisprudence of other judicial bodies such as the ECtHR and the CJEU, be it in implicit or hidden forms. So far, such rather invisible forms are under-researched from an intersectional perspective. All approaches encountered seem to tie in one way or another with the review of either direct discrimination or indirect discrimination as explored in Chapter 4 and Chapter 5, though the lines between the two may be quite fuzzy.

As taking an intersectional perspective is generally considered to be much more complicated under non-discrimination standards containing an exhaustive list of protected grounds, as is exemplified by the EU equality directives. I will address it in a separate section.[36]

---

intolerance, 2013, Article 1.3 and the Inter-American Convention against racism, racial discrimination and related forms of intolerance, 2013, Article 1.3.

33 Committee on the Rights of Persons with Disabilities, *General Comment No. 6 (2018) on equality and non-discrimination*, par. 19.

34 Bond, Global intersectionality, 2021, Chapter 3: Evolution of intersectionality in the UN Treaty Bodies, p. 54–77.

35 Idem, p. 246.

36 Cf. the report of Fredman on the many complexities involved, Fredman, Intersectional discrimination, Report EU network, 2016.

8.3.2 *Intersectional Discrimination Review along Lines of Direct Discrimination*

The importance of legally addressing cases of intersectional discrimination along lines of direct discrimination lies in the strict judicial review usually attached to the latter. If it materializes or is approached as direct discrimination, intersectional discrimination would be regarded as presumptively suspect, similar to 'ordinary' discrimination expressly based on a single, protected ground. In a variety of jurisdictions this approach is visible in cases where at least one protected ground is expressly used as the basis for an intersectional difference in treatment.

8.3.2.1 Case Law of the Inter-American Court of Human Rights

The jurisprudence of the IACtHR provides an example of this type of judicial review of intersectional discrimination in the case *Gonzales Lluy v. Ecuador*.[37] In this judgment the IACtHR expressly refers to the concept of intersectional discrimination for the first time.[38] At stake was the plight of a girl who was expelled from her school when she turned out to be infected with HIV as a result of an unsafe blood transfusion. The school motivated this measure by the best interests of the other children. It considered the girl to provide a risk of infecting the other pupils, as she had had some hemorraghes.

In assessing whether this treatment amounted to discrimination in relation to the child's right to education, the Court applies the same standard of review as in other cases dealing with discrimination (see Chapter 4, Section 4.4.2). To determine whether the prohibition of discrimination as protected in Article 1(1) of the American Convention on Human Rights is violated, the Court analyzes whether the difference in treatment can be justified by the reasons provided by the authorities.[39] Importantly, the Court identifies HIV as a protected ground under Article 1(1) ACHR, which is formulated in an open way, allowing for the inclusion of other grounds than those expressly enumerated.[40] As a consequence, the justification review must be strict, which means that 'the reasons used by the State to implement a differentiated treatment must be particularly serious and substantiated by an exhaustive reasoning'. In this strict framework, proportionality is central: does the measure have a legitimate

37 IACtHR, 1 September 2015, *Gonzales Lluy v. Ecuador* (preliminary objections, merits, reparations and costs).

38 C. Gebruers, From structural discrimination to intersectionality in the Inter-American system of human rights: unravelling categorical framings, *The Age of Human Rights Journal*, no. 20, 2023, p. 15.

39 IACtHR, Gonzales Lluy, 2015, par. 244.

40 Idem, par. 255.

or objective purpose and is it a suitable, necessary proportionate measure to achieve the purpose?[41]

Applying this justification test, the Court concludes that the treatment of the girl has violated Article 1(1). Though the aim of protecting other children is in itself legitimate, her expulsion from school was informed by prejudice and stereotyping presumptions regarding the possible risks related to HIV.[42] The real risk of infection was extremely small, whereas the measure taken was 'the most harmful and disproportionate of those available to meet the objective of protecting the integrity of the other children'.[43]

After this clear conclusion the Court could have left it at that, but in a separate section it subsequently identifies the discrimination suffered by the girl as a form of intersectional discrimination. The Court notes that the discrimination against the girl was related to other aspects that made her more vulnerable and exacerbated the harm suffered by her. The denial of her access to education 'derived from her situation as a person living with HIV, a child, a female, and living in conditions of poverty'.[44] The Court regards this interaction to arise to 'a specific form of discrimination that resulted from the intersection of those factors'.[45]

This part of the judgment shows the awareness of the IACtHR of the specific features of intersectional discrimination. It is also a way to recognize the relevance of intersectionality to the harm suffered by the girl, even if it does not seem to affect the way in which the judicial review is conducted. Though the Court identifies the intersectional nature of the discrimination as 'aggravating', it is silent on how this may have impacted the (already stringent) strictness of its proportionality review. Apparently, then, it does not make a principled difference whether discrimination is intersectional or not in the standard of review for assessing whether the state violates the ACHR, though it can of course be expected to weigh more heavily in the ultimate balance to be struck under the proportionality requirement.

8.3.2.2 Case Law of the Constitutional Court of South Africa

Several South African cases also deal with intersectional discrimination under the regular judicial review framework of discrimination if at least one protected ground is involved. Though in these cases the terminology of intersectionality

41 Idem, par. 257.
42 Idem, par. 266.
43 Idem, par. 274.
44 Idem, par. 291.
45 Idem, par. 290.

is not used, the analysis of the type of discrimination at stake clearly involves awareness of its intersectional nature.

In fact, the very first case decided by the post-Apartheid Constitutional Court under the Interim Constitution, *Brinks v. Kitshoff*, can be regarded as being of an intersectional nature.[46] It concerned a difference in treatment based on a combination of sex and marital status: married women and married men were treated differently under an insolvency act. As a consequence, in several situations married women faced distinct financial disadvantages. This seems a clear example of (potential) intersectional discrimination, as the distinct disadvantage suffered by married women flows from the intersection of sex and marital status.

Under the applicable Interim Constitution, the equality clause included a non-exhaustive list of protected grounds of discrimination in which sex was expressly mentioned, but marital status was not yet included. As under the constitutional provisions distinctions based on listed grounds are presumed to constitute 'unfair discrimination' and thus to require a particularly strong justification to pass muster, not being listed could make a difference in judicial review. As it turns out, this is not the case.

The Court considers that the difference in treatment is indeed based on two grounds, that is sex and marital status, but holds that this does not affect regarding it as 'unfair discrimination'.[47] The constitutional prohibition of discrimination does not require that discrimination is based on one ground only[48] and as it contains an open list of protected grounds, it is not necessary to assess whether marital status would also be a ground which would constitute unfair discrimination. 'It is sufficient that the disadvantageous treatment is substantially based on one of the listed prohibited grounds, namely, sex.[49] After subsequently assessing whether the difference in treatment can nevertheless be justified, the Court concludes this is not the case.[50]

The judgment in *Brinks* suggests that the involvement of at least one protected ground in a situation of intersectional discrimination is sufficient to trigger stricter scrutiny.[51] Any other grounds involved will presumably make this only easier, as seems to be confirmed in several cases regarding the particular disadvantage suffered by Muslim women married under Sharia law.

46 Constitutional Court of South Africa, *Brinks v. Kitshoff*, [1996] ZACC 9.

47 Idem, par. 43.

48 The constitutional provision explicitly prohibits discrimination 'on one or more grounds'.

49 Idem, par. 43.

50 Idem, par. 48.

51 In the wording of the South African Constitution by establishing a presumption of unfair discrimination.

The cases *Hassam v. Jacobs* and *Women's Legal Centre Trust v. President of the Republic of South Africa and others* both concerned the particular position of Muslim women married according to Muslim personal law and family law.[52] In *Women's Legal Centre Trust* the exclusion of Muslim marriages from the Marriage Act and the Divorce Act was challenged. As a result of this exclusion, Muslim women who are married under Sharia law, and not additionally under civil law, do not receive the protection afforded by these acts regarding inheritance rights, maintenance or a number of other rights during marriage and at divorce. The Constitutional Court is very clear in its recognition of the particular negative effects this creates for Muslim women. To explain this exclusion, it refers to the historical prejudice against Muslim marriage:

> It is a well-known fact that marriages concluded in accordance with the tenets of the Islamic faith have never been accorded recognition as valid marriages in South Africa. The views expressed by the courts historically were that Muslim marriages did not accord with so-called "civilised" religious practices, were potentially polygamous, were regarded as immoral and not consonant with religion and were thus contrary to public policy.[53]

The Court holds the discrimination to be directly based on religion and on marital status,[54] and indirectly, that is by its disparate impact, on the basis of sex and gender: 'the differentiation caused by the Marriage Act strikes particularly at women, and works to the detriment of Muslim women and not Muslim men'.[55] When concluding that no justification exists for the exclusion of Muslim marriages, the Court again emphasizes its particularly detrimental effects for Muslim women:

> Not recognising Muslim marriages as valid marriages sends a message that Muslim marriages are not worthy of legal recognition or protection. There is no justification for the continuing non-recognition of Muslim marriages. This is especially so having regard to the historical context of systemic violation of the rights of Muslim women.[56]

---

52 Constitutional Court of South Africa, *Hassam v. Jacobs*, [2009] ZACC 19 and *Women's Legal Centre Trust v. President of the Republic of South Africa and others*, [2022] ZACC 23.

53 *Women's Legal Centre Trust*, 2022, par. 43.

54 Idem, par. 48.

55 Idem, par. 49.

56 Idem, par. 55.

Without using intersectionality as a distinct concept in this case, the Court clearly recognizes the intersectionally shaped character of the particular situation of Muslim women married under Sharia law.

8.3.2.3 Case Law of the ECtHR

In a rather similar, though much less articulated way, a certain sensitivity to intersectional discrimination without express use being made of the concept can be found in several judgments of the ECtHR under its 'standard' discrimination review. Interestingly, under the heading 'other forms of discrimination' the *Guide on Article 14 ECHR and on Article 1 of Protocol No. 12 of the Convention* (*Guide on Article 14 ECHR* for short), published on the website of the Court, refers to discrimination 'on the basis of several grounds operating separately or interacting with each other at the same time' as a form of discrimination distinct from direct and indirect discrimination.[57] In this context, five cases are referred to, four of which are of interest here as they were subject to review under Article 14 ECHR. Being identified in this way as of an intersectional character, they merit attention if only for this reason.

The first of these cases mentioned, *B.S. v. Spain*, is also often cited in academic literature as a (still rare) example of an intersectional approach in the jurisprudence of the ECtHR.[58] In this case the Court considered that the Spanish authorities had failed to take into account the particular vulnerability of a woman when investigating her alleged harassment by the police, in view of her position as an African woman working as a prostitute.[59]

The case *Carvalho Pinto de Sousa Morais v. Portugal* is also a quite clear example of the Court using an intersectional lens for finding a violation of Article 14 ECHR.[60] The case is more interesting than *B.S. v. Spain* for shedding some more light on how the Court uses its general non-discrimination framework to include an implicitly intersectional analysis. The judgment regarded a Portuguese judicial decision on damages awarded to a woman over fifty, who could not have intimate sexual relations anymore as a result of medical negligence. The Portuguese Court had lowered the amount considering, among

57 *Guide on Article 14 of the ECHR and on Article 1 of Protocol No. 12 of the Convention*, version 31 August 2023.

58 See e.g. M. La Barbera and M. Cruells López, Toward the implementation of intersectionality in the European multilevel legal praxis: *B.S. v. Spain*, *Law & Society Review*, 2019, p. 1167–1201; Fredman, Discrimination law, 2022, p. 228; I. Solanke. The EU approach to intersectional discrimination in law, in: *The Routledge Handbook on gender and EU politics*, 2021, p. 93–104, at p. 99.

59 ECtHR, 24 July 2012, *B.S. v. Spain*, appl. no. 47159/08.

60 ECtHR, 25 July 2017, *Carvalho Pinto de Sousa Morais v. Portugal*, appl. no. 17484/15.

others, that 'sexuality is not as important for a fifty-year-old woman and mother of two children as for someone of a younger age'.[61] The Court holds this assumption to constitute a gender-based sexual stereotype and concludes that Article 14 ECHR is violated in conjunction with Article 8, as 'the applicant's age and sex appear to have been decisive factors in the final decision, introducing a difference of treatment based on those grounds'.[62]

The other two cases on intersectional discrimination referred to in the *Guide on Article 14 ECHR* seem to be more aligned to indirect discrimination and will be discussed in Section 8.3.3.2.

Though the *Guide on Article 14 ECHR* does not include references to any other cases involving 'several grounds operating separately or interacting with each other at the same time', quite a number of other cases could probably be identified as such if all Strasbourg case law would be revisited and analyzed from an intersectional angle. It is beyond the scope of this study to conduct this type of comprehensive investigation, but some obvious candidates for further exploration of how the Court has approached intersectional discrimination in more implicit and hidden ways could include, for example, cases dealing with pensions and with family relations. Both areas have been and often still are characterized by differences in treatment linked to multiple and intersecting grounds, such as sex, age, marital status, sexual orientation and gender identity, and various combinations of these grounds. If anything, intersectional discrimination is not a new phenomenon, even if the conceptual attention it has started to attract as a distinct notion in non-discrimination law is of a recent date.

8.3.2.4 Case Law of the Supreme Court of Canada

The Canadian case *Corbiere*[63] is often mentioned as an important example of how an intersectional approach to discrimination can take shape.[64] At stake was a complaint that members of an aboriginal band who did not live on the reserve were excluded from the vote in band elections. The Court recalls that enumerated grounds function as 'legislative markers of suspect grounds', and holds that the same applies to analogous grounds.[65] It adds that if a ground is held to be 'analogous', this status has a permanent character, in the same

61 Idem, par. 52.

62 Idem, par. 53.

63 Supreme Court of Canada, *Corbiere v. Canada (Minister of Indian and Northern Affairs)*, [1999] 2 SCR 203.

64 See e.g. Fredman, Intersectional discrimination, Report EU network, 2016, p. 66–67; Atrey, Intersectionality and comparative antidiscrimination law, 2020, p. 61.

65 Supreme Court of Canada, *Corbiere*, 1999, par. 7–8.

way as 'sex' or 'race' always constitute a suspect ground. This status does not depend on the specific context of a case. The specific circumstances of a case do come into play – but only then – when assessing whether a difference in treatment based on an enumerated or analogous ground can be justified.[66]

The Court subsequently identifies 'Aboriginality-residence' as it relates to band members living on or off the reserve as an analogous ground. It refers to what I called the underlying rationale for identifying grounds as protected or suspect in Chapter 4 (Section 4.3.1). For band members the distinction is linked to a 'personal characteristic essential to a band member's personal identity' and changing status from off-reserve to on-reserve is only possible at great cost. As such, it is 'no less constructively immutable than religion or citizenship'.[67] As the Court subsequently holds that the blanket exclusion of off-reserve band members cannot be justified, it violates the constitutional equality standards.

The construction adopted by the Canadian Supreme Court stands out from the approaches in the other jurisdictions discussed so far. The Court in fact recognizes the intersectional nature of the disadvantage suffered by off-reserve band members by expanding the list of suspect grounds, which in turn results in more stringent scrutiny attached to this status. This construction uses the open model of protected grounds underlying the applicable equality standards. In Chapter 4 (Section 4.3.3) this way of extending the list of protected grounds has been called expansion by categorical inclusion.

8.3.3 *Intersectional Discrimination Review along Lines of Indirect Discrimination*

With its focus on disparate impact or effects as a trigger for starting an inquiry under equality standards, the concept of indirect discrimination seems a quite logical candidate for being able to deal with intersectional discrimination. Examples from case law in several jurisdictions show this has indeed been the case. The most prominent case expressly addressing intersectional discrimination through the lens of indirect discrimination is no doubt the South African case *Mahlangu* decided in 2020. The judgment stands out for the way in which the Constitutional Court deliberately takes the opportunity to use this case for developing intersectional discrimination as a legal concept. The judgment has been heralded by Atrey as 'an exemplar in discrimination law and more broadly, constitutional law, in its treatment of intersectionality'.[68]

66 Idem, par. 8.

67 Idem, par. 14.

68 S. Atrey, Beyond discrimination: *Mahlangu* and the use of intersectionality as a general theory of constitutional interpretation, *International Journal of Discrimination and the Law*, 2021, p. 168–178, at p. 169.

8.3.3.1 *Mahlangu and Another v. Minister of Labour and Others*[69]

The case *Mahlangu* regarded the exclusion of domestic workers from a social security scheme for workers, the *Compensation for Occupational Injuries and Diseases Act 1993* (COIDA). In this act domestic workers were excluded from the definition of 'employee', so they could not claim any benefits resulting from occupational injuries. In the South African context, this group consists mainly of black women.

The Constitutional Court takes two avenues to conclude that this violates the constitutional equality standards, using both Section 9(1) and Section 9(3). As explained in Chapter 4, Section 9(1) is held to apply to 'mere differentiations', whereas Section 9(3) regards 'discrimination', that is differentiations based on protected grounds, a number of which are (non-exhaustively) enumerated in this provision.[70] The list includes, among others, race, gender and sex. 'Mere differentiations' meet with very lenient judicial review, whereas 'discrimination' is presumed to be unfair; any justifications put forward are subject to stringent scrutiny.

The Court starts by considering that the exclusion of domestic workers can be seen as a 'mere' differential treatment of two categories of workers, that is domestic workers and other categories of workers. As this differentiation is 'arbitrary' (which was not disputed by the Government) it violates Section 9(1).[71]

The Court could have left things there, but 'in the interest of justice' it continues to discuss the additional claim made in this case, that the exclusion of domestic workers constitutes (unfair) indirect discrimination. The Court seeks to take this 'unprecedented opportunity to expressly consider the application of Section 9(3) through the framework of intersectionality'.[72]

The Court endorses the claim of indirect discrimination, 'because (…) domestic workers are predominantly Black women. This means discrimination against them constitutes indirect discrimination on the basis of race, sex and gender'.[73] The Court elaborates on what this intersectional approach amounts to. In doing so it emphasizes that this approach is not anything new or alien in terms of the Court's jurisprudence:

69 Constitutional Court of South Africa, *Mahlangu and another v. Minister of labour and others*, [2020] ZACC 24.

70 Chapter 4, Section 4.4.2.

71 *Mahlangu*, 2020, par. 72.

72 Idem, par. 75.

73 Idem, par. 73.

> It means nothing more than acknowledging that discrimination may impact on an individual in a multiplicity of ways based on their position in society and the structural dynamics at play. There is an array of equality jurisprudence emanating from this Court that has, albeit implicitly, considered the multiple effects of discrimination.[74]

The Court illustrates the actual presence of intersectional perspectives in its case law with references to, among others, *Hassam* and *Brinks*,[75] cases I also briefly discussed above in Section 8.3.2.2. The Court also refers to the judgment of the ECtHR in *B.S. v. Spain*[76] before quite extensively discussing academic literature on intersectionality, including work by Crenshaw, Albertyn, Smith and Atrey.[77] From all these considerations it concludes that to establish intersectional discrimination, a qualitative and contextual analysis is needed, including 'the nature and context of the individual or group at issue, their history, as well as the social and legal history of society's treatment of that group'.[78] Applying this framework to the case at hand, there can be no doubt that in the South African context Artice 9(3) is violated by the exclusion of domestic workers from the COIDA.

8.3.3.2 Case Law of the ECtHR

As mentioned in Section 8.3.2.3, two cases identified in the *Guide on Article 14 of the ECHR and on Article 1 of Protocol No. 12* as addressing intersectional discrimination seem to align more with an analysis in terms of indirect discrimination rather than direct discrimination.

The first case, *Yocheva and Gadeva v. Bulgaria* concerned a family allowance provided to 'children with one living parent'.[79] In applying this provision, a single mother of children with an unknown father was denied the benefit. She claimed that the denial violated Article 14 ECHR (in conjunction with Article 8), as single parents of children whose legal ties to *both* parents had been established before the other parent died were eligible to it.

74 Idem, par. 76.

75 Idem, par. 79–81.

76 Idem, par. 83. No other foreign case law is mentioned.

77 Idem, par. 85–91; Crenshaw, Demarginalising the intersection of race and sex, 1989; Smith, Intersectional discrimination and substantive equality, 2016; Albertyn, Contested substantive equality in the South African Constitution, 2018; S. Atrey, *Intersectional discrimination*, Oxford, Oxford University Press, 2019.

78 Idem, par. 95.

79 ECtHR, 11 May 2021, *Yocheva and Ganeva v. Bulgaria*, appl. no. 18592/15.

The Court holds that this difference in treatment is based on two grounds. A sex-based difference in treatment is involved because the denial of an allowance disadvantages mothers far more often than fathers, 'given that, as maternity is determined by the act of birth, in the vast majority of cases it is only children's paternity that can be unknown'.[80] The second ground at stake is 'family status', as the applicant 'was treated differently on account of being a single mother, with the identity of the fathers of her children not being established'.[81] The Court draws a parallel with parental leave to note that in view of the goals of the family allowance – supporting children growing up in families who are for a variety of reasons in a vulnerable position – men and women are in an analogous situation in their role as parents.[82] This includes single parents who are carers of children with an unknown father. It adds that the same applies to single mothers of children with unknown fathers being in a relevantly similar situation to surviving mothers of children born in wedlock or whose deceased father has recognised them.[83] Reiterating that differences in treatment on the basis of sex and on the basis of birth outside marriage have to be assessed under the 'very weighty reasons' test, the Court concludes that the denial of the benefit to the complainants does not meet this test:

> [T]he Government have not shown, in the particular circumstances of the present case, that there were convincing reasons unrelated to the applicant's family status or to her sex to offset the discriminatory *effect* on the applicant's family.[84] [emphasis added].

The second case is the well-known case S.A.S *v. France*, in which the Grand Chamber of the ECtHR held that the French ban on the full-face veil did not violate the Convention.[85] Though the central focus of the Court's analysis is on Articles 8 and 9 ECHR, the Court briefly addresses whether the ban may constitute indirect discrimination under Article 14 as Muslim women may be 'particularly exposed' to the ban and the sanctions which may flow from it.[86] By posing this question the Court shows it is fully aware of the distinct detrimental impact of the ban on Muslim women at the intersection of religion and sex, but this does not seem to put any additional weight into the balance.

80 Idem, par. 111.
81 Idem, par. 112.
82 Idem, par. 107.
83 Idem, par. 108.
84 Idem, par. 125.
85 ECtHR (Grand Chamber), 1 July 2014, SAS *v. France*, appl. no. 43835/11.
86 Idem, par. 160.

The Court acknowledges that a measure which has a disproportionately prejudicial effect may indeed be discriminatory, but adds this is only the case if it lacks an objective and reasonable justification. Referring back to its considerations under Article 8 and 9 ECHR, the Court concludes that the difference in treatment is objectively justified.[87] No reference is made in this context to the 'very weighty reasons' test usually applicable in sex discrimination cases.

The judgment in *S.A.S.* seems to be a good example of the way in which all sorts of other factors may counterbalance the more stringent scrutiny which is supposed to be leading when potential direct or indirect discrimination on the basis of sex is at stake (see Chapter 4, Section 4.4.2 and Chapter 5, Section 5.4.3). These may stem from the presence of other rights and interests, the area of law or policy involved, the lack of common ground between states, et cetera. Ultimately, the proportionality test is very malleable and does not provide hard and fast rules on the proper balance to be struck when such competing factors are involved, pulling in different directions. Recognition of intersectionality, then, is not necessarily followed by more stringent scrutiny.

8.3.4 *Addressing Intersectional Discrimination under EU Law*

It is generally acknowledged that equality and non-discrimination standards including an open list of protected grounds provide more or easier space for addressing intersectional discrimination than models with a limited, exhaustive list. EU law is a prime example of the latter.[88]

Xenidis traces the origins of the development of intersectional perspectives within the EU to anti-racist advocacy movements and feminist groups 'concerned by the rise of xenophobia and racism in the EU, and by the lack of voice given to migrant and ethnic minority women'.[89] More sustained and robust attention for intersectional discrimination in EU law – or multiple discrimination as is the common EU terminology – can be linked to the coming into being in 2000 of Directive 2000/43 and Directive 2000/78. They extended the protection of EU non-discrimination law far beyond its original limitation to sex discrimination, by including race/ethnic origin, religion/belief, sexual orientation, disability and age as protected grounds.[90] As will be discussed below, the particular design of the EU directives in separate and self-contained

87 Idem, par. 161.

88 For the very limited way in which intersectional discrimination can be addressed in the US under Title VII of the Civil Rights Act, which also contains a closed list of a limited number of grounds, see e.g. Atrey, Intersectionality and comparative antidiscrimination law, 2020, p. 44–49.

89 Xenidis, Multiple discrimination in EU anti-discrimination law, 2018, p. 49.

90 Idem, p. 8–15.

compartments is generally identified as a major barrier to the development of an intersectional perspective in EU non-discrimination law. In addition, attention will be paid to an important body of case law on intersectional discrimination predating the '2000' directives, which seems mostly overlooked in contemporary discussions on how intersectional discrimination is or could be approached under the current framework provided by the directives. This lack of attention is most likely due to the fact that at the time it was not approached in terms of intersectional or multiple discrimination. This line of jurisprudence has its origin in particular forms of intersectional discrimination suffered by women, which found their way to the CJEU notwithstanding the single-axis focus on sex discrimination in the applicable legislation.

8.3.4.1 Intersectional Approaches to Discrimination in EU Law since the Turn of the Century

The extension of the protection of EU discrimination law to a much larger number of protected grounds was a watershed moment, overhauling the non-discrimination framework previously limited to sex discrimination.[91] The preambles to the two new directives refer for the first time to multiple discrimination. They do so by calling for the need to take particular care of the position of women in implementing the directives, 'especially since women are often the victim of multiple discrimination'.[92] The selective limitation to women seems a clear reflection of the strong, but limited historical focus on sex discrimination in EU law. Xenidis notes that legislative efforts to broaden the notion of multiple discrimination as relevant for all the grounds now covered by EU discrimination law in the proposal for the so called Horizontal Directive meet with opposition from the member States.[93] She concludes from this that 'the perspective of a full legislative ban [of multiple discrimination] is still distant and multiple discrimination remains a grey zone in EU legislation at present'.[94]

The gap regarding intersectional discrimination in the current legislative framework has not been filled by the CJEU. Jurisprudential clarification is at best patchy, but on the whole largely lacking. This is generally explained by the particular barriers posed by the architecture of EU non-discrimination law.

---

91 Xenidis, Multiple discrimination in EU anti-discrimination law, 2018, p. 41.

92 Recital 14 of Directive 2000/43 and recital 3 of Directive 2000/78.

93 Xenidis, Multiple discrimination in EU anti-discrimination law, 2018, p. 14. The proposed directive will extend the protection against discrimination on the basis of religion or belief, disability, sexual orientation and age from the area of employment (covered by Directive 2000/78) to the field of goods and services.

94 Idem, p. 43.

Obviously, the fragmentation of the protection against discrimination in different directives, covering different grounds, with a different scope of application and with different possibilities for justifying (potential) discrimination preclude an integrated and more holistic approach.[95] It may require intersectional discrimination to be brought under different directives and be reduced to a single-axis issue, which would go against the very core of what the notion seeks to address.

Added to these barriers in the design of non-discrimination standards, the CJEU has been noted for its apparent unwillingness to address intersectional discrimination even where it is obviously present. The judgments in *Parris* and in the 'headscarf cases'[96] are often mentioned as examples of this reluctance.[97] Other cases figuring in academic literature as possible examples of an emerging recognition of intersectional discrimination are isolated cases.[98] They do not provide much guidance towards developing a clear conceptual framework for addressing it.

Against this background it seems all the more interesting to call attention to case law on intersectional issues connected to sex discrimination, which was part and parcel of EU non-discrimination jurisprudence from the start without being gouged in terms of intersectional discrimination. It is beyond the scope of this study to revisit this quite extensive jurisprudence in full, but some examples may illustrate its potential relevance for developing a broader intersectional framework that could service the enlarged reach of EU non-discrimination law as it stands today.

8.3.4.2 Intersectional Approaches to Discrimination in EU Law Predating the 2000 Directives

A prohibition of sex discrimination figured in EU law from the very beginning in the form of a requirement of equal pay. It was driven by economic rather than human rights considerations, but it turned out to provide an important

---

95 Cf. Fredman, Intersectional discrimination, Report EU network, 2016, p. 62–65; Xenidis, Multiple discrimination in EU anti-discrimination law, 2018, p. 59.

96 CJEU, 24 November 2016, *Parris*, C-443/15; on prohibitions regarding headscarves see CJEU (Grand Chamber), 14 March 2017, *Achbita*, C-157/15; CJEU (Grand Chamber), *Wabe* and *Müller*, 15 July 2021, C-804/18 and C-341/19; CJEU, 13 October 2022, *SCRL, C-344/20*.

97 For a discussion of this reluctance see e.g. Xenidis, Multiple discrimination in EU anti-discrimination law, 2018, p. 28–33.

98 See e.g. the examples discussed by Fredman, Intersectional discrimination, Report EU network, 2016, p. 71–79 and by Xenidis, Multiple discrimination in EU anti-discrimination law, 2018, 62–64.

tool for the European women's rights movement to link its claims for equal rights for men and women to the development of the EU.

From the start, some major preoccupations of the feminist agenda revolved around intersectional discrimination stemming from the gendered division of roles between men and women in the family and in gainful employment. Several issues of this nature gave rise to important jurisprudence by the CJEU, which operated by necessity within the framework of the single-axis prohibition of discrimination on the basis of sex. To illustrate how the Court has navigated these issues, I will briefly explore some of its case law regarding the intersection of sex and marital status in social security arrangements. In line with the main structure of EU sex discrimination law, the approach taken by the CJEU to address this issue had to be along the lines of either direct or indirect discrimination.

8.3.4.3 Sex and Marital Status Discrimination in Social Security

Inequalities between men and women deriving from the gendered division of labour along lines of the traditional breadwinner-homemaker model have resulted in an important body of case law regarding discrimination on the basis of sex and marital status in social security. Quite some of these cases originated in the Netherlands.[99]

Until the late seventies/early eighties of the past century, the Dutch social security system was squarely based on the breadwinner-homemaker model, with the husband in the former role and the wife in the latter. Social security schemes were predominantly directed at protecting against loss of income of the breadwinner due to, among others, disability, unemployment or retirement. Within families, this was in the far majority of cases the husband. Reflecting this presumption of the husband being the breadwinner and the wife the homemaker, married women were mostly either excluded from a variety of social security arrangements, or would only be eligible under stringent conditions which neither unmarried women nor men (whatever their civil status) had to meet. Put differently, the category of 'married women' was used as a proxy for 'non-breadwinners'.

When an increasing number of married women entered the labour market such exclusions came under increasing attack. Dutch eyes turned to the EU regulations directed at combatting sex discrimination for help, the main one

99 For an extensive overview of the interplay between EU law and social security law in the Netherlands in the eighties and nineties see M. Driessen and A. Veldman, *Inkomenszekerheid* (Income security), in: R. Holtmaat en T. Loenen (red.), *Vrouw en Recht* (Woman and law), Nijmegen, 1997, p. 181–223. I draw largely from this publication.

in this area being Directive 79/7/EEC on the progressive implementation of the principle of equal treatment for men and women in matters of social security.

The landmark *FNV* case proved successful in tackling the reduced eligibility of married women to unemployment benefits.[100] Whereas unmarried women and all men could apply for an extended period of unemployment benefits after the regular unemployment allowance had ended, married women were excluded from this additional protection against loss of income, unless they could prove to be the breadwinner. The CJEU made short thrift with this regulation. It had no difficulty in holding that the particular provisions regarding (categories of) married women violate the prohibition of discrimination on the basis of sex as incorporated in Directive 79/7.[101]

The ruling shows that direct discrimination may not just be at stake when a difference in treatment is based exclusively on the sex of a person, but also if it is expressly used in combination with another criterion. So conceptually, under EU law a single-ground non-discrimination regulation need not pose a principled problem for what is also called 'sex plus' discrimination.[102] If at least one protected ground such as sex is expressly used for a difference in treatment, it can be dealt with through the lens of direct discrimination, with its strict regime of possible justifications.[103]

When Dutch social security law was amended to live up to the demands of Directive 79/7, differential treatment of (categories of) married women was almost completely erased from the law books. The Directive initiated a profound overhaul of the system in the eighties, and up into the nineties.[104]

Yet, making social security regulations sex neutral did not mean they had neutral effects. To counterbalance the considerable financial consequences of including married women on the same terms as men, new conditions for being

100 CJEU, 4 December 1986, *Federatie Nederlandse Vakbeweging* (*FNV*), C-71/85.

101 Idem. Cf. M. De la Corte-Rodríguez, Recent cases and the future of Directive 79/7 on equal treatment of men and women in social security, *European Journal of Social Security*, 2021, p. 44–61.

102 Cf. Fredman, Intersectional discrimination, Report EU network, 2016, p. 67. A 'sex plus' or 'race plus' approach is also accepted by several federal courts in the US under Title VII non-discrimination law, but not by all. It is limited to a combination of two grounds; S. Atrey, Intersectionality and comparative discrimination law, 2020, p. 44–49. So far, the US Supreme Court has not pronounced itself on this issue.

103 In this context it is important to note, however, that the social security directive allows for a wider range of exceptions to the prohibition of discrimination than the contemporary employment directive. Thus, for instance, in the area of statutory old-age pensions it still allowed for important exceptions to the requirement of equal treatment, see e.g. Directive 79/7 Article 7.

104 See for an overview Driessen and Veldman, *Inkomenszekerheid* (Income security), 1997.

eligible were often introduced. Such conditions could regard, for example, the level of income loss suffered or requiring longer periods of having been gainfully employed before the risk occurred. These types of conditions did not do away with the strong focus of social security arrangements on protecting loss of income of the (main) breadwinner. It still reflected the real life world, in which the breadwinner-homemaker model remained dominant in Dutch society. The uneven share of mothers and fathers in paid employment and unpaid care continued, with working mothers often being involved in small part time jobs or precarious work.

As a consequence, social security schemes often continued to have a disparate effect on married women – and on the increasing number of cohabitating women – rather than on unmarried/single women or on men, regardless their civil or family status. The disparate impact of the changes in the social security system on the intersectionally shaped group of 'non-breadwinner' women, provided an avenue to turn again to EU law, now through claims of indirect discrimination. The CJEU took up many of these cases.[105] Conceptually, the Court did not seem to find much – or at least not a principled – difficulty in addressing many of these intersectional issues through the lens of indirect discrimination. It often acknowledged the particular detrimental effects of the new sex neutral arrangements on women. Similar to its reasoning under direct discrimination analysis, this seems to imply the acceptance of a 'sex plus' discrimination approach. The real bone of contention in the social security cases brought to the CJEU under the heading of indirect discrimination turned out to be of a different kind: the application of the objective justification test. According to several Dutch and other commentators, as applied to social security cases, this test became more lenient over the years.[106] It is a good example of how the 'bite' of the concept of indirect discrimination is indeed highly dependent on the strictness with which courts apply it (see for further elaboration Chapter 5, Section 5.4.3).

This brief account of how the CJEU approached the intersectional discrimination faced by women in the context of social security suggests it would be worthwhile to investigate other parts of its extensive jurisprudence from an intersectional perspective to find out how much space a single-axis framework provides or fails to provide for this type of inquiry.

105 Idem.

106 Idem, p. 184. Ellis and Watson conclude in a similar vein in respect of the much wider body of case law they analyse in their comprehensive study, *EU anti-discrimination law*, 2012, p. 463–470.

Another obvious candidate would be the intersection of sex and age in the area of old age pension schemes. The EU case law on this topic is often extremely complex and technical, but also highly interesting from an intersectional perspective. Pension schemes are rife with intersectional issues which often have a particularly prejudicial effect on elderly women. Fredman mentions several examples of post-2000 case law in this field which she regards as an illustration of an emerging recognition by the CJEU of intersectional discrimination.[107] As the jurisprudence on direct and indirect sex discrimination in pensions has long roots going back to the eighties, a comprehensive analysis of this field with current understandings regarding intersectional discrimination in mind could probably yield some interesting insights.

8.4 Concluding Remarks

As a legal concept, intersectional discrimination is the least developed of the modalities of discrimination explored in this study. It is still in a fledgling state. The Constitutional Court of South Africa can be said to have taken the lead in filling this gap in its judgment in *Mahlangu* by its express elaboration of how it may figure as part of equality and non-discrimination analysis. At the same time, intersectional discrimination is not a new phenomenon. It may be present in case law without the terminology of intersectional discrimination being used in addressing it. Several examples given above attest to this. Revisiting existing case law through an intersectional lens may be a worthwhile exercise to gain better understanding of how intersectional discrimination can be addressed under equality and non-discrimination standards.

My *tour d'horizon* of some of the ways in which intersectional discrimination has been addressed in judicial analysis, both explicitly and implicitly, shows this can proceed along several avenues. To start with, intersectional discrimination which involves an express distinction on at least one protected ground may follow the same path which is open to claims of 'ordinary', direct discrimination. This may be a quite common way to approach it, as shown by the examples provided in Section 8.2.2. In addition to this 'ground plus' approach, the Canadian case of *Corbiere* shows how an intersectionally created criterion forming the basis of a difference in treatment may also be identified as a new suspect ground in itself, thereby also bringing it under the protection or a prohibition of 'ordinary' direct discrimination.

107 Fredman, Intersectional discrimination, Report EU network, 2016, p. 71–72.

If intersectional discrimination is not based expressly on at least one protected ground, but has a disparate effect on an intersectionally formed group protected by non-discrimination standards, it may be possible to address it through the concept of indirect discrimination, as exemplified by the approach of the Constitutional Court of South Africa in respect of the exclusion of domestic workers from certain benefits in *Mahlangu*.

The distinction between addressing intersectional discrimination through an analysis of direct or indirect discrimination may not be of great significance under equality and non-discrimination standards of a general nature, such as generally found in constitutional provisions and human rights treaties. For EU law, however, the difference is important in view of the legal framing of the directives along lines of direct and indirect discrimination. Nevertheless, also in this context room exists for addressing intersectional discrimination through either of these concepts. The exceptional difficulties presented by EU law for developing a comprehensive intersectional approach may derive most of all from the fragmentation of the legislation over different grounds with a very different scope and different possibilities for justifying direct and indirect discrimination.

CHAPTER 9

Concluding Reflections

9.1 Introduction

This final chapter will draw some lines of the analysis developed in this study together. I will do so by reflecting on some general trends in the development of conceptual approaches to equality and non-discrimination standards that have become apparent and seem to stand out across jurisdictions. This also provides room for some broader and more normative observations.

The first two trends I like to highlight regard core background factors without which developments in the legal conceptualization of equality and non-discrimination discussed in this study are difficult to fully appreciate. They concern the tremendously increased and still expanding interventions by modern states in social and economic life (Section 9.2) and what seems to be the ever more important role played by judicial bodies in shaping legal standards, including equality standards (Section 9.3).

Content-wise, the development of approaches to equality and non-discrimination as legal concepts from (more) formal towards (more) substantive understandings constitutes arguably the most important trend to pay attention to. It runs like a common thread through the previous chapters (Section 9.4). A final content-related trend which stands out, regards the increasing complexities involved in the interpretation and application of equality standards resulting from the development of the various modalities of discrimination that have taken shape, be it in a robust or as yet only fledgling form. If anything, these dynamics illustrate once more that the conceptualization of equality and non-discrimination standards is an ongoing process which is bound to continue (Section 9.5)

9.2 The Increasing Reach of Equality as a Legal Standard – Its Interconnecting Function

As discussed in Chapter 2, the increasing reach of equality standards in modern societies results from their central, interconnecting function within the prevailing legal framework.[1] They are switched on as soon as the state starts

1 Chapter 2, Section 2.2.3.

regulating society and social relations by adopting laws or policies.[2] Whether the state provides for a justice system, old age pensions or welfare benefits, or whether it regulates trade and commercial relations, if it does it has to do so without discrimination. If the latter is not the case, equality standards may work as a lever to challenge this.

As in modern societies state intervention has typically increased tremendously, the reach of equality standards has grown in its wake. Even in states with a strong liberal tradition of non-intervention by state powers, such as the US, this is at stake, but it arguably becomes most prominent in jurisdictions which have adopted human rights, including social rights, as their overarching legal framework. The reach of equality standards is often further increased by covering horizontal relations in (parts) of social life. Of old, employment is the most regulated of these areas.[3] If we take the EU as an example, a trend is discernible towards broader regulation of discrimination in the area of goods and services.

This much more expanded reach of equality as a legal standard makes it into a potentially radicalizing legal principle. Whether it actually becomes so, however, depends to a significant degree on its conceptual scope: to what extent does an extension of the material scope of equality standards combine with a conceptual development from a limited, (more) formal towards a more far-reaching, substantive approach? As has become apparent in the preceding chapters, in the far majority of jurisdictions figuring prominently in this study, an overall trend towards taking more substantive notions on board is clearly visible. Before discussing the significance of this general development, the crucial role of judicial bodies in this evolution merits some more attention.

---

2 Alkema called this the function of the equality principle as a *schakelbepaling*, which I translate here as 'interconnecting provision': it starts operating as a legal obligation for the state wherever state regulation is involved, even if the particular regulation is not legally required as such. He used this term in particular in the context of state regulation in social policy areas. In these areas, the state usually has no obligation to develop particular social programmes or grant benefits – and equality standards as such do not require it – but if the state does, such provision must conform to equality standards and as a result usually become subject to judicial review. E.A. Alkema, *Schakelbepalingen. Enige beschouwingen over samenhang en werking van de rechten van de mens*, Oratie UvA, 1981 (Interconnecting provisions. Some reflections on the cohesion and working of human rights, Inaugural lecture, University of Amsterdam, 1981); E.A. Alkema, Het internationale gelijkheidsbeginsel en de Nederlandse staatsrechtelijke verhoudingen, in: *Staatsrecht, buitenlandse betrekkingen en de internationale rechtsorde, Preadviezen Staatsrechtconferentie 1986*, Nijmegen 1987, p. 64–105 (The international equality principle and Dutch constitutional relations, in: Constitutional law, foreign relations and the international legal order, 1986, p. 64–105).

3 The ILO Discrimination (Employment and Occupation) Convention (Convention No. 111) dates from 1958. It is widely ratified by 175 states.

9.3 The Central Role of Judicial Bodies

9.3.1 *Increasing Interplay and Mutual Influencing across Jurisdictions*

The interpretation and application of equality standards by judicial bodies constitutes a driving force in the conceptual development of equality as a legal concept. What stands out in this respect and has frequently been noticed in the preceding chapters, is the increased interplay between such bodies and the mutual influence they seem to have on each other in developing the various concepts of equality and discrimination discussed in this study.[4]

This trend is part of a much more general one in human rights law.[5] Though judicial bodies are in all sorts of ways legally confined in exercising their role in adjudication and judicial review by the specific legal mandates they have been granted, they usually have quite some leeway in terms of how to conceptualize and interpret fundamental rights provisions. As these standards are often formulated in a broad and general way, they leave much interpretive space. Equality standards are no exception. As this study shows, judicial bodies have used this space time and again. In doing so they often look to other jurisdictions for inspiration and for what they may perceive as best conceptual practices, be it explicitly or implicitly.

Interaction of this nature facilitates aligning the core concepts and modalities of discrimination developed in various jurisdictions into a broadly shared, overarching conceptual framework – without, of course, doing away with the many differences between them or with the myriad peculiarities at play within each jurisdiction. This phenomenon may not be new as such – the way in which the US *Griggs* case influenced European conceptualizations of indirect sex discrimination is a case in point[6] – but it could only become a much more common practice since the information revolution took off with much increased speed after the turn of the century.

Interestingly, mutual influencing has turned out to be more than one-way traffic. Over time, judicial bodies from both the Global North and South seem to have come to operate as a web of interconnected hubs; with shifting importance or influence flowing from each of these hubs depending on the particular subject matter involved. The preceding chapters provide quite some examples of this. Whereas the initial conceptualizations of direct, indirect and positive

---

4 The US Supreme Court seems to constitute a notable exception. It does not seem to be open to transnational developments. If anything, its approach to indirect discrimination and affirmative action is moving in the opposite direction of developments elsewhere.

5 See Chapter 2, Section 2.4.1.

6 See Chapter 5, Section 5.2.1.

discrimination or positive action seem to have been dominated by Western jurisdictions, the further elaboration of these 'old' concepts as part of a more robust substantive equality perspective is much more prominently developed in Global South jurisdictions.[7] Regarding intersectional discrimination, the South African Constitutional Court has shown that it intends to take the lead in developing this largely underdeveloped concept.[8] Last but not least, the particular influence now exerted by the CRPD, a global human rights instrument, on the development of the concept of reasonable accommodation stands out.[9]

9.3.2 *Decisive Role in How Much 'Bite' Equality Standards Actually Have*

If anything, this study has shown how the critical function of equality standards in holding authorities, employers or other duty bearers to account depends to a considerable extent on the way in which judicial bodies shape the applicable review standards and apply these in concrete cases. In this regard, the strictness or leniency of the scrutiny with which the justifications put forward to save a particular rule, policy or measure are assessed is of crucial importance. The various elements of this inquiry – assessing the legitimacy of the goal; the degree of fit between means and ends, including the comparability of the cases; consideration of other rights and interests at stake – involve many normative considerations and assessments. As a consequence, the outcome of equality and non-discrimination analysis may inevitably vary with the perspectives taken.[10]

The wide interpretive space which seems to be part and parcel of applying equality standards means that judicial bodies usually exert a lot of power. How they use this power will depend on a variety of factors, but most importantly it seems to imply that any further developments may depend to a large extent on the particular composition of these bodies. Whether this is a strength or a weakness may be up for discussion, but it does suggest that advancements made so far – and I consider the development of (more) substantive approaches to equality as positive – are not to be taken for granted unless they become also more firmly embedded in solid legislative frameworks. The latest developments in the case law of the US Supreme Court, heavily restricting the space for affirmative action measures in higher education, are a case in point.[11]

7 See for further elaboration Chapters 4, 5 and 7.
8 See Chapter 8, in particular Section 8.3.3.
9 See Chapter 6.
10 See Chapter 3, Section 3.2.1; Chapter 4, Section 4.4.2.
11 See Chapter 7, Section 7.4.1.

9.3.3 *Limits of the Judicial Role within the Trias Politica*

Judicial bodies may hold governments to account and push them to act on their responsibilities under equality standards, but they cannot take over the designing and implementation of laws and policies. In the preceding chapters this was also a recurring theme, particularly when discussing the reach of the concepts of indirect discrimination, (reasonable) accommodation and positive discrimination or positive action. Where equality standards require taking difference into account by treating people differently in accordance with their particular situation and needs – in line with the second limb of the Aristotelian *adagium* – the treatment due is often open-ended. This type of equality claim is more difficult to handle for judicial bodies than claims to be accorded the same treatment as other people already receive.[12] It shows that a more fully substantive approach to equality standards depends on interventions by the legislative and administrative powers, that is ultimately on the political process.

National judicial bodies have to negotiate the tensions between their role in holding the other branches of government to account, and leaving these proper deference within the confines of the larger constitutional framework they operate in. Though the position of international courts is different, they also have to face a very similar and important issue: how much deference to leave to the national authorities.[13]

9.4 From a (More) Formal towards a (More) Substantive Approach

The process of mutual influencing between jurisdictions sketched above may well inform the overall trend in the development of legal approaches to equality and non-discrimination which has become apparent in the preceding chapters: a move from a (more) formal equality approach towards (more) substantive perspectives.

This development is core to how the various modalities of discrimination have been – and still are – shaped into multifaceted and multilayered concepts. This turn to a more articulate and more fully substantive reading of equality standards, characterized by an impact oriented approach, is of crucial importance. It takes the outcome of any treatment as the yardstick for

12 See Chapter 3, Section 3.5.2; Chapter 5, Section 5.3.5 ; Chapter 6, Section 6.6.3.

13 Cf. Y.Shany, Toward a general margin of appreciation doctrine in international law? *European Journal of International Law*, 2006, p. 907–940.

complying with equality standards, regardless the sameness or difference of the treatment involved.

This is not to say that formal equality is not important. On the contrary, it is a vital element of a substantive equality approach even if it has a limited reach only. As explored in Chapter 2, striving for formal equality was fundamental to the recognition of historically disadvantaged groups as 'like cases' deserving the equal protection of their fundamental rights and freedoms, on an equal basis with other groups who had been accorded such rights. Articles 1 and 2 of the UDHR and the equality standards included in the subsequent human rights conventions and in national constitutions attest to this.

The prohibition of discrimination expresses this by providing particular protection against all sorts of exclusions explicitly based on race, sex, religion and many other grounds which have been added to the list of protected grounds in the past decades.[14] Experience has shown that classifications on these ground have often resulted in more than incidental, structural patterns of disadvantage. For this reason distinctions based on these grounds are sensitive and to be approached with much more suspicion than 'ordinary' classifications. They should not be easily accepted. In judicial review this distinct protection offered by non-discrimination standards usually translates into more stringent scrutiny of the justifications put forward for differential treatment.

The general prohibition of discrimination – with its focus on direct discrimination and thus formal equality – has proven to be an important instrument to challenge all sorts of exclusions suffered by the groups protected by it. Formal equality is indeed still a driving force for many equality and non-discrimination claims, including, for instance, claims for equal access to marriage and pension benefits for same-sex couples, or equal legal personhood for mentally disabled persons. In such situations formal equality is a prerequisite for an equal outcome and runs parallel with substantive equality.

The examples show that the relationship between formal and substantive equality is not a zero-sum relationship; they are not always opposites. As discussed in Chapter 3, if taken on its own, however, formal equality can turn into a barrier to substantive equality.[15] This happens in particular when the conceptualization of equality is *limited* to formal equality. In Aristotelian terms this is at stake when equality is restricted to the first limb of the *adagium* that 'like cases are to be treated alike' and the second limb is discarded, which calls in addition for treating 'unalike cases unalike in proportion to their unalikeness'. Only if the two parts are accepted as operating in tandem a fully substantive

14 See Chapter 4, Section 4.3.3.
15 See Chapter 3, Section 3.3.

approach to equality comes into view, which takes unequal outcome as its core concern. A formal approach is insufficient for providing meaningful guidelines for how to deal with and accommodate difference.[16]

9.4.1 *Manifestations of Substantive Equality – Indirect Discrimination, (Reasonable) Accommodation and Remedial Measures*

Moving attention to the impact and effect of any treatment as the yardstick for identifying (potential) violations of equality standards has resulted in the development of several distinct modalities of discrimination. As explored in Chapters 5, 6 and 7, the concepts of indirect discrimination, (reasonable) accommodation and positive discrimination or positive action are all linked to a more outcome oriented, substantive equality approach.

Indirect discrimination connects to a substantive approach by bringing the disparate impact of seemingly neutral criteria under the reach of equality standards. It has become a commonly accepted part of non-discrimination analysis across a wide range of jurisdictions. Particularly in India and Canada, it has been heralded by the apex courts as an instrument to tackle structural and systemic discrimination.[17] Concrete examples of case law on indirect discrimination from a variety of jurisdictions show the concept may indeed reach more structural forms of discrimination, but whether it will actually work in this way depends ultimately on the 'bite' with which it is applied in concrete cases.[18] The examples discussed also show that tackling indirect discrimination has in addition some clear inherent limits in addressing structural and systemic discrimination which is embedded in the fabrics of society. It does not necessarily reach the underlying dominant standards and power relations shaping social realities.

The concept of (reasonable) accommodation is much less developed as the analysis in Chapter 6 shows, but it has gained more prominence since the turn of the century. In several jurisdictions it operates under the umbrella of indirect discrimination. In others a lack of (reasonable) accommodation has also appeared as a distinct *sui generis* form of discrimination. The CRPD is a prime example of the latter by formulating a duty of reasonable accommodation specifically geared to meeting the individual needs of disabled persons.[19]

Beyond the specific context of the CRPD, a duty of (reasonable) accommodation has long roots in the application of equality standards in relation

---

16 See in particular Chapter 3, Section 3.3.
17 See Chapter 5, Section 5.3.1.
18 See Chapter 5, Sections 5.3.2–5.3.6.
19 See Chapter 6, Section 6.5.

to other groups whose particular position and needs have to be taken into account, such as religious minorities.[20] As a general notion, it ties in with the second limb of the Aristotelian formulation, which requires that unalike cases are treated unalike. In this more generic form a duty of accommodation is not limited to disability but may cover any protected ground. The jurisprudence of the ECtHR provides some clear examples of this approach by stipulating that discrimination may also occur if states, without providing an objective and reasonable justification, fail to treat differently persons whose situations are significantly different.[21] In Canada and South Africa a more general duty of accommodation applicable to all protected grounds is also regarded as an integral part of a substantive reading of equality standards. Interestingly, this duty of accommodation is put on a par with a prohibition of indirect discrimination. The lines between these concepts are seen as fluid, as they both emanate from the same substantive conception of equality and are both triggered by the disparate effect of neutrally formulated rules or policies on (members of) a protected group.[22]

Affirmative action policies are also linked to a substantive approach to equality. It is the most contested of all the concepts discussed in this study. This is reflected in how remedial measures are approached under equality standards. Review models for dealing with positive discrimination or positive action vary significantly between jurisdictions. In jurisdictions in which affirmative action is approached as highly contested, judicial scrutiny tends to be very strict. In jurisdictions in which remedial measures are seen as part and parcel of a substantive equality approach, assessment is much more lenient. In this context in particular, differences between the equality approaches adhered to in different jurisdictions become most apparent.

Almost all jurisdictions figuring in this study have moved towards a (more) substantive approach to a greater or lesser extent. The most common manifestation of this development has been the broad adoption of the concept of indirect discrimination. Approaches to positive discrimination or positive action are much more mixed; those regarding (reasonable) accommodation are often still in a nascent state.

The US is an exception to this trend by adhering much more strongly to a formal equality approach. Though the US Supreme Court played an important role in the initial development of the concept of indirect discrimination, over time it has adopted a very restrictive approach to it, particularly so

20 See Chapter 6, Section 6.4.
21 See Chapter 6, Section 6.4.2.
22 See Chapter 6, Sections 6.4.1–6.4.3.

where constitutional equality standards are concerned. The Court has become equally restrictive in its approach to affirmative action. Even in the US, however, elements of a substantive approach to equality are present in respect of reasonable accommodation of disabled people and of religious groups.

9.4.2 *Intersectional Discrimination as a Crosscutting Dimension of the Other Modalities of Discrimination*

Intersectional discrimination is also informed by an eye for unequal impact, be it within and across disadvantaged groups. As a modality of discrimination it has a distinct character by its crosscutting dimensions. Intersectional discrimination can appear as part of direct or indirect discrimination analysis.[23] In addition, addressing intersectional discrimination may also figure in positive discrimination or positive action policies.[24] Though I did not come across case law regarding intersectional discrimination in the context of (reasonable) accommodation, intersectional issues can no doubt be present in this context as well.

Intersectional discrimination as a legal concept is the least developed of the concepts I discuss in this study, though its importance is generally acknowledged in academic scholarship. To indeed integrate this concept into the equality and non-discrimination framework is arguably the biggest challenge lying ahead. If anything, addressing intersectional discrimination adds another layer to the increasing complexity of legal conceptualizations of equality and non-discrimination.

9.5 Increasing Complexity – an Ongoing Process

Undoubtedly, equality and non-discrimination analysis has never been simple or straightforward. In whatever modality it appears, it involves making all sorts of assessments to decide whether distinctions made (or lack of distinction) are justified or not. Many of these include normative deliberations, which may very well vary with perspectives taken. Assessing the legitimacy of the goal of rules, policies or measures; the fit or proportionality between the means chosen and this goal, including the comparability of the cases involved; the balancing with other rights and interests which may be at stake; all these assessments are often susceptible to a wide array of normative considerations.[25]

23 See Chapter 8, Sections 8.3.2 and 8.3.3.

24 See Chapter 7, Section 7.5.

25 See Chapter 3, Section 3.2.1.

A recurring observation in this regard has been how in this type of assessment the more stringent scrutiny due when classifications are based on a protected ground may be offset by other factors which may influence levels of scrutiny applied by judicial bodies. The particular area of law or society or other rights and interests involved, as well as degrees of disadvantage suffered may all pull in different directions. This issue surfaces time and again regarding all the modalities of discrimination.[26] It helps explain why application of equality standards is often characterized as unpredictable or elusive.

The complexities of equality and non-discrimination analysis have increased over the course of time in most jurisdictions by several developments. To start with, the list of protected grounds has expanded in most jurisdictions – often quite considerably. This enhances the protection provided by non-discrimination law for a larger number of groups, but it also leads to new challenges. The most important of these may well be the development of a certain hierarchy between protected grounds, be it explicitly or implicitly. As not all forms of discrimination are as invidious, differing levels of scrutiny have been developing for different grounds of discrimination, either expressly or in more hidden form.[27] Though this seems a logical corollary of the expansion of protected grounds, it adds another layer of complexity to non-discrimination analysis. Several other complexities can be traced to the development of the particular modalities of discrimination which accompany the turn to more substantive equality approaches.

9.5.1 *Complexities Flowing from the Development of Particular Modalities of Discrimination*

Where indirect discrimination is concerned, apart from difficulties in distinguishing direct and indirect discrimination particular problems may be attached to establishing the disparate impact of rules, policies or measures on a protected group.[28] Using either quantitative or more qualitative indicators, or a combination of both, may make a considerable difference. Moving towards a more qualitative analysis – as seems to be a general trend across jurisdictions – is indispensable, as for many groups protected by non-discrimination standards no disaggregated statistical data may be available to start with. Qualitative analysis is not necessarily easier or straightforward.[29]

---

26 See Chapter 4, Section 4.4.2; Chapter 5, Section 5.4.3; Chapter 7, Section 7.4.2.

27 See Chapter 4, Section 4.4.2.

28 Chapter 5, Section 5.4.1 and Section 5.4.2.

29 Chapter 5, Section 5.4.2.

In instances of indirect discrimination which boil down to a lack of (reasonable) accommodation, application of the concept of indirect discrimination shares in the complexities deriving from the latter modality of discrimination. The most important one would seem to be the problem of the often open-ended character of (reasonable) accommodation. Where discrimination comes in the form of an unjustified difference in treatment, a point of reference exists for the treatment due. When a discrimination claim is about unjustified equal treatment, which is characteristic for a claim for (reasonable) accommodation, this is much more fuzzy. What degree of accommodation of difference is sufficient or not to avoid a violation of equality standards is often open-ended.[30]

This issue of open-endedness may not be a prime concern when individual, personalized accommodation is due. In such cases, the accommodation demanded is usually quite concrete and specific. Deciding whether it can be provided without imposing a disproportionate burden will also be quite concrete. Where more collective forms of (reasonable) accommodation are concerned, this is different. Collective accommodation usually requires the development of general policies and allocation of financial or other scarce resources. For example, improving access to all public buildings for disabled people, granting decent pregnancy and maternity leave or accommodating the religious needs of pupils to pray at school are much more open-ended regarding their achievement levels. Particularly where accommodation requires the allocation of scarce resources, the legislature and administration are in the lead in deciding the pace and level of fulfilling duties of (reasonable) accommodation. The position of judicial bodies in assessing when they are at fault in this regard seems quite comparable to their role in social rights adjudication; it brings along similar complexities and questions regarding the proper division of powers between the branches of Government.[31]

Turning to the difficulties involved when designing positive discrimination or positive action measures, the demarcation of the groups which should benefit may present particular dilemmas. Both overinclusion of those favoured by affirmative action (the 'creamy layer' problem), or underinclusion of equally disadvantaged individuals may be problematic (in India for example by excluding Christian and Muslim members of the scheduled castes because they do not belong to the Hindu religion).[32] As with (reasonable) accommodation, this problem is all the more difficult to handle where the resources to be more

30 See Chapter 3, Section 3.5.2; Chapter 5, Section 5.5; Chapter 6, Section 6.6.3.

31 See Chapter 3, Section 3.5.2; Chapter 5, Section 5.5 ; Chapter 6, Section 6.6.3.

32 See Chapter 7, Section 7.5.1.

equally distributed are scarce – which is inherently the case with places in higher education or higher functions, but also an issue in terms of the financial means available for all sorts of remedial policies. Budgets are always limited, even in affluent states. Scarcity calls for more distinct targeting of remedial measures to the most disadvantaged groups – for instance along intersectional lines – but such more narrow tailoring may also imply painful choices have to be made between those who are 'most deserving' and those who are 'less deserving'. This in turn may create unwanted competition for scarce resources between and within disadvantaged groups.

The growing attention for intersectional discrimination may well raise the most difficult challenges yet. Once you start looking for it, intersectional discrimination seems everywhere and may appear as 'the norm, rather than the exception'.[33] As intersectional discrimination cuts across all modalities of discrimination, the particular complexities it brings along are relevant for all of them.

The core value of the concept of intersectional discrimination for equality analysis may at the same time be a pitfall. Awareness of intersectionality is indispensable for problematising the inequalities existing within disadvantaged groups, which may be glossed over if the focus is exclusively on the particular list of grounds protected by non-discrimination standards. Social realities are indeed much more fuzzy and complicated. At the same time, it is unclear what degree of further delineation of subgroups is workable or desirable before it turns into unmanageable fragmentation. Each person's position in society flows from an intricate and ultimately unique mix of characteristics and experiences. If taken to its ultimate extreme, then, an intersectional approach to equality and non-discrimination would require what I have described as a substantive equality approach in an absolute sense: that is a substantive equality approach which would treat every person always and everywhere in a completely personalized way, taking all the myriad, particular differences and needs of this person into account.[34]

From the perspective of what law can deliver, this type of striving for fully individualized justice for all is an unfulfillable goal.[35] In addition, an absolute, singular focus on the unique, individual experiences of disadvantage and oppression would detract from what non-discrimination standards are at bottom about; it would risk losing sight of the broad, structural patterns

33 Xenidis, Multiple discrimination in EU anti-discrimination law, 2018, p. 42.

34 See Chapter 3, Section 3.1.

35 See Chapter 3, Section 3.2.1; Chapter 4, Section 4.4.2.

of disadvantage and discrimination shaping society and the power relations between social groups.

This brings me back to the core of what equality and non-discrimination analysis has to deal with: what is the proper level of generalization or particularity to be chosen in designing law and policies? How broad or narrowly tailored should classifications be?[36] By and large, law and policies have to be based on generalizations; the use of all sorts of proxies is inevitable. Law has to make choices between those who benefit and those who are burdened all the time. Classifying is so to speak part of the life of law. Some space exists for more fully personalized treatment for sure, but law cannot operate on this basis as matter of principle. In my view, what equality standards – and more particularly their expression in terms of a prohibition of non-discrimination – can and should do is to prevent that certain groups are time and again disadvantaged or burdened. Non-discrimination provisions intend to address structural and systemic patterns of disadvantage and exclusion suffered by particular groups, not incidental forms of unfavourable treatment. They seek to provide heightened protection for such vulnerable groups by identifying a number of grounds as suspect or protected grounds. The realities of intersectional discrimination reveal the limitations of this grounds-based approach. This is why they pose a distinct conceptual challenge. Intersectional perspectives force us to rethink how and to what extent a grounds-based approach can still be used where discrimination is compounded by the intersection of two or more of these grounds.

9.5.2 *Fuzzy Boundaries between the Various Modalities of Discrimination*

Last but not least, increasing complexities in equality analysis seem to flow from the blurred lines between the various modalities of discrimination. Fuzzy boundaries may exist between direct and indirect discrimination, and between indirect discrimination and (reasonable) accommodation.[37] In addition, remedial measures, (reasonable) accommodation and 'ordinary' social policy are sometimes hard to distinguish. There may also be quite some unclarity when such measures may turn into 'ordinary' discrimination.[38]

---

36 T. Loenen, Recht en het onvervulbare verlangen naar individuele gerechtigheid. Over verfijning van regelgeving, vage of open normen, en concrete toetsing aan grondrechten, (Law and the unfulfillable longing for individual justice. On differentiation in regulation, vague or open norms, and concrete human rights review), RM *Themis* 1996, p. 123–136.

37 See Chapter 5, Section 5.3.5.

38 See Chapter 7, Section 7.5.2 and 7.5.3.

These blurred lines show that notwithstanding efforts at further systematization and fine tuning of all these concepts to fit them nicely into coherent and consistent legal doctrines – a distinct preoccupation of legal scholars and professionals, including myself – realities on the ground are often much more opaque. Legal concepts are an indispensable tool for mapping realities and getting a better grip on them, but they cannot fully capture the complexities of either law or life.

Coming to the end of this study, a question that self-evidently presents itself is where to go from here. If anything, the preceding chapters show how the conceptualization of equality and non-discrimination as legal standards is an ongoing process. It will not stop at this particular point in time. Though this may be a platitude, it is no less true for that matter. Whatever future developments will bring, I hope the preceding analysis will prove helpful in better getting to grips with them.

Bibliography

Agathocleous, A., Conway, K., and Moore, R., *Trump on DEI and anti-discrimination law. Rolling back the clock of racial justice*, American Civil Liberties Union, 2 July 2022

Albertyn, C. and Goldblatt, B., Chapter 35. Equality, in: S. Woolman and M. Bishop (eds), *Constitutional Law of South Africa*, 2007.

Albertyn, C., Contested substantive equality in the South African Constitution: beyond social inclusion towards systemic justice, *South African Journal on Human Rights*, 2018, p. 441–468.

Albertyn, C., Section 9 in a time of COVID: substantive equality, economic inclusion and positive duties, *South African Journal on Human Rights*, 2021, p. 205–229.

Alkema, E. *Schakelbepalingen. Enige beschouwingen over samenhang en werking van de rechten van de mens*, Oratie UvA, 1981 (Interconnecting provisions. Some reflections on the cohesion and working of human rights, Inaugural lecture, University of Amsterdam, 1981); Alkema, E., Het internationale gelijkheidsbeginsel en de Nederlandse staatsrechtelijke verhoudingen, in: *Staatsrecht, buitenlandse betrekkingen en de internationale rechtsorde, Preadviezen Staatsrechtconferentie 1986*, Nijmegen 1987, p. 64–105 (The international equality principle and Dutch constitutional relations, in: Constitutional law, foreign relations and the international legal order, 1986, p. 64–105).

Altmann, A., *Discrimination*, in: *The Stanford Encyclopedia of Philosophy* (Last update 20 April 2020).

Aristotle, *Ethics*, London, Penguin Classics, 1976.

Alviar García, H., Klare, K., and Williams, L. (eds), *Social and economic rights in theory and practice. Critical inquiries*, Abingdon/New York: Routledge 2015.

Atrey, S., *Intersectional discrimination*, Oxford, Oxford University Press, 2019.

Atrey, S., *Intersectionality and comparative antidiscrimination law. The tale of two citadels*, Brill Research Perspectives in Comparative Discrimination Law, Brill, 2020.

Atrey, S., Beyond discrimination: *Mahlangu* and the use of intersectionality as a general theory of constitutional interpretation, *International Journal of Discrimination and the Law*, 2021, p. 168–178.

Babeuf, F-N., *Manifeste des égaux*, 1796. Translated from French into English and included in L.P. Pojman and R. Westmoreland (eds), *Equality. Selected readings*, New York/Oxford, Oxford University Press 1997, p. 49–52.

Balboni, M., (ed), *The principle of discrimination and the European Convention of Human Rights*, Editoriale Scientifica, 2017.

Berry, S.E., Bringing Muslim Minorities within the International Convention on the Elimination of All Forms of Racial Discrimination: square peg in a round hole?, *Human Rights Law Review*, 2011, p. 423–450.

Bond, J., *Global intersectionality and contemporary human rights*, Oxford, Oxford University Press, 2021.

Bonthuys, E., Institutional openness and resistance to feminist arguments: the example of the South African Constitutional Court, *Canadian Journal of Women and the Law*, 2008, p. 1–36.

Brems, E., (ed.), *Conflicts between fundamental rights*, Antwerp/Oxford/Portland, Intersentia, 2008.

Bribosia, E., and Rorive, I., *Reasonable accommodation beyond disability in Europe?* Report European Network of legal experts in the non-discrimination field, 2013.

Brink, M. van den, and Dunne, P., *Trans and intersex equality rights in Europe – a comparative analysis*. Report European network of legal experts in gender equality and non-discrimination., 2018.

Broderick, A., *Arnar Helgi Lárusson v. Iceland: muddying the waters on inaccessibility of public buildings*, Blog Strasbourg Observers, 30 August 2022.

Burgorgue-Larsen, L., "Decompartmentalization": the key technique for interpreting regional human rights treaties, *International Journal of Constitutional Law (I·CON)*, 2018, p. 187–2013.

Burri, S., Parents who want to reconcile work and care: which equality under EU law? In: M. van den Brink, S. Burri and J. Goldschmidt (eds.), *Equality and human rights: nothing but trouble? Liber amicorum Titia Loenen (SIM Special)*, SIM/Utrecht University, 2015, p. 261–277.

Burri, S., Protection and rights related to pregnancy and maternity in EU law, *Revue de Droit Comparé du Travail et de la Sécurité Sociale*, 2019 (English Electronic Edition).

Burri, S., Combating pregnancy discrimination in the Netherlands. The role of equality bodies, in: B. Havelková and M. Möschel (eds), *Anti-discrimination law in civil law jurisdictions*, Oxford University Press, Oxford 2019, Chapter 7, p. 158–1175.

Cameron, E., A South African perspective on the judicial development of socio-economic rights, in: L. Lazarus, C. McCrudden & N. Bowles (eds), *Reasoning rights. Comparative judicial engagement*, Oxford, Hart Publ., 2014, p. 319–338.

Carlson, L., *Comparative discrimination law: historical and theoretical frameworks*, Brill Research Perspectives in Comparative Discrimination Law, Brill, 2017.

Celorio, R., Discrimination and the regional human rights protection systems: the enigma of effectiveness, *University of Pennsylvania Journal of International Law*, 2019, p. 781–837.

Collins, H., and Khaitan, T., Indirect discrimination law: controversies and critical questions, in: H. Collins and T. Khaitan (eds), *Foundations of indirect discrimination law*, Bloomsbury, 2018, p. 1–30.

Committee on Economic, Social and Cultural Rights, *General Comment No. 20 (2012) on Non-discrimination in economic, social and cultural rights (Art. 2, para. 2 of the ICESCR)*, E/C.12/GC/20.

Committee on the Elimination of Discrimination Against Women, *General Recommendation No. 25 (2004) on Article 4, paragraph 1, of the Convention on the Elimination of All Forms of Discrimination against Women (temporary special measures).*

Committee on the Elimination of Discrimination Against Women, *General Recommendation No. 27 (2010) on older women and protection of their human rights.*

Committee on the Elimination of Discrimination Against Women, *General Recommendation No. 28 (2010) on the core obligations of States Parties under Article 2 of the Convention on the Elimination of All Forms of Discrimination against Women.*

Committee on the Elimination of Discrimination Against Women, *General Recommendation No. 39 (2022) on the rights of indigenous women and girls.*

Committee on the Elimination of Racial Discrimination, *General Recommendation No. 25 (2000) on the gender related dimensions of racial discrimination.*

Committee on the Rights of Persons with Disabilities, *General Comment No. 2 (2014), Article 9, Accessibility.*

Committee on the Rights of Persons with Disabilities, *General Comment No. 6 (2018) on equality and non-discrimination.*

Corbett, W.R., Reasonably accommodating employment discrimination law, *Penn State Law Review* 2024, p. 535–568.

Crenshaw, K., Demarginalising the intersection of race and sex: a Black feminist critique of antidiscrimination doctrine, feminist theory and antiracist politics, *University of Chicago Legal Forum*, 1989, p. 139–167.

Crowley, N., *Equality bodies and reasonable accommodation beyond the ground of disability*, Equinet report 2022.

Cruells. M., and Coll-Planas, G., Challenging equality policies: the emerging LGBT perspective, *European Journal of Women's Studies*, 2013, p. 122–137.

De la Corte-Rodríguez, M., Recent cases and the future of Directive 79/7 on equal treatment of men and women in social security, *European Journal of Social Security*, 2021, p. 44–61.

De Schutter, Olivier, Report of the Special Rapporteur on extreme poverty and human rights, *Banning discrimination on grounds of socioeconomic disadvantage: an essential tool in the fight against poverty*, 15 July 2022.

Driessen, M. and Veldman, A., *Inkomenszekerheid* (Income security), in: R. Holtmaat en T. Loenen (red.), *Vrouw en Recht* (Woman and law), Nijmegen, 1997, p. 181–223

Dworkin, R., Comment on Narveson: in defense of equality, *Social Philosophy and Policy*, 1983, p. 24–40.

Dušková, Š., *Who should we accommodate? Opening the grounds for reasonable accommodation under the European Convention on Human Rights*, Doctoral Thesis, University of Essex, 2023, https://repository.essex.ac.uk/35695/.

Ellis, E., and Watson, P., *EU anti-discrimination law* (2nd ed.), Oxford, Oxford University Press, 2012.

Equal Treatment Commission, *Advies 2004/06 inzake arbeid, religie en gelijke behandeling* (Advice 2004/06 on employment, religion and equal treatment).

Equal Treatment Commission, *Advies 2008/03 inzake gelijke behandeling in het onderwijs: 'Naar een discriminatievrije school'* (Advice 2008/03 concerning equal treatment in education: 'Towards a discrimination-free school').

Equal Treatment Commission, *Advies 2008/04 inzake gewetensbezwaarde ambtenaren van de burgerlijke stand: 'Trouwen? Geen bezwaar!'* (Advice 2008/04 on conscientious objections of civil registrars: 'Marriage? No objection!').

EU-Directives

- Council Directive 76/207/EEC of 9 February 1976 on the implementation of the principle of equal treatment for men and women as regards access to employment, vocational training and promotion, and working conditions.
- Council Directive 79/7/EEC of 19 December 1978 on the progressive implementation of the principle of equal treatment for men and women in matters of social security.
- Council Directive 92/85/EEC of 19 October 1992 on the introduction of measures to encourage improvements in the safety and health at work of pregnant workers and workers who have recently given birth or are breastfeeding (tenth individual Directive within the meaning of Article 16 (1) of Directive 89/391/EEC).
- Council Directive 2000/43/EC of 29 June 2000 on the implementation of equal treatment irrespective of race or ethnic origin in employment and regarding access to and supply of goods and services (Race directive).
- Council Directive 2000/78/EC of 27 November 2000 establishing a general framework for equal treatment in employment and occupation (Framework directive).
- Council Directive 2004/113/EC of 13 December 2004 implementing the principle of equal treatment between men and women in the access to and supply of goods and services.
- Directive 2006/54/EC of the European Parliament and of the Council of 5 July 2006 on the implementation of the principle of equal opportunities and equal treatment of men and women in matters of employment and occupation (Recast).
- Directive (EU) 2019/1158 of the European Parliament and of the Council of 20 June 2019 on work-life balance for parents and carers and repealing Council Directive 2010/18/EU.

Eyer, K., The but-for theory of anti-discrimination law, *Virginia Law Review* 2021, p. 1621–1710.

Ferrer Mac-Gregor, E., Conventionality control. The new doctrine of the Inter-American Court of Human Rights, *International Journal of American Law*, 2015, p. 93–99.

Fiss, O., Groups and the Equal Protection Clause, *Philosophy and Public Affairs*, 1976, p. 107–177.

France, A., *Le Lys Rouge*, 1894.

Fredman, S., *Discrimination law*, Oxford, Oxford University Press, 2022 (3rd edition).

Fredman, S., Review article: Coming of age: socio-economic rights as human rights, in: S. Fredman and M. Campbell (eds), *Social and economic rights and constitutional law*, Cheltenham, Elgar Publ., 2016.

Fredman, S., *Intersectional discrimination in EU gender equality and discrimination law*, Report European Network of legal experts in gender equality and non-discrimination, 2016.

Fullinwider, R., *Affirmative action*, in: *The Stanford Encyclopedia of Philosophy*, 2018.

Ganty, S., and Benito Sanchez, J.C., Equinet report, *Expanding the list of protected grounds within antidiscrimination law in the EU*, 2021.

Gebruers, C., From structural discrimination to intersectionality in the Inter-American system of human rights: unravelling categorical framings, *The Age of Human Rights Journal*, No. 20, 2023.

Gerards, J., Judicial review in equal treatment cases, Leiden/Boston, Martinus Nijhoff, 2002.

Gerards, J., The margin of appreciation doctrine, the very weighty reasons test and grounds of discrimination, in M. Balboni (ed), *The principle of discrimination and the European Convention of Human Rights*, Editoriale Scientifica, 2017, p. 27–61.

Gerards, J., Non-discrimination, the European Court of Justice and the European Court of Human Rights: who takes the lead? In T. Giegerich (ed), *The European Union as the protector of equality*, 2020, p. 135–163.

Gerards, J., *General principles of the European Convention on Human Rights*, Cambridge, Cambridge University Press, 2023 (2nd ed).

Gijzen, M., *Selected issues in equal treatment law: a multi-layered comparison of European, English and Dutch law*, Antwerp/Oxford, Intersentia, 2006.

Goodale, M. (ed), *Letters to the contrary. A curated history of the UNESCO human rights survey*, Stanford, Stanford University Press, 2018.

Goldschmidt, J.E., Staats- en bestuursrechtelijke aspecten van positieve actie (Constitutional and administrative aspects of positive action), in: W.P. Fase, J.E. Goldschmidt en B.P. Sloot, *Positieve discriminatie* (Positive discrimination), *preadviezen NJV*, 1989, p. 57–117.

Goldschmidt, J.E., 'Ms Goldschmidt, is it true you are deaf? That would really help us to meet our quota!'. Positive discrimination revisited …, In: M. van den Brink, S. Burri and J. Goldschmidt (eds), *Equality and human rights: nothing but trouble? Liber amicorum Titia Loenen (SIM Special)*, SIM/Utrecht University, 2015, p. 345–357.

Gosepath, S., *Equality, The Stanford Encyclopedia of Philosophy* (Summer 2021 Edition), Edward N. Zalta (ed).

Gunning, M.J., *Gewaande rechten. Het denken over vrouwen en gelijkheid van Thomas van Aquino tot de Bataafsche Constitutie* (Supposed rights. Thinking regarding women and equality from Thomas of Aquino to the Batavian Consititution), Zwolle, W.E.J. Tjeenk Willink, 1991.

Harrison, D., *Geschiedenis van de slavernij: van Mesopotamië tot moderne mensenhandel* (History of slavery: from Mesopotamia to modern human trafficking; translated from Norwegian), Utrecht, Omniboek, 2019.

Haverkort-Speekenbrink, S., *European non-discrimination law. A comparison of EU Law and the ECHR in the field of non-discrimination and freedom of religion in public employment with an emphasis on the Islamic headscarf issue*, Antwerp, Intersentia, 2012

Henrard, K., Duties of reasonable accommodation in relation to religion and the European Court of Human Rights, *Erasmus Law Review*, 2012, p. 59–77.

Henrard, K., Duties of reasonable accommodation on grounds of religion in the jurisprudence of the European Court of Human Rights: A tale of (baby) steps forward and missed opportunities, *International Journal of Constitutional Law* (I·CON), 2016, p. 961–983.

Hirschl, R., *Towards juristocracy: The origins and consequences of the New Constitutionalism*, Harvard, Harvard University Press, 2004.

Holtmaat, R., and Naber, J., *Women's human rights and culture: from deadlock to dialogue*, Antwerp, Intersentia, 2010.

Human Rights Committee, *General Comment No. 18: Non-discrimination*, 1989.

ILO, *Transforming enterprises through diversity and inclusion*, 6 April 2022.

Ippolito, F., *Understanding vulnerability in international human rights law*, Editoriale Scientifica, 2020.

Keane, D., and Waughray, A., Introduction, in: D. Keane and A. Waughray (eds), *Fifty years of the International Convention on the Elimination of All Forms of Racial Discrimination. A living instrument*, Manchester, Manchester University Press 2017, p. 1–31.

Khaitan, T., *A theory of discrimination law*, Oxford, Oxford University Press, 2015.

Khanna, V., Indirect discrimination and substantive equality in *Nitisha*: easier said than done under Indian constitutional jurisprudence, *International Journal of Discrimination and the Law*, 2022, p. 74–86.

Killander, M., Interpreting regional human rights treaties, 2010 *SUR – International Journal on Human Rights*, 2010, p. 145–169.

King, J., *Judging social rights*, Cambridge, Cambridge University Press, 2012

La Barbera, M., and Cruells López, M., Toward the implementation of intersectionality in the European multilevel legal praxis: *B.S. v. Spain, Law & Society Review*, 2019, p. 1167–1201.

Lakoff, S.A., *Equality in political philosophy*, Cambridge/Mass, Harvard University Press, 1964.

Lau, H., *Sexual orientation and gender identity discrimination*, Brill Research Perspectives in Comparative Discrimination Law, Brill, 2018.

Lincoln, A., *Charleston speech*, 18 September 1858.

Lippert-Rasmussen, K., The philosophy of discrimination – an introduction, in: K. Lippert Rasmussen (ed), *The Routledge Handbook on the ethics of discrimination*, 2017.

Lixinski, L., Treaty interpretation by the Inter-American Court of Human Rights: expansionism at the service of the unity of international law, *European Journal of International Law*, 2010, p. 585–604.

Locke, J., *Two treatises of Government*, 1689.

Loenen, T., *Verschil in Gelijkheid. De conceptualisering van het juridische gelijkheidsbeginsel met betrekking tot vrouwen en mannen in Nederland en de Verenigde Staten*, (Difference in equality. The conceptualization of the legal principle of equality regarding women and men in the Netherlands and the United States), Doctoral thesis, Zwolle, Tjeenk Willink, 1992.

Loenen, T., Rethinking sex equality as a human right, *Netherlands Quarterly of Human Rights* 1994, p. 253–270.

Loenen, T., Recht en het onvervulbare verlangen naar individuele gerechtigheid. Over verfijning van regelgeving, vage of open normen, en concrete toetsing aan grondrechten, (Law and the unfulfillable longing for individual justice. On differentiation in regulation, vague or open norms, and concrete human rights review), *RM Themis* 1996, p. 123–136.

Loenen, T., Indirect discrimination: oscillating between containment and revolution, in: T. Loenen and P. Rodrigues (eds), *Non-discrimination law: comparative perspectives*, The Hague/London/Boston, Kluwer Law International, 1999, p. 195–211.

Loenen, T., Indirect discrimination as a vehicle for change, *Australian Journal of Human Rights*, 2000, p. 77–96.

Loenen, M.L.P., and Goldschmidt, J.E., (eds), *Religious pluralism and human rights in Europe: where to draw the line?* Intersentia, Antwerpen/Oxford, 2007.

Loenen, T., In search of an EU approach to headscarf bans: where to go after *Achbita* and *Bougnaoui*? *Review of European Administrative Law*, 2017, p. 47–73.

Loenen, T., The impact of anti-discrimination law in the Netherlands. A case study of discrimination on grounds of religion in employment, in: B. Havelková and M. Möschel (eds), *Anti-discrimination law in civil law jurisdictions*, Oxford, Oxford University Press, 2019, p. 233–243.

MacDougall, B., Bonthuys, E., Norrie, K., and van den Brink, M., Conscientious objection to creating same-sex unions: an international analysis, *Canadian Journal of Human Rights*, 2012, p. 127–164.

MacKinnon, C., *Feminism unmodified*, Boston, Harvard University Press, 1987.

McColgan, A., *Discrimination, equality and the law*, Oxford, Hart Publ., 2014.

McCrudden, C., and Prechal, S., *The concepts of equality and non-discrimination in Europe: a practical approach* (Report European Network of experts in the field of gender equality), 2009.

McCrudden, C., Indirect religious discrimination: resisting the temptations of premature normative theorization, *Harvard Human Rights Journal*, 2021, p. 249–280.

McKean, W., *Equality and discrimination under international law*, Oxford, Clarendon Press, 1983.

Minow, M., *Making all the difference. Inclusion, exclusion, and American law*, Ithaca/London, Cornell University Press, 1990.

Morsink, J., *The Universal Declaration of Human Rights: origin, drafting and intent*, Philadelphia, Univ. of Pennsylvania Press, 1999.

Mulder, L., Voorkeursbehandeling van vrouwen en de betekenis van gelijkheidsbeginselen (Preferential treatment of women and the meaning of equality principles), *Nederlands Juristenblad* 1984, p. 1391–1397.

Mwakagali, M., *International human rights law and discrimination protections. A comparison of regional and national responses*, Brill Research Perspectives in Comparative Discrimination Law, Brill, 2019.

Mykhalchenko, O., and Isabel Santagostino Recavarren, I., In 38 countries women can still be fired for being pregnant, 13 May 2021, https://blogs.worldbank.org/developmenttalk/38-countries-women-can-still-be-fired-being-pregnant.

Neuman, G., Questions of indirect discrimination on the basis of religion, *Harvard Human Rights Journal*, 2021, p. 177–194.

Neuman Wipfler, A.J., Identity crisis: the limitations of expanding Government recognition of gender identity and the possibility of genderless identity documents, *Harvard Journal of Law and Gender* 2016, p. 491–554.

Okin, S.M., *Women in Western political thought*, Princeton, Princeton University Press, 1979.

Ooijen, H. van, *Religious symbols in public functions. A comparative analysis of Dutch, English and French justifications for limiting the freedom of public officials to display religious symbols*, Doctoral thesis Utrecht University, Antwerpen, Intersentia, 2012.

Oppenheimer, D.B., *The Ubiquity of positive measures for addressing systemic discrimination and inequality. A comparative global perspective*, Brill Research Perspectives in Comparative Discrimination Law, 2019.

Oppenheimer, D.B., What is 'systemic racism?' How is it different from racist acts caused by bigotry, prejudice or bias? Paper, 6 July, 2020; available at SSRN.

Ouald-Chaib, S., and David, V., *European Court of Justice keeps the door to religious discrimination in the private workplace opened. The European Court of Human Rights could close it*, Blog Strasbourg Observers, 27 March 2017.

Pascual-Vives, F., Evolutive interpretation as a method of interpretation in Public International Law, in: F. Pascual-Vives, *Consensus-cased interpretation of regional human rights treaties*, Chapter 4, Brill, 2019.

Phang, J., Book review of Erin F. Delaney and Rosalind Dixon (eds), *Comparative judicial review*, Edward Elgar, 2018, *International Journal of Constitutional Law* (I·CON), 2019, 721–725.

Pothier, D., Connecting grounds of discrimination to real people's real experiences, *Canadian Journal of Women and Law 2001*, p. 37–73.

Rosenblum, R., Unsex CEDAW, or what's wrong with women's rights, *Columbia Journal of Gender and Law*, 2011, p. 98–194.

Ross, R. (ed), *Racism and colonialism. Essays on ideology and social structure*, Studies in Overseas History vol. 4, The Hague/Boston/London, Martinus Nijhoff Publ., 1982, p. 1–9.

Schauer, F., Statistical (and non-statistical) discrimination, in: *The Routledge Handbook of the ethics of discrimination*, 2017, Chapter 3, p. 42–53.

Schiek, D., On uses, misuses and non-uses of intersectionality before the Court of Justice (EU), *International Journal of Discrimination and the Law*, 2018, p. 82–103.

Separation of powers, the judiciary and the politics of constitutional adjudication, *Special issue South African Journal of Human Rights*, 2020 no. 4.

Shany, Y., Toward a general margin of appreciation doctrine in international law? *European Journal of International Law*, 2006, p. 907–940.

Simons, K.W., Overinclusion and underinclusion: a new model, *University of California Los Angeles Law Review* 1988/99, p. 447–528.

Sjöholm, M., *Gender-sensitive norm interpretation by regional human rights law systems*, Brill/Nijhoff, 2018.

Sloot, B.P., *Positieve discriminatie. Maatschappelijke ongelijkheid en rechtsontwikkeling in de Verenigde Staten en Nederland* (Positive discrimination. Social inequality and legal development in the US and the Netherlands), Zwolle, Tjeenk Willink, 1986.

Smith, A., Equality constitutional adjudication in South Africa, *African Human Rights Journal*, vol. 14, p. 609–632.

Smith, B., Intersectional discrimination and substantive equality: a comparative and theoretical perspective, *The Equal Rights Review*, 2016, p. 73–102.

Solanke, I., *Discrimination as stigma: a theory of anti-discrimination law*, Bloomsbury, 2017.

Solanke, I., The EU approach to intersectional discrimination in law, in: *The Routledge Handbook on gender and EU politics*, 2021, p. 93–104.

Solum, L., Originalism versus Living Constitutionalism: the conceptual structure of the great debate, *Northwestern University Law Review*, 2019, p. 1243–1296.

Steiner, J., The principle of equal treatment for men and women in social security, in: T. Hervey and D. O'Keefe (eds), *Sex equality law in the European Union*, Chichester, Wiley, 1996, p. 111–136.

Stoljar, N., Discrimination and intersectionality, in: K. Lippert-Rasmussen (ed), *The Routledge Handbook of the ethics of discrimination*, Routledge 2018, Chapter 5, p. 68–79.

Summerfield, S., Women, war and social change: women in Britain in World War II. In: A. Marwick (ed) *Total war and social change*, London, Palgrave Macmillan, 1988, p. 95–118.

Sunstein, C.R., and Vermeule, A., *Law & Leviathan: redeeming the administrative state*, Cambridge, Massachusetts, The Belknap Press of Harvard University Press, 2020.

Timmer, A., *Strengthening the equality analysis of the European Court of Human Rights: the potential of the concepts of stereotyping and vulnerability*, Doctoral thesis, Gent University, 2014.

Timmer, A., Baumgärtel, M., Kotzé, L., and Slingenberg, L., The potential and pitfalls of the vulnerability concept for human rights, *Netherlands Quarterly of Human Rights*, 2021, p. 190–197.

Timmer, A., and Holtmaat, R., Article 5, in: P. Schultz, R. Halperin-Kaddari, B. Rudolf and M. Freeman (eds), *The UN Convention on the elimination of all forms of discrimination against women and its Optional Protocol: a commentary* (2nd ed), Oxford, Oxford University press 2022, p. 222–256.

Tobler, C., *Indirect discrimination. A case study into the development of the legal concept of indirect discrimination under EC law*, Antwerpen/Oxford, Intersentia, 2005.

Tobler, C., *Indirect discrimination under Directives 2000/43 and 2000/78*, Report European Network of legal experts in gender equality and non-discrimination, 2022.

Tussman, J., and tenBroek J., The equal protection of the laws, *California Law Review* 1949, p. 341–381.

Vandenhole, W., *Non-discrimination and equality in the view of the UN human rights treaty bodies*, Antwerpen/Oxford, Intersentia 2005.

Vickers, L., *Comparative discrimination law: age as a protected ground*, 2018, Brill Research Perspectives in Comparative Discrimination Law, Brill, 2018.

Vierdag, E.W., The concept of discrimination in international law, The Hague, Martinus Nijhoff, 1973.

Vrijheid en gelijkheid. De horizontale werking van het gelijkheidsbeginsel en de nieuwe antidiscriminatiewet (Freedom and equality. The horizontal working of the equality principle and the new antidiscrimination act), Antwerpen/Apeldoorn, Maklu, 2003.

Waddington, L., and Hendriks, A., The expanding concept of employment discrimination in Europe: from direct and indirect discrimination to reasonable accommodation discrimination, *International Journal of Comparative Labour Law and Industrial Relations*, 2002, p. 403–427.

Waddington, L., Reasonable accommodation – time to extend the duty to accommodate beyond disability? *Nederlands Tijdschrift voor de Mensenrechten*, 2011, p. 186–198.

Waughry, A., and Keane, D., CERD and caste-based discrimination, in: A. Waughray and D. Keane (eds), *Fifty years of the International Convention on the Elimination of All Forms of Racial Discrimination: a living instrument,* Manchester University Press, 2017, Chapter 6, p. 121–149.

Westen, P., The empty idea of equality, *Harvard Law Review* 1982, p. 537–590.

Wiggers, *J.H., Recht doen aan gelijkheid. Een beschouwing over voorkeursbehandeling en de betekenis van het gelijkheidsbeginsel in het grensgebied van recht en sociaal-politieke ethiek* (Doing justice to equality. A reflection on preferential treatment in the border area between law and socio-political ethics), Nijmegen, Ars Aequi Libri, 1991

Winkel, L.C., Enige opmerkingen over de geschiedenis van het gelijkheidsbeginsel in het recht (Some remarks on the history of the equality principle in law), in: C.W. Maris (red.), *Gelijkheid en recht* (Equality and law), Deventer/Zwolle, Van Loghum Slaterus/Tjeenk Willink, 1988, p. 99–112.

Wolstonecraft, M., A vindication of the rights of women, 1792.

Worldbank, *Women, business and the law, Report 2021.*

Xenidis, R., Multiple discrimination in EU anti-discrimination law. Towards redressing complex inequality?, in: U. Belavusau and K. Henrard (eds), *EU anti-discrimination law beyond gender,* Oxford, Hart Publishing, 2018, p. 41–74.

Xenidis, R., The concept of direct discrimination in European anti-discrimination law: theory, practice and limits, *iCourts Working Paper Series*, no. 285, 2022.

Index

www.ingramcontent.com/pod-product-compliance
Lightning Source LLC
Chambersburg PA
CBHW070120190926
PP18882900001B/9
* 9 7 8 9 0 0 4 5 3 7 8 5 9 *